TAMILS AND THE NATION

MADURIKA RASARATNAM

Tamils and the Nation

India and Sri Lanka Compared

HURST & COMPANY, LONDON

First published in the United Kingdom in 2016 by
C. Hurst & Co. (Publishers) Ltd.,
41 Great Russell Street, London, WC1B 3PL
© Madurika Rasaratnam, 2016
All rights reserved.

Printed in India

The right of Madurika Rasaratnam to be identified as the author
of this publication is asserted by her in accordance with the
Copyright, Designs and Patents Act, 1988.

A Cataloguing-in-Publication data record for this book
is available from the British Library.

ISBN: 978-1-84904-478-3 *paperback*

This book is printed using paper from registered sustainable
and managed sources.

www.hurstpublishers.com

CONTENTS

ACKNOWLEDGEMENTS

Over the course of researching and writing this book, I have been fortunate to have the support and encouragement of many people and I would like to say a special thanks to some of them. The book emerged from my doctoral research and my first thanks are due to John Breuilly, my supervisor, for his dedicated support. He took a deep interest in the puzzle this book addresses, and our many discussions over the years have shaped its arguments and my scholarly development. I have benefited greatly from the intellectually stimulating environments of the Department of Government at the LSE, where I completed my doctoral thesis, the Department of Politics and International Studies at SOAS, where I completed my undergraduate studies and taught for several years, and the School of Politics and International Relations at the University of Kent, where I presently teach. I am especially grateful to Mark Laffey for his mentoring and friendship. My understanding of Sri Lankan, Indian and Diaspora politics has been immeasurably strengthened by numerous friends and colleagues who share my interests. In particular I would like to thank David Rampton, James Manor, and Jan Jananayagam. My longstanding involvement with the Tamil Guardian has been a defining experience, and the countless conversations with the team, past and present, have helped me to sustain an intimate engagement with Tamil politics. They also provided insightful comments on drafts of several chapters. I am grateful to Michael Dwyer and Rob Pinney at Hurst for their enthusiasm for the project—and their patience as I completed the manuscript!

This book and the doctoral dissertation which preceded it would not have been possible without many interviews and conversations with past and present political leaders, journalists and activists in south India and Sri Lanka. The origins of this book can be traced to a chance encounter in 1998 with the

ACKNOWLEDGEMENTS

late Dharmaratnam Sivaram, the leading Tamil journalist of recent decades He encouraged me to study politics and sparked my interest in the historical depth of Tamil nationalist mobilisation and the international dynamics of Sri Lanka's conflict, of which he was known as a keen and perceptive analyst as well as a participant. I am also indebted to the late Anton Balasingham, the chief negotiator and political strategist of the Liberation Tigers of Tamil Eelam, for generously sharing with me his time, experiences and sharp insights into Tamil, Sri Lankan and international politics. His wife Adele has also been a source of warm encouragement. I am also grateful to Gajen Ponnambalam for numerous conversations on Tamil nationalist mobilisation and for introducing me to his fellow Tamil politicians in Sri Lanka.

I began work on this manuscript soon after my baby daughter was born, and its completion has depended on the goodwill, encouragement and help of family and friends. My mother has been generous to a fault, sharing caring for Maalathy with my partner Sutha to allow me the time to write. My dear friend Vino Kanapathipillai repeatedly went out of her way, extending assistance and thoughtful advice just when they were most needed—I look forward to repaying my debt as she begins writing up her own manuscript. The moral support and company of my brother Ramkumar and my other dear old friends Neil Young, Ezra Zahabi and Barira Limbada added to the pleasures whilst easing the anxieties of both motherhood and writing. Most importantly, I have relied on Sutha and his affection, humour and indefatigable enthusiasm for life. His careful and critical reading also immeasurably improved the text, though I alone am responsible for any errors. We share the pleasure of seeing it in print. Finally I am indebted to my late grandmother, Sathyabhama Cumaraswamy, who passed away while I was completing this manuscript. She shared and developed my interest in politics and history, not least because in her ninety three years she lived through and sometimes participated in many of the tumultuous events discussed in these pages. It is dedicated to her.

viii

ACRONYMS

ACTC	All Ceylon Tamil Congress
AI/ADMK	All India/Anna Dravida Munnetra Kazhagam (Anna Dravidian Progressive Association)
BJP	Bharatiya Janata Party (Indian People's Party)
CNA	Ceylon National Association
CNC	Ceylon National Congress
CP	Communist Party
DK	Dravida Kazhagam (Dravidian Association)
DMK	Dravida Munnetra Kazhagam (Dravidian Progressive Association)
FP	Federal Party
INC	Indian National Congress
ITAK	Illangai Tamil Arasu Kazhagam (Sri Lanka Tamil Government Association)
JVP	Janatha Vimukthi Peramuna (People's Liberation Front)
JYC	Jaffna Youth Congress
LSSP	Lanka Sama Samaja Party (Lanka Equal Society Party)
LTTE	Liberation Tigers of Tamil Eelam
MDMK	Marumalarchi Dravida Munnetra Kazhagam (Renewed Dravidian Progressive Association)
MEP	Mahajana Eksath Peramuna (People's United Front)
MGR	M. G. Ramachandran (leader of ADMK)
PMK	Pattali Makkal Katchi (Common People's Party)
OHCHR	Office of the United Nations High Commissioner for Human Rights
SLFP	Sri Lanka Freedom Party

ACRONYMS

TNA	Tamil National Alliance
TULF	Tamil United Liberation Front
UNHRC	United Nations Human Rights Council
UNP	United National Party

INTRODUCTION

The strikingly divergent political trajectories of the Tamil-speaking regions of south India and Sri Lanka[1] present an interesting puzzle for the study of ethnicity, nationalism and ethnic conflict. From the early decades of the twentieth century, movements and ideologies stressing a distinct Tamil political identity and interest have dominated Tamil politics in both south India and Sri Lanka. However, the relationship between these movements and their respective states has evolved in very different ways and resulted in dramatically different economic and political outcomes for the two Tamil-speaking regions. Tamil Nadu is today an economically successful and politically stable component of the Indian Union. It has good development indicators, a flourishing culture industry and has been well represented at the Union level since independence. In contrast, the Tamil-speaking regions of Sri Lanka have been devastated by thirty years of high-intensity armed conflict which ended brutally in May 2009 without resolving, and indeed exacerbating, the underlying ethnic polarisation.[2] While Tamil Nadu's relationship with the government in Delhi has at times been fractious and tense, disputes have invariably been contained within the constitutional framework and never escalated into sustained violence. In Sri Lanka, however, relations between the Colombo government and Tamil political actors since independence have been marked by confrontation, abandoned compromises and recurrent violence that escalated into protracted militarised conflict.

What is peculiar about these contrasting outcomes of south Indian ethnic accommodation and violent ethnic conflict in Sri Lanka is that they are both diametrically at odds with the historical dynamics of Tamil politics. In the late colonial period the south Indian Dravidian movement opposed Congress-led Indian nationalist mobilisation as a direct threat to Tamil identity and inter-

1

ests. Then when independence from Britain approached, Dravidian leaders even advocated separation from India as a means of securing Tamils against the alleged threats of Indian domination. This antagonism continued in the immediate post-independence period. For example, the Indian government's attempts in 1965 to replace English with Hindi as the official language led to widespread and violent protests across Tamil Nadu. Seven people self-immolated in protest against the act while two took poison, and up to 150 people were killed in ensuing clashes between protesters and police.[3] Conflict did not, however, escalate. Instead, from 1967 onwards, Dravidian parties have held power at the state level and have worked comfortably within the Indian constitutional framework. In 1976 the Anna Dravida Munnetra Kazhagam (ADMK), one of the two major Dravidian parties, even added the All India prefix to its name to signal explicitly its acceptance of the Indian constitutional framework,[4] though it has remained an exclusively Tamil Nadu party. Furthermore, the Dravidian parties were important partners in the coalition governments which governed in Delhi from the early 1990s until April 2014.

While Tamil Nadu politics have moved from separation to integration, Sri Lankan Tamil politics have moved in the opposite direction. From the late nineteenth century, Sri Lankan Tamil politicians led attempts to form pan-ethnic nationalist organisations, actively collaborating with Sinhalese politicians in these efforts. As independence approached, Tamil political leaders advocated power-sharing within a single unified constitutional structure as a means of promoting and protecting Tamil interests. Conflict between the Tamils and the increasingly Sinhala Buddhist state emerged in the wake of the 1956 Sinhala Only act, which established Sinhala as the sole language of state administration. This sparked demonstrations across the Tamil-speaking areas, blockading government offices and bringing civil administration to a standstill. Although the protests were widespread and sustained, they were nevertheless quite tame in comparison with the intensity of the language protests in Tamil Nadu. But conflict steadily escalated, despite occasional and always abortive 'pacts' between Tamil and Sinhala leaders, and in 1977 a coalition of Tamil parties, citing a history of state violence and discrimination, swept the polls in the Tamil-speaking areas on a platform of independence. At around the same time, episodic confrontations emerged between the now Sinhala-dominated military and a nascent Tamil insurgency seeking independence through armed struggle. Military repression and continuing anti-Tamil violence, culminating in the July 1983 pogrom alongside powerful international interventions, tipped the simmering insurgency into a full-blown civil war.

The turning point of the conflict came in 1977 when the newly elected United National Party (UNP) government adopted a series of pro-market economic reforms, pointedly abandoning the state-led development policies of previous governments, and thus became an enthusiastic member of the US-led anti-communist alliance, receiving both developmental assistance as well as military and diplomatic backing in its campaign against Tamil militancy. Sri Lanka's decisive shift towards the West and away from its previous 'non-aligned' stance prompted in turn Indian intervention that sought to counter the Westward tilt by providing support and training to an array of Tamil militant groups. These developments fuelled the rapid militarisation of the conflict whilst irreversibly enmeshing it in the shifting dynamics of Cold War and post-Cold War liberal order making.

These dramatic reversals, from separation to union in Tamil Nadu and in the opposite direction in Sri Lanka, despite a range of historical, social and economic similarities between the two cases, make them uniquely comparable. India and Sri Lanka have a shared history of British colonial rule followed by sustained competitive electoral democracy. They have similar social and economic systems, and electoral politics in both states continue to include patronage networks that distribute public resources of various kinds. They also have similar patterns of ethnic cleavages with overlapping differences of caste, religion, language, biological notions of race based on physical appearance and region. It has been suggested that India's more ethnically fragmented population, where the Hindu majority is cleaved by differences of language and caste, is more conducive to ethnic accommodation than Sri Lanka's binary division between a Sinhala Buddhist majority and a Tamil-speaking minority. However, the idea of a consolidated Sinhala Buddhist–Tamil conflict in Sri Lanka overlooks regional, religious and caste cleavages that have been important sites of intra-Sinhala and intra-Tamil conflict.[5] Conversely, from the early decades of the twentieth century Indian Hindu nationalists have sought to create a majoritarian Hindu political identity that incorporates intra-Hindu caste and linguistic cleavages.[6] The Hindu nationalist Bharatiya Janata Party's (BJP) victory in the April 2014 parliamentary elections relied in part on successfully mobilising cross-caste support in regions where caste identities have long been politically important.[7] In short, the political salience of an overwhelming ethnic majority in Sri Lanka and a more ethnically fragmented polity in India are themselves outcomes in need of explanation, and not pre-given variables that can underlie the divergent outcomes of the Tamil question in India and Sri Lanka.

Aims of the book

This book argues that the key to explaining this stark difference in trajectories is the dominant understanding of national identity that has come to structure political competition in the two states. The politically dominant conception of national identity in India un-problematically includes Tamils, whereas that in Sri Lanka does not. Through a comparative analysis of national identity formation that extends over time from the late colonial era to the present day, the book argues that contingent—in that they could have been otherwise—processes of political organisation and mobilisation explain the stark divergence between the two Tamil-speaking regions. The empirical chapters show how distinct patterns of political activity that emerged in comparable conditions brought to the fore very different conceptions of national identity. In India patterns of political organisation and mobilisation beginning in the late nineteenth century and reaching a crucial turning point in the mid twentieth century established the political dominance of the Indian National Congress and its pan-ethnic conception of national identity that was inclusive of Tamils. In contrast, in Sri Lanka, a different pattern of political activity over the same period and in comparable conditions established as dominant a Sinhala Buddhist conception of the nation hostile to Tamil claims and demands. The cross-case comparison sets out the contingency of the patterns of political activity, which diverged despite similar conditions, as well as their causal force in establishing very different conceptions of the nation and the attendant ethnic accommodations and conflicts that these subsequently entailed. The comparison of each case over time sets out in turn the causal force of national identity in establishing the divergent relations of ethnic accommodation in India and ethnic polarisation, leading to violent conflict, in Sri Lanka. Taken together therefore, the comparison between cases and the analysis of each case over time establish both the contingency of national identities but also their causal force in the divergent outcomes of the two Tamil-speaking regions. The analysis thus explains the dramatic reversals in south Indian and Sri Lankan Tamil politics; from separatism to accommodation in the former and from pan-ethnic nationalism to secession in the latter, as effects of contingent but temporally continuous political processes and the more or less ethnically inclusive identities that these create.

The analysis begins in the late nineteenth century and ends in the present day. It is divided into two parts. Part One examines nationalist and Tamil politics comparatively in the two cases, from their first emergence in the nineteenth century to a point of mature development in the late 1970s, when the relations of ethnic accommodation in India and ethnic conflict in Sri Lanka were both apparent and settled. The configurations of Tamil Nadu's stable accommodation in the Indian national framework have remained largely unchanged since then, sustaining its ongoing stability as well as relative prosperity and economic development. There have of course been important political developments as well as socio-economic changes, for example the mobilisation of Dalit political parties,[8] but these have not unsettled Tamil Nadu's accommodation within the Indian Union. In contrast, Sri Lanka's ethnic conflict has been through radical shifts, intensifying in violence as well as internationalising in scope, such that the configuration of actors and their relations have transformed beyond measure.

Part Two is therefore devoted to Sri Lanka, tracing the genesis, escalation and ending of Sri Lanka's armed conflict from the late 1970s to the present, as well as discussing the subsequent and post-war intensification of the underlying antagonism between the Sinhala Buddhist state and a now globalised Tamil nationalist movement. It focuses on the pivotal role of international actors and processes in the war and subsequent post-war period. The turn to the international is a departure from the framework of analysis used in Part One, but one that is grounded in the deep and transformative internationalisation of Sri Lanka's ethnic conflict. The chapters show how the rapid militarisation of the conflict was coeval with its internationalisation, and also how the unintended consequences of international action shaped in often decisive ways the capacity of Sinhala Buddhist and Tamil nationalist actors to pursue their projects, generally advantaging the former at the expense of the latter. It uses the term 'liberal peace' to capture the directionality of international interventions in Sri Lanka that continue to seek an ethnically inclusive, liberal-democratic and market-orientated state. International interventions in Sri Lanka are thus understood as part of a broader set of Western- (primarily US-) led, post-WWII international processes and institutions orientated towards securing a global pacific order based on the principles of liberal democracy and market economics. The analysis draws on the now established scholarly and policy literature on liberal order making, including the literature on Sri Lanka's conflict, that uses the term 'liberal peace' to characterise international efforts to secure peace and stability in sites of conflict and instability. In this literature the liberal peace entails a diffuse and loosely coordinated, rather than centrally planned, set of activities led by states, non-state actors and multilateral organisations orientated towards overlapping ends such as conflict management, peace-building, economic reform, development, security sector reform, human rights advocacy and democracy promotion.

The chapters in Part Two show how and why Sinhala Buddhist and Tamil nationalist movements continued to reproduce themselves and their preferred conceptions of national and ethnic order amidst powerful international efforts to secure liberal reform. They explain why international efforts failed to realise their stated ends—an ethnically inclusive liberal, democratic peace—and worked instead to fuel the militarisation of the conflict whilst inadvertently strengthening the Sinhala Buddhist character of the state and military that in turn also intensified countervailing Tamil nationalist mobilisation. The final chapter discusses the role of India and Tamil Nadu in the now international-ised post-war politics of Sri Lanka's ethnic conflict and thereby brings the divergent but now intersecting trajectories of the two Tamil-speaking regions to the present. It shows that these complex and internationalised dynamics have their origins in the contingent patterns of national identity politics that began in the late nineteenth century. Tamil Nadu actors' advocacy on behalf of Tamils in Sri Lanka is locked into a stable accommodation within the Indian national-state framework that was formed in colonial era political processes, whereas Sri Lanka's ethnic conflict—now played out across interna-tional fora—is equally rooted in contingent patterns of nationalist mobilisa-tion that established a dominant and ethnically hierarchical Sinhala Buddhist nationalism incompatible with Tamil nationalist demands for national autonomy and equality.

The politics of Tamil and national identities in India and Sri Lanka present plausible and interesting cases for comparison, not just because of the social, historical and economic similarities in which the divergent outcomes emerged, but also because of their ongoing and important connections. While both countries share a history of British colonial rule, there were also impor-tant pre British political and trade relations that embedded the island within broader Indian as well as south-east Asian ambits.[9] The social and political movements that shaped Tamil and national identities from the nineteenth century onwards were also connected. There were connections between Indian Hindu revivalists and Sinhala Buddhists in Sri Lanka and connections between the Tamil revivalisms of south India and Sri Lanka. The Indian Congress movement was also influential amongst Tamil and Sinhala political actors in Sri Lanka.[10]

While these connections are pivotal in understanding the constitution of ethnic and national identities, the analysis here nevertheless takes the two national states—India and Sri Lanka—as discrete units of comparison. It does so because conceptions of national identity and the powerful transformations of ethnic inclusion, exclusion and hierarchy that they generate are contained within the territorial boundaries of the state. Sinhala Buddhist nationalism and Indian nationalism were formed amidst cross-border processes of economic, social and political change, but Sinhala Buddhist nationalism has worked to marginalise both politically and economically the Tamils in Sri Lanka, not those in India, while Indian nationalism incorporated Tamils in India, not those in Sri Lanka. Likewise, despite their manifold and ongoing connections, Tamil politics in India and Sri Lanka have remained distinct and autonomous in their goals and objectives. Sri Lankan and Indian political leaders have in the past, and usually opportunistically, raised the spectre of a pan-Tamil irredentism crossing the Palk straits, unsettling Indian and Sri Lankan state boundaries; but Tamil political activity has always been separated by state borders and defined by the national framework of its respective state.[11] While Tamils in Sri Lanka have sought support from Tamils in Tamil Nadu, and the latter are now enthusiastic in providing it, their joint enterprise is in seeking a reorientation of power for the benefit of Tamils in Sri Lanka, rather than a joint political project as Tamils.[12] For these reasons the analysis presented here works within rather than against the territorial boundaries of the two states.

The following section sets out the understandings of nationalism and ethnicity as well as the broader theoretical framework that informs the empirical analysis presented here. The subsequent and third section reviews existing approaches to ethnicity and nationalism in South Asia and shows how the focus on national identity and political processes adopted in this study contributes to this literature. The final and fourth section then sets out an overview of the subsequent chapters, linking them to the overarching focus on the causal role of contingent political processes and the powerful—as well as more or less ethnically inclusive—national identities they create.

Framework of analysis

The nation and ethnicity are understood here as political concepts that are ubiquitous and unavoidable in the politics of the modern nation-state system. The centrality of the nation and ethnicity derive from their close connection to the doctrine of popular sovereignty, the sole principle of political legitimacy within the system of nation-states.[13] The claim to rule on behalf of the people is now ubiquitous, such that today 'rulers, however tyrannical their rule, justify their sovereignty as an expression of their nation's will'.[14] Popular sovereignty insists that authority flows directly from the people, but as the concept of popular sovereignty evolved and expanded from the late eighteenth century, the people have invariably been identified as a nation; that is a collective—rather than a collection of individuals—constituted as such by a shared history that in nationalist understandings also entails shared cultural characteristics and a shared attachment to territory.[15] The transformations of the nineteenth and twentieth centuries through the interlinked processes of capitalism, war, colonial rule and industrialisation produced a globe-encompassing system of territorial states that were at the same time also understood as national states; states that were of and for the people as nations within their boundaries. Ethnicity and nationalism were not however surplus or accidental by-products of this process; rather, as Andreas Wimmer argues, 'modernity itself rests on a basis of ethnic and nationalist principles'. That is:

> The main promises of modernity—political participation, equal treatment before the law and protection from the arbitrariness of state power, dignity for the weak and poor, and social justice and security—were fully realised only for those who came to be regarded as true members of the nation. The modern principles of inclusion are intimately tied to ethnic and national forms of exclusion.[16]

The terms nation and ethnicity are therefore linked in defining the patterns of inclusion and exclusion. Almost all national states contain culturally diverse populations that must somehow be reconciled into the ideal of a historically constituted and culturally homogenous whole. This immediately raises a set of vexed and contentious questions. Which of the various linguistic, religious, caste or regional groups contained within the boundaries of the state will come to form the national core, and which will be excluded? It is in this context of national inclusion and exclusion that terms such as ethnicity, minority, community and communal acquire their political salience and meaning. In relation to the problem of defining the boundaries of national community, ethnicity and its cognates cover the set of differences that are held to be inherited and form the basis of categories that identify multi-generational populations. These categories furthermore can become politically salient as markers of national inclusion, exclusion or hierarchical subordination.

Class, gender and sexual orientation may also be important and often violent sites of national exclusion and subordination; but the categories that are defined as ethnic are different in that they may also form the basis of national claims to political autonomy and maximally self-rule in an independent state. The ethnic identities that become politically salient contain a historically specific mix of religious, linguistic, caste and other categories. For example, Sri

Lankan Tamil nationalism mobilises support from Tamil-speaking Hindus and Christians but not Tamil-speaking Muslims, who tend to identify politically as Muslims rather than Tamils. Ethnicity, like the nation, identifies a hereditary population deemed to have a shared past, cultural solidarity and a claim to territory. As concepts the nation and ethnicity therefore overlap. While all nations are in part ethnic—even so called 'civic' or 'political' nationalisms characterise the nation as a multi-generational community with a shared past and shared 'ancestors'[17]—ethnicity may also, but does not always, form the basis of national claims. Caste is an important site of political mobilisation across India, but does not form the basis of claims to national autonomy. Ethnicity is therefore distinct from class, gender and sexual orientation not because it is more acute or more important than these other social categories; in fact in many, if not most, circumstances it may be less so. Rather, ethnicity is distinct because it can lead to specific forms of inclusion and exclusion from the national community. Exclusion on the basis of class, gender and sexual orientation is often linked to calls for greater equality or inclusion within the existing boundaries of the national state. In contrast, ethnicity may form the basis for wholesale exclusion of a multi-generational population, but may also serve as the basis of demands for national autonomy.

While ethnic pluralism thereby poses a problem that has to be overcome in the formation of a unified sense of national community, this problem can be solved in more or less inclusive ways. This is apparent in the contrast between the pan-ethnic conception of the Indian nation linked to the Congress movement and Sinhala Buddhist nationalism that has dominated Sri Lanka's politics in the post-independence era. Jawaharlal Nehru, India's first post-independence Prime Minister, describes the diversity of India as 'tremendous'. He notes in particular the difference between the 'Pathan of the North-West and the Tamil in the far South', whose 'racial stocks are not the same' and they differ in 'race and figure, food and clothing and of course language'. In between these two extremes are the myriad other groups, and he lists amongst others the Marathas, the Gujaratis, the Malayalis, the Andhras, the 'great central block' of Hindustani-speakers and the Kashmiris. But amidst all this diversity—all these groups have maintained their 'peculiar characteristics for hundreds of years'—there is also a historically constituted unity:

> Some kind of a dream of unity has occupied the mind of India since the dawn of civilization. That unity was not conceived as something imposed from outside, a standardisation of externals or even of beliefs. It was something deeper and, within its fold, the widest tolerance of belief and custom was practiced and every variety acknowledged and even encouraged.[18]

This understanding of the historical origins of the Indian nation has of course always been in conflict with one that is more exclusively Hindu[19] but was nevertheless important in defining crucial aspects of the Indian constitutional framework, particularly those related to language. In contrast the Sinhala Buddhist conception explicitly excludes Tamil-speaking groups from the conception of the national core. Successive Sinhala leaders from the early twentieth century to the present have equated the Sri Lankan nation with the Sinhala nation and drawn on a history of the island in which the Tamils are positioned as invaders from south India repeatedly threatening the flourishing Buddhist civilisation of the Sinhalese. This equation between Sri Lanka and Sinhala is evident in a speech made by J. R. Jayewardene in 1987 in which he avers:

> [The] Sri Lankan nation has stood out as the most wonderful nation in the world because of several unique characteristics. [The] Sinhala nation has followed one faith, that is Buddhism for an unbroken period of 2500 years.... The language of the King and the people 2100 years ago had been Sinhala which we speak today.... Another unique heritage is the country's history of sovereignty and territorial integrity.[20]

These depictions of national community gain force because they have become the principle axis of social inclusion and exclusion. The boundaries of national community determine the entitlement to citizenship, the distribution of economic goods and services, including welfare, military recruitment and the rights to political representation. The analysis presented in the empirical chapters shows how the relative stability and prosperity of Tamil Nadu is linked to the inclusion of Tamils within the 'unity in diversity' conception of national identity associated with the Congress movement and politically dominant in the post-independence decades. In contrast the Sinhala Buddhist conception of national identity excludes Tamils from full membership of the nation and is linked to the post-independence exclusion of Tamils in Sri Lanka from economic opportunities and political life, materially manifest in the relative impoverishment of the Tamil-speaking regions and populations compared with their earlier relative prosperity.[21] These material outcomes are linked to a hierarchical conception of national identity in which Tamils and other minorities occupy a subordinate positon and thereby are denied equal access to the rights and privileges, or the 'promises of modernity', enjoyed by the national Sinhalese. This was set out bluntly by Sarath Fonseka, Commander of the Sri Lankan Army (2005–9), credited with the May 2009 victory over the LTTE. In an interview given in 2008, Fonseka declaimed:

I strongly believe that this country belongs to the Sinhalese but there are minority communities and we treat them like our people.... We being the majority of the country, 75%, we will never give in and we have the right to protect this country. We are also a strong nation ... They can live in this country with us. But they must not try to, under the pretext of being a minority, demand undue things.[22]

The cross-case comparison of national inclusion and exclusion in India and Sri Lanka, as well as the comparison of each case over time, show that these outcomes were not inevitable, but rather dependent on contingent processes of political mobilisation through which more or less inclusive conceptions of national identity were asserted, contested and more or less securely established as the organising principles of social and political activity. The dominance of a pan-ethnic conception of Indian national identity or a Sinhala Buddhist conception of Sri Lankan identity was not assured in the late nineteenth and early twentieth centuries. In India the Congress movement competed with Hindu, Tamil and Muslim movements that were in various ways hostile to the Congress's national claims. Likewise in Sri Lanka, alongside the Sinhala Buddhist revivalist movement there were efforts to organise a pan-ethnic nationalist movement along the lines of the Congress. The Sinhala Buddhist movement was also not assured of success as it had to overcome intra-Sinhala ethnic cleavages (caste, region and religion) that were important sources of social and political conflict at this time.

What therefore distinguishes successful ethnic and national movements from ones that fail? Why for example was pan-ethnic nationalism successful in India while similar efforts in Sri Lanka failed? The empirical chapters show that successful ethnic and national movements are those that bring together three activities in a temporally sustained way: articulating an ideological framework that sets out key ideas about the boundaries of national community and national interests; incorporating politically significant and existing cleavages as well as interest groups; and finally effectively marshalling support through activities of direct political mobilisation. This framework builds on and departs from John Breuilly's comparative analysis of nationalist movements on the basis of the three functions of nationalist ideology: coordinating diverse political interests, mobilising new groups, and legitimizing the movement to influential outsiders.[23] But whereas Breuilly is concerned with the role of ideology, the focus here is on patterns of political activity, of which setting out a clear ideological framework is only one. As the example of pan-ethnic nationalisms in colonial India and Sri Lanka show, ideologically similar movements in comparable conditions can have different levels of success and therefore different outcomes; the causal difference being absence or presence of temporally continuous patterns of political activity that bring together the three activities identified above.

In setting out an ideological framework, national movements have to make claims about the ethnic boundaries of national community: which groups are included and which excluded. National movements can variously set out a vision of national identity that is inclusive of all ethnic groups, that explicitly excludes some groups whilst including others, or finally an ethnically hierarchical identity that privileges some groups while subordinating others. Along with setting out a clear ideological framework, successful political movements also have to mobilise support; this involves co-opting already powerful social and political actors and directly mobilising amongst the target population. Groups and individuals who are co-opted in such a way might support the movement for reasons that are quite apart from the movement's ideological objectives—for example, because they want political power. However, all ideological movements that have become significant social and political forces must draw in, alongside the ideologically motivated cadres, others who more or less consciously use the movement to pursue self-serving ends. Conversely, it can be seen as a sign of an ideological movement's success that individuals who are motivated to pursue social recognition or power come to see the movement in question as a reliable or even unavoidable way of securing these ends. Thirdly, all successful movements use methods such as mass protests and the channels of mass communication to reach their target audience directly. This direct mobilisation requires constant communication and often involves the use of popular and culturally resonant symbols and metonyms. The scope and medium of direct mobilisation has therefore an impact on the ethnic boundaries of national community. A movement can only build support amongst a target ethnic category if it is able directly and effectively to communicate its message by using resonant language and symbols. There is also a symbiotic relationship between a movement's proven capacity to mobilise support directly and its ability to co-opt the support of powerful actors. Politically ambitious actors are more likely to support an ideological movement, for whatever reason, if the latter has a proven capability for directly mobilising the support of a target audience that is also important to the former.

The success of ethnic and nationalist movements is thus analytically distinct from the motivations and interests of actors who participate in them. Ethnic and nationalist actors can be motivated by a wide range of interests that are quite apart from the stated objectives they pursue. Nevertheless by working to advance a particular set of ethnic or nationalism claims, even for self-consciously self-seeking reasons, they contribute to establishing the public visibility and resonance of those claims and the identities they entail.

It is important to note two important caveats about the use of the word 'success' in this context. Firstly, success does not refer here to a movement's capacity to realise its stated outcomes which, in any case, are often linked to external factors unrelated to its political salience and strength. For example, Sri Lanka gained independence from British rule primarily because of the consequences of World War Two and the related momentum of Indian independence. It was entirely unrelated to the fairly anaemic forces of the anti-colonial movement on the island. Furthermore the Sinhala leaders to whom power was transferred espoused—at least with British officials—a pan-ethnic conception of national identity; but this was extremely thin, not linked to a temporally continuous or socially expansive pattern of political activity, and as such quickly dissolved after independence, leaving no lasting impact on the dynamics of political life. In contrast, the Sri Lankan Tamil nationalist movement has utterly failed to secure its objective of Tamil self-rule despite over six decades of powerful and coordinated mobilisation, first through parliamentary politics, then armed struggle. Nevertheless Sri Lankan Tamil nationalist mobilisation cannot be described as having failed, as it has established a Tamil national identity as a dominant political reality which the Sri Lankan state, international actors and non-nationalist Tamils have to negotiate in the now internationalised ethnic conflict. Success therefore is not taken to mean a movement's capacity to achieve stated objectives, but rather its capacity to establish its preferred identity as an important, if not dominant, organising principle of social and political life. It is in this way that Sri Lankan Tamil nationalism has been successful, though having failed to secure its objective; whilst the pan-ethnic conception of Sri Lankan nationalism failed, although it secured its objective of independence from colonial rule.

A second and related caveat is that success does not imply that a movement has transformed the day-to-day subjective experiences and allegiances of its target population, or even its active adherents in its preferred ethnic or national direction. The term 'identity' is thus used in relation to nationalism and ethnicity to describe a spatially, socially and temporally consistent pattern of political activity embedded in formal as well informal institutions, everyday behaviour and patterns of speech. The assertion that an ethnic or national identity exists is not meant to imply the existence of an objective 'group' or a state of subjective allegiance and continually experienced social solidarity.

Rather it is meant to capture a pattern of activity that is publicly meaningful as ethnic or national and empirically observable over a sustained period of time. National and ethnic identities are thus sustained patterns of social and political activity that can in turn be outcomes of political mobilisation. Nationalist movements that capture state power can quickly and effectively transform social, economic and political life in their preferred direction by using the material resources and coercive apparatus of public institutions. However, even national and ethnic movements that fail to secure state power can nevertheless successfully establish their preferred identities as facts of social and political life. Through sustained political mobilisation, they can build a broad electoral base and thereby secure a lasting presence in political life. They can also mobilise mass protests and establish media and other institutions to reproduce ethnic and national rituals, symbols and rhetoric in a banal but nevertheless visible and productive way. When nationalist movements successfully mobilise support for an armed struggle, they not only challenge the state's territorial control but can also establish de facto governing institutions that reproduce national identity in a state-like way. The successful assertion of an ethnic or national identity is thus a matter of outward patterns of social and political behaviour over sustained periods of time, rather than inward experiences of subjectivity, allegiance and solidarity.

Contribution to the extant literature

The analysis of ethnicity and nationalism that is presented here is focused on political processes, contingency and the centrality of national and ethnic categories to the production, reproduction and contestation of social, political and economic order in modern national states. The growing field of ethnicity and nationalism has been described as 'unsurveyably vast'[24] but the approach here draws on two important trends. The first trend is the growing move away from 'substantialist' assumptions that presume the existence of ethnic or national groups towards a focus on the processes and dynamics that underpin nationalist and ethnic phenomena.[25] Secondly, it also draws on the now substantial body of work that links the political salience of national and ethnic categories to the modern territorial state and its allied political principles of popular sovereignty.[26] Ethnicity and nationalism matter not because they answer an innate need for group solidarity, or because they are universally important components of human subjectivity; but because they are powerful principles of political, social and economic ordering in the modern system of territorial states.

This explanation of the divergent outcomes of the two Tamil-speaking regions thus draws on but also develops important trends in the study of ethnicity and nationalism. While focusing on the contingent processes through which national and ethnic identities are constructed, it nevertheless also links these identities to the core dynamics of social and political order in modern states and shows how once established through long-run processes, they can have a powerful and directive effect on social, political and economic life. It argues therefore that while national and ethnic identities are indeed contingent and constructed, they are not ephemeral and nor are they superfluous to political contestation. Rather they are core and unavoidable components in the struggles to contest and establish the legitimate boundaries of political community and the authoritative purposes of public power and resources. This explanation also uses the comparison between the two Tamil-speaking regions to show that while nation-building amidst ethnic pluralism is a crucial and unavoidable problem, it is a problem that can be resolved in more or less inclusive ways.

This study is also a contribution to the literature on ethnicity and nationalism in India and Sri Lanka, a growing and theoretically as well as methodologically varied area of research that has sought to explain the salience and often conflictual dynamics of ethnic and nationalist mobilisation in the two states. Extant studies have focused on explaining a variety of phenomena such as Hindu–Muslim riots, caste-based political parties, the escalation of Sinhala–Tamil conflict, the production of caste and ethnic identities, the emergence of the south Indian Dravidian movement and the mobilisation of religious and linguistic identities in north India. There are also two studies that are focused on the two Tamil-speaking regions: the first, by Alfred Stepan, Juan Linz and Yogendra Yadav, analyses the impact of the different models adopted by India and Sri Lanka to manage ethnic pluralism on the two Tamil-speaking regions;[27] while the second, by Sankaran Krishna, examines how discourses of national identity in India and Sri Lanka shaped India's intervention in Sri Lanka's conflict as well as the relations between these states and their respective Tamil populations.[28]

Amidst the diverse topics of inquiry and analytical approaches, there are nevertheless four areas of focus that recur both singly and in combination in the explanations of ethnic and nationalist phenomenon in the two states. The first is the interests—material and otherwise—of political leaders and their followers and the extent to which these promote ethnic polarisation or accommodation. Closely related to this is ethnic demography, the second area of focus. A binary ethnic division of the population between two competing groups—as in Sri Lanka—is linked to ethnic outbidding by political elites and subsequent conflict, whereas a more fragmented and cross-cutting ethnic structure—as in India—is said to inhibit such polarising behaviour. The third area of focus is institutions—broadly conceived to include constitutions, but also decision-making rules and whether these are configured to promote inclusion or exclusion. Finally, a fourth area of focus has been the social and political practices—or discourses—embedded in administrative categories, patterns of speech and the day-to-day practices of states and other social and political movements that produce ethnic and national subjectivities as well as ways of being.

The comparative analysis of India and Sri Lanka, as well as each case over time, produces, however, a set of countervailing empirical examples which show that these factors cannot account for the divergent outcomes of the two Tamil-speaking regions. Very different national identities emerged in India and Sri Lanka despite similar types of interests, ethnic cleavages and discourses of identity. Furthermore, while post-independence Indian institutions have been more accommodative of ethnic differences, these institutions are in turn embedded in dominant conceptions of identity and interest that are in need of explanation. The rest of this section discusses some of the key studies to show that in focusing on the causal dynamics of ethnic and nationalist phenomena, these approaches tend to overlook the public character of ethnic and national identities as well as their pivotal role in establishing the boundaries of inclusion and exclusion in modern states. It suggests furthermore that uncovering the causal factors of ethnic and nationalist phenomena is not the same thing as explaining why in comparable circumstances some national identities are more inclusive than others, or why some ethnic claims lead to conflict and others do not.

The interests of political elites as well as those of voters have been cited as a causal force in explaining the politicisation of ethnic identities, party polarisation and violence, as well as explaining instances of ethnic moderation and efforts to contain or limit violence. Analyses that focus on elite interests include Kristian Stokke's argument that Sinhala Buddhist and Tamil nationalist identities were mobilised by political elites from the dominant class who used nationalist appeals as a means of diverting demands for more substantive forms of economic redistribution.[29] David Washbrook and Christopher Baker likewise cite the economic interests of rural bosses and urban magnates to explain the emergence of the Dravidian movement and Indian nationalism in south India.[30] They argue that these powerful elites adopted party labels as vehicles for pursing political power, employing 'publicists' to produce ideologically charged propaganda but also frequently shifting their allegiance from Congress to the Dravidian movement and back again as it suited their interests. In a related argument, Paul Brass foregrounds the character of the political arena and political elites' struggle for power in determining whether ethnic symbols become mobilised in politics or not.[31]

While intuitively appealing, the limitations of elite instrumentalism are apparent when placed in comparative perspective. For example, Stokke's analysis does not explain why Tamil and Sinhala elite interests in political power and securing a highly unequal economic order had to be secured through competing nationalist frameworks rather than in any other way. During the same period and amidst the same economic inequality and class interests, Sri Lankan Muslim, Indian and south Indian Tamil elite interests in power and ongoing economic inequality were similarly secured through other types of political projects. Likewise Baker and Washbrook's focus on magnate interests as exhaustive of political mobilisation fails to explain why Congress was able to build support amongst some magnates (Tamils) but not others (Muslims), which can only be understood by focusing on the symbolic and cultural content of its political mobilisation in different regions. Paul Brass's focus on elite actors selectively mobilising and manipulating ethnic symbols overlooks the varied substance of elite demands which in turn actually cause outcomes of conflict or accommodation. Sri Lankan Tamil elites' mobilisation of a distinct linguistic and cultural identity to demand political autonomy has led to conflict, but the similar Sri Lankan Muslim mobilisation of a distinct religious identity to demand greater representation as Muslims within the Sinhala Buddhist system has generally been accommodated. What matters is not which ethnic symbols elites choose to mobilise, but why some of these symbols come into conflict and others do not.

While the above approaches focus on the interests of leaders in mobilising ethnic sentiments, another set of approaches begins with the presumption that ethnicity is an important source of voter allegiance independent of the machinations of political elites. These approaches link ethnic conflict to ethnic demography and the character of political institutions. In Kanchan Chandra's analysis of ethnic parties, she argues that ethnicity is a rational source of electoral allegiance in patronage democracies such as India, where access to political power facilitates the personalised flow of public goods but also notes that parties can incorporate multiple ethnic groups if they institute intra-party democracy and allow leaders from upwardly mobile ethnic groups to rise up their ranks.[32] However, voters' expectations of patronage cannot explain the very different types of demands that ethnic parties make. For example, the main Sri Lankan Tamil parties have consistently sought autonomy and stayed out of government, even though this limited their access to the public resources which could be distributed as patronage, although they have not suffered electorally for this. In contrast, the main Sri Lankan Muslim political parties have consistently joined whichever government is in power and thereby always secured access to public goods.

In a similar vein, Sumantra Bose and Neil DeVotta have argued that Sri Lanka's ethnic conflict is driven by a combination of voters' ethnic allegiances, ethnic demography, majoritarian institutions and elite behaviour.[33] The numerical dominance of the Sinhalese in Sri Lanka's majoritarian constitutional framework has incentivised Sinhala leaders to pursue Sinhala voters exclusively by progressively outdoing each other in their efforts to promote Sinhala rights and interests at the expense of Tamil ones. This in turn fuelled Tamil resentment and an escalating Sinhala–Tamil conflict. Likewise, Kenneth Bush has argued that intra-ethnic competition is key to explaining key moments of escalation in Sri Lanka's civil war that were spurred by fierce outbidding as competing elites sought to out-manoeuvre each other by taking successively more uncompromising positions.[34]

Competitive ethnic outbidding has been an important feature of Sri Lanka's escalating conflict. However, it has only been effective because it operated within politically dominant conceptions of Sinhala Buddhist and Tamil conceptions of national identity that were by no means a guaranteed or self-evident outcome of earlier political processes. As the historical analysis presented here shows, for most of the colonial era, intra-Tamil and intra-Sinhala ethnic conflict along religious and caste lines was far more important and politically salient than Tamil–Sinhala conflict. Caste cleavages were so strong that in 1911 upper-caste Sinhalese voters preferred an upper-caste Tamil candidate over a lower-caste Sinhalese one in elections to choose a Ceylonese representative for the legislative council; and as a consequence the Tamil candidate (P. Ramanathan) won.[35] The possibility of Sinhala ethnic outbidding and the production of a dominant conception of Sinhala hierarchy required, first, the political consolidation of intra-Sinhala caste, regional and religious differences; and second, the emergence of a Tamil national identity demanding Tamil–Sinhala equality. Neither of these outcomes was inevitable and turned on contingent but temporally extended processes of political organisation and mobilisation. It is only because of the existence of these stable identities that intra-ethnic outbidding could produce an escalation of ethnic conflict.

Elite and popular interests have also been used to explain ethnic accommodation in south India. Marguerite Ross Barnett cites the pragmatism of Dravidian leaders to explain the moderation of the movement's demands from secession to accommodation.[36] She argues that Dravidian leaders dropped the demand for independence in November 1960—against the wishes of their followers—to prevent the movement being targeted by the Indian government, which was increasingly hostile to secessionist demands in the midst of border tensions with China. In contrast, Narendra Subramanian points to the interests of Dravidian movement supporters as moderating the more extreme ethno-nationalism of their leaders.[37] He argues that the Dravidian parties' main support base—upwardly mobile middling peasants, small shopkeepers and clerical workers—used the open and flexible structures of the Dravidian parties to blunt their leaders' ethno-nationalism and radical demands for secession (contra Ross Barnett) whilst pursuing their own social and political advancement within the Indian constitutional framework. He further argues that the more authoritarian Tamil and Sinhala Buddhist nationalist parties in Sri Lanka were less open to being changed by their supporters and thus retained their focus on upholding exclusive ethnic identities.

These explanations, whilst citing contrasting sources of moderation for the relative stability of south Indian ethnic politics, are nevertheless equally problematic as they overlook the importance of national identity in sustaining relations of conflict and accommodation. Ross Barnett's arguments about the moderation of Dravidian leaders cannot be applied to Sri Lanka, where even relatively 'moderate' Tamil demands for autonomy, rather than independence, have provoked resolute and angry rejections from Sinhala Buddhist leaders. Furthermore, Sri Lankan Tamil nationalist demands that Tamil identity and interest be treated equally to those of the Sinhalese are no more or less 'extreme' than core Dravidian demands for the cultivation of Tamil identity and interests. Yet in Sri Lanka conflict emerged because Tamil and Sinhala Buddhist conceptions of national identity are incompatible; while in India stability ensued because the politically dominant conception of Indian national identity could accommodate Dravidian demands.

Subramanian's argument about the moderation of Dravidian party supporters also cannot be used to explain Sri Lanka's ethnic conflict. Sri Lankan political parties—Tamil and Sinhala—are also not centralised and authoritarian, but quite susceptible to pressure from below. James Manor along with

Katharine Adeney and Andrew Wyatt have argued that it is the weakness of the main Sinhala parties that rendered them unable to withstand the force of Sinhala Buddhist mobilisation; they also point to the relative strength of the Indian National Congress as a source of India's more inclusive and stable democracy.[38] However, linking strong party structures with ethnic accommodation is also problematic as it ignores the Congress movement's ethnically inclusive conception of national identity, which developed in tandem with its organisational coherence.[39] Had Sri Lanka evolved a similarly organisationally robust movement with an ethnically inclusive conception of national identity, then conflict would have been avoided. However, if the Sinhala parties had evolved cohesive organisations on a Sinhala Buddhist platform, the problem of mutually incompatible Tamil and Sinhala national identities would have remained, but with the added feature of organisational stability.

The varied incidence of Hindu–Muslim violence has also been explained in terms of the elite as well as grass-roots or civil society interests. Ashatoush Varshney has argued that intra-communal civil society associations that cross the Hindu–Muslim divide have the capacity to prevent and contain Hindu–Muslim violence at a local level in the aftermath of exogenous shocks, such as the destruction of the Babri Masjid in 1992 that led to violence in several cities and towns across India.[40] Varshney argues that these networks and associations, which were unevenly established during the anti-colonial wave of mass mobilisation in the 1920s and 1930s, can effectively contain violence by halting the spread of rumours and providing timely information to the law enforcement authorities. In contrast Steven Wilkinson has suggested that key to explaining the varied incidence of ethnic riots and violence are the electoral and political interests of political leaders who are able to control law enforcement authorities. Where these leaders have an interest in creating ethnic polarisation, they will allow violence to unfold; but where they have an interest in containing violence—because they are dependent on the votes of ethnic minorities—they will use law enforcement authorities to halt and prevent violence.[41]

These explanations equally overlook the causal force of identities in shaping actors' proclivity to provoke and restrain mass violence. Ashatoush Varshney's argument about the capacity of civil society networks relies on the presumption that the state—or the law enforcement mechanism—is ethnically neutral and inclined to prevent violence. As he himself states, his framework cannot be applied to situations where the state and military are 'bent on ethnic pogroms' in which identities and the compulsions they create are clearly important.[42] Identities rather than civil society networks are therefore key to explaining the officially sanctioned anti-Tamil violence of the 1977–83 era that was an important factor in the escalation of Sri Lanka's conflict.[43] Identities may also override electoral incentives and provoke violence against minorities, even where minority votes have become an important component of exercising power. In June 2014, for example, when a Buddhist organisation close to the government triggered anti-Muslim violence in a southern Sri Lankan town, the security forces were slow to intervene to protect Muslims and their property, even though Muslim political parties were members of the then President Mahinda Rajapaksa's ruling coalition.[44] The anti-Muslim violence was coeval with a resurgent and triumphalist Sinhala Buddhist nationalism that has dominated Sri Lanka's politics since the end of the war, and the government chose to consolidate Sinhala Buddhist support even though this meant alienating Muslim voters. The loss of Muslim support was not without electoral consequences and subsequently contributed to Rajapaksa's defeat in the January 2015 elections.[45] Likewise, in the April 2014 general elections, the Hindu nationalist BJP built an electorally successful cross-caste Hindu alliance in the north Indian state of Uttar Pradesh following an eruption of Hindu–Muslim violence in September 2013, the worst in over a decade, which organisations linked to the BJP have been accused of instigating.[46] The electoral growth of parties representing lower castes and their efforts to build support amongst Muslim voters had previously worked to contain Hindu–Muslim violence in the state, but countervailing mobilisation towards an alternative Hindu conception of identity that marginalises Muslims has been associated with the return of such violence.[47]

Analyses that focus on institutions have stressed India's more accommodating constitutional design and forms of governance for its relative success—when compared with Sri Lanka—in managing ethnic differences. Alfred Stepan, Juan Linz and Yogendra Yadav argue that Indian leaders' decision to adopt what they term 'state-nation' policies that explicitly recognise cultural plurality fostered stable accommodation, while Sri Lanka's ethnic conflict is caused by 'nation-state' policies which forcibly sought to create cultural homogeneity out of deeply entrenched cultural heterogeneity.[48] James Manor has argued that India's federal design has worked to quarantine conflicts within state boundaries and thereby prevented them from turning into challenges to the central government.[49] Paul Brass has also provided an explanation of India's success in managing ethnic pluralism that focuses not so much on formal constitutional design but rather on broad rules through which demands for recognition are managed. He suggests that these rules—which recognise linguistic but not religious demands, requiring broad support and consent from all sides—will slowly work towards the consolidation of a stable 'multi-national' state in India, comparable to that in Switzerland.[50]

Although India's institutions have been more accommodating of ethnic difference than those in Sri Lanka, this is not merely a matter of institutional design or choice. India's formal recognition of ethnic pluralism derives from decades of Congress's anti-colonial mobilisation, which sought to secure political support from multiple and politicised caste, linguistic and religious groups.[51] This produced a series of accommodative measures and practices within the Congress movement itself that were subsequently incorporated into the Indian constitution, because Congress dominated the Constituent assembly.[52] The absence of such measures in Sri Lanka is not mere oversight that can be corrected with appropriately framed constitutional reforms, but rather is linked to the political dominance of the Sinhala Buddhist conception of national identity and the simultaneous absence of a pan-ethnic one. The argument that India has adopted a multi-national identity is likewise problematic, as it confuses ethnic claims and ethnic accommodation with the acknowledgement and making of national demands. India's management of ethnic differences, where this has been successful—as in the Tamil case—has depended on symbolically and organisationally including these ethnic identities within an overarching conception of the nation as a historically formed entity. Assertions of linguistic and caste identity have generally sought recognition within the Indian framework, rather than political autonomy, and are therefore better described as ethnic rather than national groups. The 'unity in diversity' conception of the Indian nation described in the quote above describes a national identity in which the acknowledgement of ethnic difference is nevertheless bounded by the idea of a shared past and importantly a shared future. India's management of ethnic difference is therefore due to the emergence of an ethnically inclusive sense of national identity, rather than a multi-national one.

Approaches that focus on identity-shaping discourses also offer little scope for comparative explanation, as broadly similar discourses are evident across both states and influenced by cross-cutting intellectual trends, for example the Aryan/Dravidian dichotomy.[53] These studies have focused on the discourses of the state as well as those of social and political movements. Nicolas Dirks and Nira Wickramasinghe have discussed the colonial state in India and Sri Lanka respectively: Dirks the importance of British practices and ideas in producing caste identities;[54] and Wickramasinghe the role of official practices and interests in producing Sinhala, Tamil, Muslim and Kandyan ethnic identities.[55] Sankaran Krishna's study of India's intervention in Sri Lanka's ethnic conflict argues that the discursive production of a unified national 'self' in India and Sri Lanka has also created a series of ethnic 'others' that in turn have sustained violent conflicts in both states.[56] Finally, Sumathi Ramasway's study of south Indian Tamil linguistic nationalism explains its passion—for example, adherents' willingness to self-immolate to defend the official status of Tamil against Hindi—through the rhetorical tropes, images and metonyms of this literature that constitutes a Tamil-speaking subject defined by service to the Tamil language.[57]

However, a comparative perspective highlights the limitations of these approaches in accounting for the divergent outcomes that are the focus of this study. Dirks' foregrounding of British rule in producing caste identities could equally be applied to British and Dutch practices in Sri Lanka.[58] But whereas in India caste has become an important vector of mobilisation, allied to but independent of language and ideas of race, in Sri Lanka caste divisions remained important but are largely incorporated within Sinhala Buddhist and Tamil nationalist mobilisation. Similarly Wickramasinghe's focus on colonial attitudes and policies in constituting ethnic identities in Sri Lanka cannot account for the very different political trajectories of these similarly constituted categories. Twentieth-century Tamil politics have been dominated by the demand for collective Tamil–Sinhala political equality, while Muslim political leaders have largely accepted and worked within the Sinhala Buddhist framework. Krishna's notion of self–other conflicts similarly overlooks the differentiated nature of relations between the national self and various ethnic groups, only some of whom become others. For example, the accommodation of Tamil identity within the Indian 'Unity in Diversity' conception and the simultaneous exclusion of Muslim identity was contingent on patterns of mobilisation rather than the working out of self–other logic inherent to the discursive production of identities. Finally, while the Tamil protests that Ramaswamy seeks to explain were undoubtedly intense and passionate, they were not uniquely so. There was, for example, a wave of upper-caste self-immolations in the early 1990s against positive discrimination measures to benefit lower-caste groups, but these were not associated with a previous history of thick and emotive literary expression.[59] Also, as previously noted, while the Tamil language rights protests were violent and intense in India, the issue has been largely resolved. In comparison, Sri Lankan Tamil language rights protests were relatively tame, involving in the main limited acts of civil disobedience, but these protests nevertheless provoked lethal bouts of anti-Tamil violence and the language issue become part of a broader and escalating Sinhala–Tamil conflict that finally led to civil war in 1983.

The analysis presented here offers therefore a novel explanation for the divergent outcomes of the two Tamil-speaking regions that departs from extant analyses. Instead of focusing on the factors that cause specific ethnic phenomena, it analyses national identity as an organising principle of the modern state, but one that can be variously inclusive or exclusive of the ethnic pluralism found within the boundaries of almost all states. It also shows that while interests, institutions and discourses are important in the production and reproduction of national and ethnic identities, only a focus on contingent—in that they could easily have been otherwise—but temporally extended political processes can explain why more or less ethnically inclusive national identities emerge in comparable conditions. The comparative analyses of national identity formation presented here show how initial and contingent differences in the patterns of national and ethnic politics beginning in the late nineteenth century but subsequently sustained over several decades produced in India a dominant conception of national identity inclusive of Tamils, and in Sri Lanka one that was hostile to Tamil demands. The analyses also show how these differently inclusive conceptions of national identity and their relations of accommodation and conflict with Tamil political actors explain the stark disparities between the relative prosperity and stability of the south Indian state of Tamil Nadu and the war-shattered impoverishment, state repression and militarisation that characterise the Tamil-speaking regions of Sri Lanka. The empirical chapters that follow trace the emergence, contestation and development of Tamil and national identities comparatively from the late colonial period to the present day. Each of the empirical chapters is organised around a puzzle that foregrounds the causal role of contingent political processes in producing unexpected patterns of national and ethnic politics. The final section of this chapter provides a brief summary of the chapters that follow and shows how the argument unfolds.

Overview of chapters

Chapter 1 provides an overarching view of the emergence and development of ethnic and nationalist politics and shows how the process of national identity formation in India and Sri Lanka emerged in comparable conditions and had to accommodate a similar range of ethnic differences. The subsequent four empirical chapters of Part One deal in turn with colonial and post-independence politics in India and Sri Lanka. Chapter 2 discusses colonial India: it explains how and why Congress's pan-ethnic nationalism became dominant, despite countervailing mobilisation by Dravidian and Muslim nationalists, and also explains why it was able to incorporate Tamils but not Muslims. Chapter 3 turns to colonial Sri Lanka and shows why pan-ethnic nationalism did not develop in Sri Lanka despite arguably more propitious conditions. It also shows that intra-Tamil and intra-Sinhala ethnic conflict along caste and religious lines was the principal axis of conflict at this time and describes how the consolidation of distinct but incompatible Sinhala Buddhist and Tamil national identities overcame these divisions. Chapter 4 then returns to India and traces the post-independence competition between the Dravidian movement and the Congress party and argues that this was agonistic rather than antagonistic because of their shared objectives—namely promoting Tamil identity and interests. It further argues that the Dravidian movement's accommodation within the Indian constitutional framework occurred because this constitution accommodated and recognised these core objectives—rather than because of the relative moderation of Dravidian leaders. Chapter 5, the last in Part One, then moves back to Sri Lanka and shows that escalating conflict in Sri Lanka was driven by the mutual incompatibility between Sinhala Buddhist conceptions of an ethnically hierarchical order and Tamil nationalist demands for collective equality. It argues that Tamil nationalist mobilisation was not simply a response to exclusion but rather required active and temporally continuous political mobilisation.

Part Two focuses on the escalation and ending of Sri Lanka's civil war, as well as subsequent post-war developments. The extant analyses of the conflict and its relentless militarised escalation over three decades have tended to be 'internalist', focusing on the belligerents and their interests and blaming in particular the LTTE and its allegedly extremist, uncompromising and militaristic character. However, these explanations struggle to account for important post-war developments. They cannot explain the deepening ethnic polarisation that continues despite the demise of the LTTE or the ongoing and militarised domination of the Tamil-speaking areas by the almost exclusively Sinhala armed forces. They also cannot account for the important shifts in the international alignments of the conflict that have seen growing tensions post-war between the Sri Lankan government and its former key allies in the war against the LTTE, principally Western states and India over the latter's insistence on accountability for wartime abuses, demilitarisation and political autonomy for the Tamil-speaking regions. At the same time it is also important to explain the new and emergent linkages between international state and non-state actors pursuing liberal reform and Tamil nationalists on the ground and in the diaspora, who were previously viewed with suspicion as aligned to the 'extremist' LTTE and often subject to repressive anti-terrorism proscriptions intended to stifle and contain the LTTE's capacity to mobilise support.

These chapters offer a fresh explanation for the conflict that accounts for these post-war developments by focusing on the interaction between powerful international interventions on the one hand and on the other hand the sustained processes of Sinhala Buddhist and Tamil nationalist mobilisation. The chapters show how and why sustained international interventions into the conflict beginning in the late 1970s fuelled the processes of both Sinhala Buddhist and Tamil nationalist mobilisation whilst failing to secure their stated end: an ethnically inclusive liberal–democratic state. The analysis draws from the now established analysis of international peace-building and liberal intervention in sites of conflict to argue that dominant policy and academic frameworks which securitise and de-politicise conflict worked in Sri Lanka to produce an asymmetrical pattern of intervention that generally strengthened the Sinhala Buddhist nationalist project whilst seeking to contain and marginalise the armed Tamil nationalist threat to the Sri Lankan state. Three chapters trace these developments in chronological order. Chapter 6 focuses on the Cold War era (1977–94) and shows how Western interventions under the rubric of anti-communism and Indian intervention to secure regional dominance interacted with the then simmering insurgency to produce a full-blown civil war that entrenched the Sinhala Buddhist character of state and society whilst prompting radical shifts in the configurations of Tamil nationalist politics. Chapter 7 then turns to the post-Cold War era (1994–2009) and shows how international actors' focus on containing or defeating the LTTE, viewed as the principal obstacle to liberal reform, concealed the stark contradictions between international expectations of liberal reform and the entrenched dominance of Sinhala Buddhist nationalism in Sri Lanka's state, society and crucially the military. These contradictions that have come to the fore in Sri Lanka's post-war era are discussed in Chapter 8, which shows how shifting international alignments have opened up new spaces for the now globalised Tamil nationalist movement, whilst presenting new challenges for Sinhala Buddhist nationalism which faces increasingly forceful international demands for liberal reform that can no longer be delayed by citing the LTTE's obstructions. The Conclusion discusses the implications of these findings for the study of ethnicity and nationalism as well as efforts to manage ethnic conflicts through constitutional reform and broader peace-building efforts.

PART ONE

1

THE ORIGINS

Introduction

This chapter provides a historical overview of ethnic and national politics in India and Sri Lanka, showing that despite the differences of geographic and demographic scale, the problem of ethnicity and national identity in the two states are comparable. It traces the simultaneous emergence of ethnic and national politics in India and Sri Lanka during the nineteenth century. This occurred alongside the uneven processes of social, economic and political transformation associated with British colonial rule. The chapter shows that the question of national identity in the two colonial states required the accommodation of a similar range of ethnic identities that included differences of religion, caste, race, region and language. Along with a broad synchronicity in the timing of important landmarks in the development of ethnic and national politics in the two states, there were also strong ideological overlaps in many of the movements concerned. The very different resolutions of the national question in India and Sri Lanka could not have been predicted from the range of political movements and positions visible during the early decades of the twentieth century. Thus, despite the apparent differences of geographic and demographic scale, India and Sri Lanka are comparable case studies that reveal the causal force of autonomous, open-ended and competitive political processes in shaping the more or less inclusive resolutions of the national question.

The first part of the chapter establishes the historical trajectories through which modern ethnic and national politics first became conceptually meaningful in late-nineteenth-century colonial India and Sri Lanka. These conditions are usefully analytically separated into the following two related and synchronous processes: first, the establishment of the colonial state and the adoption of concepts such as popular sovereignty and representative government; second, the conceptual and social translation of the existing cultural and social diversity of the population into modern ethnic categories. The emergence of national and ethnic politics was also dependent on the social, technological and economic changes that occurred during the nineteenth century. These include the introduction of mass communication technologies, beginning with the printing press; the shift to modern forms of education and the emergence of a Western-educated segment; changes in transportation infrastructure; and the integration of India and Sri Lanka into regional and global commodity, labour and financial flows.[1] These changes did not replicate the transformations that took place across western Europe and north America. Indeed, the expansion of colonial rule in the early decades of the nineteenth century was associated with de-urbanisation and de-industrialisation across many parts of India.[2] Nevertheless, by the end of the nineteenth century, concepts such as popular sovereignty and the nation, along with the political institutions of the colonial state, became crucial and established facts of social and political activity in India and Sri Lanka. The third and final part of the chapter provides a broad outline of ethnic and national politics in the two countries.

British colonial rule and modern politics

The antecedents of formal British colonial rule in India and Sri Lanka can be traced to 1611, when the East India Company first began its trading activities on the Indian subcontinent. The English company was not the first to arrive in the region and was not for many centuries the most politically or militarily dominant.[3] An early lead was taken by the Portuguese, who established trading posts primarily on the western coast of India from the early 1500s[4] and the south-western coast of Sri Lanka in 1501.[5] In India European traders, including the French and the Danes, acted within a vibrant and competitive Indian political system in which Indian rulers vied for control over territory and taxable resources, including trade.[6] From the dissolution of the Mughal Empire and until the mid-eighteenth century, European trading companies occupied subsidiary political, economic and military roles in relation to competing Indian rulers who sought to expand and consolidate their state-building projects. The shift from trade to formal colonial rule on the Indian subcontinent took place in the context of eighteenth-century French and

British rivalry in which India became one of the theatres of globalised military conflict. From the 1740s, troops from the British and French state armies and navies regularly supplemented the troops of their respective trading companies in battles for control of Indian trading posts. By the late eighteenth century, the expansion of the French and British military presence in India and the perceived importance of Indian trade to French and British national interests altered the balance between the European companies and Indian rulers. The French and British companies increasingly used their military and financial resources to intervene in conflicts between Indian rulers and in Indian succession disputes which left their Indian allies heavily indebted to European company officials. The East India Company's decision in 1757 to depose the Nawab of Bengal, replacing him with a succession of dependants and finally in 1771 directly assuming the governance of Bengal, was the culmination of a series of events in which British ideals of absolute sovereignty, Indian political rivalries, Indian indebtedness, as well as the global imperatives of Anglo-French competition, were all present.

From the initial base in Bengal and trading posts in Madras and Bombay, British territorial possessions gradually expanded over the next century through a mixture of logistics and motivations that included the need to expand and secure the 'turbulent frontier'[7] against possible Indian and French threats and the growing indebtedness of some Indian rulers, as well as the expanding territorial ambitions of others. British expansion was punctuated by a series of intense military encounters with Indian rulers, principally the Marathas and Mysore, who were themselves expanding their territories through the logic of militarised state-building. A decisive victory over Mysore was finally achieved in 1799, while the Marathas were defeated by 1818. Some of the annexed territory was brought under direct British rule and administered through the Presidencies of Madras, Bombay and Calcutta. Alongside this, a large number of Indian kingdoms were incorporated as Princely States, ruled by hereditary monarchs who retained a veneer of autonomy within the overall structure of the British Empire. British colonial expansion continued through the nineteenth century; by 1891 it covered an area of 1.3 million square miles, with a total population of over 280 million people.[8]

For much of the eighteenth century the Tamil-speaking areas of south India were the site of intense and violent contest between post-Mughal successor states and European powers. The clashing territorial ambitions of Mysore (ruled by Haider Ali and Tipu Sultan), the Nawab of Arcot and the Maratha-ruled kingdom of Tanjore led to frequent battles in which European companies were increasingly involved as allies and often adversaries of Indian rulers. By the 1760s, the ruler of Arcot had become a dependant of the East India Company; and by the 1780s, the same was true of the ruler of Tanjore. With the final defeat of Tipu Sultan at the turn of the nineteenth century, the Tamil-speaking areas were incorporated into Company rule and contained within the borders of the Madras Presidency. The vast majority of these areas, excepting the small princely state of Puddukotai and the French-administered enclave of Pondicherry, were incorporated as directly administered territories. The Madras Presidency covered an area of 141,001 square miles, an area calculated at the time to equal the United Kingdom and Greece combined and containing a polyglot population of almost 36 million, of which just over 15 million were Tamil-speakers.[9]

Formal colonial rule and the rapid incorporation of India into a British-centred global economy from the early decades of the nineteenth century[10] wrought important changes in south Indian society as well as its economic patterns and linkages.[11] Principally the growing commercialisation of the south Indian economy, evident from the fifteenth century, and the well-established links of trade and culture with the Arab Gulf and South East Asia began to wither. The twin impacts of the industrial revolution and the intensification and consolidation of British rule produced an economic depression during the early decades of the nineteenth century.[12] The overseas and internal markets for south Indian textiles and other artisanal goods, along with a nascent local iron and steel industry, were soon taken over by British goods. Meanwhile, the defeat of Indian rulers also dampened demand for artisanal goods, soldiers and other forms of cultural specialists as the courts and their armies were dismantled. Large numbers of former artisans and soldiers[13] were therefore forced back onto the land just as the Company was seeking to consolidate its rule by extracting often penal levels of revenue from agricultural production. The overall effect was predictably to depress prices and crush economic activity, such that by the time the 'depression lifted, in the 1850s, what once had been one of the early modern world's great commercial economies had been turned into a "backward" agricultural dependency'.[14] South India's own trading and cultural links with the rest of the world were thus curtailed and rearticulated along the lines of Britain's growing political and economic dominance. The Company's south Indian troops, financed in large part by agricultural revenue, were used in Sri Lanka (1795), Java (1811–15) and Burma (1822–4). At the same time the growing population combined with a depressed local economy centred on agricultural production led to pressure on the land and net labour emigration from south India, including to the expanding plantation economy of Ceylon.[15]

The island of Ceylon was also incorporated into the British Empire against the background of global Anglo-French rivalry and was prompted by the French invasion of Holland in 1794.[16] At that point most of the island, except for the inland and inaccessible Kandyan kingdom, had been under European political and economic dominance for almost three hundred years. The Portuguese initially established a trading base on the south-western coast of the island in 1501, but by the end of the century had annexed the territories associated with the south-western Sinhala kingdom of Kotte (later Colombo) and the northern Tamil kingdom of Jaffna as Portuguese dominions. Portuguese rule lasted until the mid-seventeenth century when first Colombo (1656) and then Jaffna (1658) fell to the Dutch East India Company. Dutch rule in its turn was brought to an end when the French deposed the Stattholder of Holland and installed a friendly republican government, prompting British fears that the Dutch territory on the island, particularly the natural harbour at Trincomalee, would be used by the French to attack India.[17] East India Company troops laid siege and captured Trincomalee in August 1795, and by February the next year all the Dutch possessions on the island had been surrendered to the British. The newly captured territories in Ceylon were initially administered by the East India Company in Madras, but in 1802 were incorporated as the Crown Colony of Ceylon and brought under the control of the recently established Colonial Office.[18]

In 1815 the hitherto independent kingdom of Kandy was annexed and brought under British rule. The Kandyan areas were linguistically Sinhalese and religiously Buddhist, like the low country or south-western Sinhalese regions that had been under European rule since 1501. However, the different historical experience of the Kandyan areas produced an important regional distinction between the low country and Kandyan Sinhalese. The low country Sinhalese areas and people were more commercially developed and had been under Western and Christian influence for a much longer period; this cultural and economic difference also became at times politically salient.[19] The capture of the Kandyan areas furthermore triggered an important change in the island's economy and demography by opening up the interior areas to plantation agriculture: initially coffee and then, from the 1880s, tea. Labour for the plantations was sourced from south India, particularly the Tamil-speaking areas. The increasing commercialisation of the island's economy, stimulated by its integration into global trade flows, also brought large numbers of other

Tamils and Indians more generally who came to take advantage of the opportunities in trade and commerce. By the late nineteenth century there were thus two distinct Tamil-speaking populations on the island. The first was the population that had migrated in the nineteenth century and settled mainly in the central and south-western parts of the island. The second was the population in the north-eastern parts of the island that had been established there for several centuries.[20] The 1891 Census of Ceylon recorded the population of the island, a territory of 25, 333 square miles, at just over 3 million.[21] Of this, the majority were Sinhalese (2,041,158) and just under a third were Tamils (723,853).[22] The other significant minorities were the Muslims, called Moormen (197,166); and Malays (10,133), migrants from Malaysia.

Although they were administered separately, the political development of the two colonies, and in particular the emergence of ethnic and national politics, was crucially shaped by what Thomas Metcalfe has called a 'distinctive ideology of imperial governance shaped by the ideals of liberalism'.[23] This ideology was linked to the emergent industrial revolution and the associated reform and evangelical movements that were transforming social, political and economic life in Britain, and replaced the earlier more conservative and purely extractive mercantilist orientation of British rule.[24] British rule was legitimised as a means of effecting social and economic progress and development. This sentiment is clearly expressed in Queen Victoria's proclamation of 1857, issued to mark the end of the Indian mutiny or rebellion and the beginning of the British Crown's direct rule over India, replacing the previously existing indirect rule through the East India Company. The proclamation stated that it was 'our earnest duty to stimulate the peaceful industry of India, to promote works of public utility and improvement, and to administer its government for the benefit of all our subjects resident therein'.[25] The influence of liberal imperialism is also clearly evident in Sri Lanka. The 1833 report of the Commissioners W. M. G. Colebrooke and C. H. Cameron, appointed to recommend reforms on the government, judiciary and economy of Ceylon, was optimistic about the prospects for advancement on the island. The Commissioners stated that Ceylon was 'the fittest spot in our Eastern Dominions in which to plant the seeds of European civilization whence we may not unreasonably hope that it will hereafter spread over the whole of these vast territories'.[26]

Self-government through representative institutions was a crucial component of the liberal imperialist notions of advancement towards European standards of civilisation. Thomas Macaulay, English parliamentarian, historian and law member of the Governor General's Council in India, stated in 1833 that the day when India's 'public mind', expanded by 'our system', sought self-government, 'it will be the proudest day in English history'.[27] The contemporaneous Colebrooke–Cameron report also recommended a legislative council with representatives—nominated rather than elected—chosen to represent interests in Ceylon society. The Commissioners noted that while the prevailing 'ignorance and prejudice' would prevent the government from adopting the Ceylonese representatives' views, a representative legislature was nevertheless consistent 'with the policy of a liberal government'.[28]

By the mid to late nineteenth century, the early-nineteenth-century optimism of liberal imperialism had given way to more conservative attitudes, and British officials were generally reluctant to grant the possibility of progress towards self-government in both India and Sri Lanka.[29] Despite official resistance and sometimes outright hostility to the possibility of self-government, increasing numbers of Indians and Sri Lankans were nevertheless adopting the language of liberal representative politics to make demands of their respective states. In India from the 1830s onwards[30] and in Sri Lanka from the 1860s,[31] political and social activity was increasingly orientated towards the colonial state and sought to reform, influence and mobilise the power of the state towards their various projects: projects always framed in terms of the ultimate ideals of progress, development and legitimate government. In the last quarter of the nineteenth century, political organisations emerged in both countries that claimed to be national in scope; they made at first extremely circumscribed but later more expansive demands for greater Indian and Sri Lankan participation in the business of government. The Indian National Congress (INC), formed in 1885, initially sought minor constitutional and administrative changes[32] but by the early 1920s had adopted the demand for 'swaraj' or self-rule.[33] A similar organisation called the Ceylon National Association (CNA), formed in 1888, also sought minor constitutional changes. It was supplanted by the Ceylon National Congress (CNC) in 1917 which in turn was replaced in 1946 by the United National Party (UNP). The problem of national identity and ethnic diversity was conceptually hard-wired into this politics and was ever present, more or less explicitly, in the wrangling and manoeuvring of all significant actors, official and unofficial alike.

While British officials were often hostile and dismissive of the claims of these organisations, they nevertheless framed their objections in the language of popular sovereignty. That is, while British officials might have eschewed the possibility of democratic self-government, they nevertheless had to rest the legitimacy of British rule ultimately in its ability to protect and promote the interests of its Indian and Sri Lankan subjects. As Michael Billig notes, for the modern state, 'sovereignty has descended from heaven to earth, from the clouds to the soil of the homeland and to the collectively invoked bodies of its inhabitants'.[34] British officials often claimed that they had a much clearer understanding of the needs of the Indian and Sri Lankan populations than Indian or Sri Lankan politicians who simply sought their own self-interest. A clear expression of this sentiment was made by the Viceroy Lord Dufferin (serving 1884–8) who dismissed the INC by stating that it was a 'microscopic minority' and that it was impossible to entrust to such an organisation the 'safety and welfare' of the 'majestic and multiform empire' for which the British stood responsible 'in the eyes of God and before the face of civilization'.[35] At the same time, British officials also invoked the ethnic pluralism of the Indian and Sri Lankan politicians to challenge these politicians' national claims. In India, Congress's claim to be nationally representative was challenged along the lines of religion and caste by Muslim[36] and lower-caste representatives[37] with more or less explicit British support. Similarly in Sri Lanka, the CNC's claims to be nationally representative were challenged along the lines of region and language by Kandyan Sinhalese and Tamil representatives—again with more or less explicit British support.[38]

Eventually the transition from British colonial rule to independence was effected through constitutional changes that saw a gradual expansion of elected Indian and Sri Lankan representation in the political institutions established during the early decades of the nineteenth century, along with greater executive power for elected representatives. These changes invariably involved contestation over the extent and balance of ethnic representation. During most of the nineteenth century, until the reforms of 1920, constitutional change was slow and incremental. In India the first substantive step came with the 1909 Indian Councils Act (also called the Morley–Minto reforms) which introduced for the first time the elective principle to the Imperial and Provincial legislative councils, with representatives elected indirectly from the members of local district and municipal boards. The 1909 reforms also introduced the principle of separate Muslim electorates; that is, Muslims voters were formed into a distinctive electoral college to facilitate the election of specifically Muslim representatives. The intention was to ensure adequate Muslim representation, as in most electoral constituencies Muslims were a minority of the eligible voters. Constitutional change in Sri Lanka was also slow during much of the nineteenth century.[39] There was little change to

the nominated legislative council created in 1833 by the Colebrooke–
Cameron reforms, save for the addition of two extra representatives in 1886:
one for the Muslims and one for the Kandyan Sinhalese, the latter seen as
requiring separate representation from the low country Sinhalese.

The pace of reform in the twentieth century was comparatively more rapid
than that in the nineteenth century. In India, just a decade after the 1909 act,
the Montague–Chelmsford reforms of 1919 allowed for the direct elections
of Indians (from largely territorial constituencies) to the Provincial legislatures, and indirectly from the Provincial legislature to the Imperial legislature,
now moved to the new capital in Delhi. The 1919 act also devolved a limited
amount of executive responsibility to Indians at the provincial level. These
reforms were rejected by the INC and other nationalists, including a significant number who sought to use political violence as a means of directly over-
throwing British rule. The push for more extensive reform led to the 1935
Government of India Act which expanded the franchise further and granted
responsible government, albeit under the final executive authority of the
Viceroy, at provincial and central levels. India was governed under the provisions of the 1935 act until independence and partition in 1947, following
which, in 1952, the Indian Constituent Assembly adopted India's post-independence constitution and elections were held for the first time with a universal franchise.

The pace of reform in Sri Lanka in the twentieth century was equally rapid,
with important changes to the constitutional structure coinciding with major
reforms in India.[40] The electoral principle was gingerly introduced to the legislative council in 1909, with the creation of an additional educated Ceylonese
seat selected by an electorate restricted on the basis of education and property.
The August 1917 Montague–Chelmsford announcement of reforms in India
spurred the creation of the Ceylon National Congress (CNC) to press for an
expansion of the electoral principle and territorial rather than communal
representation. These demands were resisted by Kandyan Sinhalese and Tamil
politicians, who insisted on special electoral provisions to offset the demographic majority of the low country Sinhalese translating into electoral dominance. A series of reforms throughout the 1920s contained a mixture of
territorial and communal electorates, a limited franchise and extra weighting
to increase the representation of the minorities—principally the Tamils and
the Kandyan Sinhalese. The next stage of reforms in Sri Lanka, as in India, was
tasked to a commission, the Donoughmore Commission, which remarkably
arrived on the island in November 1927 just as the similarly-tasked Simon

Commission arrived in India to protests and boycotts by Indian nationalist groups, including Congress. The Donoughmore Commission, unlike its equivalent in India, met with a full and exhaustive range of Sri Lankan politicians and formulated a far-reaching set of proposals. It set out a constitutional structure based on the London County Council system, in which executive committees elected by the entire legislature—named the State Council—were tasked with responsibility for the major areas of government. The state councillors were to be elected primarily on the basis of territorial constituencies and universal franchise.

The clear emergence of ethnic and national politics in India and Sri Lanka was not associated with the transformative social and economic changes that accompanied the expansion of representative politics and the elective principle in North America and western Europe. In India as in Sri Lanka, for the duration of the nineteenth century and well into the twentieth century, the proportion of the population engaged in political activity that was framed through the concepts of nation and ethnicity was small and limited. This is apparent in the size of the proportion of the electorate that was eligible for the franchise when it was restricted through literacy and property qualifications; the 1919 reforms in India extended the franchise to just two per cent of the population, while in Sri Lanka the 1921 reforms extended the franchise to just over one per cent of the population.[41]

The emergence of mass political movements in the early decades of the twentieth century also did not signal the creation of a uniform public culture. Shahid Amin's study of peasant perceptions of Gandhi in the 1920s shows that the official statements set out by Congress Party workers and Gandhi himself were starkly dissonant with millennial expectations and ambitions for social mobility through which Gandhi's rural audience reframed his message.[42] Similarly, the prevalence of significant economic inequality meant that even during the periods of limited franchise, electoral contestation was organised through vote banks and the often coercive mobilisation of patron–client networks.[43] Patronage networks were therefore crucial to the production of ethnic accommodation in India and ethnic conflict in Sri Lanka, and therefore cannot be used to explain the divergence.

Framing ethnic diversity in India and Sri Lanka

The colonial states of India and Sri Lanka brought together populations containing a diversity of social and cultural groups. By the late nineteenth century this diversity was framed and understood through the categories of caste, language, religion and race; categories that were built into the structures of the colonial state.[44] There is an ongoing debate on the relationship between modern ethnic categories and pre-modern cultural differences. An influential body of post-colonial scholarship suggests that modern ethnic identities and therefore ethnic antagonisms are largely the products of colonial rule. However, these arguments are challenged by others who suggest that these categories were politically and socially significant in the pre-British period and their salience in modern politics is the result of Indian and Sri Lankan agency as much as colonial systems of governance.[45]

The approach adopted here sidesteps questions of colonial power, historical continuity and the agency of colonial subjects at the centre of debates on the meanings and subjective experience of cultural difference. Rather, it suggests that by the late nineteenth century, many of the cultural practices touched by the social, political and economic transformations associated with the colonial state would inevitably have been translated into the modern categories of religion, caste and language. The long-established institutions, philosophical traditions and ritual practices that were incorporated into the Buddhist, Hindu, Muslim and Saivite religious revivalisms of the late nineteenth century could not have simply disappeared or avoided contact with modern conceptions of religion as a confessional system and potentially 'national' institution. Similarly, the established Sanskrit, Tamil, Sinhala and Urdu literary traditions and practices would also not have disappeared or avoided translation into modern languages, reproduced through print and studied through modern conventions of literary analysis. In Ernst Gellner's terminology, this process involved the translation of pre-modern high cultures into modern, academy-produced culture, rather than the translation of pre-modern wild culture into modern high culture.[46] In other words, the transformation of pre-modern cultural difference into modern categories of religion, language and caste is understood here as a matter of inevitable conceptual translation, leaving aside questions of agency and continuity. Furthermore and what is important for this study is that the social and cultural diversity of the Indian and Sri Lankan populations was framed, administered and discussed through remarkably similar ideas and categories. As a consequence, the problem of national identity in India and Sri Lanka had to contend with the same range of ethnic categories that included caste, language, religion, race; and in Sri Lanka, also region.

By the late nineteenth century, modern ethnic categories were an established part of colonial public culture. They were not only extensively used in the administrative practices of the state, but also formed the basis of the expanding range of social and political activities undertaken by Indians and Sri Lankans themselves. The decennial census operations undertaken by the colonial governments of both states organised the population according to categories of language, religion, race and caste. These categories were also important in routine administrative practices such as recruitment to state agencies—including the police and military, the distribution of public funds for education and the administration of civil law. At the same time social reform movements and political associations also based their activities on these very same ethnic categories. Religious and linguistic revival and reform movements, as well as caste associations, worked within the same frameworks and sets of assumptions as the colonial state.[47] An important and influential set of ideas that influenced the use of ethnic categories—by officials as well revivalists and nationalists—claimed that the Indian and Sri Lankan populations could be divided into racially distinct Aryan, Dravidian and Muslim populations on the basis of language, race, religion and caste. This racial categorisation was used by a wide range of actors in both countries to set out the substance of national identities and national histories that included some linguistic, religious and caste groups, but excluded others.

The Aryan/Dravidian distinction, with Muslims as civilisational outsiders, evolved from the late-eighteenth-century study of Sanskrit by British scholars who were based mainly in Calcutta and were identified by themselves and others as Orientalists.[48] Noticing the structural similarities between Sanskrit and European languages, particularly Latin and Greek, Sir William Jones argued that they must have come from the same root language at some stage, and furthermore that speakers of these languages shared common ancestors. The term Aryan, a Sanskrit word meaning 'noble' or 'honourable', was introduced by the Sanskritist Max Muller in the 1840s and it quickly acquired nineteenth-century racial implications absent from the eighteenth-century work of the Calcutta Orientalists.[49] Thomas Trautmann has argued that Sir William Jones' study of Sanskrit was situated within a larger biblical ethnology that emphasised the unity of mankind. In keeping with this, eighteenth-century perspectives of Indian society generally viewed all Indian languages and cultures as derived from the same Sanskritic roots. The Orientalist characterisation nevertheless saw the Muslims as outsiders and invaders responsible for the destruction and degradation of Sanskritic Hindu civilisation; a theme that became important to Hindu nationalist interpretations of Indian history.

The notion that all Indian languages were derived from Sanskrit was challenged by scholars working on south Indian languages, in particular Tamil and Telugu. First Francis Ellis Whyte in 1816, and then Robert Caldwell in 1856, argued that the south Indian languages were independent of Sanskrit and had an alternative source. Caldwell used the term Dravidian, also derived from Sanskrit and originally used to designate south Indian Brahmin groups, to label the south Indian language group, language speakers and their cultural and literary heritage.[50] The distinction between the Aryan and Dravidian components of Indian society gave rise to two competing understandings of Indian civilisation and history: one in which the Aryans became the bearers of civilisation, and in the other the Dravidians. The Aryan/Dravidian distinction also mapped broadly onto a north/south regional divide separating the Aryan north from the Dravidian south. From the late nineteenth century, proponents of both accounts began to draw on then popular biological conceptions of race in which racial types, identified through physical features, particularly skin colour, were used to explain intellectual and cultural or 'civilisational' attainment.

In the Aryan narrative of Indian history, Indian civilisation is created by the foundational act of Aryan migration. In this view, light-skinned or Caucasian Aryans who migrated to India from the central Asian and Caucasian regions brought with them the Sanskrit language and Hindu religion.[51] Upon entering India they found less civilised and darker-skinned people—identified as Dravidian—whom they variously either exterminated, pushed into the mountainous regions or incorporated within their social structure as low-caste labourers. In India the Aryan idea was taken up by Hindu nationalists and used to characterise Indian national culture and history as racially Aryan, religiously Hindu and based on Sanskrit culture and language. The golden age of Indian civilisation was identified with the Vedic period when key Sanskrit texts were first thought to have been composed. In the Hindu nationalist conception, this Vedic–Aryan golden age was brought to an end by Muslim 'invasions' that subsequently triggered the decline of Aryan social order and led to corruptions in Hindu thought and practices. Practices such as caste and gender inequality were thus blamed on the decline triggered by the Muslim 'invasions'. Indian Muslims were thereby rendered outside the national core and, along with Muslim culture and religion, seen as an ever threatening cultural, religious and even demographic threat to the Hindu–Indian nation.

This view of the non-Aryan peoples as less civilised was challenged by south Indian scholars, particularly Tamils (Sri Lankan and Indian) who, building on

Caldwell's Dravidian ideas, created an alternative Dravidian view of Indian society and history.[52] The Dravidian view reversed the hierarchy of the Aryan view and argued that the original Dravidian society had attained a high level of civilisation based on egalitarian and humanist principles, but was destroyed by the Aryan invasions. The Aryans, far from civilising the subcontinent, brought with them the uncivilised practices of caste and gender hierarchy associated with Hinduism. From the early decades of the twentieth century, the Dravidian category became politically significant in south India and was used to frame south Indian, particularly Tamil, language, culture, literary history and people as racially Dravidian. Using the Aryan association with Sanskrit and Hinduism, Dravidian activists argued that Hinduism, the caste structure and Sanskrit were all alien impositions on an otherwise egalitarian and religiously plural Tamil society. The Dravidian idea was also used by anti-caste movements across India to identify lower-caste groups with the original Dravidians conquered and enslaved by the invading Aryans.

As discussed further in Chapters 2 and 3, while the Dravidian idea was an important pole of south Indian Tamil social and political life, it was less influential amongst the Sri Lankan Tamils. Nonetheless, the Aryan/Dravidian dichotomy did have consequences in Sri Lanka. Linguistic analysis in the early nineteenth century established that the Sinhala language had more in common with Sanskrit and the north Indian languages than Tamil and the south Indian or Dravidian languages. The Sinhalese people were thereby classified as Aryan and this led a number of British officials and scholars, along with Sinhala revivalists, to produce an Aryan narrative of the island's history and national identity, one that was structurally identical to the Hindu nationalist vision.[53] From the late nineteenth century, Buddhist revivalists, like their Hindu counterparts in India, used the Aryan idea to characterise Sri Lankan national identity and national history as religiously Buddhist, as well as linguistically and culturally Sinhalese. The foundational act of the island's history was deemed the migration from north India of Aryan Sinhalese, who subsequently adopted Buddhism. In this narrative, the flourishing Sinhala Buddhist civilisation, with its developed system of irrigated rice farming, was destroyed by the invading south Indian Dravidian Tamils. As with the Muslims in India, the Tamils in Sri Lanka were thereby rendered outside the Sinhala Buddhist core and equally seen as a cultural, religious and demographic threat to the Sinhala Buddhist nation.

Finally, the Aryan/Dravidian dichotomy was also influential in framing ideas about caste, particularly in south India. A complex, regionally as well as historically, varying phenomenon, caste practices and norms nevertheless contain a number of similarities across the subcontinent that extend to Tamil and Sinhalese society in Sri Lanka. The English term 'caste' covers two separate indices of social hierarchy: jati (or birth group) and varna (or social class).[54] The varna classification of society into four hierarchically ranked groups is derived from Hindu theology and set out in a series of Sanskrit texts which ascribe to each group a set of qualities and a related set of social roles and functions. The highest-ranking groups are Brahmins (priests and ritual specialists), then Kashatriyas (rulers and warriors), followed by Vaishyas (commercial groups and other wealth creators) and finally the Shudras (or servile toilers). In Sanskrit theology an individual's position in the varna scheme is determined by the merits of their previous life, while their relative status in the next life is determined by their fulfilling the obligations that arise from their varna status in this life. An individual's rank is contained within the substance or essence of their body, such that people of higher caste are regarded as of purer and more auspicious substance. For those of high caste, the bodies of low castes are polluting, as is any food prepared or touched by them.

Although substance is determined by birth (such that Brahmin bodies are always more auspicious and pure than those of Shudras), it can also be affected by daily conduct; contact with substances that Sanskrit texts deem pure impart a quality of auspiciousness, while contact with substances deemed polluted can render the substance of a body polluting to others. This division of the universe of substances into pure and polluting has also created a fifth order, not formally recognised in the varna status, who deal with especially polluting substances— dead flesh (animal as well as human) and human waste. Caste groups or jatis associated with polluting activities such as removing and treating dead human and animal bodies, working with animal flesh (leather workers for example) and removing human waste are subject to a set of practices known by the term 'untouchability'. Untouchable groups were—and in many places continue to be—denied access to public spaces such as schools, temples, common wells and public roads. From the early decades of the twentieth century the term Dalit, meaning oppressed or broken, has also been used by caste groups treated as untouchable as a term of political and cultural resistance.[55]

The bodily practices of caste hierarchy—particularly taboos about food, engaging in work associated with untouchable groups and the prohibitions on untouchable groups' access to temples and other public spaces—became the objects of social and political protests in India and Sri Lanka from the early decades of the twentieth century. They have also produced three important political and social strategies for overcoming caste hierarchy. One approach argued that caste hierarchies and the violent exclusion of untouchable groups were inherent to Hinduism, and therefore the only way of excising caste was to abandon Hindu thought and practice wholesale.[56] In the Tamil-speaking regions, this approach was closely associated with the Self-Respect Movement and later the Dravida Kazhagam (DK). The Self-Respect Movement and the DK, both working within the Dravidian framework, encouraged their followers to abandon Hindu lifecycle rituals, caste names and Hindu worship whilst staging acts of iconoclasm—book burning and idol smashing—as a means of shattering the ritual status of Hindu objects of worship. A second approach was to suggest that caste hierarchy and particularly the practices of untouchability were later corruptions of Hindu theology. In this approach, most closely associated with Gandhi, caste taboos could be overcome by reforming both upper-caste and lower-caste behaviour whilst all castes remained within the fold of Hindu belief and practice. Political and social associations that adopted this approach encouraged activities such as inter-caste dining, public upper-caste performance of lower-caste work, access for lower castes to privileged upper-caste spaces and more controversially encouraged lower-caste groups to adopt upper-caste practices—such as vegetarianism, teetotalism, orthodox lifecycle rituals and the worship of gods from the high Hindu pantheon. The third approach, linked to Nehru, saw caste along with other 'communal' divisions as relics of a pre-modern era that would inevitably be eroded by the forces of modernity and industrialisation.

While the varna hierarchy provides the theological basis of caste hierarchy and was incorporated into colonial administrative structures, the actual experience of caste is through a second category of human community, known across most of south Asia by the term jati or its equivalents. The term jati identifies a clear social group bound generally by practices of intermarriage and interdining. There are innumerable named jati groups: some confined to small locales and identifying a population of only a few thousand, and others ranging across vast regions and numbering in the millions.[57] Only Brahmin and untouchable jatis are clearly identifiable with their respective varna. For most other jati identities, social position and status has rarely been a matter of fixed inheritance. Instead the social status of a particular jati has been determined by relative political and economic power and has allowed for a great deal of social mobility. Groups that have gained prestige and status through arms-bearing, control of land or commercial wealth have often been able to convert this to social status by adopting varna norms, that is by restricting their marriage practices, worshipping the gods of the high Hindu pantheon and adopting appropriately Kshatriya-like lordly lifestyles (for arms-bearing groups) or the Vaishya-like lifestyle of the pacific and settled man of worth (for commercial and landowning groups).[58] The varna hierarchy is therefore better understood as an ideal index of social ranking than a description of social practice. The Brahmin's ritual status was only ever a means to legitimise the already existing wealth and power of upwardly mobile groups and many Brahmins were the dependants of their wealthy landowning or commercial patrons.[59]

From the late nineteenth century onwards, caste in both its varna and jati manifestations was an established part of colonial public culture. In India the varna hierarchy was incorporated into colonial legal codes as part of Hindu personal law and also used to categorise jati groups in the census enumerations.[60] This led to a number of caste associations demanding an upward revision of their varna status.[61] Even in Sri Lanka where varna was not formally incorporated into colonial administrative practice, jati groups such as the Sinhala Karava and Salagamas sought official recognition for their claims to Kshatriya and Brahmin status respectively.[62] The increasingly public prominence of the varna hierarchy had specific implications for south Indian society, including the Tamil-speaking areas. Here commercial and artisan groups as well as large landowners, many of whom had very restrictive and varna-like social practices, nevertheless did not perform rituals, in particular the investiture of males with the sacred thread, which marked Kshatriya and Vaishya status in north India. Except for the Brahmins and the untouchables, the vast majority of south Indian Hindu jati groups were therefore classified as Shudras in the fivefold varna scheme.[63] This division between Brahmins and the rest of south Indian society implied therefore a racial division between Aryan Brahmins and Dravidian non-Brahmins. A number of south Indian scholars argued that caste was brought to south Indian society by the racially Aryan Brahmins as a means of enforcing social and political dominance over the previously egalitarian Dravidian society.[64] The Aryan (Brahmin)/Dravidian (non-Brahmin) divide also became an important pole of political activity during the early decades of the twentieth century. This Brahmin/non-Brahmin duality was not, however, influential within Sri Lankan Tamil politics. Instead, as Chapters 3 and 5 show, the Gandhian and Congress approach to transforming caste hierarchy has been far more influential in Sri Lankan Tamil society than the radical reform agenda of the Dravidian movement.

The ethnic diversity of the Indian and Sri Lankan populations was therefore framed in comparable ways that invoked the categories of race (Aryan,

Dravidian and Muslim), religion, caste, language and, in Sri Lanka, region (low country versus Kandyan Sinhalese). These categories were used by colonial officials as well as Indians and Sri Lankans themselves to make claims about the national identities and national histories of these societies. They have remained central to the question of national identity and ethnic diversity in both states. While the politics of national identity are discussed in terms of the same categories of ethnic difference, it has been argued that the structure of ethnic demography is different. That is, India's more fragmented ethnic demography, in which the Hindu majority is intersected by divisions of caste and language, is more conducive to ethnic accommodation than the binary Sinhala–Tamil division that has dominated Sri Lankan politics in the post-independence period.[65]

However, this argument overlooks the important extent to which the axis of ethnic conflict within both states has shifted over time. The earliest forms of modern associational activity in the south Indian Tamil-speaking areas (emerging in the early nineteenth century) were Hindu revivalist organisations[66] and this activity produced often violent conflict with Tamil-speaking Christians and Muslims.[67] However, Hindu revivalism in the south Indian Tamil areas did not develop into a substantial political force, and by the early decades of the twentieth century had given way to the competing, though ideologically overlapping, Congress and Dravidian movements. The Dravidian movement also accommodated and incorporated Muslim identity, such that the Hindu–Muslim divide has not been as politically significant as it has in north India.[68] The Hindu–Muslim division has not however disappeared, and in post-independence India the Hindu nationalist movement has sought to consolidate a Hindu national identity by overcoming intra-Hindu caste and linguistic divides.[69] Furthermore, the absence of Hindu nationalist mobilisation in the Tamil-speaking areas is not guaranteed, and there is a debate as to whether contemporary Hindu nationalist mobilisation is eroding the largely secular political culture established by the Dravidian parties in Tamil south India.[70]

Similarly in Sri Lanka, while the majority population could be identified as linguistically Sinhalese and religiously Buddhist, the Sinhala Buddhist category is internally divided by caste as well as the distinction between high country Kandyan and low country Sinhalese. Importantly, for much of the colonial period, intra-Sinhala and intra-Tamil distinctions were far more significant as axes of social and political conflict than the distinction between Tamils and Sinhalese. In the late nineteenth century, politics amongst Sinhala elites involved caste-based conflict between the landowning Goyigama caste, on the one hand, and on the other, the non-landowning but commercially successful caste complex known by the acronym KSD—standing for Karava (fishing), Salagama (cinnamon peelers) and Durava (toddy tappers).[71] In the 1911 elections the Goyigama Sinhalese preferred to vote for a Tamil from the landowning Vellala caste than for a Sinhalese candidate from the Karava caste.[72] Meanwhile amongst the Tamils there was acute political and social conflict between Hindus from the landowning Vellala caste and Christians from non-landowning castes.[73] The analysis in Chapters 3 and 5 shows how the consolidation of competing Sinhala Buddhist and Tamil nationalist projects in post-independence Sri Lanka was effected by processes of political mobilisation and contestation that actively worked to overcome intra-Sinhala and intra-Tamil divisions.

Conclusion

The emergence of very different conceptions of national identity in India and Sri Lanka thus occurred despite comparable and connected histories of British colonial rule and national identity in the two states having to encompass a similar range of ethnic pluralism that was framed through the shared ideas of Aryan and Dravidian historical origins. The politics of national and ethnic identities were also played out in both states through electoral competition, in which patronage networks played an important role. The divergent outcomes of the two Tamil-speaking regions cannot therefore be explained by temporally static variables such as material interests, structures of ethnic demography or political institutions. Rather they are the effects of patterns of political activity sustained over long periods of time through which more or less inclusive conceptions of national identity are asserted, contested and more or less securely established.

2

BECOMING NATIONAL

TAMILS, MUSLIMS AND CONGRESS IN COLONIAL INDIA

Introduction

This chapter explains why the pan-ethnic conception of Indian national identity and national interest associated with the Indian National Congress (Congress or INC) was able to mobilise support in the Tamil-speaking areas, and therefore symbolically include Tamil identity, but could not do the same with Muslim politics. The key moments at which to judge Congress's ability to incorporate these distinct identities are the elections that took place between 1934 and 1937 and again in 1945. Before and during these elections there were significant social and political movements in the Tamil-speaking areas and amongst Muslims across India denouncing Congress and Indian nationalism as antithetical to Tamil and Muslim interests respectively. In the Tamil-speaking areas, first the Justice Party (founded in 1916), and later the Self-Respect movement (founded in 1925), both describing the Tamils as Dravidian, denounced Congress as a vehicle of north Indian, Aryan and Brahmanical domination. Amongst the Muslim electorate, the Muslim League characterised Congress as a Hindu body and a threat to Muslim political interests. Despite this symmetrical—in rhetoric at least—opposition, Congress's ability to mobilise support amongst the two electorates was very different. In the 1937 elections it scored one of its most impressive victories in the Tamil-speaking areas securing 159 out of a total of 215 seats.[1] In contrast, in the same elections Congress failed to demonstrate Muslim electoral support and secured only 26 of the 482 provincial legislature seats elected from Muslim constituencies across India.[2]

This failure cannot be explained by the different strengths of the Tamil and Muslim movements; both the Muslim League and the Justice party had weak party structures and very little ability to mobilise direct political support. Similarly, it cannot be explained by a fundamental difference in the salient economic and social structures of the Tamil and Muslim electorates; in both, the key to electoral success was winning over important rural and urban notables or magnates able to mobilise significant vote banks through patron–client networks.[3] Importantly, the political behaviour of Tamil and Muslim patrons was equally motivated by considerations of personal advantage, rather than sustained allegiance to ethnic identity or political party. Instead of looking to structural forces, the argument presented here is that the difference lies in the extent to which Congress activists incorporated Muslim and Tamil identities in their activities of direct mobilisation and communication. In the Tamil-speaking areas, from the late nineteenth century, regional Congress politicians used the Tamil language as both the medium and expression of Indian nationalism and thereby symbolically and organisationally incorporated Tamil practices and symbols into a wider Indian nationalist project. The explanation for the absence of similar sustained efforts to present Congress and Indian nationalism in Muslim religious and cultural terms is located at the regional levels of the Congress organisation. In Punjab, Bengal and the United Provinces (UP)—the three areas that contained the majority of Indian Muslims[4]—the regional Congress was dominated by groups that were also closely associated with Hindu nationalism and therefore propagated and understood the Indian nation in largely Hindu terms.[5]

Despite the importance of patronage networks, rather than political affiliation, in deciding electoral outcomes, direct mobilisation using ethnic categories is a crucial factor in explaining this difference. Congress's sustained efforts at direct mobilisation through Tamil linguistic and cultural categories, heightened during the mass protests of Non-Cooperation (1920–22) and Civil Disobedience (1930–34), established the movement as an important and visible presence in Tamil political life. This presence did not necessarily translate directly into voter motivation and behaviour. Rather, when Congress entered electoral competition, many powerful rural and urban bosses who could command extensive patronage networks and who previously had other affiliations switched to Congress, sensing that it was an attractive vehicle for electoral success and therefore one that could be utilised against them.[6]

Congress simply did not have this effect on Muslim magnates—and nor, importantly, did the Muslim League until 1945.[7]

Congress's contrasting ability to mobilise amongst the Tamil and Muslim populations in India is not simply a matter of electoral outcomes. Rather, the inclusion of publicly asserted and politically significant ethnic identities is realised through these processes of political organisation and mobilisation. The inclusion of Tamil political and associational activity within a pan-Indian framework occurred because of activities that actively sought to mobilise popular support for Indian nationalism in the Tamil-speaking areas. In adopting the Tamil language and Tamil cultural forms as vehicles of Indian nationalism, Congress activists also adopted them as interests of Indian nationalism; the organisational and substantive content of Indian nationalism in the Tamil-speaking areas took on distinctly Tamil concerns and interests. In other words, Indian national identity is today unproblematically inclusive of Tamils (and linguistic diversity more generally) but problematically so of Muslim identity because of the contingent historical processes of political organisation and mobilisation. The antagonism between Hindu and Muslim associations and interests at the regional levels, while important, was not the only or even dominant vector of social and political conflict in Punjab, Bengal and UP. What was decisive for the relationship between Congress and Muslim groups, however, was the dominance of Hindu nationalist sentiment and associations at the regional level of the Congress organisation.

The first section of this chapter describes the ideological content and organisational structures of pan-ethnic Indian nationalism, the competing Dravidian and Indian nationalisms in the Tamil-speaking areas as well as Hindu and Muslim nationalism. The following section then describes Congress's development from 1885 to become by 1947 arguably the central institution of Indian politics in terms of three key activities of political mobilisation: ideological articulation; co-option of existing sources of power and influence; and the direct mobilisation of support. It discusses in turn the Congress movement's relationship to Tamil/Dravidian, Hindu and Muslim nationalisms to reveal the differential ways in which the identities espoused by the movements were incorporated within the larger vision of a pan-ethnic Indian national identity and national interest. The chapter ends by explaining why ethnic demography and rational calculation alone cannot account for the different patterns of Congress mobilisation amongst Muslim and Tamil voters.

Context

Congress and pan-ethnic Indian nationalism

Addressing the first session of the INC, held in Bombay in December 1885, G. S. Iyer, a delegate from Madras, expressed his sense of the momentous nature of the occasion. He stated that the assemblage of 'my chosen countrymen from Calcutta and Lahore, from Madras and Sind, from places wide apart and difficult of intercommunication' indicated 'the beginning of national political life'. For Iyer, Congress was national because it was pan-Indian, and the fact that such a meeting could be held meant that Indians could 'with greater propriety than heretofore speak of an Indian nation, of national opinion and national aspirations'.[8] The attempt to create a pan-Indian 'national' political body had been a feature of Indian politics from the early decades of the nineteenth century.[9] These attempts gained momentum in the late 1870s and early 1880s because of a series of government decisions that were crystallised in Indian politics—through the activity of regional organisations and the press—as revealing of the contradiction between Indian and British interests, with the latter seen as unduly driving official policy. Under the Conservative Viceroy Lord Lytton (served 1876–80) government decisions on civil service recruitment, famine response, cotton tariffs and the rising expenditure on military campaigns in Afghanistan, along with the extravagant 1876 Delhi Durbar to celebrate Queen Victoria's golden jubilee at a time of devastating famine, were widely condemned as inimical to Indian interests. Subsequently, the Liberal Viceroy Lord Ripon's (served 1880–84) attempts to introduce the elective principle at local government elections and equalise racial anomalies in the status of European and Indian judges produced a clear divide between Indian and European opinion and led to India-wide demonstrations of support for Ripon when he made a last tour of the country near the end of his tenure.[10]

The move towards holding a pan-Indian meeting was led by regional organisations in Calcutta, Madras, Poona and Bombay—all areas with a growing Western-educated population.[11] Two separate pan-Indian meetings were held in December 1885: one in Calcutta, called the National Conference; and one in Bombay, called the Indian National Congress. At the time the Bengali political leader S. N. Banerjea remarked on the perceptible level of political activity that 'all India seemed at the present moment to have met in solemn conclave to think out the great problem of national advancement'.[12] The second session of the INC was held in Calcutta, where it was nominally merged with the National Conference and subsequently became 'the matrix of the later nationalist movement'.[13]

Over the following years, the activities of the INC expressed and established an understanding of Indian national identity and national interest that was organised around a core set of principles. The most important of these principles was that the diverse ethnic and regional identities found within the Indian population were nevertheless united by shared interests. The INC claimed to be the body that expressed these shared interests because it contained within its organisational structure the ethnic and regional pluralism of the Indian population; the official report of the first session noted the regional, professional and ethnic diversity of its delegates as a mark of the representative character of the proceedings.[14] The notion that India's ethnic and regional pluralism existed alongside a unity of purpose and interest remained a constant theme of Congress's claims and activities. The unified Indian national interest and identity, shared by India's plural population, was defined by Congress's activities over the following years as consisting of three broad objectives: the first was to secure Indian economic progress and development; the second was greater equality; and the third was demands for greater self-government, leading eventually to calls for political independence.

Although the idea that British rule was economically detrimental to India was apparent from the early years of the nineteenth century,[15] in the later part of the century these arguments were, importantly, expressed in terms of the national developmental paradigm, first developed by Friedrich List as a challenge to the neo-classical model associated with Britain's global economic dominance.[16] List's ideal of a national developmental state was explicitly taken up by Indian intellectuals and political activists. For example, Govind Mahadev Ranade, an Indian judge and member of Congress's 'inner circle' for the first two decades of its existence,[17] described the ideal state as the 'national organ taking care of national needs'.[18] Importantly, the ideal of the national developmental state also framed criticisms of British policy. Most famously, Dadabhai Naoroji, another member of the inner circle, who produced early estimates of India's national and per capita income, argued that British rule was facilitating a net drain of wealth from India to Britain.[19] Naoroji's arguments led to an ongoing debate with British officials, who countered by publishing their own 'official' estimates of per capita income, and from 1890 onwards, for the 'next several decades, the accurate determination of per capita income became a sub-industry of its own'.[20] Importantly, the economic arguments between Indian nationalists and British officials reified the ideal of the state as the agent of national economic progress and established economic growth as a key element of a unified national interest. This was evident in Congress and wider nationalist politics from the late nineteenth century. Resolutions and speeches on economic issues were a regular feature of the annual Congress sessions[21] as were exhibitions and fairs on industrial development.[22] The national development paradigm and the 'territorial isomorphism of economy and nation'[23] it implied also provided the basis of mass political participation. The boycotting of foreign goods and the use of alternative indigenous or Swadeshi products became key features of mass nationalist mobilisation in the twentieth century.[24]

The demand for equality between Indians and Europeans was also an important element in forming the idea of a unified Indian national interest and identity in the public culture of the late nineteenth century. By the late nineteenth century, assumptions of racial superiority were a crucial feature of the way many Europeans in India, government officials as well as non-official, interacted with Indians.[25] The attitude of racial superiority was also expressed in support of policies that discriminated against Indians. Issues that were important in late-nineteenth-century Indian political life—and subsequently taken up by Congress—included: the demand that the recruitment examinations for the civil service be held in India as well as in England; the ability of Indian judges to hear cases involving European subjects;[26] the admittance of Indians to the Indian Volunteer Reserve Force; and lifting restrictions on Indians carrying firearms.[27] While Congress sought equality between Europeans and Indians, the principle of equality also became a means of regulating the internal pluralism and diversity of the Indian population. A broad notion of equality was expressed in a number of ways. Firstly, Congress adopted an approach of non-discrimination and sought to include all major ethnic groups within its platform—which eventually translated into an inclusive and territorial framing of citizenship in the Indian constitution.[28] Secondly, Congress also slowly adopted measures to address the various social, political and economic inequalities amongst the Indian population. The Nehru report of 1928 adopted universal franchise as policy,[29] and from 1932 Gandhi explicitly adopted measures to ameliorate the social and economic conditions of caste groups subject to the practices of untouchability.[30] The post-independence Constitution (adopted in 1950), framed by a Congress-controlled Constituent Assembly, explicitly prohibited the exclusionary and violent practices through which individuals were treated as untouchable and committed the Indian state to measures addressing economic and social inequality.[31]

The link between self-government and national identity was apparent in the founding of the INC. The circular note sent to regional associations inviting them to attend the first session of the INC stated: 'Indirectly this Conference will form the germ of a Native Parliament and, if properly conducted, will constitute in a few years an unanswerable reply to the assertion that India is still wholly unfit for representative institutions.'[32] The demand for self-government became an increasingly important part of the Congress platform. Beginning in the late nineteenth century with calls for modest reforms of the existing constitutional structure, by the late 1920s Congress was demanding independence for an Indian government elected on the basis of universal franchise from territorial constituencies.[33] Congress's constitutional demands were initially made on the public platform, at the annual December sessions, through petitions and proposals for constitutional reform. From 1920 onwards, however, as Congress switched to become a mass party, the imperative of constitutional reform became the nominal trigger for mass agitation, the key issue of contestation between Congress and the Indian government and—as discussed below—a source of conflict within Congress itself.

At the time of the Congress founding, however, this pan-ethnic understanding of Indian national identity and interest was not the only or even the most important political project in Indian politics. Alongside and often in direct collision with Congress were other forms of social and political activity which asserted very different understandings of national identity and national interest. Three that are in themselves politically significant and also significant for understanding the political trajectory of modern national and ethnic politics in the Tamil speaking areas are Hindu, Muslim and finally Tamil/Dravidian nationalisms. These are discussed in the following sub-sections, whilst the next section will discuss the organisational and ideological presence of these three movements in the late nineteenth century.

India as a Hindu/Aryan nation

By the time of the first Congress session in Bombay, the understanding of India as an exclusively Hindu nation was already a well-established trope in Indian political life. Key to Hindu nationalism was the Aryan idea of a flourishing Hindu- and Sanskrit-based civilisation corrupted and degraded by centuries of Muslim rule.[34] By the late nineteenth century, the term Arya or Aryan was central to Hindu nationalist thought and activities[35] and came to represent 'a renascent Hinduism, a reformed Hinduism excised of corrupting external currents, and the traumatic imprimatur of what were seen as successive colonial intrusions'.[36] The increasing use and wide circulation of the Sanskrit term Bharat to describe India, along with the more evocative image of the nation as mother goddess or Bharatmata, also established a clear and unmediated equation between Aryan (Hindus) and the Indian national past and national interest.[37] Non-Hindus, and Muslims in particular, became therefore non-nationals, and a potential cultural as well as demographic threat who could only be brought into the national core through cultural assimilation.[38]

The relationship between Hindu nationalism and the Congress movement can be understood through two associations: the Arya Samaj and the Theosophical Society. The Arya Samaj was founded in 1875 in Gujarat by Dayananda Saraswati (1824–83) but had most support in Punjab and the United Provinces.[39] The movement set out to reform Hindu practice to be in line with an idealised, pristine and reformed religion—labelled Arya Dharm— that did away with idol worship, practices of caste hierarchy and caste exclusion, Brahmin priests and priestly ritual, whilst also introducing a novel ritual of purification (or Shuddi)—used to 're-convert' Muslims and Christians to their 'original' Aryan religion.[40] By 1921 the Samaj had a significant social and cultural presence, with an estimated half a million members[41] and a network of schools, colleges and hospitals across the country that were also used by non-Arya Samaj Hindus.[42] The Arya Samaj was closely associated with Congress in Punjab[43] and the United Provinces[44] where its activities contributed to social and political antagonism along Hindu–Muslim lines. The Samaj vigorously promoted efforts to protect cows, including prohibitions of slaughter that not only characterised Muslims as sacrilegious but also sought to outlaw the customary sacrifice of cows at Muslim religious festivals.[45] The Samaj also championed the use of Hindi (written in the Sanskrit or Devanagri script) over Urdu (written in the Persian script), identifying the former as authentically 'national' and the latter as a foreign imposition.[46]

The promotion of an Aryan and Hindu conception of Indian national identity in south India was prominently associated with the Theosophical Society. The Theosophical brand of Hinduism was socially far more conservative than the Samaj's Arya Dharm, defending, for example, caste hierarchy and the notion that lower-caste bodies were inherently polluting and polluted 'purer' upper-caste bodies by their mere presence.[47] Despite these differences, the Theosophists treated the revival and cultivation of an idealised Vedic or Aryan Hinduism as a national mission.[48] Colonel H. S. Olcott, the co-founder of the society, speaking in Madras described the Aryan religion as the 'national religion',[49] stating that Indian national regeneration demanded the revival of

Aryan science and religion.[50] The society soon established an important presence, with branches and Sanskrit schools in many districts and small towns across the Tamil-speaking areas.[51] Furthermore, from the late nineteenth century, the society also built up a presence in the print media.[52] These assets proved useful in the society's close association with pan-ethnic Indian nationalist politics. The Madras Mahajana Sabha, the organisation that sent delegates to the first Congress in Bombay, timed its first provincial conference in December 1884 to coincide with the society's annual meeting.[53] The society continued to have close links with the predominantly Brahmin Madras politicians, known as the Mylapore group,[54] who effectively controlled the provincial Congress organisation until 1920.[55] Annie Besant,[56] the society's president after the death of Olcott in 1907, played an important role in Congress-led efforts for Indian self-rule during the 1910s and 1920s.

Muslim nationalism

Along with the idea of a pan-ethnic Indian national identity and a Hindu national identity, the notion that Indian Muslims also constituted a distinct social and political group, and potentially a national group, was also well established in late-nineteenth-century Indian politics. The Muslims of India, who constituted almost twenty per cent of the total Indian population at the 1892 census, were unevenly distributed across the provinces. The majority of Indian Muslims lived in Bengal, whilst in Punjab Muslims formed a majority of the population and in the United Provinces Muslims constituted a socially and culturally significant minority. Along with this regional variation, there were also other important divsions amongst the Muslim population: 'Language, caste and economic standing worked together to divide Muslim from Muslim no less than Hindu from Hindu.'[57] The idea of a distinct Muslim identity uniting these disparate groups and carrying conceptual and institutional implications for modern political activity can be understood as the outcome of three distinct sets of activities that took place during the nineteenth century. The first were the Muslim revival and reform movements of the early nineteenth century that worked amongst ordinary Muslims; the second were the collective pronouncements of British officials; and the third were the efforts of Muslim leaders and intellectuals who sought to establish a Muslim political identity that cut across regional, class and sectarian differences.

Peter Hardy describes the activities of Saiyid Ahmed (1786–1831) and his followers across northern India, and those of Haji Shariatullah (1781–1840), as well as his son Dudu Miyan (1819–62) in Bengal, as directing a message of

Islamic revival and reform that sought to consolidate a sharply differentiated religious identity.[58] Preaching against customs that many Muslims shared with Hindus, such as 'intercession at the tombs of saints, consultation of Brahmins, even vegetarianism and aversion to the remarriage of widows', these movements were 'essentially rejections of medieval Indian Islam in favour of early Islam in Arabia'.[59] Unlike the Hindu reform movements, these reformists directed their message at non-elite groups. In the case of Saiyid Ahmed, there were small landowners, teachers, small shopkeepers and minor officials, and in Bengal 'depressed Muslim cultivators sinking into the sea of landless labourers'.[60] These activities sought to consolidate a distinct identity by making Muslims aware of 'what they did not share with their non-Muslim neighbours'.[61]

While Islamic reformers were attempting to consolidate an Islamic social and religious community, British officials from the mid-nineteenth century also began to adopt the category of an all-India Muslim religious community and an all-India Muslim political interest in administrative practice and official communications. At the all-India level, this first became visible in a 1871 Government of India regulation calling for the official encouragement and support of Muslim education: classical, vernacular and in the English language. The resolution, prompted by incidents of what appeared to be Islamist-inspired violent opposition to the colonial state, was intended to foster Muslim loyalty to British rule.[62] A report published in the same year, and prompted by the anxiety about widespread Muslim disloyalty, categorised Muslims in total as 'in all respects ... a race ruined under British rule'.[63] Although this judgement was probably only applicable to certain groups of Muslims, it was nevertheless adopted as a blanket assessment that Muslims had not prospered and were relatively 'backward' when compared to Hindus. This assessment of relative 'backwardness' was important and, following the resolution of 1871, there were two further Government resolutions in 1873 and 1885 sanctioning official support for Muslim education.[64] The introduction of elections for local governments from 1882 also led to the adoption of separate electorates for Muslim voters, thus recognising Muslims as a separate political constituency.[65]

Finally, activities of political organisation and mobilisation were also crucial in establishing in public life the concept of a Muslim political identity. Important in this regard were the activities of Sir Syed Ahmed Khan (1817–98), a judge and Muslim reformer, who sought to reconcile Islam and Western education and thereby establish a modern and progressive Muslim identity. Through his writings, Syed sought to demonstrate that Islam was 'compatible with progress, as a Victorian liberal understood it', and also that 'Islam was modern progress and modern progress was Islam properly understood'.[66] One of his most significant achievements was the founding of the Muhammadan Anglo-Oriental College at Aligarh in 1875. The college, founded with Government backing, educated elite Muslims along Western lines whilst also providing a Muslim religious education.[67] Similarly, in 1863 in Calcutta, Abdul Latif, a civil servant, established the Muhammadan Literary and Scientific Society to 'impart useful information to the higher and educated classes of the Mahomedan Literary Community'. By 1877 the society had over 500 members.[68] There were also attempts to establish pan-Indian Muslim associational linkages. In 1877 Amir Ali, a Calcutta barrister, established the National Mohammedan Association, and by 1888 it had fifty branches across India, including five in Madras.[69] As a consequence of these three types of activities, by the time the INC held its first session in Bombay, the understanding that Muslims constituted a distinct interest and identity was well established in colonial politics. The Muslim identity was a reality that Congress politicians, both Muslim and Hindu, had to negotiate in their attempts to establish a pan-ethnic Indian national platform from which to negotiate with the British state.

Tamil as Dravidian and Tamil as Indian

By the late nineteenth century there was also a well-established Tamil public culture established through the circulation of printed journals, texts and related political and revivalist activity.[70] These activities were organised around two distinct poles, and while both asserted the existence of a Tamil linguistic identity, they sought to transform Tamil social, religious, linguistic and later political practices in different and mutually incompatible ways. One set of activities, hugely influenced by the Dravidian idea, argued that Tamil and the other south Indian languages formed a single Dravidian language family that was distinct from Sanskrit and the Aryan family of languages.[71] Like the Aryan idea, the Dravidian idea expanded from its initial linguistic association and became by the second half of the nineteenth century a theory of south Indian society, religion, language and history. Analogous to the Vedic golden age of the Aryan theory destroyed by Muslim rule, the Dravidian theory posited a lost Dravidian golden age destroyed by the Aryan invasion.[72] In the multiple uses of the Dravidian idea by religious and social reformers, the Aryan invasion is blamed for corrupting an initially pristine Dravidian religion (Saivism) and for introducing unsavoury social practices such as the subjugation of women and caste hierarchy.[73] Alongside and often in competition with the notion of a Dravidian Tamil identity were activities that promoted Tamil language, culture and religion as components and expressions of a wider Indian tradition.[74] While the Indian-orientated Tamil revivalist activities sometimes characterised Tamil as having ultimately Aryan origins,[75] the Tamil language was also presented as the equivalent of Sanskrit in its literary and linguistic merit.[76]

During the nineteenth century the Tamil-as-Dravidian idea was associated mainly with Tamils from upper non-Brahmin castes, usually educated in English and often employed as government officials or as educationalists.[77] These activists produced printed editions of Tamil texts from the palm leaf manuscripts and sought to cultivate the production of literary knowledge about these texts by founding journals and literary associations. The notion of Tamil-as-Dravidian prompted efforts to purge Tamil speech and writing of Sanskrit inflections and Tamil religious practice of alien accretions to what was considered to be authentic Saivite theology.[78]

Linguistic and religious reappraisal also implied a reappraisal of racial origins and, thereby, caste hierarchy in Tamil society. The Tamil-as-Dravidian project challenged the lowly position assigned to non-Brahmin Tamils in the fivefold Varna hierarchy and reiterated in the Aryan theory of Indian civilisation. The latter, adopted in colonial law codes and census operations, and also widely prevalent in colonial social and political life, categorised Tamil society into three distinct groups.[79] At one end of the caste and racial hierarchy were Tamil Brahmins, identified as descendants of the early Aryan colonists who carried Vedic civilisation to the south. At the other end of the hierarchy were the Untouchable groups, identified as racially Dravidian and in daily practice treated as ritually polluting. In the middle, all the other non-Brahmin Tamil groups were identified as Shudras, the last of the four Varna categories and ascribed to perform menial labour. The Shudra category, as it was used in the Tamil-speaking areas, included many high-status and often wealthy mercantile, landowning or soldiering groups. From the late nineteenth century, Tamil revivalists used the Dravidian idea to challenge this classification and instead presented Tamils as outside caste and descendants of a worthy Dravidian civilisation.[80] Tamil Brahmins, in contrast, were seen not as civilising colonisers but as deceptive outsiders who had corrupted a once flourishing and egalitarian society with their ritualism and caste hierarchies.[81] In the twentieth century the Dravidian idea was used by the Self-Respect movement, later DK, to challenge the Congress movement on the grounds that the latter was associated with Brahmins, Sanskrit and Hinduism (see below).[82]

While the Indian and Dravidian Tamil revival and reform projects were organisationally distinct and based on mutually contradictory assumptions, there were nevertheless two important areas of overlap. Firstly, they both shared an interest in the cultivation and promotion of the Tamil language and literature, albeit for different ends. The promotion of a Tamil-as-Indian identity was closely associated with pan-Indian nationalism and was therefore geared towards promoting mass political mobilisation. This orientation prompted the creation and dissemination of a more demotic and accessible Tamil that could also serve as a vehicle for the popular spread of Indian nationalism.[83] This was in sharp contrast to the Tamil-as-Dravidian project, which was generally concerned with scholarly and religious activities as well as linguistic forms that were accessible in the main to elite non-Brahmin groups.[84] Furthermore, the Tamil-as-Dravidian project presumed the existence of a sharp racial, cultural and caste divide between Tamils, on the one hand, and north Indians, Hindus and Brahmins, on the other. Despite these differences, the competing Tamil-as-Indian and Tamil-as-Dravidian projects nevertheless together contributed a varied and complex Tamil cultural and political life in which Tamil literary and cultural forms were presumed to be aesthetically valuable and adopted as political interests.

The two projects also overlapped on the need to reform social practices and address social inequalities—such as caste hierarchy and the position of women—that were increasingly understood as out of keeping with wider ideals of progress and improvement. Again, the problem of social reform was framed through mutually contradictory frameworks. While the Tamil-as-Dravidian project blamed unpalatable social practices on Aryan Hinduism and Brahmin dominance, reformists[85] within the Tamil-as-Indian project presented social reform as a means of returning to a more authentic and socially enlightened Hindu order.[86] Like the promotion of Tamil literature and culture, the different assumptions were less important for the political relationship between Dravidian and Indian nationalist politics in the Tamil-speaking regions than the objectives they shared. These shared objectives allowed these projects to compete politically and socially in a way that was agonistic rather than antagonistic (as shall be referred to frequently in this chapter), and meant that this competition could be accommodated within Congress's evolving framework of pan-ethnic Indian national identity and national interest.

Process

Political history of the Congress movement

Congress's political development from its foundation to independence in 1947 can usefully be considered in two phases: the first up to 1920 and the second from 1920 to 1947. In the first phase, its activities were limited to articulating a set of political claims and co-opting the support of established interests and associations. It was only after 1920, and the adoption of the strategy of mass protest through non-cooperation, that the Congress organisation formally adopted the third prong of public associational activity: direct political mobilisation in an effort to build popular support. For forty years, therefore, Congress was mostly an annual gathering, held in different towns and cities across British India. Despite the limited nature of its activities, the fact that they were continuous was sufficient to establish Congress as a significant social and political presence asserting the existence of a pan-Indian national identity and national interest. The success of Congress during this period was not in its ability to realise any of its stated objectives—for example the introduction of simultaneous examinations,[87] the expansion of the elective principle,[88] or the adoption of economic policies that could stimulate Indian industrial expansion and growth.[89] On all of these counts, Congress can be regarded as a failure. Rather, the success of Congress was that it slowly became an unavoidable political presence, for both its detractors and supporters alike.

Congress's ability to establish itself as an unavoidable, whether problematic or potentially useful, presence in Indian political life was not the result of any a priori structural givens; those factors, such as the growing levels of education, political and administrative centralisation, or advances in communications and transportations technologies that facilitated pan-Indian integration as well as Indian integration into global economic flows, were also all present in Sri Lanka during the same period.[90] Rather, the gradual institutionalisation of Congress as an accepted fact of political life was realised through coordinated and temporally continuous activities within a shared conceptual framework in which the claim to be a pan-ethnic Indian nationalist entity was both meaningful and carried political legitimacy. The crucial elements of this activity were the predictability and regularity of the annual Congress in December; the fact that the annual event was held at a different location every year;[91] and the reasonable level of commitment by nationalist politicians to maintaining the unity of the Congress organisation.

In this first phase of Congress's political history, there were significant Hindu and Muslim challenges to the project of establishing the annual sessions as *authoritative* statements of pan-ethnic Indian national opinion and interest. Muslim associations argued that Congress demands for an expansion of competitive examinations would lead to Hindu domination and charged that Congress was therefore inimical to Muslim interests.[92] Congress leaders sought to meet this challenge by attempting to demonstrate Muslim support and by adopting a rule at the 1888 session stipulating that it would not discuss issues or adopt resolutions that were opposed by a majority of either Hindu or Muslim delegates.[93] The attempt to create unity by excluding issues that caused disagreement was also evident in the conflict between social reformers and their opponents. For many Congress figures, Indian progress demanded not just self-government, but also the reformation of Indian, particularly Hindu, social practices that contravened the principles and standards of enlightenment humanism.[94] Efforts to reform Hindu practices—particularly those of child marriage and enforced widowhood—were vociferously opposed by Hindu revivalist organisations that sought to protect Hindu orthodoxy from alien (i.e. Western) intervention.[95] By 1895 orthodox opinion had prevailed and social reformers—who from 1887 had met as the National Social Conference after the normal sessions—were prohibited from holding their meetings in association with the annual Congress sessions.[96]

The 1888 rule and the 1895 expulsion of social reform issues did not conclusively resolve the relationship between Congress and Muslim political organisations, or indeed between Congress and the issue of Hindu social reform. These efforts nevertheless reveal a key dynamic of Congress's attempts to maintain unity. Importantly, the effort to create a national—in the sense of pan-ethnic—platform involved an explicit recognition of distinct ethnic groups combined with an attempt to incorporate these groups within the organisation. For example, the 1888 rule explicitly recognised Hindus and Muslims as distinct entities. Similarly, the 1895 expulsions confirmed the argument made by prominent Congress leaders[97] that Congress should confine itself to political issues, leaving social questions to the relevant social (ethnic) groups, an implicit characterisation of the Indian population as containing a multiplicity of socially self-regulating groups. The pan-ethnic national identity sought by Congress involved, therefore, first the explicit recognition of ethnic pluralism and, second, an attempt to create a political space acceptable to all the groups concerned. In other words, the creation of a pan-ethnic national identity involved the incorporation, rather than negation or transcendence, of publicly established ethnic pluralism. Accommodation was also sought at the organisational level; Congress encouraged Muslim participation at the annual sessions, invited the prominent Bombay Muslim politician Badruddin Tyabji to be President at the 1887 session and held its sessions in cities with substantial Muslim populations—such as Allahabad, Lucknow and Lahore.[98] Similarly, the expulsion of social reform issues did not entail the expulsion of reform-minded Congress politicians—many of whom remained in the Congress's 'inner circle',[99] and in 1905 one of their number, G. K. Gokhale, was elected Congress president, at that point the youngest person to have held that post.[100]

The persistence of the Congress's yearly activities, and its efforts to maintain unity, established it as an important and unavoidable presence in Indian political life. The annual sessions attracted a growing number of delegates as well as non-delegates. Delegates arriving by train from other provinces were met by large, enthusiastic crowds and then taken in procession to the pandal (tent) in which the sessions were held.[101] The sessions were also well reported in the press and, by the 1920s, the coverage was so exhaustive that the government called off its covert surveillance.[102] Conversely, the annual sessions also became a tangible object through which government officials could attack the notion of a pan-Indian national identity. In 1888, the Viceroy Dufferin formally warned princes and chiefs of the native states not to contribute to Congress,[103] and there were repeated claims that government officials worked to prevent large wealthy landowners from contributing to Congress funds.[104] Lord Curzon (served 1899–1905) set out pointedly to ignore Congress and thereby reduce it to irrelevance during his tenure.[105] The antipathy towards Congress during this initial phase signalled its growing importance in Indian political life and presaged its eventual status as the key interlocutor in the negotiations that brought British rule to an end.

Eventually, the most important split in Congress during this period was not based on ethnic or regional divisions, but rather on the approach that should be adopted in challenging British policy. The section labelled 'moderate' by British officials wanted to retain Congress as primarily a body coordinating and expressing educated Indian opinion whilst engaging in measured constitutional negotiation with the state. In contrast, those deemed 'extremists' sought to mobilise the Indian population directly, using language and symbols that would be readily understood by the largely rural and illiterate population, for the purposes of gaining greater Indian self-rule, or swaraj.[106] The split between the extremist and moderate factions came in the wake of the 1905 Bengal partition that triggered mass protests and isolated terrorist attacks against British targets, particularly in Bengal, but also across India, including the *Tamil*-speaking areas.[107] Following a violent and fractious session in Ahmedabad in 1907, where the two groups came into open conflict, key extremist leaders were arrested and then sentenced to imprisonment for inciting violence against the state.[108] At the 1908 session the moderates locked in their control of Congress by adopting a constitution that created provincial units through which the selection of delegates for annual Congress sessions would be organised.[109] This was not, however, a permanent rupture, and the eventual return of the extremists to the Congress fold in 1915[110] confirmed its centrality in Indian political life.

The transformation of Congress into a mass movement that engaged in direct political mobilisation took place in the context of changes associated with the First World War. The Indian contribution to the First World War led to a growing sense, amongst Indians and British officials alike, that there would have to be constitutional concessions in exchange.[111] British officials were also working to the logic that the economic hardship associated with the war—including spiralling prices and the increased taxes imposed to pay for wartime debt—could translate into serious political discontent unless checked by political concessions.[112] This sense of imminent political change also prompted a spurt of nationalist activity. Congress and the Muslim League convened simultaneously in Bombay in December 1915 and worked to produce a common agreement on constitutional reform.[113] Meanwhile Bal Gangadghar Tilak, the extremist leader recently released from prison, formed a mass agitation through the Home Rule League in Bombay, while Annie Besant did the same in Madras.[114] The anticipated reforms were finally enshrined in the 1919 Government of India Act. Under a system termed 'dyarchy', the act provided for a level of self-government at the provincial level by transferring control of some government departments to elected representatives, whilst retaining official control over key areas such as defence, revenues and foreign affairs.[115] The reforms were welcomed by Congress[116] and satisfied the ambitions of many Congress politicians who were eager to contest the 1920 elections for the newly empowered legislatures.[117] However, crucial events of 1919–20[118] that sharply polarised Indian and British opinion led to Congress adopting Gandhi's strategy of mass protest through non-cooperation, at a special Calcutta session of the Congress in September 1920.[119]

Gandhi introduced a series of organisational reforms that provided the infrastructure for Congress's transformation from an annual convention into a mass movement.[120] The provincial Congress committees, which previously followed the polyglot administrative structures of the colonial state, were divided into linguistic units, thereby creating for the first time a modern Tamil political unit, the Tamil Nadu Provincial Congress Committee.[121] At the same session, an executive—the Working Committee—was also established which met regularly and provided for a less sporadic organisational presence.[122] Finally, Gandhi's reforms introduced a small and nominal membership fee[123] symbolic of Congress's stated ambition of expanding beyond the educated middle classes and wealthy patrons to reach the vast mass of the Indian population directly.

In the eventful years between 1920 and 1947, Congress engaged in three phases of mass India-wide anti-colonial protest: the Non-Cooperation movement (1920–22), the Civil Disobedience movement (1930–34) and finally the Quit India movement (1942–5). These movements saw an expansion of Congress's nominal membership, but invariably drew on resentments, conflicts and aspirations that were independent of Congress's formal programme.[124] In Madras, for example, the popularity of picketing liquor shops as a tactic of protest during the Non-Cooperation movement probably owed as much to the social ambitions of upwardly mobile caste groups as it did to the publicly stated objective of targeting the liquor excise tax, a crucial element of the government's finances.[125] Similarly, participation in the 1930–34 Civil Disobedience movement across the Tamil-speaking areas was driven in part by the economic distress caused by the Depression.[126] Despite the gap between Congress's rhetoric and the multifaceted reality of mass protest in an uneven and complex society,[127] the protests were nevertheless important. By demonstrating its ability to coordinate and mobilise political activity across India, Congress established itself—in the eyes of many ordinary and politically ambitious Indians,[128] as well as the British establishment in India and London—as a powerful actor in Indian political life.[129] Crucially, Congress also gained publicity, not just within India but also internationally; Gandhi's salt march gained widespread coverage and consequently became an iconic moment in Indian political history.[130]

Through the work of organising and conducting protests—marches, picketing of cloth and liquor shops, Satyagraha (openly violating official policy to entice arrest and sometimes violent repression)—Congress built a network that was to become useful during subsequent electioneering. A section of the Congress party—labelled the Swarajists—contested elections during the 1920s for provincial and national legislatures. During the 1920s the principle of magnate power and patron–client relations remained paramount, and successful candidates were only nominally grouped under party labels.[131] By

1935, however, whilst magnate power remained important, many candidates actively sought out Congress nominations, and in some areas the negotiations between vote-bank brokers that preceded electoral contests took place within the Congress party structures.[132] This trend was accentuated during the 1945 elections as it became clear that serious negotiations for the transfer of power were imminent and many vote-bank brokers sought out parties who were likely to wield power.[133]

Congress in the Tamil-speaking areas

Congress's electoral victories in the Tamil-speaking areas during 1934–7, and again in 1947, were built on decades of Indian nationalist-orientated political activity, beginning with the twenty-one Madras delegates who attended the first Congress session in Bombay.[134] Congress's activities in the Tamil-speaking areas from the late nineteenth century took place alongside countervailing activities that sought to promote an alternative Dravidian understanding of Tamil identity and interest.[135] There were, however, two important differences between the Congress and Dravidian projects that explain the former's electoral triumph over the latter, evident in 1926,[136] but more so from 1934.[137] Firstly, in realising its electoral victories, Congress brought together all three activities of successful political mobilisation: namely ideological articulation, co-option of existing interests and direct political mobilisation. In contrast, social and political movements espousing a Dravidian identity did not, during this period, effectively coordinate these three types of activity. Secondly, whereas Congress's efforts to mobilise support directly were designed to reach a mass audience and used widely familiar cultural forms,[138] the Dravidian movement was less inclined to adopt popular culture as a vehicle of mass mobilisation. During the nineteenth century, the Dravidian idea was used to frame Tamil identity and interests by individuals and organisations who were preoccupied with scholarly activities and tended to promote elite cultural and religious forms.[139] The Self-Respect movement, which became the most visible vehicle of the Dravidian idea in the early decades of the twentieth century, repudiated many of the religious and literary concerns of the early Dravidian activists.[140] It did engage in direct mobilisation, often staging dramatic acts of iconoclasm, but these were focused on social transformation and the eradication of Hindu practices, rather than the capture of political power.[141]

As discussed above, as a consequence of their shared objectives (the promotion of Tamil literature and culture as well as social reform), the competition between Congress and the Dravidian movement was more agonistic than antagonistic. Crucially, these two objectives could also be accommodated within the broader and evolving framework of the Congress movement. Indian nationalists associated with the 'extremist' approach within the Congress movement promoted Tamil culture and language in the late nineteenth and early twentieth centuries as expressions of an indigenous Indian tradition, and a means of mobilising mass support.[142] With Gandhi's linguistic reorganisation of Congress units, the use and promotion of the Indian languages was formally tied to the objective of greater self-government.[143] Congress policy remained ambiguous on the question of a single national language—Hindi or English—as well as the redrawing of provincial boundaries. However, the adoption of linguistic units within Congress meant that India's linguistic diversity was firmly established as a reality, and value, within Congress's vision of pan-ethnic Indian nationalism. Similarly, the 1895 expulsion of the Social Reform conference did not permanently exclude social reform issues from the Congress agenda. In the Tamil-speaking areas, the poet and Indian nationalist Subramania Bharathi (1882–1921), attacked the practice of untouchability and engaged in activities to undermine caste hierarchy.[144] In 1933 Gandhi initiated a campaign to eradicate untouchability[145] and the practice of untouchability was legally prohibited in the Indian constitution.[146] Eventually a conflict over caste segregation within the Tamil Nadu Congress led to the formation in 1925 of the Self-Respect movement, which set out a programme of radical social reform based on the Dravidian idea. These conflicts continued in the post-independence era but could be ideologically accommodated within the pan-Indian Congress framework.

The widespread expectations of constitutional reform associated with the First World War provoked intense political activity in the Tamil-speaking regions. In September 1916 Annie Besant (president of the Theosophical Society), along with Congress-affiliated politicians, launched the Home Rule League in Madras city.[147] The League engaged in a campaign of direct mobilisation and used the press, pamphlets and speaking tours to reach the population in both English and Tamil.[148] The League's vociferous campaigns provoked the Madras government into issuing an order excluding Besant and two of her associates to rural areas outside Madras city between June and September 1917.[149] The punishment of Besant furthered the League's appeal: its membership increased from 7,000 to 27,000 between March and December 1917,[150] and on her release Mrs Besant was elected president of the forthcoming Calcutta Congress. Soon after the founding of the League in November 1916, a counter-political organisation, the South Indian Political

Association, was formed, also in Madras City.[151] SIPA set out its opposition to the League's demand for Indian self-rule in the 'Non-Brahmin Manifesto' that was published by the leading English language nationalist newspapers in the province.[152] Invoking ideas associated with the Dravidian theory, the Manifesto claimed that south Indian society was characterised by the social, ritual and political dominance of Brahmins over non-Brahmins and called for a continuation of British rule to hold the scales between the antagonistic interests of Indian society.[153] To propagate its message, SIPA launched two newspapers—the English language *Justice* (which led to SIPA being referred to as the Justice Party) and the Tamil language *Dravidian*—as well as acquiring an already established Telugu paper, the *Andhra Prakasika*.[154] Like the League, it held conferences and conducted speaking tours, and encouraged the formation of local Dravidian organisations to engage in activities—such as running night schools, reading rooms and libraries—to promote education amongst non-Brahmins.[155]

Although the non-Brahmin manifesto pointed to the disproportionate number of Brahmins employed in the public sector to substantiate its thesis of Brahmin domination, the actual political economy of caste across Madras, including the Tamil-speaking areas, prevented any simple division into Brahmin and non-Brahmin blocks. Social, economic and political power during this period was organised around landowning or commercial magnates who controlled productive wealth.[156] The vast majority of magnates were from non-Brahmin castes, as revealed by income tax figures,[157] and their networks of dependants were cross-caste and often multi-religious.[158] The low representation of non-Brahmins in the public sector was more easily explained by elite non-Brahmin reluctance to enter public service employment, despite official encouragement, than Brahmin exclusivity.[159] Despite the economic implausibility of the non-Brahmin manifesto, it nevertheless drew on familiar themes in south Indian public culture, namely the cultural and racial divide between Brahmins and non-Brahmins asserted by the Dravidian theory of south Indian civilisation.[160]

Congress responded to the Justice Party by establishing the Madras Presidency Association (MPA) in September 1917, an organisation representing non-Brahmins within the party. The MPA acquired its own newspapers—the English language *Indian Patriot* and the Tamil language *Desabhaktan* (patriot)—and claimed a membership of 2,000.[161] While the MPA was more of a political gesture than a serious organisation,[162] it was nevertheless significant in symbolising Congress's attempts to incorporate differences of caste within the organisational structure. The formation of the MPA acknowledged the existence of an ethnic divide but also brought this rift within the organisational structure of the Congress organisation. As with the 1888 rule and the 1895 expulsions of the social reformers, the decision to form the MPA stemmed from a pan-ethnic national project in which ethnic differences were conceptually and organisationally incorporated and accommodated, rather than ignored or excluded.

Throughout the 1920s, Congress at the all-India level decided either to boycott the newly empowered legislatures created by the 1919 Montague–Chelmsford reforms or sought to obstruct their work from within.[163] As a consequence, in Madras, until the 1935 elections, the legislature was nominally at least dominated by the Justice Party. This was not, however, a position built on a cohesive party machine. Rather, successful elections throughout this period were dependent on the votes controlled by magnate networks, and successful candidates more often than not chose party allegiances only after securing their election and often switched allegiances once elected.[164] The Justice's activities were therefore restricted to a thin form of co-opting interests: it co-opted the interests of a number of magnates to oppose Congress and the Home Rule League and did this (by distributing patronage) primarily to retain a nominal majority in the legislature. Although it held annual conferences, the Justice's efforts to mobilise political support directly were not sustained or particularly successful; its two newspapers struggled to compete, in terms of circulation, with Congress-allied nationalist papers[165] and were continuously in financial difficulties, finally closing in 1932.[166]

Meanwhile, outside the legislature, Congress was engaged in ongoing campaigns of direct political mobilisation. The spurts of activity during the all-India Non-Cooperation[167] and Civil Disobedience[168] movements saw marches, picketing of cloth and liquor shops as well as other acts of defiance against official restrictions, many of which were beyond the official Congress programme. Alongside these protests, and ongoing throughout this period, Congress politicians and allied groups worked to promote the Congress message through cultural channels. The work of the Indian nationalist Tamil poet Subramania Bharathi became popular during the 1920s following his death.[169] Bharathi's songs and poems on Indian nationalist themes and symbols—calling for independence, denigrating caste, glorifying Gandhi—were written in clear and demotic Tamil and were easily accessible to a mass audience,[170] contrasting sharply with the arcane style and inaccessible vocabulary that often characterised Tamil literary production.[171] Tamil Congress politicians built links with the touring companies which performed plays, invariably musicals, to audiences across the Tamil-speaking areas.[172] From the 1920s onwards plays were stages that extolled nationalist figures, for example Tilak and Bhagat Singh, or used familiar religious or historical stories and figures as thinly veiled metaphors of the struggles between foreign (British) oppression and indigenous resistance. The plays were always accompanied by songs, which were printed and sold in affordable song books, in praise of a similar nationalist litany of themes.[173] These activities established the symbols of Indian nationalism as unavoidable badges of political legitimacy. By 1926, even the Justice Party, which had formerly denounced Gandhi and his campaign of Khaddar or home-spun cloth, was decorating its meetings with placards reading 'Love Live Mahatma Gandhi' and encouraging the use of Khaddar.[174]

The Tamil Nadu Congress was also associated with the revival and reform of south Indian forms of dance and music that have since become characterised as emblematic of Indian 'classical' traditions. An alliance between Congress politicians and nationalist performers transformed dance styles and instrumental as well as vocal music previously performed in the temples and courts by specialist caste groups into standardised forms, performed in modern concert halls. The Madras Music Academy, founded alongside the 1927 Madras Congress, was crucial in supervising the formation of modern south Indian Bharathanatyam, from the previously plural traditions known as Sadir, and creating a standardised style of classical Carnatic music. Through these activities, forms of music and dance that were practised in south India and particularly the Tamil-speaking areas were made emblems of Indian 'national' culture and civilisation.[175]

While the Justice Party did not venture onto the streets to contest the Congress mobilisation, the Indian nationalist framing of Tamil identity and interest was challenged during this period by the Self-Respect movement, which sought a radical reform of south Indian, particularly Tamil, social and religious practices.[176] The movement was founded by E. V. R. Ramaswamy Naicker, a Congressman and active campaigner during the Non-Cooperation campaigns. Ramaswamy resigned from the Tamil Nadu Congress Committee in 1926 after falling out with the Committee members and Gandhi over separate dining arrangements for Brahmin and non-Brahmin students at a Sanskrit school funded by Congress; on learning of the separate eating arrangements Ramaswamy insisted that all caste-based distinctions should be abolished and resigned after senior Congress leaders refused to enforce common dining.[177] Ramaswamy worked within the Dravidian framework and sought to transform Tamil society by arguing that social practices such as caste and the denigration of women had been brought into south Indian society by north Indian, Aryan Hinduism. The message of the movement was unequivocal: south Indian and Tamil society would only be truly liberated and reformed once it had shed all alien Hindu practices including the use of caste names, caste marks, Hindu life-cycle rituals, Brahmin priests and idol worship.[178] Ramaswamy toured extensively and wrote voluminously, seeking to transform individual behaviour. The movement achieved a significant presence in the Tamil-speaking areas.[179] Ramaswamy's activity, however, was solely focused on direct mobilisation to realise social transformation and was not aimed at capturing political power; Subramanian argues that Ramaswamy 'lacked a clear conception of state power and a strategy to acquire and exercise it'.[180]

While the Justice Party and the Self-Respect movement were engaged in elite co-option and direct social evangelisation respectively, Congress abandoned Civil Disobedience in 1934 and decided to enter electoral politics, bringing together all three components of successful political mobilisation. This organisational capacity had been created by the years of direct mobilisation that began from 1920. The 1935 reforms granted full responsibility for all heads of government to elected provincial legislatures, although retaining a great deal of official control at the national legislature in Delhi.[181] In the Tamil-speaking areas, Congress's successful electoral campaign brought together the three sets of activities and cemented Tamil Nadu's integration into a pan-Indian and pan-ethnic conception of politics. In terms of ideological articulation, Congress's direction at the all-India level was set out in the election manifesto 'A call to the nation'. It detailed a programme that was framed by the core principles of unity amidst diversity, equality, progress (primarily through economic development) and Indian independence that had been the core of Congress's activities from the late nineteenth century. Importantly, this framework contained objectives that overlapped significantly with Dravidian politics, i.e. broadly the need to address social inequality, particularly caste hierarchy, and the recognition and cultivation of India's plural linguistic identities.

Meanwhile, the work of co-opting interests and mobilising support was conducted at the provincial levels, and here Congress's activity over the previous decade wrought important changes in the dynamics of electoral campaigns. S. Satyamurti, a senior Tamil Nadu Congress politician, observed in January 1937 that the forthcoming provincial elections would be a test 'not only of patriotism but also of our business capacity'.[182] The INC campaign was a synergy of mass mobilisation and magnate interests. On the one hand, Congress used its organisational networks to register newly enfranchised voters, held public meetings and used devices such as processions and songs to set out its programme and even offered transport to polling stations. Well-known Congress politicians—including national figures like Nehru and Vallabhbhai Patel—also toured south Indian districts.[183] On the other hand, Congress also sought out as candidates individuals able to command local votes, in other words magnates or patrons, whatever their previous affiliation.[184]

However, Congress activity over the previous years, along with the activities of mass mobilisation it initiated for the campaign, changed magnate behaviour if not magnate interests. Local power-holders, who previously waited till after the elections to choose a party allegiance, began to associate with Congress in preparation for the elections, because this appeared a viable and attractive vehicle in the competition between rival magnate factions for political power.[185] In other words, Congress had built up a presence and a perceived capacity for electoral mobilisation that was to an extent autonomous of local interests. For example, in some districts local power-holders with competing networks and vote-banks competed for the party's nomination and unsuccessful candidates withdrew from the electoral contest,[186] unwilling to match the organisational resources at the official Congress candidate's disposal. The career of Kamraj Nadar, a Congress activist from a non-elite background who joined during the Non-Cooperation movement, exemplifies the extent to which the Congress structure itself became a source of power.[187] In the 1937 elections a successful businessman stood aside to let Kamraj compete as the official candidate from a southern Tamil Nadu constituency, even though Kamraj himself did not possess a factional network tied to the control of economic resources.[188] Kamraj subsequently rose through the party's ranks, serving as both Chief Minister (1954–63) of the province and later All-India Congress President (1963–7).[189]

While the new type of organisational infrastructure mobilised by Congress meant that the Justice Party disintegrated, Dravidian politics and the assertion of an anti-Indian Dravidian Tamil political identity and interest did not disappear. The Tamil-as-Dravidian identity was invoked to challenge the INC project on two separate issues. On the first occasion, the Self-Respect league allied with other Tamil revivalists and Muslim organisations to oppose Congress's legislation, introduced in July 1937, making Hindi a compulsory subject in the Madras school curriculum. Indian nationalists from the late nineteenth century had sought to replace English with the indigenous Hindi as the link language between the different provinces, and in 1918 Gandhi had founded an institute for the propagation of Hindi in south India.[190] While Congress advocated Hindi as an indigenous Indian language, the anti-Congress alliance invoked the Dravidian theory to characterise Hindi as a north Indian, Aryan and Hindu imposition. The agitation drew significant support and led to 683 arrests, more than the 504 arrests that took place during the Congress-led Quit India (1942–5) movement.[191]

Again in June 1940 Ramaswamy and the Self-Respect league invoked the Dravidian idea to challenge Congress's claim to represent Indian demands for independence by organising a Dravidanad separation conference. At the conference Ramaswamy unveiled a map showing the whole of south India as Dravidanad whilst north India was divided into Muslim India and Aryavarta. The Dravidian idea was not, however, used to mount an effective electoral challenge to Congress until the post-independence period. The remnants of the Justice Party merged with the Self-Respect league in 1944 to form a new organisation: the Dravida Kazhagam.[192] Ramaswamy took leadership of the new organisation and retained his policy of staying out of electoral politics. The DK's activities consisted therefore of articulating a clear and unequivocal social world view along with direct mobilisation to realise that world view. This left the field open for Congress; its organisational base was further strengthened by the 1942 Quit India movement, and in the 1946 elections it won its second convincing electoral victory in Madras.[193]

Congress's electoral victory should not, however, be interpreted as a repudiation of Dravidian politics. Instead—and as a consequence of their overlapping objectives—the competition between Congress and the Dravidian movement was more agonistic than antagonistic and crucially contained within Congress's framework of pan-ethnic Indian national identity and national interest. Furthermore, the Tamil Nadu Congress developed these objectives—the cultivation of Tamil culture and issues of social reform, particularly the question of caste hierarchy—through its efforts to mobilise the Tamil-speaking population directly. As is argued in Chapter 4, it was the overlapping objectives of the Dravidian and Congress movement—rather than the relative extremism or moderation of the parties concerned—that explains the post-independence accommodation of Dravidian parties within the Indian constitutional framework. The next section of this chapter briefly discusses the relationship between Congress and Muslim politics. It argues that the absence of Congress efforts to mobilise the Muslim population directly explains Congress's failure to mobilise Muslim electoral support, despite the importance of patronage networks in determining electoral behaviour.

Congress, Muslims and Hindu nationalism

By the First World War, the idea of a distinct all-India Muslim political identity was well established in colonial politics. A clear expression of this was the
provision for separate Muslim electorates for the provincial and all-India
legislatures in the 1909 Morley–Minto reforms.[194] Congress sought to reconcile this political reality with the need to present a unified—and therefore
national—demand for constitutional reform by engaging in negotiations with
the All-India Muslim League.[195] The principal issue of negotiation was the
means of securing adequate Muslim representation in the central and provincial legislatures. Between 1915 and 1924 Congress and the League met simultaneously as they first jointly pursued constitutional reform and then, with the
adoption of Non-Cooperation, mass protest.[196] With the end of the Non-
Cooperation movement, Congress and League again began to meet separately.
Negotiations were again attempted in 1928, 1934, 1938 and 1944, but always
failed to produce an agreement on the measures that would allay Muslim fears
of being overwhelmed by an elected Hindu majority.[197] The final round of
negotiations after the elections of 1946 also failed to find agreement and led
eventually to an acceptance of partition.

This outcome was not inevitable and cannot be seen as an unmediated
expression of the growth of Hindu and Muslim nationalist sentiments or
Hindu–Muslim antagonism. Rather, the political trajectory that led to partition has to be understood partly in terms of Congress's failure to mobilise
direct support amongst the Muslim electorate. As a consequence, Congress
did not establish itself as a viable and attractive option for political mobilisation amongst the Muslim electorate. This meant that the changes that took
place in Tamil magnate behaviour were absent amongst provincial Muslim
magnates and politicians. Muslim political behaviour in the 1935–7 elections
continued to be conditioned by magnate competition and factional networks,
unencumbered by the constraints and possibilities of extensive party mobilisation.[198] This behaviour only changed with the 1945–6 elections when Muslim
political leaders and magnates switched their allegiance to the Muslim
League; in the 1935–7 elections the League had secured only 4.4 per cent of
the Muslim votes cast in provincial elections, but in the 1945–6 elections it
won nearly 75 per cent.[199]

The League's victory in the 1945–6 elections was not however built on a
robust party structure that brought together the three core components of
successful political mobilisation. The decision to switch to the League was
prompted by local considerations and conflicts along with the growing sense

that momentous constitutional changes were about to take place and Muslims needed representation at the centre.[200] The League's slogan of Pakistan had different meanings in different provinces: in Punjab it was tied to the idea of a general threat to Islam and an ideal of Muslim community,[201] whilst in Bengal it was linked to agricultural grievances and specifically an undivided Bengal province.[202] Ayesha Jalal notes that Muhammed Ali Jinnah himself left the notion of Pakistan unspecified and argues that he intended to use the idea of Pakistan as a bargaining chip to secure representation for Muslims at the centre of a strongly centralised Indian state.[203] She suggests that Jinnah was finally forced to accept partition because of Congress's determination to secure its own control at the centre, at the expense of partition, and the British determination to transfer power as quickly as possible; neither of which had been part of Jinnah's calculations.[204] Ironically, the vague resolution calling for Pakistan passed by the League in March 1940 led to the creation of new state boundaries; whilst the June 1940 Dravidanad demand, spelt out as a definite territory with map included, has become a historical curiosity. The crucial factor in explaining the different outcomes of the two demands is the Congress's contrasting history of political mobilisation amongst the Muslim and Tamil electorates.

In the Tamil-speaking areas, regional Congress politicians familiar and conversant with Tamil cultural forms were crucial to the activities of direct mobilisation that established Indian nationalism's cultural as well as political presence amongst the population. However, in areas such as Bengal, Punjab and UP with substantial Muslim populations, regional Congress politicians often had strong ties to Hindu nationalist movements and were therefore ideologically opposed to incorporating Muslim identity with the Congress movement. In the Punjab, Congress was closely allied to the Arya Samaj;[205] in Bengal it was dominated by Hindu Bengalis, who increasingly defined themselves in Hindu nationalist terms;[206] whilst in the United Provinces the Congress structure was closely associated with the Hindu Mahasabha[207] and the Arya Samaj.[208] As a consequence, in the three provinces that constituted the majority of the Muslim electorate—Bengal, Punjab and UP—Congress pushed Hindu nationalist issues such as banning cow slaughter and the promotion of Hindi in the Sanskrit script over Urdu that symbolically excluded Muslims from the core Indian national community.

The joint Hindu–Muslim mobilisation that took place during Non-Cooperation was presented by Congress and the Muslim leaders as a symbolic partnership between the cow and khilafat; Hindus agreed to protest in support of the Ottoman khalif and in return Muslims agreed to stop slaughtering cows.[209] When this participation ended, Muslim participation in anti-colonial mass protest declined and Congress's subsequent campaign—Civil Disobedience—had a very Hindu character in areas such as UP. Mass meetings were held in temples and at Hindu festivals, the propaganda invoked Hindu symbols and activities such as picketing often specifically targeted Muslim shops, leaving their Hindu competitors undisturbed.[210] As a consequence of these activities, even Muslim politicians who wanted to switch to Congress in 1937 found they could not because of the antipathy this generated within the Muslim electorate.[211]

The Hindu nationalist character of the regional Congress does not, however, indicate a clear or enduring Hindu–Muslim antagonism in politics. While there were bouts of Hindu–Muslim violence, these were episodic and separated by periods of calm and cooperation.[212] Similarly, there were also instances of Hindu–Muslim political cooperation, as in Subash Chandra Bose's ill-fated Indian National Army.[213] There were also ongoing intra-Hindu and intra-Muslim tensions. For example, amongst Hindus there were important differences between the reformist Arya Samaj and more orthodox movements such as the Sanatan Dharma.[214] There were also significant differences of interest between Muslims, including between the Muslims in the Muslim majority provinces and those in UP where Muslims formed a small but significant minority;[215] between Shias and Sunnis;[216] and sometimes between the political and religious leaderships.[217] Alongside these differences were the important differences of class and economic interest that separated Muslim and Hindu landowners from their tenants.[218]

While all these differences became politically or culturally contentious at different historical moments, the crucial factor that determined Congress's failure to build support amongst the Muslim electorate was the Hindu nationalist character of its regional structures. This became evident during the Muslim Mass Contacts campaign led by Nehru in 1937 to reach the Muslim electorate directly. The campaign had some success in UP, Bengal and Punjab and was able to recruit new Muslim members,[219] enough to alarm Muslim politicians.[220] It was, however, severely handicapped by regional and district level Congress politicians who refused to grant funds and lend manpower to the efforts to reach Muslims directly.[221] Within months the campaign was called off and the Congress leadership switched back to the tactic of direct negotiation, with Subash Chandra Bose opening talks with Jinnah.[222]

The importance of Hindu nationalists at the provincial level does not thereby mean that Congress can simply be equated with Hindu nationalism.

There are significant ideological and organisational differences between Congress' pan-ethnic Indian nationalism and the varied currents of Hindu nationalism. As discussed in Chapter 4, this became evident in the Constituent Assembly debates that framed India's post-independence constitution. It is also significant that the incidence of Hindu–Muslim communal violence, extremely high in the months leading up to and following partition,[223] reduced significantly in the decades following partition.[224] The rising incidence of Hindu–Muslim violence (primarily collective violence by Hindus against Muslims) from the early 1980s coincides with the decline of Congress as a cohesive political structure and the simultaneous growth of Hindu nationalist political, social and cultural forces.[225]

Conclusion

This chapter has argued that the emergence of Congress as a cohesive, pan-ethnic national movement was the result of temporally continuous efforts that brought together the three key activities of ideological articulation, interest co-option and direct political mobilisation, rather than simply the structurally determined coincidence of interests. It showed that the relationship between Tamil politics and the Congress movement was shaped by two related factors. The first was the development of Congress's explicitly multi-ethnic and multi-lingual ideological and organisational framework that could accommodate the principal issues of anti-Congress Dravidian Tamil politics: the cultivation of Tamil culture and social reform. Importantly, this pan-ethnic ideological and organisational framework emerged when Congress-led efforts to create a pan-ethnic platform were confronted with ethnic organisations opposing Congress's efforts. The second factor was Congress's efforts at direct political mobilisation in the Tamil-speaking areas that established Congress and pan-ethnic Indian nationalism as key brands in Tamil social and political life. In short, the key factor in creating a politically significant pan-ethnic national identity that incorporated Tamils was the outcome not of structural factors, but of competitive and agonistic, rather than merely antagonistic, processes of organisation and mobilisation. Furthermore, these processes did not so much transcend ethnic divisions as incorporate them within a wider pan-ethnic politics. Finally, the chapter discussed the relationship between Congress and Muslim politics and argued that the absence of Congress efforts to mobilise support directly amongst the Muslim population meant that Muslims were not ideologically and organisationally incorporated into the Congress national project in a way comparable to the Tamils. The following chapter analyses ethnic and national politics in colonial Sri Lanka and suggests that by the moment of independence, an ethnically exclusive Sinhala Buddhist understanding of national identity and interest had become electorally dominant and, while not organised through a single political structure, was nevertheless to become the organising principle of Sri Lanka's post-independence politics, a development that had important consequences for Sri Lankan Tamil politics in the post-independence period.

3

BECOMING NATIONAL

TAMILS AND SINHALESE IN COLONIAL SRI LANKA

Introduction

Unlike in India, at the moment of Sri Lanka's independence, the question of the political status of the Tamil-speaking people and Tamil-speaking areas within a wider conception of national identity remained unresolved. There was no organisation comparable to the Indian National Congress with a developed political programme capable of mobilising electoral support across the island. The United National Party (UNP), which came to power at independence, was formally multi-ethnic. However, as discussed below, it was a loose alliance formed in the last months of colonial rule, and its driving force was the authority and stature of its founder leader, D. S. Senanayake.[1] During the Second World War, Senanayake had established a reputation amongst British officials as a reliable leader to whom power could be transferred, despite his close and visible relationship to Sinhala Buddhist revivalism.[2] Although the UNP had a multi-ethnic list of candidates, it did not have a developed political framework that reconciled the island's ethnic pluralism within a unified conception of national identity and national interest. The party's organising principle was instead a tacit understanding and acceptance of Senanayake's leadership, and of majority rule.[3]

In the absence of a developed and institutionalised conception of pan-ethnic national identity and interest, it was the Sinhala Buddhist and Tamil conceptions of national identity and national interest that together shaped the

81

dynamics of politics in the Tamil-speaking regions. These two had mutually contradictory understandings of the history of the island's ethnic plurality, the relative historical and cultural claims of the various ethnic groups and, therefore, of the ideal means through which ethnic pluralism ought to be reconciled with the need for a unified conception of national identity and national interest. Although the two conceptions had their intellectual, and even organisational, roots in the nineteenth-century religious and linguistic revivalist movements, there was very little overt conflict or antagonism between the Tamil and Sinhala revival movements during most of the colonial period, and their relationship was mostly one of mutual indifference, with instances of collaboration, support and encouragement. It was only the advent of tangible political power tied to the conceptual framework of popular sovereignty and the nation that brought the contradictory assumptions of these two frameworks into conflict. From 1920 onwards, as self-government became a distinct and plausible prospect, there was often pointed and sometimes acrimonious political conflict between Tamil and Sinhala political leaders. Conflict took place on issues such as the citizenship rights of Indian-origin plantation labourers, constitutional reform and the distribution of public resources[4]—all of which raised divisive but conceptually unavoidable questions about the ethnic characteristics of national identity and the substance of national interest. As independence approached, these questions remained unresolved and the key political actors—Tamil, Sinhalese and British—all shared the view that a crucial factor in deciding the island's political future would be the relations between the Sinhala majority and the Tamil minority.

The appearance of two incompatible Tamil and Sinhala conceptions of national identity and national interest was not, however, an outcome made inevitable by ethnic demography or indeed the passions of ethnic revivalisms. Neither the growth of Tamil nor Sinhala Buddhist nationalisms as political platforms can be understood as the simple expressions of a pre-existing ethnic sentiment. Instead, both could only present a unified political platform—and even then not reliably so—by more or less successfully negotiating differences of religion, caste and region that remained points of intra-Tamil and intra-Sinhala conflict. The gradual political and electoral ascendance of these movements alongside the failure of pan-ethnic nationalism are not therefore structurally given outcomes but contingent upon political processes that could have been otherwise.

This chapter is organised in the following way. The first section examines the emergence of Sinhala Buddhist and Tamil conceptions of national identity and national interest from the religious and revival movements of the late nineteenth century. The next section then sets out the trajectory of ethnic and national politics in two parts, the first from the late nineteenth century to 1920, and the second from 1920 to independence. It also examines the pivotal role played by British officials in shaping the reforms leading to independence, but also explains why differences in British policy cannot account for the relative successes and failures of pan-ethnic anti-colonial politics in India and Sri Lanka. In the discussion of colonial Indian politics in Chapter 2, the year 1920 was a useful marker that separated Congress's pre-1920 phase of primarily elite-centred development from the post-1920 phase of mass mobilisation. In Sri Lanka, 1920 does not mark a clear divide between phases of elite-centred and mass mobilisation politics; it nevertheless signals an important shift in the island's ethnic and national politics. From 1920 onwards, constitutional reforms consistently adopted the principle of territorial as opposed to communal or group-based representation as the basis for self-government. From then on, the political consequences of the Sinhala demographic majority and the Tamil demographic minority became crucial factors in the island's politics. The relationship of mutual indifference alongside moments of collaboration was from 1920 replaced by ongoing contestation between Tamil and Sinhala politicians over issues that vitally touched the ethnic framework of national politics. The argument presented below links the failure to find a robust and clear resolution to these issues to the processes of political contestation, organisation and mobilisation.

Context

Sinhala Buddhist nationalism

The social and political ascendance of Sinhala Buddhist nationalism can be traced to the Buddhist revivalist and reform movements which, amongst the revivalist trends of the nineteenth century, Stanley Tambiah describes as the 'most complex, weighty, powerful and fateful for the history of the country'.[5] The Buddhist movement, like its Hindu counterparts in India and Sri Lanka, was a response to the intellectual and social challenges posed by Christian missionary activity. Buddhist revivalists, like their Hindu and Muslim equivalents, responded to missionary charges of the inferiority, irrationality and superstitious nature of their theology and ritual by adopting the very standards and definitions against which Buddhism was often held to be wanting. Buddhist revivalist activities sought to establish a separation between what they held to be 'true' Buddhism—a pristine and rational confessional religion, compatible with modern science and progress—and the 'false' Buddhism of popular practice, debased by the corrupting influence of south Indian (Tamil) invasions and British colonial rule.[6]

To propagate and defend this 'true' religion, Buddhist activists used print technology to mass produce tracts and pamphlets whilst engaging in public debates with Christian missionaries. The transformation of Buddhism was thus associated with the emergence of a consolidated Sinhala Buddhist national identity that fused language, race and religion with a powerful claim to the entire territory of the island. K. N. O. Dharmadasa describes the Sinhala Buddhist ideological tradition as having an 'explicitly stated identification of the island with one ethnic group and one religious identity—Sinhalese and Buddhist'.[7] The import and consequence of Buddhist revival and reform activities was therefore 'not so much the implementation of social reform as the forging of an ideology and consciousness of nationalist identity, destiny, and majoritarian privilege'.[8]

From the late nineteenth century onwards, Sinhala Buddhist organisations, newspapers and magazines set out a clear vision of the ethnic boundaries of national community and the relative claims of different ethnic groups. This vision was derived from a narrative of the island's history that, as in India, was closely linked to the concerns and categories of Orientalist scholarship.[9] From the early nineteenth century, a set of Pali texts, known as vamsas or chronicles that were written from the sixth century onwards,[10] were translated into English and came to be viewed as authoritative sources by British officials, scholars and Sinhala Buddhist activists.[11] Nineteenth-century interpretations of these texts set out a narrative of the island's history that were remarkably similar to the Hindu nationalist conceptions of Indian history of Aryan migration and Aryan civilisation followed by invasion and destruction. In the Sri Lankan version of the Aryan theory, an initial act of migration by north Indian Aryan Sinhalese founds a thriving classical civilisation based on Buddhist piety and an advanced practice of irrigated agricultural production able to support a substantial population, speculated to be greater than the nineteenth-century population levels on the island.[12] Whereas in the Hindu nationalist conception, the classical Vedic civilization was destroyed by Muslim invasions, the Sinhala Buddhist narrative had the south Indian Tamils as the 'principal alien and antagonist' of the Sinhala people responsible for destroying and degrading the classical glory of Sinhala civilisation.[13]

The officially sponsored archaeological study of the ruins at Anuradhapura and Polonnaruva (sites related in the Mahavamsa and other chronicles) that began in the 1870s[14] lent material weight to the Aryan theory of the island's history, for both Sinhala Buddhist revivalists and British officials alike.[15] With the opening of the railways, Anuradhapura in particular became a modern site of pilgrimage,[16] and by the early twentieth century the notion that the Sinhalese had a great and unbroken history on the island had become commonplace.[17] The chronicles were thus transformed by a modern interpretation through categories of nation, civilisation, progress and race into the basis for a national conception of history and collective agency that provided a clear matrix for social and political action, but crucially excluded non-Sinhala Buddhists, particularly the Tamils.

In response to Christian missionary proselytising, Buddhist monks engaged in a series of public debates with Christian preachers, and set out to produce printed material to defend their own doctrine and attack Christian theology, often using the arguments of Western secularists and rationalists. The debates caught the attention of Colonel Olcott, one of the founders of the Theosophical Society, who visited the island in 1880, following the Society's move to India the previous year.[18] The Theosophists' efforts gave 'organizational muscle and propagandistic efficacy' to revivalist activities[19] that were further developed by Anangarika Dharmapala (1864–1933), a revivalist who 'first found his vocation and acquired his propagandist skills in association with the Theosophists'.[20] Olcott explicitly encouraged his Buddhist audiences to adopt the organisational models of the Christian missionaries and following their visit, Buddhist societies, newspapers, schools and Young Men's Buddhist Associations (YMBA) were established across the Sinhala districts.[21] The myriad and expanding Buddhist organisational activities were the sites at which a new and reformed 'national' Buddhist religion was expressed. Tambiah describes the core features of Dharmapala's reformed religion in the following way:

> ... a selective retrieval of norms from canonical Buddhism; a denigration of alleged non Buddhist ritual practices and magical manipulations ... enunciation of a code for lay conduct, suited to the emergent Sinhalese urban middle class and business interests, which emphasized a puritanical sexual morality and etiquette in family life; and most important of all, an appeal to the past glories of Buddhism and Sinhalese civilization celebrated in the Mahavamsa and other chronicles.[22]

In this way, by the early twentieth century, Buddhism had become established as the national religion within an emergent Sinhala Buddhist identity in which language, race, religion and territory were closely intertwined. The nationalisation of Buddhism was thus coeval with the simultaneous nationalisation of Hinduism and Christianity in India and Britain respectively.[23] The social and economic context of Buddhist revivalism—and thereby emergent Sinhala nationalism—was the rapid growth and commercialisation of the economy associated with the opening up of the Kandyan[24] areas to plantation agriculture and the incorporation of the island into British-centred global flows of finance and trade. This produced a new commercial elite formed by low country Sinhala caste groups—the Karavas, Salagamas and Duravas (KSD)— who had formerly been associated with the relatively low-status occupations of fishing, cinnamon peeling and toddy tapping respectively. During the course of the nineteenth century these groups acquired new wealth and status through a variety of activities such as contracting labour to clear forests, supplying food and alcohol for the new plantations, graphite and gem mining, supplying furniture, small-scale retail and investing in urban property.[25]

The three low country caste groups—labelled the KSD—formed the initial core of the Buddhist revivalism.[26] During the twentieth century, however, Sinhala Buddhism became the dominant framework through which Kandyans, upper-caste landowners or Goyigamas and even Sinhala Christians organised their political activities. In this way, Sinhala Buddhism followed the trajectory of Hindu nationalism, which emerged first amongst urban upper-caste groups but subsequently expanded to include a wide array of non-elite groups across northern India.[27] An important difference between India and Sri Lanka was, however, that in India the force of Hindu nationalist mobilisation was contained by Congress's pan-ethnic conception of national identity and interest.

Tamil revivalism

Nineteenth-century revival and reform activities in the Tamil-speaking areas established a form of politics in the Tamil language through which Tamil cultural, as well as political, interests were contested and debated. Unlike nineteenth-century Buddhist revivalism, however, Tamil revivalist activities did not produce a clear sense of Tamil identity that brought together claims about language, religion, people and territory. Tamil revivalism was instead organised into multiple strands, connected to the strands of Hindu and Tamil revivalist activities in India. A key figure in shaping the religious movement was Arumugam Navalar (1822–79) who sought to counter Christian proselytising by reasserting the value of the Tamil Saiva Siddhanta tradition. While Navalar's activities placed the Saiva Siddhanta system of beliefs and rituals at the core of Tamil interests, later Tamil revivalists focused on the cultivation and promotion of Tamil language, literature and culture. By the early decades of the twentieth century, there was a consensus amongst Tamil organisations that the Tamils constituted a distinct ethnic group and were, like the Sinhalese, indigenous to the island;[28] but this was not linked to clear historical narratives or territorial claims. The growing consensus amongst Tamil leaders on Tamil–Sinhala political equality nevertheless led to a conflict over strategy between those who sought to work with the Sinhalese to produce a pan-ethnic Ceylonese nationalism, akin to the one in India, and their rivals who equated the situation of Tamils with those of Muslims in India, and sought political safeguards for Tamils and other minorities against the threat of Sinhalese domination.[29]

Sri Lankan Tamil revivalism in the colonial period was influenced by Hindu revivalism and the Congress brand of Tamil revivalism. However, the Tamil-as-Dravidian idea, while sometimes asserted, did not become a pole of sustained social reform or political activity, as it did in south India.[30] In short, while the Dravidian idea was often asserted, it was not linked to a sustained organisational structure, as in south India. This relative absence, which is particularly striking given the importance of the Aryan idea to Sinhala Buddhist nationalism, makes clear that mutually incompatible ethnic and national claims are not necessarily mirror-images of each other or indeed diametrically opposed. For example, while the Tamils figured prominently in Sinhala Buddhist nationalist narratives, the Sinhalese were largely absent from Tamil revivalist conceptions for most of the nineteenth century, and Navalar himself rarely mentioned the Sinhalese at all.[31] The different configurations of race, territory, language and religion in Tamil and Sinhala nationalism demonstrate that the content of the ethnic and national claims that become politically or socially dominant cannot be seen as merely the oppositional and reactive pairings of self and other. Instead, Sinhala Buddhsit and Tamil revivalists were not so much responding to each other as responding to the emergence of a new set of categories (religion and language) and concepts (nation, history, progress) through which they had to reconfigure existing ideas and practices. As discussed in Chapter 1, while the translation of pre-modern Tamil and Sinhala religious and literary systems into modern categories was inevitable, the subsequent conflict between Sinhala Buddhist and Tamil nationalist frameworks was not.

The career of Arumugam Navalar has a number of evident similarities with that of Anangarika Dharmapala and Indian Hindu nationalists like Dayananda Saraswati. The son of a Jaffna poet, Navalar was taught Tamil by his father before entering a mission school at the age of twelve to study English. He was a talented student, and after completing his studies, was asked by the principal, Peter Percival, to help with translating the Bible and Prayer Book into Tamil. Navalar's education and later work at the mission school took place in the midst of the tensions and debates associated with missionary proselytising. Although initially attracted to Christianity,[32] he was eventually moved by the desire to promote Saiva Siddhanta or the Tamil Saivite tradition and protect it against missionary attacks and criticism.[33] His efforts to defend and cultivate Saivism were comparable to those adopted by Dharmapala, Saraswati and other revivalists. He preached sermons, published tracts, edited and produced reliable printed editions of key religious texts and established schools that provided a modern curriculum within a Saivite religious atmosphere.[34] While Navalar's efforts sought to reproduce Saivism as a modern confessional faith, in the image of Protestant Christianity, the outcome of this work did not establish a sustained public equation of Saivism as the 'national' religion of the Tamil people.

The competition between Christian missionaries and their Saivite opponents was crucial to the early development of modern politics and revivalism in the Tamil-speaking areas of south India and Sri Lanka.[35] However, by the early decades of the twentieth century, Saivism had become less prominent as a means of identifying Tamil cultural and political interests—in contrast to the growing importance of Buddhism and Hinduism in Sri Lankan and (north) Indian politics respectively. There are three reasons for this. The first was that Navalar and his followers promoted Saivism primarily as a form of salvation and did not clearly elaborate a set of claims linking Saivism with Tamil political and social interests more broadly, in a manner comparable to Buddhist and Hindu revivalists.[36] Secondly, in the later decades of the nineteenth century, efforts to cultivate Saivism were increasingly undertaken under the broader label of Hinduism, abandoning Navalar's explicit focus on the Saiva Siddhanta tradition.[37] Finally, and most importantly, the relative decline of Saivism and religion more broadly as a basis for social and political community is a consequence of the growing importance—from the early decades of the twentieth century—of language, literature, Bharathanatyam and Carnatic music as means of identifying Tamil cultural, social and even political interests. This is not to say that religion disappeared as a locus of activity; quite the reverse. Temple committees, churches, religiously affiliated schools, newspapers and welfare associations continued to play a central role in the political and cultural activities of the Tamil-speaking areas.[38] However, as discussed below, the promotion of Tamil culture, broadly defined, was a concern shared by Hindu, as well as Christian organisations.

The expansion or revivalist activity in the Tamil-speaking regions began in the Jaffna peninsula and was closely associated with the dominant landowning caste, the Vellalas. At the onset of British rule, the social dominance of the Vellalas had already been consolidated by their position within the previous Dutch administrative structures and participation in south Indian and southeast Asian trade networks.[39] During the nineteenth century, agricultural production in Jaffna was increasingly turned to cash crops and the wealth accruing from this was invested in education.[40] Employment in the British administration, on the island but also in south India and in British Malaya, became further sources of income for the peninsula. Organisational activity followed the linkages of employment and administration created by colonial rule. Christian and Hindu schools were established in the Tamil-speaking districts of Trincomalee and Batticaloa, whilst the Jaffna-based press began routinely to report events from these areas, as well as from Colombo.[41] There were also efforts to encourage investment and migration from the over-populated and capital-rich Jaffna peninsula to the relatively under-populated areas of Vanni and the eastern province.[42]

Organisational activity amongst the Tamil-speaking population did not, however, establish a clear narrative of national identity that integrated claims about language, religion and territory. There was no single association that could mobilise mass activity and support across the Tamil-speaking population. Indeed, for much of this period, religious competition and theological conflict between Hindus and Christians dominated political and cultural life. Religious controversy was also closely related to the issue of caste. Christian missionary proselytising challenged Vellala dominance of low-caste groups who were often dependent labourers of Vellala landlords. While Christians and Hindus engaged in theological debates through the print media, at a more corporeal level, upper-caste Hindus sought violently to maintain the practices of caste hierarchy against efforts by low-caste groups to establish their cultural autonomy and assert social equality.[43] However, at the moment of independence, the principal political division was not over the issue of caste or religion. Instead, this was centred on whether the Tamils should seek minority safeguards that would protect against the possibility of Sinhala political domination or, instead, work with Sinhala leaders to set out a common demand for political independence.

Process

Ethnic and national politics up to 1920

Chapter 2 traced the emergence of a pan-Indian form of nationalism able to accommodate the clear sense of a distinct Tamil cultural identity and interest formed through nineteenth-century revival and reform activities. The chapter argued that crucial to this outcome was Congress's temporally continuous activity in the period between its foundation in 1885 and 1920 which established it as an unavoidable—for its detractors and supporters—presence in Indian political life. The analysis presented below shows that a comparable pan-ethnic Ceylonese national organisation failed to appear primarily because of the absence of temporally sustained activities that brought together the elements of ideological articulation, co-option of interests and direct mobilisation. There were recurrent and fitful attempts to establish a pan-ethnic Ceylonese national organisation from the late nineteenth century that were supported by Sinhalese and Tamil political actors. Some associations, like the Ceylon National Association (CNA) formed in 1888, the Ceylon National Congress (CNC) formed in 1918 and the Liberal League formed in 1932 resembled the 'moderate' section of the pre-1920 Congress in confining their activities to formal meetings and petitions, eschewing direct or mass political mobilisation.[44] On the other hand, there were also organisations like the Ceylon Reform Society formed in 1905–6, and the Jaffna Youth Congress formed in 1924, which like the 'extremist' section of Congress, emphasised social reform and the revival of indigenous cultural forms as crucial to political independence.[45] The Youth Congress also engaged in direct political mobilisation. While all the elements of a pan-ethnic national movement were present, what was absent was an organisational structure that brought them together in a temporally sustained way.

Political activity during this period (late nineteenth century to 1920) was—as in India—the preserve of a small elite defined by education, property and income concentrated around Colombo, along with a significant presence in Jaffna. The existence of substantial social and economic disparities is evident in the smallness of the electorate, which was, until the introduction of universal franchise in 1931, based on property and income qualifications. In 1912, for example, an electorate restricted to adult males literate in English contained just 2,934 voters from a population of just over 4 million.[46] In 1924, when the electorate was expanded to include adult males with literacy in Sinhala, Tamil or English along with a minimum level of property or income, the number of voters expanded to 204,997, or 4 per cent of the total population of 4 million.[47] Education and economic prosperity were also unevenly distributed. The Ceylon Tamils were disproportionately represented amongst the English educated; although only 11 per cent of the population,[48] in 1918, for example, they made up almost half of the constituency for the electorate based on English language literacy.[49] Meanwhile, wealth created by the plantation economy was concentrated primarily in the hands of the low country Sinhalese, those of the KSD castes, while the Kandyans were under-represented amongst groups that could be said to have elite status.[50]

The uneven expansion of education and commercialised prosperity meant that political activity also relied heavily on wealthy patrons. P. Ramanathan (1851–1930),[51] descendant of a wealthy Jaffna Vellala family and Tamil representative in the legislative council from 1879 to 1893, financed—largely from his own funds—the construction and, for a number of years, the maintenance of the Ponnampala-Vanesvarar temple in Colombo and the Ramanathan College for women in Jaffna.[52] Similarly the Hapitigam complex of temperance societies, which often held meetings with crowds of over 20,000, was largely funded by Don Spater Senanayake,[53] whose fortune was built on the proceeds of an early enterprise in the distillation and selling of alcohol.[54] This concentration of wealth also played out in electoral politics where, as in India, magnate power and patron–client networks played an important role in deciding electoral outcomes.[55] Successful political organisation—especially in the context of universal franchise—relied, therefore, on the co-option of magnate interest, along with articulating a political framework and direct political mobilisation.

It was in this context that the Ceylon National Association was formed in 1888 with a stated goal 'to help in the formation of a healthy public opinion on all questions of public importance and to promote by every legitimate means the political, intellectual and material advancement of the people'.[56] These objectives worked within the framework of a pan-island political identity and political interest, and the organisation brought together political actors from two of the most politically active groups on the island, the low country Sinhalese and the Sri Lankan Tamils. The organisation's first President was P. Ramanathan, the Tamil representative in the legislative council, while the CNA had much of its organisational roots in the Ceylon Agricultural Association, an organisation that was set up to promote the interests of low country (primarily Karava) planters.[57] The CNA continued to exist until December 1919 when it was merged with the Ceylon Reform League (formed in 1917) to form the Ceylon National Congress (CNC).[58] While the CNA's founders were certainly aware of the INC in India,[59] they did not emulate that pattern of activity by holding an annual meeting in different parts of the island. As discussed in Chapter 2, it was as a result of the problems encountered in this activity that Congress was compelled to formulate a framework for pan-Indian politics that could accommodate ethnic pluralism. It was forced to confront the difference between social reformers and conservatives, as well as the problems of co-opting Muslim support in the context of countervailing anti-Congress mobilisation by Muslim political actors. The CNA did not engage in this process and therefore did not have to resolve the problem of reconciling the claims of Sinhala Buddhist associations in the south with those of Tamil associations in Jaffna. Instead, the CNA continued primarily as a label, invoked to host speakers or lobby the government on specific issues.[60] As a consequence, by 1920, when constitutional reforms precipitated a shift towards mass electoral politics, political activity on the island had not generated a stable and institutionalised framework through which the ethnic pluralism could be accommodated with the need for a unified national identity and national interest.

The absence of a pan-ethnic framework on the island's politics turns crucially on the absence of political processes; primarily that of temporally continuous political organisation and mobilisation that seeks actively to incorporate a plurality of ethnic groups in an effort to present a pan-ethnic political platform. This absence cannot be explained as the outcome of a fundamental difference from India in the structure of the island's politics. The factors that were associated with Congress's political trajectory up to 1920 were also present in Sri Lanka. By the early decades of the twentieth century, ideas such as self-government, discrimination, progress, the need for patriotism and economic nationalism were circulating in the island's journals, magazines and political organisations whilst also being used to criticise the British government.[61] There was also a variety of local interests that sought to influence the government in Colombo. While the Ceylon Agricultural Association sought to lobby the government in Colombo on behalf of planters, the Chilaw Association protested against the policy on waste lands, whilst also seeking to influence the direction of government investments in railways.[62] In 1859 a group of Kandyan chiefs lobbied the government for a change in the marriage ordinances.[63] Meanwhile in Jaffna, Arumugam Navalar campaigned against the perceived maladministration of W. C. Twynam, the government agent for the province, and provided information in this regard to the Tamil representative in the Colombo legislature.[64] Finally, from 1890, Jaffna associations, including associations of Jaffna Tamils who had emigrated to work as civil servants in Malaysia, petitioned the Colombo government to demand an extension of the railway to Jaffna; the decision to construct the line was finally taken in 1898 and it was completed in 1905.[65]

Sri Lankan political actors eventually addressed the problem of establishing a pan-ethnic national demand for self-government in the context of the rising expectations of constitutional reform in India generated by the First World War. The Ceylon Reform League was founded in Colombo by P. Arunachalam (1853–1924),[66] with the explicit objective of securing constitutional reform towards self-government, at the same time as Congress and the Muslim League were holding simultaneous sessions in Bombay in an effort to find agreement on constitutional reform. The League set about attempting to formulate a common set of proposals that included the CNA and the Jaffna Association (formed in 1905).[67] The inclusion of the Jaffna association was a clear attempt to present a platform that was representative of the Sri Lankan Tamils and the Sinhalese, and was explicitly endorsed as such by the *Hindu Organ*,[68] an English and Tamil language publication that also had the largest circulation on the peninsula.[69] When an agreement was eventually reached, a new umbrella organisation, the Ceylon National Congress (CNC), was launched in December 1919 with a clear set of proposals for constitutional reform. A CNC delegation travelled to London in 1920 to make the case for constitutional reform. The delegation was led by P. Arunachalam, also elected as the first president of the CNC.[70]

The agreement with the Jaffna association turned, crucially, on the means of ensuring adequate representation for the Tamils, given that the Sinhalese were in a demographic majority and the Tamils a demographic minority. The question gained particular urgency as reformists, led by Arunachalam, sought to transform the existing system from one in which individuals were nominated by the Governor to represent specific ethnic groups into one of elected representatives chosen by territorial rather than communal (or ethnic) constituencies. Such a move would necessarily transform the existing system of balanced representation into one where a majority of delegates elected from Sinhala constituencies could potentially control the legislature. Sinhala and Tamil political leaders eventually agreed that in return for the Jaffna Association assenting to territorial rather than communal constituencies and joining the CNC, a seat in the Western Province, which had a substantial Tamil minority,[71] would be allocated to a Ceylon Tamil candidate.[72] The agreement was broken in the 1921 elections which returned three Tamils and thirteen Sinhalese to the newly constituted legislative council, without a Tamil representative from the Western Province.[73] Soon afterwards, the Jaffna Association and Arunachalam resigned from the CNC, and the latter formed a new organisation called the Tamil Mahajana Sabhai.[74] There were no subsequent formal agreements in the colonial period between Tamil and Sinhala political organisations.

The brevity of the agreement between the Jaffna Association and the CNC, as well as the abruptness of its termination, does not however indicate a pervasive or intractable Sinhala Buddhist/Tamil political divide. Although ethnic categories were a key part of political life in the period up to 1920, the crucial divides and conflicts were within the Sinhala and Tamil categories. The Sinhala Buddhist revival led to violent confrontations between Sinhalese Buddhists and Sinhalese Christians in 1883 near Colombo.[75] In 1903 there were violent clashes between Sinhalese Buddhists and the Catholics in Anuradhapura.[76] The Sinhalese category was also regionally divided between low country and Kandyan Sinhalese. In 1889 the Kandyan Sinhalese were given separate representation in the legislative council, plausibly as a counter to the emergent forms of political activity linked primarily with low country Sinhalese.[77] Finally there was caste competition within the low country Sinhalese category between the KSD groups and the landowning Goyigama caste.[78]

There were similar divides within the Tamil category. Conflict, often violent, occurred between Hindu Vellalas and low-caste groups as the latter attempted to leave the hierarchical social order through conversion to Christianity.[79] In common with the Sinhalese, there was also political competition between Tamil Hindus and Tamil Christians to be selected as the Tamil representative in the legislative council.[80] The 1889 reforms also granted separate representation to the Muslims, undermining the claim of P. Ramanathan, the existing Tamil representative in the legislative council, that the Muslims ought to be considered part of the Tamil category.[81]

Finally, the most significant episode of ethnic violence took place in 1915 and was primarily one of Sinhalese groups attacking Muslim traders in the central and low country areas of the island.[82] The violence—triggered by a confrontation over the routing of a Buddhist procession near a newly expanded mosque—was closely associated with the Buddhist revival movement, particularly the temperance movement. Sinhala Buddhist nationalist magazines and periodicals—particularly those associated with Anagarika Dharmapala—portrayed the Muslims as foreigners increasingly usurping the rightful place of the Sinhalese.[83] Although Dharampala and his associate

Walinsinha Harischandra excoriated the Tamils (in terms similar to those used against Muslims),[84] the violence was directed almost exclusively at Muslims, leaving unaffected the Tamils resident in those areas.[85]

While violent ethnic conflict was present, albeit not along a Tamil–Sinhala axis, there were also, during this period, notable instances of Tamil–Sinhala cooperation. P. Ramanathan and P. Arunachalam, as well as cooperating with Sinhalese politicians in attempts to form political organisations, also encouraged Sinhala Buddhist revivalist activities. Ramanathan addressed Buddhist associations, encouraging his audience to speak Sinhalese in place of English;[86] supported moves to get the observance of Vesak (the birthday of the Buddha) recognised as a national holiday;[87] and sought to establish a Buddhist–Hindu school in Colombo.[88] Ramanathan also travelled to the Colonial Office in London following the 1915 violence to protest against the harsh measures taken by the government against prominent Sinhala Buddhist leaders and organisations thought to be responsible for the rioting.[89] Similarly, Arunachalam also spoke publicly on the virtues and wonders of Sinhala Buddhist civilisation and in 1919 addressed the Lanka Mahajana Sabha, a Sinhala Buddhist revivalist association, in Sinhalese.[90] Finally, in 1911, Ramanathan was elected to represent the educated Ceylonese from an island-wide constituency of 'native' Ceylonese literate in English. His opponent was Sinhalese, but from the Karava caste, and many of the Goyigama Sinhalese preferred to vote for a high-caste Vellala Tamil over a Karava Sinhalese.[91]

Despite the apparent lack of Sinhala–Tamil conflict and the instances of clear collaboration, the problem of reconciling the publicly established Tamil and Sinhala ethnic identities with the need for a unified conception of national identity and national identity remained conceptually unavoidable. It also became politically unavoidable because of the strength of organisational activity that established distinct and incompatible conceptions of national identity and national interest in the Tamil- and Sinhala-speaking areas. Increasingly, Tamil and Sinhala associational activity sought to accommodate—though not necessarily successfully—differences of caste and religion within larger conceptions of Tamil and Sinhala identity and interest respectively. That is, Sinhala and Tamil political activity was coming to identify the Sinhala and Tamil categories as platforms that unified internal diversities of caste, religion and region.

Anagarika Dharmapala emphasised the unity of the Aryan Sinhalese identity that overcame the divisions of caste, stating that the 'Aryan nationals belonging to the Govi caste, Karuva caste, Dura caste, Vahumpura caste, Uli caste, Berava caste and Rada caste should take heart to maintain Aryan codes of conduct'.[92] Meanwhile, attempts were also made to overcome the Buddhist–Christian divide, as when prominent Buddhist and Christian Sinhalese organised a 'national' day on 15 April 1914. One of the organisers, E. T. de Silva (also a Christian), described the day as one of 'introspection by the Sinhalese of themselves as Sinhalese ... for the celebration of our past glory and to breathe our hopes for the future'.[93] The following year another 'national day' was organised on 2 March to mark the centenary of the Kandyan convention—as a result of which the formerly independent Kandyan kingdom came under British rule. The events of the day, including the hoisting of the Kandyan lion flag as the national flag, were attempts to build a symbolic bridge across the gaps between the low country and Kandyan Sinhalese areas. In the process the Kandy kingdom and the Kandyan identity more generally were increasingly viewed as authentic representatives of a glorious Sinhala and thereby Sri Lankan past, by both Sinhalese and many British officials alike.[94]

These attempts to forge an overarching Sinhalese conception of national identity and national interest of course necessarily excluded the Tamils. In Sinhala Buddhist revivalist activity, the Tamils were depicted as the 'barbaric races of south India'[95] responsible for destroying the once glorious Sinhala civilisation, whilst Anagarika Dharmapala noted that the Sinhalese were a 'unique race, in as much as they have no slave blood in them, and never were conquered by either the pagan Tamils or European vandals'.[96] Dharmapala's vision of the island as a Sinhala Buddhist territory expressed a hierarchical ordering of ethnic groups in which the Tamils, and other groups, could only have a secondary claim:

> The island of Lanka belongs to the Buddhist Sinhalese. For 2455 years this was the land of birth for the Sinhalese. Other races have come here to pursue their commercial activities ... for the Tamils there is South India; for the moors Egypt ... But for the Sinhalese there is only this island.[97]

Alongside the Sinhala nationalist conception of a hierarchical ordering of ethnic groups on the island, Tamil political activity was also increasingly coalescing around a conception of Tamils and Sinhalese as equally indigenous to the island. There was a general presumption in Tamil politics—also adopted by P. Ramanathan and P. Arunachalam—that the Tamils were one of the two 'founding races' of the island.[98] The *Hindu Organ*, not only the largest circulating but also the most influential of the peninsula's newspapers, welcomed the pact between the CNC and the Jaffna Association, characterising it as an agreement between the 'Sinhalese and the Tamils, the people (inhabitants) of this country'.[99] When the pact broke down, many of the Tamil politicians associated with the negotiations asserted that Tamil political interests required a focus on securing Tamil rights, rather than the attempt to bury differences in an attempt to secure self-governance. To this end, a number of political organisations were formed with a focus on securing and promoting Tamil interests. Arunachalam, speaking at the inauguration of the Ceylon Tamil League in 1923, noted that while the Tamils would not 'abandon the proud duty and privilege of service to all our brothers of every race and creed', they did nevertheless 'object to being bullied or terrorised' and intended 'to defend ourselves and make ourselves strong'.[100] Furthermore, Tamil political interests were also projected as incorporating differences of caste and religion. At the inaugural meeting of the Jaffna Association, the *Hindu Organ* expressed the hope that the organisation would function 'with full unity and all earnestness, without involving caste and religious prejudices'.[101] Later political organisations, such as the Jaffna Youth Congress and the All Ceylon Tamil Conference, had prominent Hindu and Christian participants.[102]

In contrast to the situation in India, Sri Lankan politics in 1920 lacked a developed pan-island organisational structure with a worked-out conception of pan-ethnic national identity and national interest. Instead, Tamil and Sinhala associational activity from the late nineteenth century had produced two conceptions of national identity and interest that were mutually incompatible, while not diametrically opposed. The Sinhala conception—akin to the Hindu nationalist conception in India—was one of ethnic hierarchy in which the Sinhala Buddhists had a privileged historical, social and political position on the island. In contrast, the Tamil position was increasingly one of ethnic equality between the Tamils and Sinhalese, the two 'founding races' of the island. As discussed below, the dominant conception of Tamil identity and interest apparent in Tamil political activity was closer to the Indian pole of south Indian Tamil revivalism than the Dravidian pole. Although the distinct Tamil and Sinhala conceptions were not each associated with robust organisational structures—many of the organisations established during this period were short-lived[103]—they were nevertheless influential and came to inform efforts to mobilise mass political participation and electoral support in the decades leading to independence. These two distinct and mutually incompatible conceptions of national identity and national interest thus became established parts of the island's political landscape.

1920–47: Towards independence

A crucial component of the process of constitutional reform during this period was the question of ethnic representation. In 1945 a Commission, headed by Lord Soulbury and appointed by the Secretary of State, made public its recommendations for constitutional reform on the island.[104] The Commission described the 'problem of the Ceylon Constitution' as essentially one of 'reconciling the demands of the minorities for an adequate voice in the conduct of affairs' with the obvious fact that the constitution must 'preserve for the majority that proportionate share in all spheres of Government activity to which their numbers and influence entitle them'.[105] This characterisation contained the recognition that ethnic identities remained important to electoral politics.[106] From 1833 to 1920 representation in the legislative council had been communal (ethnic): individuals were nominated by the Governor to represent the interests of ethnic groups. Initially individuals were chosen to represent the Sinhalese, the Tamils and the Burghers. In 1889 additional representation for the Kandyans and Muslims was also granted. The elective principle was introduced on a limited basis in 1911 for the educated Ceylonese seat, but from 1920 onwards there was a rapid shift away from communal representation towards territorial representation.[107] The political consequences of the Sinhala demographic majority and the Tamil demographic minority became therefore key issues of debate, discussion and mobilisation for Tamil and Sinhala political leaders as well as for British officials.

Two dynamics were at play in shaping ethnic and national politics during the final decades of colonial rule and in determining the constitutional structure through which the island became independent. The first was the ongoing consolidation—though not erasure—of the religious, regional and, to some extent, caste divisions within the Tamil and Sinhala Buddhist conceptions of national identity that was coeval with a shift towards mass mobilisation associated with the rapidly expanding franchise. As direct political mobilisation became a more important feature of political contestation, ethnic and national identities were increasingly communicated in the Tamil and Sinhala languages and through popular cultural forms. This was comparable and even connected to events in India, but in the absence of a pan-ethnic framework produced very different outcomes.[108] The second crucial dynamic in determining the final shape of constitutional outcomes was the perceptions and decisions of British officials. The views of British officials, rather than the force of political mobilisation on the island, were crucial in the decisions to abandon communal representation in favour of territorial constituencies, to adopt universal franchise[109] and to appoint D. S. Senanayake as the key interlocutor in the negotiations for the transfer of power.[110] These decisions were justified by two slightly contradictory strands of reasoning. The first was that the island had a Sinhala Buddhist character and that inevitably the Sinhalese would be politically dominant. The second strand of reasoning was that the emergence of a pan-ethnic national framework to politics was desirable and would eventually develop on the island.[111]

The shift towards territorial representation that began with reforms implemented in 1921 initially produced a conflict between the political interests of the Kandyans and those of the low country Sinhalese politicians, largely represented by the CNC. Kandyan politicians took the position that further self-government would simply mean domination by the low country Sinhalese, many of whom worked in the Kandyan areas as traders and suppliers servicing the plantation economy.[112] As a consequence, the Kandyans remained aloof from the CNC and lobbied to retain communal representation, which they were granted in the first set of reforms in 1921. However, in the following set of reforms, implemented in 1923, the Kandyans lost the communal safeguards and found that many of the Kandyan electorates were won by low country Sinhalese politicians. In response, a Kandyan National Assembly was formed that demanded a federal autonomy for the Kandyan areas: the KNA's scheme envisaged a threefold division of the island into Tamil, low country and Kandyan federal states.[113]

This political division between the Kandyans and the low country Sinhalese was, however, bridged during the 1930s through a shared interest in excluding Indians—plantation labourers and traders—from the economic and political life of the island. The shift was precipitated by the decision in 1931 to adopt the recommendations of the Donoughmore Report on constitutional reform that advocated universal adult franchise—including women—and territorial constituencies. The reforms enfranchised the south Indian, mainly Tamil, plantation labourers, arousing the hostility of both Kandyan and low country Sinhalese politicians and associations, all of whom complained that the Indians would demographically 'swamp' the Sinhalese.[114] In 1921 the Indian Tamil population (who lived and worked mainly in the tea plantations in the Kandyan districts) was almost two-thirds the size (just over 600,000) of the Kandyan Sinhalese population (just over 1 million). The Kandyans complained that if the Indians were given the right to vote, Kandyan candidates would not be elected. Kandyan hostility to the Indian Tamil plantation labourers was therefore political and not economic: plantation owners had sought out labour from south India because the Kandyans, relatively prosperous and with abundant land, did not want to work on the plantations that were opening up from the mid nineteenth century.[115] At the same time, by the late nineteenth century, economic stagnation and landlessness in south India was leading to labour emigration.

In contrast, the Sri Lankan Tamils, who had been resident in the north-east of the island for several centuries, supported the Indian Tamils' right to vote. Sri Lankan Tamils were not competing for work on the plantations; there was a relatively prosperous agricultural economy in the north-east[116] which supported a growing demand for education, particularly English education. As noted earlier, this led to an over-representation of Sri Lankan Tamils in the public services[117] and also led many Sri Lankan Tamils to emigrate to Singapore and Malaysia in search of similar white-collar work.[118] Sri Lankan Tamil support for the Indian Tamils was interpreted by Sinhala political leaders as a means of 'defeating the majority community'.[119] The Donoughmore Commissioners recommended adult franchise as a means of alleviating the social and economic conditions of workers and other impoverished sections of the population, specifically mentioning the plantation labourers.[120] However, from 1929 onwards, the franchise conditions were repeatedly revised specifically to exclude Indian labourers by the Colonial Office and the Governor General at the insistence of Kandyan as well as low country Sinhalese politicians.[121]

The alliance of Kandyan and low country Sinhalese was facilitated by the widening use of Sinhala Buddhist rhetoric and symbols in the techniques of mass political mobilisation. Sinhala Buddhist conceptions of national identity and national history were circulating through an expanding vernacular print culture and also through forms such as the popular theatre.[122] The nationalist message exhorted the Sinhalese to change their names, forms of dress and other cultural habits to be more authentically Aryan,[123] and at the same time focused attention on the threat posed by Indian labourers and traders.[124] Sinhalese labour leaders also mobilised against the Indian threat, organising boycotts of Indian-owned business, calling for landlords to evict Indian tenants, encouraging businesses not to employ Indians and even exhorting the Sinhalese not to engage in mixed marriages as it would diminish the purity of the Sinhalese.[125]

The increasing political viability of a pan-Sinhalese identity is evident in the behaviour of S. W. R. D. Bandaranaike, a low country politician and future Prime Minister of independent Sri Lanka. Bandaranaike initially supported the Kandyan demand for federation in the hope of securing Kandyan backing.[126] By 1936, however, he abandoned this and adopted a Sinhala Buddhist platform forming the Sinhala Maha Sabha as a means of bridging the gap between the low country and Kandyan Sinhalese.[127] Through the SMS, Bandaranaike adopted a very shrill note on defending Sinhalese interests, stating for example that 'I am prepared to sacrifice my life for the sake of my community, the Sinhalese. If anybody were to try to hinder our progress, I should see that he should never forget.'[128] The conscious attempt to consolidate a regionally unified Sinhala identity was also exemplified at the 1940 annual session of the CNC, where it adopted independence as its eventual goal and unfurled the Kandyan lion flag as the national flag.[129]

The shift from communal to territorial electorates also precipitated a divide in Tamil politics, albeit one that was based on differences of approach, rather than differences of region, caste or religion. On the one side Tamil politicians, most prominently P. Ramanathan and from 1934 G. G. Ponnambalam[130] (1901–77), sought to retain a balance of ethnic representation in the legislative council. On the other side was a new organisation called the Jaffna Youth Congress that was formed in 1924.[131] The JYC attacked its Tamil opponents as 'communalists' and sought instead to build a pan-ethnic form of Ceylonese nationalism that explicitly used techniques of mass political mobilisation. Despite the bitter, and often violent, conflicts between the two groups, they nevertheless shared an understanding of the Tamils as indigenous to the island and sought a multi-ethnic political future for the island in which the Tamils and Sinhalese could coexist as equal collectives.[132] Their tactics to realise this end differed: the JYC sought to build political alliances with Sinhalese politicians,[133] while P. Ramanathan and later G. G. Ponnambalam sought to build alliances with other minority representatives;[134] but both were orientated towards a similar political vision.

The JYC, for example, at its first session in 1924 promulgated a political framework of national identity that was very much like that of the early Indian Congress. Asserting that it was possible for 'people of all religions to work of the welfare of the mother land', the JYC resolved that 'no distinction be made between or preference shown to any one of the various religious bodies in the country and that no sectarian issue be ever raised' by the JYC in its meetings or publications.[135] In a similar vein, G. G. Ponnambalam, in a 1939 speech setting out the case for balanced representation, argued that 'we are a composite of different races and nationalities who have to live and move and have our being in this country'. He went on to state that the 'rights of every component part must be accepted and the claims recognised if this country is to march on for the highest good of the greatest number if not of the people as a whole'.[136]

The JYC was strongly influenced by the Indian Congress, particularly the adoption of mass mobilisation and questions of social reform, poverty and the promotion of indigenous cultural forms that occurred under Gandhi's leadership. During the height of its political presence between 1924 and 1931, the JYC held sessions addressed by prominent Indian leaders including Gandhi and Nehru as well as the Tamil Nadu Congress leaders Satyamurti and V. Kalyanasundara Mudaliar. The JYC also promoted Gandhi's campaign of using homespun cotton or Khaddar over imported cloth, encouraged the use of the Tamil language in public life, led campaigns to end caste discrimination in Jaffna's educational institutions and raised issues of imperialism and economic underdevelopment in its annual sessions.[137] The JYC's cultivation of Tamil language and culture—an explicit part of its programme since its founding—was part of a broader movement of Tamil cultural promotion that was shaped by the Indian pole of south Indian Tamil revivalism. In the course of the 1930s, for example, Bharathanatyam and Carnatic music—the south Indian traditions of dance and music adopted and reformed by the Indian Congress as 'national forms'—replaced Western classical music and dance in the curricula of Jaffna schools and colleges.[138]

Over a period of six years, the JYC established a presence in the island's political life—concentrated in Jaffna[139]—by setting out a clear framework of national identity and national interest and directly mobilising political support. As a consequence, it was also briefly able to influence ambitious politicians seeking election in a manner comparable to the Indian Congress in the elections. In 1931 the JYC called for a boycott of the elections to the State Council created by the Donoughmore Commission reforms. The decision was taken on the basis that the reforms did not go far enough towards independence and echoed the Indian Congress's campaign of Civil Disobedience taking place at the same time.[140] Within days of the JYC announcing its decision and holding public meetings to dissuade people from voting, a large number of the more notable candidates withdrew their nominations.[141] The fact that some candidates withdrew, despite the electoral landscape in which patronage networks were crucial, suggests that the JYC brand had nevertheless become an independent source of electoral legitimacy within northern electoral constituencies.[142] The boycott was also, however, the cause of the JYC's eventual demise. Its optimistic hopes of a reciprocal boycott in the Sinhalese areas were entirely unfounded[143] and indeed its activities were even misrepresented by many, though not all, Sinhalese politicians and later by British officials as a demand for communal electorates.[144] By 1934 Tamil politicians who sought to negotiate balanced ethnic representation, most prominently G. G. Ponnambalam, had persuaded the then Governor, R. E. Stubbs, to hold elections in the areas affected by boycott and enter the state council. From that point on, the demand for balanced representation between the majority Sinhalese and non-Sinhalese in any future constitutional reforms became an important—though not dominant—platform in Tamil politics. The demand, commonly known as 50–50,[145] was promoted as a means of protecting the non-Sinhala minorities against discriminatory acts by ensuring a balance of political power between the majority and the minorities. Although the JYC and its members remained politically active, they lost their former influence. When two key JYC members stood for election in 1947, they fared dismally and lost their deposits. In the meantime, the notion that Tamil political interests were threatened by Sinhala domination gained momentum. At the 1947 elections Ponnambalam's All Ceylon Tamil Congress (ACTC) won six seats (out of nine) in the northern province and one seat (out of seven) from the eastern province[146] on a platform of seeking 'responsive co-operation'[147] with Sinhala leaders. In the elections, Ponnambalam abandoned his home constituency of Point Pedro and directly challenged A. Mahadeva, standing as a candidate for D. S. Senanayake's UNP in the Jaffna town constituency. In what he described as an 'ordeal by election', Ponnambalam beat Mahadeva,[148] demonstrating that his argument of the threat posed by Sinhala majority rule to Tamil interests had gained traction in Jaffna town, an important locus of Tamil politics.

British perceptions and the transfer of power

The Donoughmore Commission's recommendations were intended to overcome the ethnic divisions that were apparent in the island's politics. However, ethnic divisions continued in the period between 1931 and 1947, when the Donoughmore constitution functioned, and more importantly mutually incompatible Tamil and Sinhala conceptions of national identity and interest became established in political life. From 1931 the Sinhala Buddhist framework also became the basis for economic policy. D. S. Senanayake, as the Minister for Agriculture and Lands,[149] implemented a policy of state support for peasant colonisation of the largely under-populated Dry Zone areas in the north central, northern and north-western areas of the island.[150] The colonisation schemes resonated with the Mahavamsa vision of the island's history, in which the glorious Buddhist, hydraulic civilisations centred on the cities of Anuradhapura and Polunnaruwa were destroyed by Tamil invaders. The schemes were widely presented as the reconquest of Buddhist land, and Senanayake presented himself as a direct descendant of an old Rajarata (or King's country) family.[151] Tamil politicians criticised these policies as discriminating against Tamil interests. The emphasis on (Sinhala) peasant colonisation led to a radical reduction in public funds spent on irrigation works in the north-east, where previous investments had produced rapid increases in productivity.[152] At the same time they also noted that rates of landlessness in the Jaffna peninsula were comparable to those in the over-crowded south-western parts of the island.[153] Meanwhile, the public services also became hugely politicised as Sinhala politicians criticised Tamil over-representation, while Tamil politicians complained of administrative measures that discriminated against Tamil candidates.[154] A 1943 debate in the State Council on the issue of replacing English with a national language also revealed deep differences between Sinhalese and Tamil representatives.[155]

The Soulbury Commission, appointed in 1944 to recommend further constitutional reforms, recognised that ethnic categories continued to dominate the island's politics.[156] The commission noted Tamil and other minority complaints of discrimination but suggested that these were simply the effects of the Sinhalese majority correcting for previous deficiencies. The Commission was however optimistic that a more ethnically inclusive form of politics would naturally develop in the post-independence period and encouraged Sinhalese leaders to take minority concerns into account.[157] From 1943 onwards D. S. Senanayake emerged as the leader to whom power would be transferred, and from that point onwards Tamil politicians were largely excluded from discussions on constitutional reform.[158] The Soulbury Commission's recommendations—approved in early 1946—set out a parliamentary system with cabinet government and territorial, rather than communal, constituencies. Senanayake's demand for dominion status and finally independence were eventually granted, largely as a consequence of the pace of events in India and as a means of shoring up Senanayake's political credibility on the island in the face of growing labour unrest.[159] The problem of reconciling the island's ethnic pluralism into a singular national framework was left to the future: strikingly it was agreed that if the minorities no longer had a third party to whom appeals could be made, compromise was more likely.[160]

Conclusion

The analysis of the Indian Congress movement in Chapter 2 demonstrated that the emergence of a pan-ethnic framework of national politics was not an act of compromise or statesmanship. Rather, it emerged through continuous efforts of political mobilisation and organisation. In Sri Lanka, a pan-ethnic political platform failed to develop because of the absence of these processes. Organisations such as the CNA and the CNC did not engage in continuous political activity to build pan-ethnic support across the island. As a consequence, they were easily ignored and quickly supplanted by new organisations. In April, in preparation for the first elections to be held under the auspices of the Soulbury constitution, Senanayake bypassed the CNC and formed the UNP.[161] Most of CNC's parliamentary candidates simply switched allegiances to the UNP, which won 42 out of a total of 95 seats in the 1947 elections.[162] The UNP did not have a developed framework of national identity and national interest and functioned primarily as a label that coordinated the interests of ambitious politicians of local standing; its chief asset was Senanayake's status as the most likely future Prime Minister.[163]

The failure of pan-ethnic politics in Sri Lanka is in many ways surprising, as the pattern of ethnic politics on the island was in some ways more favourably disposed than in India. Unlike the relations between leading Congress and Muslim political leaders, important Tamil politicians and Tamil associations were central to efforts to create a pan-ethnic form of politics. The brothers P. Ramanathan and P. Arunachalam played important roles in the founding of the CNA and the CNC respectively, both of which sought to advance pan-ethnic politics. Later, Jaffna politics were for a period dominated by the Youth Congress, which also sought to create a popular movement in support of a pan-ethnic form of anti-colonial nationalism; its 1931 boycott was the only instance of anti-colonial mass protest in the island's history comparable to the pan-Indian agitations through which Congress built its support and organisational structure.[164] However, these activities had no broad-based counterparts amongst the Sinhalese, and as consequence politics came instead to be organised around two incompatible—though not diametrically opposed—conceptions of national identity and national interest.

The Muslim and Tamil politicians who endorsed Senanayake's leadership and the UNP explained their decision in terms of the legitimacy of accepting majority Sinhala rule—not as a means of evolving a pan-ethnic–national identity. However, the understanding of the island's national character as essentially Sinhala Buddhist failed to gain traction in Tamil politics. Instead, as discussed in Chapter 5, in the post-independence period Tamil politics were dominated by the Federal Party, which continued to insist on the notion of Tamils and Sinhalese as equally indigenous to the island. The escalating conflict between this momentum in Tamil politics and the Sinhala Buddhist framework that was systematically being incorporated into state structures became a central component of the island's politics in the post-independence decades.

4

TAMILS IN THE NATION

POST-INDEPENDENCE INDIA

Introduction

This chapter discusses the relationship between political dynamics in the Tamil-speaking areas and Indian national identity in the post-independence era. It will first outline the understanding of Indian national identity contained in the Indian constitution. The constitution was an expression of Congress doctrine and set the dominant framework through which ethnic pluralism was reconciled into a unified national whole. The chapter will argue that the electoral competition between the Dravidian movement and Congress in the Tamil-speaking areas took place in terms of shared notions of Tamil identity and interest that were compatible with constitutional understandings of Indian national identity. The chapter explains Congress's electoral decline in the Tamil-speaking areas as the outcome of the Dravida Munnetra Kazhagam's (DMK) more effective mobilisation, compounded by an economic crisis and contingent political factors that worked against a Congress revival. It will suggest that the political accommodation of Tamil identity within Indian nationalism was due to the political dominance of an ethnically plural understanding of Indian national identity, rather than the federal provisions of the constitution or the political moderation of the Dravidian parties.

In the post-independence era, the Indian state was redefined in national terms. A key act in this formal redefinition was the drafting of a new Indian constitution. The constitution expressed and enshrined an understanding of

Indian national identity that recognised the internal ethnic pluralism of the Indian population, but reconciled this within a shared and unifying national interest in economic and social development.[1] This understanding of Indian national identity and national interest captured in the phrase 'unity in diversity' was the outcome of Congress's ideological and political development from its inception in the late nineteenth century.[2] In the decades following independence, Congress's electoral and political dominance established the twin principles of ethnic pluralism along with a unifying national constitutional framework and commitment to economic development as central facts of Indian political life.[3] Whilst Congress eventually lost power at the national level in 1977, the constitution has remained in force to become the most durable of the constitutions that succeeded British colonial rule in south Asia. The constitution's understanding of Indian national identity has likewise remained a critical force in Indian political dynamics, acting as both a restraint and a resource for social and political movements that have sought to capture or exercise state power in line with their preferred understandings of national identity and national interest.

In the Tamil-speaking areas, the Congress party and its articulation of Indian national identity was challenged by the political growth of the DMK, a party that had its ideological roots in the once separatist and outspokenly anti-Indian Dravida Kazhagam (DK).[4] However, the growth of the DMK and its replacement of Congress as the governing party in the Tamil-speaking areas by 1967 took place without a fundamental redefinition of Indian national identity in the Tamil-speaking regions or indeed a complete reorientation of Dravidian ideology. This accommodation was possible because there was sufficient ideological overlap between Dravidian and Indian notions of Tamil identity: an ideological overlap that was developed through the Congress movement's mobilisation in the Tamil-speaking areas. Although not infinitely elastic, the constitution's characterisation of the Indian nation has been capacious enough to withstand the ascendance to political power of the once separatist Dravidian movement in the Tamil-speaking areas.

Congress party dominating the Indian constitution

The framing of the Indian constitution and its relative stability are inseparable from Congress's organisational, ideological and electoral dominance of Indian political life from the late colonial period until 1977. While the political values that eventually defined the constitution reflected the party's political doctrine, its ability to dominate discussions in the constituent assembly reflected its electoral strength.[5] The values of democracy, socialism, pluralism and unity that guided the framing of the Indian constitution were outcomes of Congress's political development and its struggle to present itself as the legitimate representative of Indian national identity and interests.[6] Although there was a diversity of views within the constituent assembly, the drafting of the constitution was closely controlled by a few key individuals whose authority rested on their status in the Congress party.[7] There were important differences between these key figures on crucial issues such as land reform, economic policy[8] and caste, but their political careers had all been at a pan-Indian rather than provincial level, and they all agreed on the need for a strong centralised state capable of securing national unity and directing the processes of economic development and social transformation.[9]

The Indian constitution, and the process of constitution-making, established an authoritative framework for reconciling the ethnic pluralism of the Indian population with the need for a unified national identity. This framework combined the need to manage ethnic pluralism with the overarching objectives of preserving Indian unity and securing Indian national interests in social and economic progress and development. During the constituent assembly debates, as during the anti-colonial struggle, the need for unity was often juxtaposed to the fissiparous tendencies of ethnic/communal pluralism and demands.[10] There were, however, two antagonistic views on how ethnic pluralism ought to be reconciled within a unified Indian national whole. The first was the Hindu nationalist conception that was most forcefully expressed during the debates on the question of national language. Hindu nationalists sought to cement the dominance of a Sanskritised version of Hindi that would lead to the linguistic, and therefore cultural, assimilation of Muslim Urdu speakers and the speakers of south Indian Dravidian languages.[11] During the assembly debates, Hindu nationalists insisted on a Sanskritised version of Hindi, purged of Urdu references and the Arabic script,[12] whilst demanding that south Indians learn Hindi.[13] In contrast to this ethnically assimilationist project, the Congress leadership, along with most south Indian, Muslim and other ethnic minority members, advocated the idea of 'unity in diversity' in which political relations between plural ethnic groups could be managed in a non-antagonistic manner.

The 'unity in diversity' conception of the Indian nation as a pre-political and organic whole that was nevertheless marked by great pluralism is most closely associated with Nehru and was eventually dominant in framing the

Indian constitution. Although the constitution did contain some Hindu nationalist inflections, notably the inclusion of the Sanskrit term Bharat and an injunction on the state to work towards the prohibition of cow slaughter,[14] it also contained a large number of provisions that formally recognised and entrenched the existence of religious, caste and linguistic diversity.[15] It is these latter provisions that are invoked by Stepan, Linz and Yadav in describing the Indian polity as 'robustly multinational' in its institutional framework. Furthermore, these provisions have also resisted later Hindu nationalist attempts to overturn them. The measures through which the categories of caste, religion and language were recognised varied—and included a number of positive and negative rights—but all the measures were legitimised and mediated by the need to secure Indian unity and Indian interests in progress and development.

One of the most contentious issues was the political representation of caste and religious groups. Soon after partition, the constituent assembly abandoned the colonial policy of separate electorates for religious groups on the basis that this undermined a unified national identity.[16] It did, however, retain a form of special representation for Dalits and tribal groups, known as Scheduled Castes and Tribes, as they were listed in a schedule of the constitution. A number of constituencies were marked as reserved and in these only SC and ST candidates could be elected. Furthermore, SC and ST groups were also granted a reserved quota of spaces in public sector employment and higher education. Both these measures were initially adopted for a limited period of time as a means of ameliorating the 'backward' condition of these groups.[17] While the political representation of religious groups was rejected as incompatible with national unity, the constitution nevertheless sought to protect and encourage the religious pluralism of Indian society. Not only was freedom of religion guaranteed as a fundamental right, public subsidies were also granted to religious activities, such as education and pilgrimage—including subsidies for Muslims undertaking the Haj.[18] Religious freedom was not, however, sacrosanct and was instead circumscribed by the imperative of social reform: Hindu religious freedom was circumscribed by laws explicitly prohibiting the practice of untouchability;[19] whilst Muslim religious freedom was circumscribed by the state's obligation to work towards the creation of a uniform code of civil law, one that would override separate Hindu and Muslim personal laws.[20] In making these incursions, the constituent assembly accepted that the 'right freely to practice religion should not prevent the state from making laws providing for social welfare and reform'.[21]

The problem of reconciling linguistic diversity and national unity was also acutely contested within the constituent assembly and involved two separate issues. The first was the need to define a national or official language and the consequent problem of the political status afforded to the non-national and non-official languages. The second issue was that of the linguistic reorganisation of India's provincial boundaries. Questions of language again polarised debate between Hindu nationalists, on the one hand, and, on the other hand, those advocating a 'unity in diversity' conception of Indian identity.[22] Hindu nationalists (within Congress) demanded official/national status for Sanskritised Hindi over and above the claims of English and the other Indian languages. Those advocating a 'unity in diversity' approach, including Nehru and most of the actors identified as crucial in the constitution-making process, favoured a long-term switch from English to Hindustani, understood very much as a composite of its Persian and Sanskrit roots. Nehru and most south Indian delegates also favoured the continued use of English as the state language and were unwilling to insist that south Indians learn Hindustani/Hindi. The eventual agreement on language was in keeping with the broad Congress doctrine of 'unity in diversity': Hindi was ascribed the prosaic title of 'official' language in place of the more emotively resonant 'national' status; while English was also retained as a recognised official language, initially for a period of fifteen years until 1965, when the switch from English to Hindi for all official purposes was to be effected. The constitution also went on to list thirteen regional languages, including Tamil, which could be adopted by the state or provincial legislatures. According to Durgabi Deshmukh, who helped draft the language provisions, this was done for 'psychological reasons and to give these languages status'; Nehru suggested that formally listing the languages in the constitution would ensure 'their due place' in the new India.[23] As 1965 approached, conflict continued between Hindi advocates insisting on an immediate switch to Hindi and non-Hindi speakers demanding the continued use of English. The conflict was eventually resolved, under Nehru's leadership, by the passage of legislation in 1963 that mandated the continued use of English alongside Hindi for official purposes after 1965.[24]

The assembly also had to decide whether to undertake the linguistic reorganisation of provincial units along with the promulgation of the new constitution. Linguistic reorganisation had been a consistent part of the Congress platform since 1920 and Congress itself was organised on linguistic lines from that time. At independence there were also growing and insistent calls, especially from the Telugu-speaking areas, for immediate reorganisation.[25] The linguistic reorganisation of provinces was initially promoted as a necessary element of democratic self-governance. The 1928 Nehru Report envisioned a system of linguistic provinces on the basis that language 'corresponds with a special variety of culture, of traditions and literature' and argued that in linguistic provinces 'all these factors will help in the general progress of the province'.[26] As independence approached, however, the Congress leadership increasingly began to see demands for immediate linguistic reorganisation as divisive; in a December 1948 note, Azad deplored 'the demand for linguistic provinces and other particularistic tendencies'.[27] In response to the insistence of assembly members demanding immediate linguistic reorganisation, two commissions were formed during the term of the Assembly to report on the issue; and both, influenced by Nehru, advised against immediate linguistic reorganisation as inimical to the national interest.[28] The first report, submitted in December 1948, allegedly drafted by Nehru, found that linguistic reorganisation was 'not in the larger interests of the Indian nation'.[29] The second commission, of which Nehru was a member, reported in April 1949 that any reorganisation of provincial boundaries must be 'subject to certain limitations in regard to the good of India as a whole'.[30] The new constitution was adopted in January 1950 with the provincial boundaries of the colonial era largely in place. The process of linguistic reorganisation was only reluctantly initiated by Nehru in 1953 following mass protests in the Telugu-speaking areas, demanding the immediate creation of the Telugu-speaking state of Andhra Pradesh with the city of Madras as its capital.[31] This movement triggered a more widespread process of linguistic reorganisation and the creation of new states across India,[32] including the Tamil-speaking state of Madras being renamed Tamil Nadu in 1967.[33]

Although linguistic reorganisation transformed India into a union of largely linguistically-defined states, federalism was not envisaged or indeed created as a mechanism for accommodating linguistic identities per se. The new constitution did organise Indian government along federal lines, but this was more an outcome of the institutional history of the colonial state than an expression of federalism as a component of Indian national identity. While concepts such as democracy, progress, unity and socialism had been core components of Congress's development, federalism had not. In terms of national identity, the principle of unity was far more important in organising the constitution than the principle of federalism. In keeping with colonial administrative practices, power was centralised in Delhi and the federal autonomy of the state governments could easily be over-ridden; Ambedkar, chair of the drafting committee, described the constitution as avoiding the 'tight mould of federalism' able to be 'both unitary as well as federal according to the requirements of time and circumstances'.[34] As such, control over the boundaries of the states rests entirely with the central government which, acting through the President, can redraw existing boundaries to create new states or merge existing states regardless of the linguistic principle. The constitution requires only that the President ascertain the views of the states concerned, rather than secure formal consent through majority votes in state legislatures. The federal provisions of the constitution have therefore been less important in accommodating linguistic identities within a national whole than the notion of India's linguistic diversity, firmly embedded in Congress doctrine and expressed through the official and national language provisions of the constitution.

The overarching objective driving the framers of the Indian constitution was to create a strong and centralised unitary state that would secure Indian political unity and the drive for economic development.[35] A central part of this process was the constitutional recognition of the Indian population as ethnically plural. This constitutional recognition was not, however, an act of shrewd statesmanship, wise moderation or enlightened policy-making, but rather an outcome of process: the long and temporally continuous process of anti-colonial nationalism that had established the Congress party as the dominant political force in India, the only institution capable of mobilising pan-Indian political activity. This process created and established an ideology of Indian national identity and national interest in which the Indian population was conceived as a plural but ancient and historically unified people with a shared interest in realising a future of development and progress. The political recognition of ethnic pluralism was in line with this vision of progressive development; religious groups were granted social and cultural rights, but not political recognition; SC and ST groups were granted political representation and positive discrimination quotas as a means of alleviating their 'backwardness'. Linguistic pluralism was acceptable in so far as it expressed India's 'composite culture', but resisted if it expressed 'divisive' tendencies.

Tamil cultural nationalism and Tamil Nadu electoral politics

Post-independence political developments in the Tamil-speaking regions of south India are often characterised as the electoral defeat of Congress's vision of pan-Indian nationalism and its replacement with a specific form of regional or cultural national identity. In the two decades following independence, the Congress party gradually lost its electoral dominance in the Tamil-speaking regions to the DMK, an ideological and organisational offshoot of the DK—an organisation that had open secessionist objectives and in the post-independence period staged public burnings of the Indian flag and constitution. Although Congress won comfortable majorities in the three sets of elections following independence, in the 1967 elections it was defeated by a coalition of parties headed by the DMK. The DMK-led coalition won the majority of seats in national elections and in the state assembly elections, pushing the Congress party into opposition in the Tamil-speaking areas for the first time since 1935. After the 1967 elections the Congress's electoral fortunes in the Tamil-speaking areas went into permanent decline; it has subsequently never won a majority of seats in either the national or state assembly elections. Congress's political position in the Tamil areas was further marginalised in 1972 when M. G. Ramachandran (or MGR as he is commonly known), a popular actor, left the DMK to form the ADMK. In 1976 MGR added the prefix All India to the ADMK as a gesture of explicitly accepting the pan-Indian framework and identity, although the party remained a Tamil Nadu entity.[36] The DMK and ADMK have subsequently become the two largest parties in the Tamil areas, acting as the major partners in the electoral coalitions contending in the state and national assembly elections. Congress, along with the Communists and other minor regional parties, has been reduced to the position of alliance partner to either the DMK or the ADMK.

Explanations of the Dravidian movement's ascendance have suggested that the DMK offered a more culturally resonant understanding of Tamil identity and interest than Congress's vision of Tamils as a component of a pan-Indian nation struggling for progress and development. In N. Subramanian's study of Dravidian politics, he characterises Nehruvian nation-building as attempting to build a shared national identity on the basis of the strategy of economic development and industrialisation at the expense of a more cultural understanding of nationhood. When Nehruvian nation-building did attempt to characterise the state-bearing nation in cultural terms, it 'drew on the syncretic Mughlai culture of the North Indian elite, with which few Tamils felt an affinity'.[37] In contrast, Tamil or Dravidian 'mytho-history' was central to the DMK's vision of Tamil identity as it presented itself as the vehicle of a Tamil plebeian class left out by Congress's vision of economic development.[38] In an earlier study of south Indian Tamil politics, Marguerite Ross Barnett makes a similar argument equating Tamil cultural nationalism with the DMK:

> The founding of the Dravida Munnetra Kazhagam ... in 1949 was a turning point in the political history of Tamil Nadu, south India, because it ushered in the era of

Tamil cultural nationalism. Nationalism existed before 1949, but in nascent form, encompassed and overshadowed by other political themes. In the hands of the DMK, Tamil nationalism became an ideology of mass mobilisation, and has shaped the articulation of political demands for a generation.[39]

David Washbrook adopts a similar explanation, suggesting that there existed a 'cultural gap, centuries wide, between Indian nationalism and the Dravidian ideology'. As a consequence, the Dravidian movement simply had 'no means of comprehending policies and arguments geared to the development of a modern bourgeois nation state'.[40] The timing of the DMK's victory, just two years after an intense and widespread wave of protests across the Tamil-speaking areas against the adoption of Hindi as India's official language, adds to the impression of the DMK as representing a growing Tamil nationalist sentiment at odds with Congress's pan-Indian vision of national identity. The DMK declared 26 January 1965, the date on which the constitution sanctioned the switch from English to Hindi, as a day of mourning, and called on its supporters to raise black flags and engage in protest. The protests quickly gathered momentum and expressed a deep and generalised antipathy to the introduction of Hindi. Between 26 January and early February, five people self-immolated and two more took poison. Although the DMK leaders were placed in preventive detention to avoid unrest, the anti-Hindi agitations triggered violence and rioting that was comparable in scale and intensity to the 1942 Quit India agitations. There were widespread attacks against public buildings, leading to confrontations between the police and protesters and police firing; according to the government 70 people were killed, while the DMK put the figure at 150.[41]

The apparent ideological divide between the DMK and Congress on the language issue was compounded by the fact that the latter was in government (in Tamil Nadu and in Delhi) at the time of the anti-Hindi protests, while the DMK was the largest opposition party in Tamil Nadu. Although Congress leaders from Madras frequently expressed their preference for retaining English as the official language, along with Hindi, they were nevertheless associated with the national government's language policy. The Congress Chief Minister at the time, M. Bhaktavatsalam, who refused to meet protesters and discuss their demands, was also prominently associated with the Dakshina Bharat Hindi Prachar Sabha, the organisation founded by Gandhi to promote the learning of Hindi in the non-Hindi-speaking areas.[42] However, the appearance of an intense and passionate confrontation between the Congress-led state government and the DMK on the language issue did not signal an irrevocable ideological gap.

Rather than representing disparate and incompatible visions of Tamil identity and interest, the DMK and Congress may be interpreted as working within a shared set of ideological norms that could be accommodated within the constitutional framework of Indian national identity. The Congress and DMK ideologies, while distinct, overlapped in two important areas: the promotion of Tamil speakers' interest in progress and development, and the encouragement of Tamil language and culture.

The notion of progress and development shared by the DMK and Congress was broadly defined and included the need to promote economic growth and industrialisation of the Tamil-speaking areas, abolish poverty and improve living conditions, whilst also encouraging social change in line with egalitarian and liberal norms focusing in particular on the eradication of caste oppression and exclusion.[43] For Congress, these commitments were encompassed in the term Socialism, which united a variety of groups and interests whose specific economic policies and priorities were often quite divergent.[44] Whilst the DMK never articulated an explicit position on industrialisation or economic growth that was comparable to its emphasis on protecting and promoting Tamil cultural interests, notions of progress and development were nevertheless implicit in its vision of Tamil identity and interests and particularly its criticisms of Congress rule. The DMK regularly asserted that the Congress party prioritised the economic development of north India whilst neglecting the south, and argued that the ordinary Tamil people were excluded from the benefits of Congress's developmental strategy.[45] Meanwhile, both parties committed themselves to abolishing the exclusions and hierarchies of caste and presented themselves as championing the interests of socially and economically marginalised lower-caste groups.

The two parties were also comparable in their approach to the promotion of Tamil language and culture in the public/political sphere. As discussed later, the Tamil Nadu Congress and Congress-affiliated organisations were far more important than the Dravidian movement in the efforts to create a Tamil-speaking state out of the polyglot Madras presidency. Congress leaders were crucial in efforts to ensure that Madras city remained within the Tamil-speaking Madras state, rather than the Telugu-speaking Andhra Pradesh, and were also important in other border disputes over areas claimed by more than one of the soon-to-be-formed linguistic states. The Dravidian movement, at that stage committed to the idea of a pan-south Indian Dravidian identity, remained aloof from these essentially intra-Dravidian disputes. While the DMK played an important role in the anti-Hindi agitations, Congress's commitment to Hindi as the official language was not incompatible with the Tamil Nadu section promoting Tamil language and culture as appropriate emblems of India's 'composite culture'. The DMK's efforts to promote the Tamil language as an emblem of a Dravidian heritage when it finally took power were not radical departures from Congress's previous policies.[46]

The electoral ascendance of parties associated with the Dravidian movement cannot therefore be interpreted as the displacement of the Congress vision of Tamil identity with a notion of Tamils as Dravidian. Rather the growth of the DMK has to be interpreted in the light of pan-Indian social and political factors that produced electoral defeats in 1967 for Congress across India, including Tamil Nadu. The short-term factor that produced these defeats was the acute food crisis that affected India from 1964 as a result of droughts and poor harvests. The food crisis led to shortages, spiralling prices and also compulsory requisitioning of grain from farmers.[47] The DMK made the food crisis an important part of its electoral strategy: party activists regularly held protests outside ration shops, and reducing the price of rice was a prominent part of the election manifesto.[48] Congress's electoral demise was therefore contingent on these and other developments, rather than being an expression of a structural shift away from pan-Indian politics to Tamil cultural nationalism.

The DMK's success is also closely related to expanding political participation amongst the Indian population and particularly amongst groups variously labelled as the intermediate or Backward Classes/Castes (BCs). Marguerite Ross Barnett identifies the DMK support base in class/caste terms as 'the rising urban lower middle class, the educated unemployed youth, and the middling (film-going) farmer in the backward castes'.[49] Narendra Subramanian characterises the groups who formed the DMK's early support base as small shop-keepers, small peasants, artisans and the new white-collar worker all of 'intermediate caste origin'. This newly important electoral demographic comprised a substantial component of the Tamil Nadu population; in caste terms the BCs account for 51–67 per cent of the state's population, whilst in class terms small property-holders and white-collar workers comprise 50–60 per cent of the population.[50] In the decades since independence, these groups have been granted affirmative action quotas similar to those granted to SCs and STs: first at state level and then from the early 1990s at the union level.[51] The caste groups eligible for these benefits are identified in official documents as in much political discussion as Other Backward Classes (OBCs).[52] The mobilisation of Backward Classes/Castes across south India from the 1940s onwards prefigured their mobilisation across northern India during the 1980s.[53]

The relative electoral successes and failures of Congress and the Dravidian parties within these changed political conditions can be analysed in terms of the three facets of successful political mobilisation: ideological articulation; co-option and direct political evangelisation; and conversion. In terms of the first two facets, the performance of Congress and the Dravidian parties was broadly comparable; Dravidian and Congress notions of Tamil identity and interest could be contained within the Indian constitutional frameworks while the DMK, AIDMK and Congress attempted to co-opt the support of actors, groups and institutions with established sources of power. The relative success of the Dravidian parties can therefore be attributed to their more effective techniques of direct mobilisation, which included the use of the growing Tamil print media, cinema, street theatre and popular oratory. As a consequence, the Dravidian parties were more effective at presenting themselves to voters, particularly from OBC groups, as custodians of Tamil economic and cultural interests, even though Dravidian policies were not vastly different from those pursued by Congress.

Tamil identity and interests in Congress and Dravidian ideology

According to the Dravidian ideology, as articulated by the DK, Tamil society's interests demanded the rejection of Hindu theology and ritual and the adoption of modern, rational and secular practices and norms, as well as improvements in the material wellbeing of economically oppressed Dravidians. Like the Congress party, the Dravidian movement also conceived of the state as an important agent of social and economic transformation. This was, however, deemed impossible in a Congress-dominated India. The DK, particularly its chief ideologue E. V. Ramaswamy, characterised Congress as a vehicle of north Indian, Brahmin interests and sought a separate independent state of Dravidanad in which a full programme of social reform could be pursued, unencumbered by the Hindu-dominated Congress. This radical social reform agenda was less interested in the promotion of Tamil culture and literature than in removing the signs and symbols of Hindu and Brahmin domination. As such, the ideal state and political realm was envisaged by the DK as a vehicle of rational, secular, progressive and scientific symbols and values.

Despite the DK's opposition to Congress rule, its conceptions of the state were not diametrically opposed to Congress doctrine and the constitutional understanding of Indian national identity. In both Congress and DK doctrines, the state was an agent of social transformation and the political realm ideally an arena of secular, rational, modern values.[54] Where the DK and Congress differed was on the relationship between Hinduism and social reform; while the DK sought to eradicate Hindu symbols and practices from Tamil society, Congress commitments to social reform, including the reform of Hinduism, were balanced by the state's responsibility to recognise and protect the plurality of existing norms and practices in Indian society. As a consequence of these overlaps, and despite the DK's avowedly secessionist demands, it was not subjected to the same levels of repression as parties such as the National Conference in Kashmir or the Akali Dal in Punjab which were deemed secessionist by the Congress government.[55]

The formation of the DMK produced a new conception of Tamil society, interest and identity that was less orientated towards social reform and more concerned with promoting Tamil culture as well as the interests of the OBC category. In 1949, C. N. Annadurai (1909–69), one of Ramaswamy's principal lieutenants, split with his former leader over ideological and organisational differences; the bulk of the DK membership left with him and joined the newly formed DMK. The DMK retained a conception of Tamil society as Dravidian, rather than Indian, but welcomed Indian independence as a step towards realising Tamil interests, and also saw electoral contest as a viable means of capturing political power. In contrast, Ramaswamy observed Indian independence as a day of mourning and condemned electoral politics as a distraction from the more important work of social reform. The new party insisted on its ideological loyalty to the DK, and the presidency of the party was left symbolically vacant, to be occupied by the DK leader when he chose to do so.[56]

In its early years, the DMK's activities complemented the DK's emphasis on social transformation and the eradication of Hindu ritual and symbolism. During the 1950s, for example, the DMK participated in DK protests over visible symbols of caste hierarchy, and attacked polytheism and superstition; also the party's first election manifesto, produced for the 1957 polls, emphasised social reform themes. However, during the 1960s the emphasis of the party's electoral campaigns shifted to focus on issues such as the supposed economic neglect of the south, measures to improve the welfare of the Tamil Nadu 'common man' and expanding reservations for the BCs. The Dravidian political parties have since been associated with an expanding sphere of welfare provision. Successive DMK and ADMK governments have expanded the scope of reservations for OBC and SC/ST groups, such that they now account for 50 per cent of all public sector employment and publicly controlled higher education institutions in the state.[57] Meanwhile, the ADMK's electoral success during the 1980s was closely associated with a series of high-profile welfare measures, such as free midday meals for children.[58]

Social reform issues were not completely abandoned; the DMK government did, for example, enact legislation to provide legal recognition for Self-Respect marriages[59] and sought, unsuccessfully, to open up the Hindu priesthood to all castes.[60] However, DMK leaders have distanced themselves from the DK's trademark iconoclasm; in 1971 M. Karunanidhi (1924–), the then DMK chief minister, openly censured a DK campaign of publicly mocking and attacking Hindu deities and scriptures, saying the DMK government would not tolerate 'anti God activities'.[61] ADMK leaders have gone even further and explicitly associated themselves with Hindu rites and rituals. In 1968 M. G. Ramachandran (1917–87) organised special poojas (or ritual offerings) in Hindu temples across Tamil Nadu for the speedy recovery of C. N. Annadurai who had fallen ill.[62] When M. G. Ramachanran fell ill in 1984, Jayalalitha, the ADMK second in command, organised similar poojas. Although Jayalalitha is a Brahmin and regularly engages in public acts of Hindu piety, this has not precluded her from assuming the role of a Dravidian leader, revealing the shifting meanings and associations of the term Dravidian from its early-twentieth-century links to the non-Brahmin movement.[63]

In abandoning social reform, the DMK and subsequently the ADMK have adopted and promoted Tamil culture, language and literature as emblems of Tamil identity and Tamil interest. This is a notable departure from the DK, and particularly Ramaswamy, who often denounced the Tamil language as 'barbaric' and sought to modernise and liberate Tamil society, rather than return it to a more authentic cultural past.[64] During the 1960s the DMK prominently associated itself with the movement against Hindi as a means of burnishing its Tamil credentials; although, as Marguerite Ross Barnett notes, the anti-Hindi movement was a much wider coalition that the DMK actually struggled to control.[65] Once in power, the party sought to promote the Tamil language; it changed the official name of Madras to Tamil Nadu, adopted a new flag and also instituted a song in praise of the Tamil language to open state assembly sessions, rather than the customary prayer.[66] In February 1968 it hosted the international Tamil studies conference in Chennai, attended by scholars from around the world, and used the event to present itself as custodian and advocate of the Tamil cultural and literary heritage.[67] In 1970 the party introduced proposals to make Tamil, rather than English, the language of instruction at secondary and tertiary levels, but withdrew the proposals after protests from students.[68]

Although the DMK's association with Tamil language and popular culture along with its advocacy of Tamil economic interests, particularly those of the intermediate social groups, were important in its electoral rise, these factors did not radically distinguish the Dravidian parties from Congress. On the promotion of a specifically Tamil political and cultural interest, on welfare measures and promotion of OBC interests and on promoting the economic development of the Tamil-speaking areas, Congress's record was comparable to that of the Dravidian parties. While the Dravidian movement was closely associated with the anti-Hindi protests, Congress leaders and Congress-linked activists played an active role in the move to create a Tamil-speaking linguistic state.

Nehru reluctantly agreed to linguistic reorganisation in December 1952, following the death of an Andhra activist who had undertaken a protest fast insisting on both the creation of a Telugu-speaking state and the incorporation of Madras city as the capital of the new state.[69] The wider process of linguistic reorganisation opened up a series of disputes not just on the Tamil/Telugu border but also on the Tamil/Malayalam border.[70] The DMK and the DK were absent from these protests and campaigns as they continued to work within a pan-south Indian Dravidian framework. In the absence of the DMK, an important role was played by Congress figures as well as organisations and activists with close affiliations to the Tamil Nadu Congress. The linguistic boundaries of the southern states was finally agreed in September 1955, but until that point there were constant protest marches and meetings on the political status of the 'border areas'. These campaigns were led by the Tamil Arasu Kazhagam (TAK), an organisation that had close affiliations with Congress.[71]

In January 1946, when the TAK organised a public celebration of the Tamil harvest or Pongal Festival in Madras to reinforce the Tamil claim on Madras city,[72] both Kamraj Nadar and Chakravarti Rajagopalachari attended, despite their then factional differences.[73] Soon after independence, the TAK launched a campaign to retain the northern districts that bordered the Telugu-speaking areas within a Tamil-speaking state. The TAK also worked with the Travencore Tamil Congress, when the latter initiated protests in 1954 demanding the merger of the Tamil-speaking areas of that state with Tamil Nadu. The status of Madras city was finally decided by Rajagopalachari, the then Congress Chief Minister, and the DMK was largely absent from the Tamil campaign, although the city later became a DMK electoral stronghold. As both Tamil and Telugu Congressmen were equally insistent in their respective claims, a commission was formed to adjudicate. Before the commission could formally announce its results, however, Rajagopalachari forced Nehru's hand by threatening to resign unless Madras city was retained as the sole capital of the Tamil-speaking Madras state. Nehru relented, and in October 1953 announced the formation of Andhra Pradesh, excluding Madras city.[74]

The Tamil Nadu Congress party and affiliated figures were also closely associated with campaigns and protests to promote and cultivate the Tamil language. Following the process of linguistic reorganisation, the Tamil Nadu Congress adopted Tamil as the official language of the state.[75] Tamil Nadu Congress leaders also consistently demanded the continuation of English alongside Hindi as the official language at the Union level,[76] and Rajagopalachari, after leaving the Congress party in 1958, played a prominent role in the anti-Hindi protests of 1965 and 1967.[77] Moreover, the initiative and planning for the 1968 World Tamil Studies Conference, hosted with great pomp by the DMK government, actually began under the previous Congress administration. The public promotion of Tamil literary heritage even extended to the ADMK, which was more explicit in its acceptance of a pan-Indian identity. In 1984 the then ADMK government again hosted the World Tamil Studies Conference amidst great fanfare, with party founder and Chief Minister M. G. Ramachandran playing a visible and prominent role.[78] Arguably, Congress had a much stronger record during the 1950s of promoting and protecting Tamil cultural and political interests than the DMK and DK, which were still closely linked to the protection and promotion of Dravidian interests in radical social reform.

Congress could also plausibly present itself as promoting and protecting Tamil economic interests. Contrary to the DMK's criticisms of northern prosperity and southern neglect, during the period of Congress dominance Tamil Nadu experienced higher than average rates of economic growth and industrial development. The state became one of the most urbanised in India, had high levels of literacy and started to bring down population growth to replacement levels. Tamil Nadu's high levels of economic growth and investment during this period reflected the state-level Congress leadership's success in bargaining for resources from the central government and party hierarchy.[79] The regime of planned economic development implemented through the five-year plans that started from 1951 was meant to direct economic and industrial investment through nationally orientated priorities. In reality, however, the process of national planning became a national framework of bargaining through which powerful state-level Congress leaders fought over economic resources that could be used to maintain support bases and patronage networks within their respective states. Tamil Nadu's success in securing resources was related to the power of Kamraj Nadar (1903–75)—the Tamil Nadu Congress President 1946–52 and Chief Minister 1954–63—in the national-level Congress organisation. Kamraj was known to be close to Nehru and was an important figure in the group of state Congress leaders, known as the syndicate, who controlled the Congress organisational machine at the regional level.[80] Tamil Nadu's economic performance during this period reflected therefore a relatively powerful position within the national Congress structure, rather than a position of marginality as claimed by the DMK.

Finally, Congress could also make credible claims to be challenging caste hierarchy and exclusion whilst promoting the welfare of under-privileged groups. Kamraj Nadar came from a non-elite background and had worked his way up through the Tamil Nadu Congress structure. Although Kamraj's immediate family had been small traders, the Nadars traditionally were engaged in the relatively low-status occupation of toddy tapping and were included within the BC category.[81] During his tenure as Chief Minister, Kamraj launched a midday meal scheme as a welfare measure and also built over 12,000 schools in rural areas; school attendance between the ages of six and eleven increased from 45 to 75 per cent in the seven years after he became Chief Minister in 1954.[82] Both Kamraj and his predecessor as Congress Chief Minister, C. N. Rajagopalachari, included in their cabinets ministers from both Backward and Scheduled caste groups.[83] Kamraj explicitly committed the Tamil Nadu government to promoting the interests of the SCs, and in 1951 Madras became one of the first state governments in post-independence India to introduce reservations for BCs in education and public sector employment. Congress introduced a quota of 25 per cent for BC groups, later expanded by a DMK government to 31 per cent, and then by ADMK government to 50 per cent.[84]

Electoral competition between Congress and the DMK was not, therefore, a conflict between two competing visions of Tamil identity and interest; rather, it took place within a shared political culture in which the promotion of Tamil political, cultural and economic interests were unquestioned norms. The DMK quietly abandoned the link between Tamil identity and the rejection of Hinduism once central to DK ideology, and, like the Congress party, linked Tamil identity to language and literature. Congress and the Dravidian parties also defined Tamil economic interests via similar types of policies: infrastructure and industrial investment in the Tamil-speaking areas, as well as the provision of special economic benefits to SC and BC groups. While Congress sought political legitimacy from the large-scale infrastructure and industrial projects that were implemented in the Nehruvian period, the DMK also associated itself with Tamil interests in progress and development. While in opposition, the DMK criticised Congress policies for the apparent industrial underdevelopment of the south in relation to areas such as Bombay and Allahabad; for example, the central government's failure to provide investment for a steel plant in Salem was an important part of the DMK's 1967 electoral campaign. When the DMK came to power, it adopted a high-profile policy of slum clearance and urban housing provision that was promoted as an indicator of development.

Ideology and Congress decline in Tamil Nadu

The electoral demise of the Congress party in Tamil Nadu was not therefore the result of a radical ideological conflict and is better explained as the outcome of contingent factors working alongside the more effective strategies of mobilisation deployed by the Dravidian parties. Congress's electoral hegemony between 1937 and 1967 rested on the co-option of powerful groups and the distribution of patronage through networks that brought together landlords, industrialists, business people, bureaucrats and their dependants into a relatively stable coalition.[85] During the 1960s this system of electoral dominance was undermined by a series of economic problems and a split within the Congress party. As a result of these manifold crises, Congress's 1967 defeat in Tamil Nadu was mirrored in electoral reversals across India: the party's vote at the national level fell by 5 per cent[86] and it failed to gain a majority in eight other states, in which a variety of coalition non-Congress governments came to power.[87]

The electoral success of the Dravidian parties was also associated with expanding political participation in Tamil Nadu, particularly amongst the backward or intermediate classes, a development that prefigured similar changes across northern India during the 1980s.[88] The entry of these groups into politics was signalled by the growing use of the vernacular media, popular mobilisation around linguistic identities and demands for positive discrimination policies tailored to BC groups in employment and education. This new political culture was described by Selig Harrison as the 'pulp culture of popular writers who will address themselves to the swelling millions of new literates in the regional languages'.[89] The relative success and failure of Congress and Dravidian parties in the context of these pan-Indian contingent and structural factors can best be explained in relation to the three facets of successful political mobilisation; ideological articulation; co-option of powerful groups and individuals and direct political evangelisation.

As discussed above, there was an enormous amount of ideological overlap between Congress and the Dravidian parties. This was evident not only in the remarkably similar policies they pursued when in power and advocated when in opposition; it could also be seen in the political alliances that brought together actors across the Congress/Dravidian organisational divide.[90] There was, for example, a long-standing personal friendship between Ramaswamy and Rajagopalachari which from 1959 also produced a political alliance on opposition to Hindi as the official language. Meanwhile, between 1954 and 1963, Ramaswamy and the DK officially supported Kamraj and the Congress party with DK activists actively canvassing for Congress party candidates. The differences between Congress and the Dravidian parties can best be explained therefore in relation to their relative effectiveness in co-opting individuals and groups and mobilising support through direct political evangelisation. An analysis of Tamil Nadu electoral dynamics in terms of these two factors suggests that Congress decline and Dravidian ascendance were the result of successful Dravidian mobilisation compounded by contingent factors that fatally hampered Congress's revival in the Tamil areas.

The DMK's electoral rise in the post-independence decades was associated with a steady expansion in electoral participation, particularly amongst intermediate or backward caste groups that were largely outside the Congress's networks of support. The expanding political participation of this intermediate class/backward caste cluster significantly changed the electoral dynamics of the Tamil-speaking areas. There was a substantial expansion of voter participation, from 49 to 67 per cent between 1957 and 1967, and simultaneously the proportion of votes gained by independent candidates, who invariably relied on networks of personal loyalty and deference, declined from 25 to 7 per cent in the same period. In the context of these changing dynamics, while Congress's electoral support remained steady, from 45 to 41 per cent of the popular vote between 1957 and 1967; the DMK's support expanded from 13 to 41 per cent in the same period.[91] In effect the DMK expanded its vote, in part by attracting Congress supporters but also by increasing voter turnout.[92] The Congress network, excessively dependent on aggregating the support and dependent networks of notables and magnates, did not accommodate these newly emergent groups. In contrast, the DMK built support amongst those of 'less wealth and status,'[93] engaged in voter registration drives[94] and pursued an electoral strategy that had a strong element of direct political mobilisation:

The DMK attempted to win support by aiming appeals at castes and classes not already politicized by Congress; by trying direct rather than indirect methods of mobilization in order to erode that portion of the Congress vote based on social deference; and by penetrating new regions and rural areas that the Dravidian movement had not as yet thoroughly organised.[95]

The DMK communicated directly with this newly enfranchised group through a variety of media and cultural forms. The party had close associations with the film industry: C. N. Annadurai and M. Karunanidhi[96] were scriptwriters for plays and films, and many of the major figures of the 1950s cinema were associated with the DMK. M. G. Ramachandran, who went on to become 'the most popular film star and public figure of modern Tamil Nadu', joined the DMK in 1953 and starred in a number of films scripted by Karunanidhi that contained several allusions to the DMK and the Dravidian movement.[97] Along with cinema, in its early years of expansion, the DMK also used street performances to reach the illiterate and semi-literate majority with even the major leaders 'wearing the players' makeup'.[98] DMK leaders also popularised their messages through numerous magazines and newspapers, which were not just intended for private reading but were also discussed and circulated at street-corner meetings and the 'talk shops' that were central to the DMK's early growth. The social base of the DMK's expansion facilitated this type of mobilisation:

> The shops of some early activists served as the party's primary recruiting grounds, where Dravidianist journals were available, people congregated to gossip and discuss social issues, and the latest statements and directives of party leaders were made known.[99]

Although the Congress movement used a variety of popular and high cultural forms to communicate its message from the 1930s, by the 1950s the party had lost most of its links with the film industry and the print media. This was partly due to the death of S. Satyamurti in 1943, the key figure in forging links between the Congress movement and the Tamil popular theatre and fledgling cinema during the early part of the twentieth century.[100] His successor, K. Kamraj, was less enamoured of actors and musicians,[101] and as a consequence Congress also failed to cultivate its association with Sivaji Ganeshan, a popular actor of the 1950s and 1960s, to the extent that the DMK cultivated the film image of MGR.[102]

However, the DMK's electoral growth and dominance was not entirely built on a strategy of direct mobilisation. As the party expanded, not only did it seek alliances with sources of existing power, it also became a route to power and influence. As Narendra Subramanian suggests, as the DMK grew it attracted more substantial merchants and landlords to augment its base of small property-holders, and all those who joined the party 'gained greater social eminence through their role in the DMK's social networks'.[103] Once the party was in power, like the previous Congress administration, it used its control over public resources to build support by co-opting local notables, magnates and their dependants.[104] The continuing importance of strategies of co-option in the DMK's and also the ADMK's success suggests that the expansion of political participation and the more widespread use of direct political communication associated with the Dravidian movement did not produce a wholesale transformation in the political economy of electoral competition. As with the previous Congress system, the distribution of patronage through local notables remained an important element of Dravidian party-building. Finally, the DMK's adeptness at forming electoral coalitions with other political parties was also consequential. The DMK first adopted this tactic in a systematic way in 1962, but it subsequently became an important feature of Tamil Nadu politics. From the late 1970s the electoral dominance of the two Dravidian parties has reduced Congress—and the Communists—to the role of minor alliance partners in DMK- or ADMK-led electoral coalitions.

Although Congress's relative ineffectiveness in direct political mobilisation was an important element in the Dravidian parties' electoral dominance, Congress's electoral demise was far from inevitable, and cannot be predicted from the sheer force of Dravidian ideology. Not only was Congress's share of the vote in 1967 (41.4 per cent) slightly higher than that of the DMK-led coalition (40.6 per cent), Congress's support also remained steady at about 30 per cent during the 1970s. Congress's electoral success was therefore contingent upon pan-Indian factors that hampered the party's electoral revival during the 1970s. This included a series of poor harvests that led to nationwide food shortages and prompted an unpopular system of grain requisitioning. The general malaise caused by food shortages was compounded by a wider economic crisis that produced a breakdown of the system of five-year plans inaugurated in 1951 and forced a devaluation of the rupee in 1969.[105] In Tamil Nadu this led to a downturn in industrial output that preceded a similar downturn across India. Although the DMK-led coalition successfully capitalised on the manifold discontents produced by the economic and food crisis, Congress might have recovered power in Tamil Nadu had it not been for the national split in 1969 and a series of factors that constrained Congress's ability to mobilise growing opposition to DMK rule in the early 1970s.

The Congress party split in 1969 following a series of disagreements between Indira Gandhi, the Prime Minister, and a powerful group of regional Congress leaders, including Kamraj, of the aforementioned syndicate.[106] The Congress (R) faction led by Indira Gandhi retained the support of most Congress parliamentarians, but the Congress (O), or Organisation faction, led by the state-level party bosses including Kamraj, retained most of the organisational assets.[107] In particular, while some Tamil Nadu Congress parliamentarians joined Congress (R), the bulk of the Tamil Nadu Congress party remained within the Congress (O) structure. Thus, the split in the national Congress organisation in 1969 for the first time created a division between the national and state-level Congress organisations. In 1971 Congress (R), which had little organisational presence in the Tamil areas, formed a seat-sharing alliance with the DMK for the state and parliamentary assembly elections. Under the agreement, the Congress (R) refrained from competing in the state assembly elections in exchange for a proportion of Tamil Nadu seats in the national elections. Meanwhile, the Congress (O) formed an alliance with other smaller Tamil Nadu parties and competed in both state and parliamentary elections against the DMK alliance, which included the Congress (R). These strategies arguably worked to divide the Congress vote in the parliamentary elections and prevented Congress from capitalising on Indira Gandhi's growing popularity in the state assembly elections. From the early 1970s until his death in 1975, Kamraj attempted to bring about a reconciliation of the two factions but was opposed by other Congress (O) leaders at the national level. In 1977, following the end of the emergency, the Congress (O) joined the national Janata Coalition, and from that point Congress in Tamil Nadu more or less disintegrated into a set of factions that competed for the national leadership's attention and favour.

Another factor that compounded Congress's ability to recover was the emergence of the ADMK in 1972. The ADMK's popularity was assured by the star appeal of its leader, M. G. Ramachandran, whose films communicated a message of benevolent paternalism to groups such as the scheduled castes, women and the rural and urban poor who were largely excluded from the DMK's base of small property-holders and white-collar workers. The ADMK proved its appeal in a series of spectacular electoral victories following its formation, in some places forcing the DMK into third place behind Congress.[108] Congress's strong electoral showing in elections after 1972 suggests that the party's fate in Tamil Nadu was finally sealed as a consequence of national political alignments, rather than an ideological sea change in Tamil

Nadu politics. The importance of contingent rather than structural factors is further underlined by suggestions that following the split with the DMK, MGR had initially thought of joining the Congress (O), but was dissuaded by Kamraj's well-known aversion to film stars and the presence of the rival actor, Sivaji Ganeshan, within the Congress organisation.[109] Thus, it is possible that if MGR had joined the Congress (O), electoral politics in Tamil Nadu might have taken an entirely different course.

Tamil Nadu politics and the pan-Indian framework

The shared framework of Tamil cultural nationalism that structured electoral competition in Tamil Nadu was compatible with the Indian constitution. The peaceable accommodation of the Dravidian parties was therefore not a matter of the moderate choices of its leaders, or the moderate preferences of its followers, but rather the DMK's decision to switch from an agenda of Dravidian social reform to one of Tamil cultural nationalism. The Dravidian agenda of radical social reform jarred with the constitutional understanding of Indian society and interest in two key areas. Firstly, its insistence on a thoroughgoing purge of Hindu symbol and ritual from Tamil society sat uncomfortably alongside constitutional protections of religious practice in social life. Secondly, its demand for a separate Dravidanad transgressed the demand for unity that was central to the constitutional construction of Indian national interest. In moving away from the DK's radical social reform agenda, the DMK adopted a position on Hindu social reform closer to the constitutional position that sought to balance the interests of progress and development with the protection of religious rights in the private sphere. However, the DMK's decision to abandon secession was not an act of political moderation, but linked to its decision to shift away from radical social reform as the key marker of Tamil collective identity and interest. In the DK's ideology, the demand for Dravidian self-determination was always tied to the imperative of social reform: the Indian state dominated by north Indian Hindu interests would be an obstacle to radical social reform which could only be achieved in a separate state. Conversely, the DK's insistence on social reform led to its ambivalence on the creation of a Tamil linguistic federal state; a state that would not address the fundamental issue of Hindu/Brahmin dominance.

The call for a separate Dravidian state was central to the DMK's 1957 election manifesto, but by the early 1960s DMK leaders had privately decided to abandon the separatist demand,[110] a decision made public in 1963 following

India's border war with China and the promulgation of central government regulations that penalised parties suspected of separatist tendencies.[111] Since abandoning separation, the DMK has sought greater state autonomy for Tamil Nadu within the Indian union: a demand that brought the DMK into ideological alliance with organisations like the TAK, which explicitly combined the demand for a Tamil state with a commitment to preserving Indian unity and territorial integrity.[112]

An examination of the TAK's position on Dravidian ideology helps explain the significance of the DMK's shift from secession to Tamil Nadu. The TAK sought a Tamil Arasu, or Tamil state, within the Indian union in order to strengthen its promotion of 'Tamil language and literature in every field of human activity' and encourage the 'development of the art and culture of the Tamils'. In this vision, Tamil society was identified through language and culture, rather than caste and the reform of caste, and the TAK disavowed the Brahmin/Non-Brahmin conflict as 'communal' declaring that 'all those who spoke Tamil as their mother tongue and considered Tamil Nadu as their mother land would be treated as Tamils'.[113] The TAK, whilst insisting on Tamil Nadu, opposed the demand for Dravidanad and participated in the anti-Dravidanad movement in collaboration with Congress and the Communists. In shifting from Dravidanad to Tamil Nadu, the DMK was therefore adopting an acceptable and therefore non-communal form of cultural nationalism over its previous radical, unconstitutional and therefore 'communal' commitment to social reform. The DMK has intermittently reiterated its commitment to greater state autonomy; however, autonomy is now sought for a Tamil-speaking state and justified as necessary to facilitate better governance and greater fostering of Tamil in the public/political realm, rather than to expedite social reform.

The Dravidian movement's drift towards a purely cultural understanding of Tamil identity and explicit identification with the Indian union can be said to have reached an apotheosis when in 1976 the ADMK officially changed its name to the All India Dravida Munnetra Kazhagam, in an effort to signal an explicit acceptance of the Indian constitutional framework. The ideological inconsistency between the all-India framework and the Dravidian ideology, as articulated by EVR and the DK, is less important than the fact that one of the two largest parties in Tamil Nadu, at the moment of its ascending popularity, explicitly identified its commitment to the all-India framework. The ADMK also disavowed the search for greater state autonomy,[114] but this has not signalled a departure from the norm of promoting Tamil language/literature in the public/political sphere; not only did MGR visibly identify himself with specifically Tamil causes and issues such as the 1984 World Tamil Conference, the ADMK has also joined other Tamil nationalist parties and associations in opposing moves to enforce greater use of Hindi in place of English at the national level. As Subramanian notes, the 'ADMK joined the Tamil nationalist chorus on such occasions, even pre-empting it at times'.[115]

Conclusion

In 1976, just as the ADMK was embracing the All India prefix, the main Sri Lankan Tamil party, the Federal Party, was abandoning its then almost three decades-old demand for federalism in favour of outright independence or secession. This chapter has argued that the ADMK's decision, and the wider incorporation of the Dravidian movement into the all-India framework, cannot be understood in terms of the relative moderation of its leaders or followers. Rather the peaceable accommodation of the separatist Dravidian movement is a consequence of the overlaps between Dravidian and Indian nationalist conceptions of Tamil identity and interest, which meant that the Dravidian parties and Congress could engage in agonistic rather than antagonistic political competition. The Dravidian parties and the Congress in Tamil Nadu competed within a political culture in which promoting the Tamil language and culture, as well as securing Tamil interests in economic development, social reform and welfare provision, were accepted as norms. Furthermore, these shared norms were compatible with the constitutional definition of Indian national identity and national interest that had evolved through Congress's political struggle to establish a pan-ethnic platform, beginning in the late nineteenth century.

5

NATIONS APART

TAMILS AND SINHALESE IN POST-INDEPENDENCE
SRI LANKA

Introduction

Chapter 4 argued that the political contestation between the Dravidian movement and the Congress in Tamil Nadu was framed by large overlaps in their
competing understandings of Tamil identity and Tamil interest. In contrast, in
Sri Lanka, political contestation from independence to 1977 consolidated two
mutually incompatible Tamil and Sinhala conceptions of national identity and
national interest, leading to a violently escalating ethnic conflict. The results of
the 1977 general elections crystallised this opposition. The United National
Party (UNP) won a landslide victory (140 out of 168 seats) but its conception
of the 'national' had by this stage become explicitly Sinhala and Buddhist.[1] In
the north-eastern Tamil-speaking areas, the Tamil United Liberation Front
(TULF)—a coalition of Tamil parties whose platform was seeking an independent state (Tamil Eelam)—won 17 out of the 19 seats[2] with Sri Lankan
Tamil majorities,[3] and as a consequence of the fragmentation of the opposition
Sinhala parties, became the official opposition party. The UNP—along with
the other major Sinhala parties—worked within an ethnically hierarchical
conception of national identity and national interest in which the state is
understood as an instrument of and for the preservation of Sinhala Buddhist
identity and interests.[4] In the post-independence period, Sinhala Buddhist
nationalist mobilisation and political action were increasingly directed in

opposition to the Tamils, who were seen to pose a social, economic, political and even demographic threat to the Sinhalese.[5] The result of these processes was that by the late 1970s Sri Lanka had 'regressed into an illiberal, ethnocentric regime bent on Sinhalese super-ordination and Tamil subjugation'.[6]

Quite apart from producing a stable ethnic hierarchy, the steady consolidation of this Sinhala first order produced an enduring orientation of Tamil politics around the demand for Tamil–Sinhala collective political equality. Tamil political actors sought a variety of means to give form to this equality; initially balanced representation, then federal autonomy and, by the mid-1970s, political secession. Sri Lanka's post-independence constitution was unitary and centralised, with all effective power concentrated in the parliamentary government in Colombo. This was effectively the same structure created by the 1833 Colebrooke–Cameron reforms. In the colonial period, leading Sinhala politicians had often advocated alternatives to this, including federalism, greater devolution to local government (S. W. R. D. Bandaranaike) and even federation with India (J. R. Jayewardene). However, as Tamil politics consolidated around the demand for territorial autonomy, initially through federal reform, Sinhala Buddhist opposition to Tamil demands converged on the need to maintain the unitary and centralised structure of the state. Tamil political autonomy was framed as an existential threat to Sinhala national identity and interest, whilst entrenching centralised administrative and, increasingly, military control over the Tamil-speaking areas became a central concern of Sinhala Buddhist politics.

This chapter traces the emergence of sustained conflict between these two antagonistic and mutually incompatible conceptions of national identity and national interest. It argues that there are two crucial factors in explaining this. The first is the clear incompatibility between the two conceptions of national identity and national interest. Unlike the Dravidian and Indian nationalist conceptions of Tamil identity and interest, in Sri Lanka there are no points of overlap between the Sinhala Buddhist and Tamil conceptions of Tamil identity and interest. Secondly, these two conceptions of national identity and interest were not just ideas or even subjectively experienced identities, but concrete political projects that were embodied in cohesive and robust organisations. The Sinhala Buddhist conception was embodied in the major Sinhala parties and soon in the Sri Lankan state itself, such that the state became a vehicle and agent of Sinhala Buddhist transformation. At the same time, the Tamil conception became consolidated through oppositional mobilisation to the state, led from 1956 by the Federal Party (FP). The ideological antagonism between the Tamil and Sinhala conceptions of national identity was expressed and made visible in concrete instances of confrontation over specific issues, and mobilised by Sinhala Buddhist and Tamil organisations and actors.

The following two sections trace in turn the organisational consolidation of Sinhala Buddhist and Tamil conceptions of national identity and national interest. This shows that the consolidation of these projects was a matter of process that brought together a diversity of interests and motivations. Furthermore, once consolidated the Sinhala Buddhist and Tamil national identities became the dominant frameworks within which actors could pursue unrelated interests. These projects also cannot be understood as the simplistic articulation of Sinhala or Tamil ethnic identity respectively, as both acknowledged and sought to accommodate—more or less successfully—internal divisions of caste, region and religion. Furthermore and once consolidated as dominant frameworks, the competing Tamil and Sinhala conceptions of national identity and interest came to shape the conditions of plausible public action for their adherents and opponents alike. The third section analyses the escalating confrontation between these two projects; one that increasingly involved the use of overt force. The argument is that escalation cannot really be understood in terms of the relative moderation or extremism of the protagonists. Rather, the escalation of confrontation into the regularised use of violence is the inevitable outcome of the conceptual incompatibility of the two conceptions of national identity and interest, the significant support that both projects could mobilise amongst their target populations and fortuitous international circumstances that supported the use of force by the Sri Lankan state and Tamil militants alike.

Consolidation of Sinhala Buddhism

The consolidation of the Sinhala Buddhist framework was twinned with the consolidation of the fairly stable system of party competition amongst the Sinhala-speaking electorates. The rising importance of political parties can be seen in the declining share of the vote won by independent candidates. In the 1947 elections, independent candidates won just under 30 per cent of the vote, but by 1970 this had fallen to a low of just under 5 per cent. At the same time, the share of the vote won by the two largest political parties—the UNP and the Sri Lanka Freedom Party (SLFP)—averaged around 70 per cent between 1952 and 1977.[7] The third major force in Sinhala party politics during this period were the two Marxist parties, the Trotskyite Lanka Sama Samaja Party (LSSP) and the pro-Moscow Communist Party (CP). The Marxist parties had their best performance in the 1947 elections with 23 per cent of the vote, but this subsequently declined and from 1960 averaged about 11 per cent, reaching a low of just 5 per cent in the 1977 elections. Since 1965 the Marxist parties have generally been in coalition with the Sri Lanka Freedom Party (SLFP), formed by a split from the UNP in 1951. This steadily consolidating system of competition primarily between the UNP and SLFP was framed throughout by a shared commitment to a Sinhala Buddhist framework; in Michael Billig's terminology, Sinhala Buddhism became the 'banal' and taken for granted ground of political contestation.[8] In other words, the differences between and within parties on specific policies were framed by a shared commitment to a conception of Sri Lanka as a Sinhala Buddhist country. Sinhala Buddhism was thus not 'a particular political strategy' but 'the condition for conventional strategies, whatever their particular politics'.[9]

The consolidation of the Sinhala Buddhist framework can be usefully broken into two phases: the first is that of the UNP-dominated government of 1947–56, and the second the period of alternating UNP-led and SLFP-dominated governments of 1956–77. In the first phase, a Sinhala Buddhist conception of national identity and interest sat uneasily alongside a more multi-ethnic framework. In the second, after the escalation of Tamil demands for federal autonomy and the success of the Federal Party in 1956, there was a more determined commitment to a Sinhala Buddhist transformation of the state and polity. The two phases were also marked by two distinct political economies of contestation: the first predominantly revolved around patronage and the dispensation of welfare, while the second saw the emergence of a 'state controlled economy' regulated through a system of 'licenses, quotas and permits'.[10] The second phase was also marked by escalating conflict along the Tamil–Sinhala axis. Although intra-Sinhala and intra-Tamil conflict along caste, region and religious divisions continued during this period, these were more or less successfully contained within the wider Tamil and Sinhala categories. In contrast, conflict along the Tamil–Sinhala axis escalated and opposing Tamil political demands became an increasingly central focus of Sinhala Buddhist mobilisation; this was captured by Srimavo Bandaranaike, Prime Minister during 1960–64 and again 1970–77, who declared in 1967 that 'the Tamil people must accept the fact that the Sinhala majority will no longer permit themselves to be cheated of their rights.'[11]

1948 to 1956

The consolidation of Sinhala Buddhism during these two phases of electoral contestation was the outcome of the activities of political contestation in a

NATIONS APART

context where the Sinhala Buddhist framework had been established as the unavoidable marker of national identity and interest in Sinhala public culture. From independence up to 1956, electoral politics continued along a pattern that was established with the introduction in 1931 of universal franchise. During the 1930s party structures were absent and electoral mobilisation relied primarily on candidates' established ties of patronage and dependence within their locality. The politics of vote-banks and dependent networks was, however, quickly augmented by an expanding range of welfare provisions.[12] Elected politicians then used the powers newly available to them within the Donoughmore constitution (1931–47) to establish a range of welfare services, such as free medical and educational facilities, milk for infants and expectant mothers and, most importantly, subsidies and rations for rice and wheat flour.[13] Welfare provision thus came to occupy a crucial place in representative politics as politicians used their control over the distribution of public goods as a key asset in their electoral campaigns. As Mick Moore explains, not only did this establish individuals' and groups' access to welfare goods as crucial issues in party politics, it also introduced a strong 'welfarist' element to political language and legitimacy, such that:

> ... government support for any activity, locality or population is commonly couched in terms of the granting of 'relief' or of 'due privileges', while allegations of past failures to provide support are termed 'Cinderella' or 'step-motherly' treatment.[14]

The Sinhala Buddhist framework was also, however, an important element in the combination of welfare provision and patronage networks that drove representative politics. It sat uneasily alongside a more pan-ethnic conception of national identity and national interest. Sinhala Buddhist rhetoric and metonyms played an important role in electoral campaigns and in the public activities of Sinhala politicians. Electoral candidates invoked their Buddhist credentials, sought support from the Buddhist clergy and, in the case of S. W. R. D. Bandaranaike, the future Prime Minister, converted from Christianity (Anglican) to Buddhism[15] whilst making shrill statements about his commitment to defending the Sinhala 'race.'[16] The Sinhala Buddhist framework was also important in forging a political alliance between the low country Sinhalese and the Kandyans that included not just a commitment to a common set of symbols—notably the Kandyan lion flag as the national flag—but also a commitment to excluding Indian Tamil labourers from the franchise. Sinhalese political leaders were notably careful to invoke pan-ethnic conceptions of national identity and interest, particularly during the colonial period when the establishment of an inclusive national identity was the stated

137

objective of British officials in decisions on constitutional reform. However, the ideal of a pan-ethnic national identity was invoked only in discussions on constitutional reform and in dealing with Tamil politics (voters and politicians alike) and not as a means of mobilising mass electoral support or indeed legitimising government policy in the Sinhala areas.

The post-independence governments headed by the UNP from 1947 to 1956 produced a mixture of policies that were inspired by the Sinhala Buddhist framework as well as a more pan-ethnic conception of national identity and interest. In keeping with the Sinhala Buddhist conception, the government passed legislation in late 1948 and 1949 that stripped Indian Tamil labourers of citizenship rights and the franchise. In 1951 it adopted the Kandyan lion flag as the country's national flag. Finally, the UNP also continued with land colonisation in the Dry Zone as the mainstay of its economic development policy.[17] Although colonisation was justified in terms of easing landlessness and improving agricultural productivity,[18] there was a clear purpose of settling Sinhalese peasants in Tamil and Muslim areas.[19] However, the UNP-led governments backed off from other nationalist demands being made by leading Buddhist associations and activists. These were principally for Sinhala alone—rather than Tamil and Sinhala—to be awarded the immediate status of official language; for the Christian denominational schools to be brought under state control; for preferential treatment to be given to Buddhist students in access to higher education; and for senior posts in the civil administration and military hierarchy to be reserved for Buddhists. The UNP government therefore only partially accommodated the Sinhala Buddhist programme.

1956 and beyond

The 1956 elections abruptly established Sinhala Buddhist nationalism as the dominant framework of electoral competition and indeed government policy, and by the general elections of July 1960 a new pattern of politics was evident. This pattern was one of two-party competition between coalitions led by the UNP and the SLFP, with both parties committed to policies aimed at securing the social and political dominance of the Sinhala Buddhists, expanding state control over economic activity, along with ongoing Sinhala colonisation in the Tamil and Muslim areas of the island. The trigger for the rapid switch was the official language issue. The 1952 general elections supported a policy of having both Tamil and Sinhala as the official languages. This was opposed by a variety of Sinhala Buddhist associational actors who sought a policy of Sinhala Only. Eventually, in the run-up to the 1956 elections, both the UNP and the opposition led by the SLFP advocated the policy of having Sinhala only, rather than both languages, as the national language.[20]

S. W. R. D. Bandaranaike, Prime Minister 1956–9, played a crucial role in this radical change. In mid-1951 Bandaranaike resigned from the UNP government, largely from a sense that his ambitions to be Prime Minister would be frustrated within the UNP,[21] and formed the SLFP, which he positioned as taking an economic middle course between the right-wing UNP and the Marxist parties of the left.[22] The party's founding manifesto, issued in September 1951, committed the party to a policy of Tamil and Sinhala as official languages, stating that such a policy was necessary to ensure that 'the people of this country may cease to be aliens in their own lands'.[23] This policy remained in place until late 1953, and Bandaranaike himself sometimes expressed an ambivalent attitude towards the Sinhala language.[24] However, in the run-up to the 1956 general elections, the force of Sinhala Buddhist opposition to the two-language policy strengthened in the atmosphere of the Buddha Jayantha celebrations, marking 2,500 years since the enlightenment of the Buddha.[25] The Sinhala Buddhist challenge was also strengthened by growing hostility to the UNP, not just over its hugely unpopular and soon reversed decisions to cut subsidies in 1953, but also because of the high-profile and decidedly non-Buddhist lifestyle of the Prime Minister, Sir John Kotelawala.[26] In this charged atmosphere, which included defections from the UNP, Kotelewala made a speech in Jaffna in late 1954 committing the UNP government to ensuring parity of status between Tamil and Sinhala.[27] This was seized upon by major English and Sinhala language newspapers as suggesting that the Sinhalese would be forced to learn Tamil.[28] By late 1955 the SLFP had switched its position to that of Sinhala Only, with Bandaranaike explaining his decision in terms of the Sinhala Buddhist trope of the perpetual Tamil threat and warning that parity of status would 'mean disaster to the Sinhalese race' because the Tamils 'with their language and their culture and the will and strength characteristic to their race ... would come to exert their dominant power over us'.[29] By early 1956 the UNP had also switched its position to Sinhala Only,[30] but it was too late and the advantage was with the opposition. An SLFP-led coalition of parties, called the People's United Front (known by its acronym in the Sinhala language as the MEP), won the election, gaining just over 40 per cent of the vote and a majority of 51 seats in a legislature of 95. The UNP's share of the vote fell from 44 per cent in 1952 to 27 per cent, and it was able to retain only 8 seats.

At every election between 1956 and 1977 there was a change in government between left-leaning governments headed by the SLFP and right-leaning governments headed by the UNP. Having come to power in April 1956, the new SLFP-led government promptly passed legislation in June to make Sinhala the only official language. The bill passed with the support of the UNP and was opposed by the Tamil MPs, predictably, but also by MPs from the two Marxist parties (the LSSP and the CP) who had campaigned on a policy of equal status for Tamil and Sinhala, and between them won just over 15 per cent of the vote. By the early 1960s, however, both the LSSP and the CP had also switched their positions to Sinhala Only, and in the following years their 'attitude towards the Tamil minorities could scarcely be differentiated from the strident bigotry of the SLFP'.[31]

In 1972 the SLFP-led government introduced a new constitution that changed the name of the country from the colonial Ceylon to the new Republican Sri Lanka, whilst unequivocally affirming the Sinhala Buddhist character of the state. The constitution enshrined the status of Sinhala as the sole official language and declared that the 'Republic of Sri Lanka' would 'grant to Buddhism the foremost place, and accordingly it shall be the duty of the state to protect and foster Buddhism'. It also explicitly described Sri Lanka as a 'unitary' state,[32] thereby constitutionally excluding the Tamil demands for territorial autonomy. In 1978 the newly elected UNP government again changed the constitution, importantly replacing the system of parliamentary government with a powerful and directly elected executive presidency. The 1978 constitution nevertheless retained the articles enshrining the status of Buddhism, the Sinhala language and the unitary and therefore Sinhala-dominated nature of the state.[33]

Votes and voters

This rapid rise of the Sinhala Buddhist framework cannot, however, be linearly correlated with voting behaviour. The 1956 elections saw widespread mobilisation by Buddhist monks and Sinhala public sector workers on behalf of the MEP; and yet, as Mick Moore notes, the overall voter turnout actually dropped slightly to 71 per cent from a high of 74 per cent in 1952, suggesting that the language campaign did not draw any new voters into politics. (A more significant increase in voter turnout took place between 1947 (56 per cent) and 1952 (71 per cent), and Moore explains this as a result of 'the rapid spread of state welfare activities, especially the rice ration, in the war and post-war periods and fears that the government was contemplating cutting the rice ration for financial reasons'.)[34] Furthermore, the relationship between MPs and their constituents continued to be dominated by questions of access to resources. During this period MPs characterised their role 'as largely, if not wholly, relating to the satisfaction of their supporters' demands, the solution of their problems ... by personal intervention and the securing of tangible benefits for their constituents'.[35] In other words, politics at the local level was 'about who will be employed by the Ceylon Transport Board as bus conductors'.[36]

However, this localised and transactional politics did not entail the exclusion of wider political categories or the national context. As Janice Jiggins explains, 'neither the voter nor the MP is typically seen in isolation as an independent entity capable of staking a claim on resources or winning votes solely in his own right'.[37] Political parties thus became increasingly important to electoral contestation[38] and, along with a decline in independent candidates, party allegiance also become increasingly important to individual candidates' electoral success.[39] The entrenched localism of political bargaining has therefore co-existed alongside the consolidation of party labels and a stable pattern of two-party politics. It is at this wider national level of party politics that Sinhala Buddhism became established as the unavoidable and profoundly consequential framework of political contestation. In other words, the Sinhala Buddhist framework thus set the context within which local struggles over public goods and services could be linked to wider national frameworks.

Closing intra-ethnic divisions

As the overarching framework of political contestation, Sinhala Buddhist nationalism was also able to contain divisions by caste, region, religion and socio-economic strata within the Sinhala category, whilst also accommodating the representation of Muslim and Indian Tamil, but not Sri Lankan Tamil, votes. The UNP and SLFP drew electoral support from distinct regional and socio-economic strata: the UNP was concentrated in the low country and urban areas, and drew support from the slightly better-off sections of rural society; whilst the SLFP was dominant geographically in the largely 'dry zone' areas and was identified with the less well-off sections. Caste divisions were also important in political allegiance and determining political behaviour; political leadership in the UNP and SLFP has been exclusively with the dominant landowning or Goyigama castes, while the Karava, Durava and Salagama (KSD) castes found mainly in the low country regions are generally identified with the Marxist parties. Furthermore, both major parties combined their commitment to Sinhala Buddhist nationalism with the recognition that caste continued to be a tangible category of political mobilisation and representation. Since 1958 both parties have used the constitutional provision that allows for the appointment of MPs to represent minority groups to appoint members from low-caste Sinhalese groups who would normally struggle to be elected from the largely Goyigama-dominated Sinhala districts.[40] The UNP's striking electoral victory in 1977 (when it gained just over 50 per cent of the total popular vote) included an explicit attempt to divest itself of the image of being the party of the Goyigamas and build support amongst the KSD caste groups.[41] Relatedly, the failed armed insurrection by the Janatha Vimukthi Peramuna (JVP) against the state in April 1971—which combined revolutionary Marxism with strident Sinhala Buddhism[42]—had its support base mainly amongst the non-Goyigama youth of the low country and some Kandyan districts.[43] Sinhala Buddhism was therefore a political category, rather than an expression of ethnic sentiment, as it sought to include—more or less successfully—a plurality of Sinhala Buddhist caste groups.

While caste and regional divisions within the Sinhala category were relatively easily reconciled within the Sinhala Buddhist framework, the shifts produced by the 1956 electoral victory were associated with a series of confrontations that threatened sustained and ongoing conflict along the Tamil–Sinhala axis and separately along the Catholic–Buddhist axis, which was contained primarily within the Sinhala category. Between 1956 and 1961 two successive SLFP-led governments passed legislation and effected the administrative changes to make Sinhala the only official language, including the language of the law courts in the predominantly Tamil-speaking areas. To protest against these changes, the FP, now the largest Tamil party following the 1956 general elections, launched mass participation civil disobedience demonstrations in 1956, 1958 and 1961.[44] The 1956 and 1958 demonstrations led to anti-Tamil violence across many areas of the island that were framed—whatever the actual motivations of individual rioters themselves—by participants, victims and political actors as expressing Sinhala antipathy to Tamil political demands. The 1961 protests by the FP, which involved occupations of government offices across the north-east bringing the civil administration to a standstill, were ended with repressive use of the military, the declaration of a state of emergency in the north-east and the imprisonment of FP politicians, including the ageing leader, S. J. V. Chelvanayagam.[45]

In the same period, there was also escalating conflict along the Catholic–Buddhist axis. The flashpoint of this conflict was the nationalisation of denominational schools undertaken by the SLFP government of Srimavo Bandaranaike in late 1961. The move led to protests by Sinhala Catholics who occupied the schools, refusing to hand them over to educational authorities.

Eventually a confrontation was avoided by the intervention of the Catholic hierarchy, namely Cardinal Valerian Gracias from India (reportedly sent by Nehru), who persuaded Catholics on the island to relent.[46] Since the flashpoint of Catholic–Buddhist confrontation in the 1959–62 period, however, conflict along this axis has been largely accommodated within the Sinhala Buddhist framework. In contrast, conflict along the Tamil–Sinhala axis has inexorably escalated. To begin with, the Catholic church through the 1960s continued the process of 'nationalising' itself with masses conducted in Tamil and Sinhalese,[47] and this trend was reflected in voter allegiance. From the 1947 elections onwards, there was a trend of Catholic support for the UNP, partly as a result of the Catholic hierarchy's antipathy to Marxist parties— heightened in the context of the Cold War.[48] The conflict over denominational schools also appeared to strengthen Catholic support for the UNP.[49] However, by the time of the 1970 elections, there were swings against the UNP-led government in the majority Christian districts of the Sinhala areas, reflecting patterns across the Sinhala districts more generally.[50] Following the landslide victory of the SLFP-led United Front in 1970, the Roman Catholic bishops of Ceylon called on the faithful to give 'loyal and enlightened support to the new government', and similarly supported the UNP government that came to power in 1977.[51]

The narrowing of the Catholic–Buddhist divide can be seen in the shifting categories used to define educational entitlement. In the early 1950s leading Buddhist educationalists had demanded special quotas for Buddhist students in higher education to compensate for the disadvantages they suffered under British rule, allegedly because they 'have stuck to the religion which binds them to their native soil'.[52] However, in the early 1970s, when the United Front government adopted policies to correct Tamil over-representation in the coveted Medical and Engineering faculties, the measures were framed to benefit not the Buddhists but the Sinhalese. The schemes worked by lowering the entrance marks for students studying in the Sinhala language stream and those from rural districts. As a consequence, the ethnic composition of the Medical and Engineering faculties was substantially altered, but along a Tamil–Sinhala rather than a Catholic–Buddhist axis.[53]

Finally, these rapid changes provoked an attempted coup—the first of two—in late 1961 by a group of officers in the military and police forces who were motivated primarily to stem the ascendance of Sinhala Buddhism and the conflict it was causing, as well as the ethnic transformations it was effecting on the civil service.[54] The coup was discovered in early 1962—and hence referred to by that year—and arrests were made throughout February. Despite the mixed ethnic backgrounds of the coup plotters, it was framed in terms of the over-representation of Catholics and Tamils in the military. Successive governments have since then followed a policy of creating an 'ethnically pure' Sinhala Buddhist military.[55] As a consequence, the proportion of Tamils employed in the Police and Armed Services dropped from 40 per cent in 1956 to 4 per cent in 1980.[56]

The political ascendance of Sinhala Buddhism cannot be linearly related to ethnic demography. The fact that the majority of electorates on the island contained a Sinhala majority facilitated, but did not cause, the ascendance of Sinhala Buddhism. To begin with, mediating access to public goods was a vital part of representative politics at the local level, and increases in voter turnout were more associated with the expanding scope of public goods provision than with the stridency of Sinhala Buddhist rhetoric. Furthermore, adopting a strident Sinhala Buddhist stance did not produce direct electoral results: for example between 1956 and 1960, the UNP's share of the vote increased by just over 2 per cent (from 27 to 29 per cent), despite the party having visibly and vociferously adopted Sinhala Buddhist rhetoric. Sinhala Buddhist nationalism did not function as a means to mobilise voter sentiment, but worked instead as the underlying framework within which political contestation occurred.

Sinhala Buddhist 'reconquest'

The explanation for the dominance of Sinhala Buddhism, firmly established by the mid-1960s, must be sought in the processes of political organisation and mobilisation, rather than in the static variables of ethnic demography. The Sinhala Buddhist ethnically hierarchical conception of national identity and national interest were well established in Sinhala public culture through ongoing social and political activities that began with the late-nineteenth-century Buddhist revival. Nevertheless, these activities were not organised into a single organisation with a well-established political structure that could mobilise support across the Sinhala districts. The organisational weakness of the Sinhala Buddhist movement was however matched by the weakness of its principal oppositional target, the pan-ethnic conception of national identity and interest then associated with the UNP. As discussed in Chapter 3, the attempts by Sri Lankan politicians to form pan-ethnic nationalist associations in the late nineteenth century did not generate the temporally continuous activities that in India were associated with the establishment of Congress as a dominant and unavoidable presence—for Indian politicians and British officials alike—in colonial Indian politics. As a consequence, a pan-ethnic conception of national identity and interest had a very weak organisational presence in Sri Lankan politics. The UNP, hastily formed just before independence and including the overtly Sinhala nationalist Sinhala Maha Sabha, used the pan-ethnic conception primarily as a rhetorical device in negotiations with British officials and to coordinate the activities of its Muslim and Tamil members. The party did not develop or deploy a pan-ethnic conception of the island's history (comparable to that invoked by Nehru) to compete with the Sinhala Buddhist narrative, and nor did it have a developed framework that accommodated the island's ethnic pluralism within a shared set of interests and values. Instead, its senior Sinhala leaders regularly invoked the Sinhala Buddhist framework and were closely linked with Sinhala Buddhist associations. Furthermore, UNP candidates in the Sinhala districts explicitly invoked their Buddhist credentials during electoral campaigns. A pan-ethnic conception of national identity was therefore absent in Sinhala popular culture. It is in this historically produced, rather than demographically determined, context that when the SLFP demonstrated electoral success by adopting the Sinhala Buddhist framework and then introduced legislation to give it effect (such as the 1956 Sinhala Only act), the other political parties rapidly followed suit.

Once established as the dominant framework of political contestation, Sinhala Buddhist nationalism became a powerful and constraining presence in the island's social, political and economic life. Political contestation among the Sinhala parties was bounded by the commitment to preserving the Sinhala Buddhist character of the island, particularly against the threat posed by Tamil demands for political autonomy. There were important differences between the parties, for example on economic policy, with the SLFP and the Marxist parties favouring greater state control, while the UNP was willing to allow space for private enterprise. However, compromise with Tamil political demands could not be accommodated in this framework. An attempt in 1957 by the SLFP Prime Minister, S. W. R. D. Bandaranaike, to negotiate an agreement with S. J. V. Chelvanayagam, the FP leader, was abandoned after sustained Sinhala nationalist opposition, spearheaded by the UNP. A similar agreement in 1966 between the UNP Prime Minister, Dudley Senanayake, and S. J. V. Chelvanayagam was also abandoned, but this time as a result of sustained mobilisation by the SLFP and its Marxist partners, the CP and LSSP.[57] The Sinhala Buddhist framework thus came to dominate, even though many actors may have at times used it tactically and without any conviction.

S. W. R. D. Bandaranaike, for example, played a crucial role in initiating the switch to the Sinhala Buddhist framework, but then found that his efforts to come to an agreement with the FP were thwarted by Sinhala Buddhist mobilisation. J. R. Jayewardene, the UNP politician who led a high-profile and symbolic march to mobilise popular Sinhala opposition to the agreement between Bandaranaike and the FP, subsequently played an important role in the abortive 1966 negotiations between the UNP and the FP. The actual intentions and the motivations of the politicians themselves are therefore less important in explaining outcomes than the constraining conceptual boundaries within which they must operate.

Although the electoral dominance of Sinhala Buddhism was driven through a system of representative politics dominated by local arenas and serving often parochial interests for public goods and services, the consequences were nevertheless systemic. The changes triggered by the 1956 elections produced an expanded state. However, this state was one that was in personnel and ethos increasingly Sinhala. While membership of public sector trade unions expanded from 52,000 in 1952 to over 257,000 in 1968, the proportion of Tamils employed in the various sectors of the public sectors fell.[58] By the early 1980s public sector trade unions played a crucial role in organising anti-Tamil collective violence. Public rituals and spaces were marked by Buddhist symbols and rituals, while the nationalisation of schools introduced the Mahavamsa narrative of Sinhala civilisation and Tamil invasion to all students in the Sinhala stream. The 1956 elections also triggered the rapid creation of a 'state controlled' economy regulated through 'licenses, permits and quotas' that were needed for all forms of commercial and manufacturing activity. Although these economic rewards were distributed through patronage networks—which were determined more by factional and kinship considerations than ethnicity—Tamils found it difficult to access the necessary resources, and as a consequence were largely squeezed out of private sector activity as well.[59] The sum effect of these changes could be seen in average income figures: in the decade between 1963 and 1973, average Sri Lankan Tamil income fell from 327 rupees per month to 309, that of the low country Sinhalese increased from 292 to 343 and that of the Kandyan Sinhalese increased from 219 to 277.[60]

Following the 1962 coup attempt and the subsequent policy of establishing an 'ethnically pure' military and police, these institutions also came to operate within the Sinhala Buddhist framework and were at the leading edge of the state's confrontation with Tamil opposition, both political and later armed.

Emblematic of this change is a shift in the stated motivations of the two attempted coups of Sri Lanka's post-independence history. The 1962 coup was led by officers—multi-ethnic and cosmopolitan in outlook—who sought to check the rising dominance of the Sinhala Buddhist framework. One of their complaints was the escalation of ethnic tension: they blamed the 1958 anti-Tamil violence on 'Bandaranaike's yielding to crude communal feelings'.[61] The officers involved in the coup were also critical of the decision to send in the military to break the FP-led civil disobedience protests (known as Satyagraha after Gandhi) across the north-east. As the Satyagraha was peaceful, the officers believed the 'government was using unnecessary force in handling it' and 'some officers felt the government was even attempting to provoke violence'.[62] In a further incident, the two Tamil commanding officers in the regiment sent to quell the protests in Jaffna were ordered not to accompany their troops; a move that 'impressed the officers more deeply than the regime's needless use of troops or its excessive repression of peaceful protest'.[63] The 1966 coup, by contrast, was launched by 'extreme Buddhist elements' who were opposed to the UNP's negotiations with the FP over its demands for regional autonomy and official status for the Tamil language.[64] The overwhelmingly Sinhala military and police were subsequently deployed in increasing numbers in the Tamil-speaking areas from the early 1970s to confront the then incipient insurgency.

The ascendance of Sinhala Buddhism involved therefore the wholesale transformation of the state, society and the economy. This affected a variety of ethnic categories—including Sinhalese Catholics, Muslims and Indian Tamils, as well as Sri Lankan Tamils. However, Catholic, Muslim and Indian Tamil political actors in practice acquiesced to the dominant Sinhala Buddhist framework. In contrast, amongst the Sri Lankan Tamils the ascendance of Sinhala Buddhism was associated with countervailing mobilisation by the FP, which sought to establish political equality between the Tamils and the Sinhalese in opposition to the Sinhala first ethnic hierarchy of the Sinhala Buddhist framework. The FP's growth was in part a result of the impact of post-independence state policies on a diversity of interests within Tamil society: Jaffna students denied access to higher education; Colombo-based civil servants working within an increasingly Sinhala Buddhist hierarchy; and eastern province farmers living alongside growing state-aided colonisation schemes. However, discriminatory policies alone are insufficient to mobilise opposition. For example, the category that arguably suffered the most at first from Sinhala Buddhist policies were Indian Tamil labourers. They were also the easiest to mobilise: the large majority living and working in identical conditions and in a concentrated geographical area. Yet Indian Tamil political leaders, many of them plantation-owners, collectively sought to cooperate with the Sinhala leadership rather than mobilising opposition from their constituents' disenfranchisement and ongoing conditions of relative economic servitude.[65] The consolidation of Sri Lankan Tamil opposition must therefore be understood as the outcome of step-wise and temporally continuous processes of organisation and mobilisation that established the idea of a Tamil national identity as a dominant and unavoidable presence in Tamil political life.

Federal Party and Tamil nationalism

The electoral and political consolidation of Sinhala Buddhism occurred through contestation to gain control of the state, and then through the agencies of the state itself. It was not associated with a single organisation or party. In contrast, the consolidation of the Tamil nationalist framework during the same period was associated with the electoral growth and expansion of the FP. The party's main efforts were in seeking election to Sri Lanka's parliament. It did this primarily as a means of negotiating with the government on its core demands for territorial autonomy and gaining official recognition for the Tamil language. To this end, the FP from its foundation stated that it would not accept cabinet posts until its demands had been met; M. Thiruchelvam, an FP MP, served briefly as a minister in the UNP-led government of 1965–9, but resigned because of failure to progress on the issue of territorial autonomy and the government's refusal to categorise a Hindu temple in Trincomalee as a site of cultural importance.[66] The FP also initiated mass protests against the Sinhala Only policy—in 1956, 1958 and again in 1961—and used the support it was able to demonstrate through these, as well as through its electoral campaigns, as a means of expressing Tamil sentiment to the government and to the larger world.[67]

The period of the FP's electoral rise and dominance (1952–77) was certainly linked to the rising material impact of the policies of Sinhala Buddhist majoritarian dominance. As discussed above, following the adoption of the 1956 Sinhala Only act, Tamils were rapidly excluded from the public sector,[68] their access to the private sector was restricted,[69] the military and police were transformed into overwhelmingly Sinhala 'ethnically pure' structures[70] and Tamils' access to higher education was also curtailed.[71] Meanwhile, Sri Lankan governments funded and subsidised ethnically Sinhala colonies in the Tamil-speaking regions.[72] These programmes produced—as they were intended to[73]—significant changes in the ethnic demography of the Tamil regions. These changes were punctuated by bouts of collective anti-Tamil violence (1956, 1958, 1977, 1981, 1983) in which the ethnically transformed police and military were increasingly complicit (1977, 1981, 1983).[74]

While the impact of escalating Sinhala majoritarianism certainly provided the conditions for the rising dominance of the Federal Party, this cannot be seen as a natural consequence. The Sri Lankan Muslims, for example, who are equally outside the Sinhala Buddhist framework, have adopted an 'almost entirely instrumentalist approach to politics' evident in 'repeated party changing, support for independents and refusal, in the main, to be the captive of either of the major parties'.[75] A distinct Muslim political party, the Sri Lankan Muslim Congress (SLMC), was only formed in 1981, and until that point Muslim politicians joined either the UNP, the SLFP or stood as independents.[76] This approach has had tangible material benefits and there have been Muslims in every cabinet from independence.[77] However, Muslim political participation has been on the basis of, publicly at least, accepting the Sinhala Buddhist framework.[78]

Sinhala political leaders have sought to convince Tamil politicians and voters of the virtues of accommodation and acquiescence, rather than the FP path of opposition. Governments led by both the UNP and SLFP sought to co-opt Tamil politicians and engineer defections from the FP and ACTC.[79] Meanwhile, the Marxist parties and the SLFP often nominated candidates in the northern constituencies who campaigned on the platform that the FP's 'methods had worked against the interests of the Tamil majority who still persisted in voting for them'.[80] These efforts met with limited success; defections were rare.[81] Meanwhile in the constituencies of the north-east the vote share of candidates and parties not adopting a platform of Tamil–Sinhala political equality remained low: it fell from a high of 25 per cent in 1952 and then remained between 14 and 17 per cent.[82] There are two factors that explain the relative failure of efforts to establish Sinhala Buddhist dominance as a principle of Tamil politics, and the simultaneous electoral and political consolidation of the Tamil demand for territorial autonomy. The first is that the principle of Tamil–Sinhala equality was already well established in Tamil politics, particularly in the Jaffna peninsula, from the early decades of the twentieth century. This principle would have been available to any actor seeking to capitalise on the diverse discontents created by the escalating Sinhala majoritarianism. However, as noted earlier, the experience of exclusion does not necessarily provoke sustained opposition. Instead, the activities of the FP were decisive in translating diverse Tamil experiences of Sinhala Buddhist majoritarianism into a sustained demand for territorial autonomy as a means of ensuring collective equality between the Tamils and the Sinhalese. From its formation in 1949 until it merged with smaller Tamil parties to form the TULF coalition in 1976, the FP brought together the three processes of successful political mobilisation in a temporally sustained way. The temporally continuous as well as spatially and socially extensive character of the FP's activities established the principle of Tamil nationhood and territorial autonomy as both an enabling resource and constraining framework for all political actors—whatever their actual intentions or motivations—who sought to mobilise political support in the Tamil-speaking regions.

FP agenda and strategy

The central plank of the FP's agenda was the demand for territorial autonomy through a federal re-ordering of the Sri Lankan state. In justifying this demand, the FP explicitly used the language of nationhood and self-determination and invoked a narrative of historical continuity to assert a Tamil 'homeland' in the north-eastern Tamil-speaking areas of the island. At its first convention in 1951, the FP adopted a resolution claiming that the Tamil-speaking people had an 'unchallengeable title to nationhood' to be realised within a 'federal union with the Sinhalese' that included a 'separate historical past ... at least as ancient and as glorious as that of the Sinhalese' and 'territorial habitation of definite areas'.[83] The FP's explicit adoption of the legal and political language of nationhood was both a development of, and departure from, Tamil politics in the colonial period. As discussed in Chapter 3, Tamil politics before independence turned on a conception of the Tamils as equally indigenous to the island as the Sinhalese. There were disagreements between politicians and organisations (such as the JYC) that sought to advance Tamil interests by building a pan-ethnic form of Ceylonese nationalism and those who (like G. G. Ponnambalam and the ACTC) sought specific political guarantees of Tamil rights within an all-island political framework. These conceptions cannot easily be categorised as Tamil nationalist as the Tamils do not appear within them as the subject of national rights, but rather as a component—albeit on equal terms with the Sinhalese—of a broader Ceylonese national unity. The notion of territorial autonomy had been occasionally raised during the colonial period—most notably by P. Arunachalam [84]—but it had not become the basis of a sustained campaign of political organisation and mobilisation. For the FP, however, territorial autonomy was its core demand, as well as a crucial aspect of its organisational strategy. The rationale for territorial autonomy nevertheless retained the logic of Tamil–Sinhala political equality developed during the colonial period, but sought a different means of securing this end. As C. Vanniasingham, an FP leader, argued, the federal principle was necessary to preserve the mutual non-domination of the Tamils and the Sinhalese; a federal union would be 'fair by the Sinhalese, as Tamils did not want to dominate them even as they, the Tamils, did not want to be dominated by them ... federalism would enable them to live as equal partners of a new union'.[85]

The demand for territorial autonomy, while continuous with previous politics, was not automatically resonant: the FP did very poorly in the 1952 elections,[86] and during the campaigning the ACTC derided its claims, arguing that if Tamils achieved an autonomous state, the trains from Colombo would not pass through the narrow isthmus of the Jaffna peninsula.[87] However, in the run-up to the 1956 elections, the ACTC's strategy of securing Tamil rights by working with UNP had visibly failed and it was in this context that the FP's alternative demand for territorial autonomy gained ground. In August 1948 G. G. Ponnambalam agreed to join the UNP government in return for a cabinet portfolio, namely industry and fisheries. Chelvanayagam, then an ACTC MP, reluctantly supported this decision, having already made public statements on the need for territorial autonomy, and even secession, as a means of ensuring Tamil rights.[88] Chelvanayagam split with Ponnambalam in December 1949 and formed the FP following the UNP government's decision to strip the Indian Tamil plantation labourers of their citizenship and franchise rights. Ponnambalam stayed on in the cabinet, pointing to the material benefits of cooperation, namely a number of publicly funded projects across the north-east.[89] However, by October 1953 Ponnambalam had been expelled from the cabinet by the new Prime Minister, John Kotelawala,[90] and in February 1956 the UNP abandoned its commitment to Tamil–Sinhala linguistic equality, prompting the resignation of Tamil party members.[91] The FP's rise to political dominance occurred therefore in the context of the failure of the ACTC's strategy of 'responsive co-operation', while the mainstream Sinhala parties could offer only limited material benefits in exchange for acceptance of the Sinhala Buddhist framework.

Unlike the ACTC, the FP made direct political mobilisation a crucial component of its strategy, and at its inaugural meeting, its leader Chelvanayagam stated that the FP was not an ordinary political party but a 'movement', and its ultimate purpose was the mobilisation of the Tamil-speaking people. Even if the FP did not realise its key demand, namely Tamil autonomy, it should nevertheless 'at the very least mobilise and marshal our younger generation to carry the banner forward and fulfil our mission'.[92] To this end, the FP held public meetings to set out its views, published a weekly newspaper, the *Suthanthiran* (advocate of freedom), held yearly conventions in different locations across the north-east and also mobilised mass protests in 1956, 1958 and in 1961. At the same time, it also sought to win parliamentary seats as a means of creating a disciplined parliamentary block that could be used to extract concessions from Sinhala leaders. Agreements, albeit abortive, were reached on three occasions between the FP and Sinhala political leaders (with the SLFP in 1957 and 1960 and then with the UNP in 1965).

By the early 1970s it was evident that the FP's project had singularly failed to realise any of its stated objectives. The FP's three mass protests ended with violence directed primarily at Tamils, the imprisonment of FP leaders (1958 and 1961) and the imposition of emergency rule in the Tamil areas (1961). At the same time, the three pacts it negotiated ended in abrogation and two (1957 and 1965) were abandoned amidst vociferous opposition framed in Sinhala Buddhist terms. The 1970 constitution also entrenched the unitary and Sinhala Buddhist character of the state, thus apparently closing off the possibility of constitutional change through the parliamentary process. The FP's failure to realise its stated objectives turned out, however, to be an integral component of the consolidation of a territorial Tamil national identity. Indeed, FP political mobilisation and the responses it generated from Sinhala political actors were linked in an escalating dialectic of protest and violent response, negotiation and abrogation that consolidated the Tamil and Sinhala Buddhist nationalist projects and their mutually incompatible conceptions of the 'right' ethnic ordering of the island.

By 1976 the ACTC, which had once derided the idea of federalism, had joined the FP in demanding an independent Tamil state. The growth of a Tamil militant movement that sought independence through armed struggle also showed that the territorial conception of Tamil identity had escaped the bounds of the FP's politics. Importantly, this process was also important in consolidating Sinhala Buddhist nationalism. Until the late 1970s, opposing and resisting the FP's demands was a crucial element of the Sinhala Buddhist platform. From the early 1980s onwards, confronting and containing the growing Tamil insurgency, and later the LTTE's armed state-building project (early 1990s-2009), along with Tamil demands for independent statehood, became a central component of the Sinhala Buddhist domestic, as well as international agenda.

The FP's first protest was held in June 1956 as the Sinhala Only act was being enacted into legislation. Three hundred FP volunteers who staged a sit-down protest in front of the parliament in Colombo were attacked by an assembled crowd and thrown into a nearby lake. There followed several days of rioting, principally attacks against Tamils and Tamil property in Colombo but also notably in the areas of the eastern province that contained Sinhala colonies.[93] In August of that year the FP held its convention in the eastern port city of Trincomalee and set out its core demands: a federal re-ordering of the constitution, parity of status for Tamil and Sinhalese, an end to Sinhala colonisation in the Tamil-speaking areas and the restoration of citizenship and franchise rights for Indian Tamil plantation workers. It also threatened to launch a mass civil disobedience campaign unless these demands were met. In order to recruit volunteers for the campaign, Chelvanayagam and C. Vanniasingham, two key leaders, toured the towns and villages of the north-east establishing branches and setting out the FP's programme and strategy.[94]

The FP's demands and Prime Minister Bandaranaike's own personal inclination to compromise led to an agreement in July 1957 (the Bandaranaike–Chelvanayagam or 'BC' pact). There was immediate resistance: in October 1957 J. R. Jayewardene led a march from Colombo to the Temple of the Tooth in Kandy (which contains a relic believed to be the Buddha's tooth). The march was loaded with symbolic meaning and was staged as a 'pilgrimage to worship and to protest at that shrine, where the relic that served as the palladium of earlier Sinhalese kingdoms, and by extension, of the modern polity rested'.[95] As Bandaranaike hesitated, the FP took the initiative and in January 1958 launched civil disobedience protests across the north-east, with volunteers courting arrest by publicly tarring Sinhala characters on vehicle license plates in the Tamil-speaking areas. Chelvanayagam participated in such a protest in Batticaloa, was arrested and imprisoned for a week.[96] By April that year, and following a protest by a group of Buddhist monks in front of his private residence, Bandaranaike agreed to abrogate the pact. There followed a second, more intense, as well as spatially widespread episode of ethnic violence, primarily Sinhala violence against Tamils.[97] The violence has been explained in a variety of ways; Manor has for example argued that economic interests that had 'suffered during Bandaranaike's two years in power contributed to the rioting in order to destabilise the government'.[98] However, the violence also has to be read against the framework of Sinhala Buddhist nationalism and its project of establishing a Sinhala first hierarchy of ethnic relations on the island. As Sankaran Krishna suggests:

Viewed against this hierarchy, the periodic pogroms and explosions of collective violence against the Tamils (1956, 1958, 1977, 1981, 1983) in Sri Lanka represent efforts to put them back in their place on grounds that they need to be taught a lesson, according to an oft-used phrase. It is hardly coincidental that the bouts of collective violence in recent times have all occurred immediately after or during efforts to open a dialogue on redressing minority grievances in Sri Lanka.[99]

The final FP mass protest lasted from February to April 1961 and was again in response to government policy on the language issue. An SLFP-led government elected in July 1960 announced that it would bring the Sinhala Only act into full effect by January the following year and included provisions to make Sinhala the language of the law courts in the north-east. In response, the FP led mass demonstrations across the north-east. Protesters sat in front of government offices in Jaffna, Vavuniya, Trincomalee and Batticaloa, the largest population centres in the north-east, blocking all government functions until late April.[100] The protests were eventually ended by the use of military force; all of the FP MPs were arrested and detained for two months and a state of emergency existed in the Tamil-speaking areas for two years.[101]

Although the protests ended without any substantial gains in terms of securing the FP's objectives, they were nevertheless important in demonstrating—to opponents and allies—the party's capacity to mobilise support. As Chelvanayagam stated, the purpose of the Satyagraha had been 'to demonstrate to the world that the Tamil speaking people were united in the defence of their language rights and in their opposition to the government's discriminatory policies'.[102] The protests consistently drew large crowds and the increasing political centrality of a Tamil political identity based on national demands for territorial autonomy were also evident in the FP's improving electoral performance. In 1952 the party secured only two seats of the eleven with Tamil majorities; by 1956 it secured six and in July 1960 it secured twelve out of an available sixteen (a fresh delimitation of constituencies in 1960 added the extra seats). At the same time, its share of the vote in Tamil majority constituencies expanded from 16 per cent in 1952, to a high of 59 per cent in July 1960.[103]

The FP was about to launch a second civil disobedience campaign in 1964 when the SLFP government fell as a result of defections.[104] The FP then entered into negotiations with the UNP leader, Dudley Senanayake (son of the former leader, D. S. Senanayake), ironically at the home of Dr M. V. P. Pieris, who had served as the medical adviser on Jayewardene's 1957 protest march to Kandy.[105] The negotiations led to a second agreement, labelled the Senanayake–Chelvanayagam (SC) pact, which contained provisions on limited self-government for the north-east and some limitations on Sinhala colonisation in these areas. The FP subsequently became a partner in the UNP-led coalition government of 1956–69, and M. Thiruchelvam took the local government portfolio as a means of implementing the SC pact. However, by 1968 it was evident that Senanayake was backsliding, again in the face of growing Sinhala Buddhist hostility, and the provisions of the SC pact remained unimplemented.[106] The FP finally left the government in late 1968 when the Prime Minister overrode Thiruchelvam's decision to designate the area around the historic Thiru Koneswaram temple in Trincomalee a Hindu religious site, thereby preserving it from commercial development and colonisation. Senanayake acquiesced to Sinhala Buddhist opposition to the designation, led by a Buddhist monk from Trincomalee, who argued that if the land was designated as a Hindu religious site it would 'get into the hands of those who were neither Sinhalese nor Buddhist'.[107]

The SLFP-led coalition's landslide victory in 1970[108] and the adoption of the new constitution in 1972 was simultaneous with a radicalisation of Tamil politics as the FP itself abandoned federalism for secession. In 1972 Chelvanayagam resigned his seat in protest at the new constitution and stated that he would fight the by-election on the platform of independence. When the by-election was finally held in 1975, he won with 72 per cent of the vote; his opponent, a candidate for the Communist Party (an SLFP ally), got 26 per cent of the vote.[109] In the 1977 general elections, an FP-led coalition, the Tamil United Liberation Front (TULF), stood on a platform of independence, citing a history of violence, discrimination, economic exclusion and colonisation along with the failure of political compromise.[110] The TULF won 17 out of the 19 constituencies with Tamil majorities, with 59 per cent of the vote.[111]

At the same time there was growing militancy amongst Tamil youth seeking independence through armed struggle. This included, amongst numerous others, the Tamil New Tigers (formed in 1972), the organisation that subsequently became the Liberation Tigers of Tamil Eelam (LTTE) and came to dominate the armed movement from the mid-1980s.[112] The militancy was first expressed in widespread student protests against government ministers and other officials visiting the north-east, particularly Jaffna. There was also a spate of bank robberies, assassinations of police officers and Tamil politicians seen to be collaborating with the Sri Lankan state.[113] The state responded with intensified police and military repression in an escalating cycle of violence.[114] A notable incident was the police firing into the crowd attending the fourth World Tamil Conference hosted in Jaffna in 1974 (the first was held in

Malaysia in 1966, the second in Tamil Nadu in 1968 and a third in Paris in 1970). The police firing left nine dead and hundreds injured[115] and signalled the growing centrality of violence in defining relations between the Sri Lankan state and Tamil political as well as cultural activity.

Votes and voters

The consolidation of a territorial conception of nationhood in Tamil politics cannot be seen as the unmediated expansion of nationalist sentiment. In a pattern that reflected trends in the Sinhala-speaking areas, voter turnout in the Tamil-speaking areas appeared to correlate more closely to expanding welfare provision than FP mobilisation. The largest expansion in turnout was between 1947 (55 per cent) and 1952 (71 per cent) a period which saw the expansion of welfare provision, particularly rice subsidies, along with fears that this might be withdrawn. The 1956 elections were, however, an important landmark in the FP's trajectory; it expanded its vote share to 40 per cent of the vote in the Tamil majority constituencies. But average voter turnout at the 1956 elections across the Tamil constituencies (as in the Sinhalese ones) was actually slightly less in 1956 (69 per cent) than in 1952 (71 per cent). This was despite the FP's successful mobilisation of mass protests in 1956 and 1958 and the anti-Tamil violence this provoked. Welfare provision was therefore an important factor in mobilising Tamil votes. Meanwhile FP MPs, when they were not leading protests, behaved much like other parliamentarians and worked to mediate their constituents' access to publicly provided goods and services; some also used their parliamentary positions as a means of advancing personal interests.[116]

Like Indian and other Sri Lankan political parties, the FP did not rely on direct political mobilisation alone to mobilise support. Instead, it often co-opted locally powerful individuals as a means of building and expanding its support base. Although many FP candidates were individuals of local standing who often financed their campaigns with personal resources, the party label and the Tamil nationalist framework did make an important difference. In the Jaffna constituency, the independent candidate Alfred Duraiappah, who was elected in the 1960 elections for the Jaffna town constituency, nevertheless felt constrained to identify himself with the FP-led Satyagraha in 1961 and made high-profile visits to the protests on several occasions.[117] (Duraiappah later joined the SLFP, and as mayor of Jaffna ordered the police raid on the World Tamil Conference, which is said to have led to his assassination in 1975 by militants.) C. Arulampalam, the successful candidate for the ACTC in the

Nallur constituency (Jaffna) during the 1970 elections polled 46.6 per cent of the vote.[118] However, he subsequently crossed over to the SLFP and in 1977 stood as the SLFP candidate, but this time polled just over 3 per cent of the vote. Similarly in the Jaffna constituency, C. X. Martyn, who stood in the 1970 elections as the successful FP candidate, gained 35 per cent of the vote. However in the 1977 elections, standing as independent, he also gained just over 3 per cent of the vote.[119] The FP's failure to mobilise new voters does not, however, diminish its political significance. Instead, its activities worked to establish Tamil nationalism as the dominant framework of political contestation.[120] In other words, the FP's activities were decisive in establishing the principle of territorial autonomy as core to Tamil politics, a principle that has since to be invoked by all actors seeking Tamil support, whatever their actual political motivations.

Closing intra-ethnic divisions

The Tamil nationalist platform, like Sinhala Buddhism, was also not a mere assertion of organic ethnic solidarity but a complex political project that involved a recognition of, and effort to mediate, the pluralism within. While seeking equality with the Sinhalese, the FP also sought to regulate the differences of caste, region and religion within the Tamil category through the principle of equality, expressed through the notion of 'non-domination'; that is, no one section (however defined) would dominate the other. In terms of religion, for example, the party made explicit commitments to secularism.[121] As discussed in Chapter 3, the differences between Christians and Hindus had largely been overcome by the late colonial period through a shared understanding of Tamil identity and interest as political and cultural; Chelvanayagam, the pre-eminent Tamil leader of this period, was Anglican,[122] whilst one of his principal lieutenants, C. Vanniasingham, was an orthodox Hindu.[123] The notion of secularism was therefore not an abstract principle but a way of capturing this historically created accommodation, and was intended as a means of also including the Tamil-speaking Muslim population. Although the FP had some success in mobilising Muslim support, it was not able to incorporate Muslim voters successfully and stably into its electoral base. This is primarily because Muslim political activity from the late nineteenth century had primarily identified Muslim cultural and political interests in terms of religion[124] and as therefore distinct from Tamil public culture organised around language and culture. At the same time Muslim political leaders have also worked within the Sinhala Buddhist framework as a means of advancing their electorate's interests.

The principle of non-domination was also intended to cover the issue of caste.[125] Caste hierarchy continued to exist in much of Tamil social and cultural life, particularly in the Jaffna peninsula, and was to some extent reflected in voting behaviour. For example, the CP and LSSP had a base amongst caste groups subject to the practices of untouchability in two Jaffna constituencies: Udipudy and Nallur.[126] The issue rose to prominence in the late 1960s as a number of associations amongst caste groups treated as untouchable began to organise protests demanding entry into temples, often met by organised violence from upper-caste temple patrons.[127] By the early 1970s, partly as a result of these protests, caste began to figure more prominently in the FP's activities. Caste figured in the six-point programme adopted by an FP-led coalition of Tamil parties in 1972,[128] and a number of FP leaders began to suggest positive discrimination measures such as those adopted in India to alleviate the effects of caste hierarchy and exclusion.[129]

The attitudes of FP politicians towards caste were mixed; most, including S. J. V. Chelvanayagam, were members of the dominant landowning caste, and some were known to be rigidly observant of caste hierarchy in their own lives. Others, such as Navaratnam, the FP MP for Chavakachcheri, engaged publicly in activities—such as inter-caste sharing of food and the cleaning of latrines in lower caste houses—that were intended symbolically to overturn caste hierarchy.[130] These activities copied Gandhi's approach to caste: by publicly engaging in activities that broke caste taboos, such as cleaning latrines (a task normally reserved for castes treated as untouchable), Gandhi sought to undermine upper-caste prejudice whilst retaining other aspects of Hindu practice and belief. The FP's approach to caste was therefore very much in keeping with the dominance of the Indian rather than Dravidian strand of Tamil revivalism; the DK's wholesale rejection of Hindu belief and practice remained absent as a substantial or visible part of Tamil political activity in Sri Lanka in the post-independence period. Caste also became a category of political representation; in the 1977 elections T. Rajalingam, the successful TULF candidate for Udupiddy (Jaffna), was from a caste subject to untouchability. His campaign involved extensive canvassing by members of the FP's youth wing, who were deployed to win support for their candidate amongst the predominantly upper-caste voters.[131]

Caste remains an important aspect of Tamil society, influencing, for example, marriage patterns amongst both Christians and Hindus. However, successive Tamil nationalist actors—the FP and the LTTE—have explicitly sought to address the question of caste. The LTTE, for example, adopted positive

NATIONS APART

discrimination measures within its own military and political structures, which by the mid-1990s were well developed.[132] Caste issues have therefore been contained, rather than erased, by Tamil nationalist actors' efforts to create a pan-Tamil national movement, inclusive of caste. This mirrors the situation in India where caste has not disappeared, but instead caste-based demands are contained within the Indian constitutional framework.

The attempt to create a unified Tamil national platform also had to address the differences of region. From the mid-1920s onwards, the Jaffna peninsula had become an important centre of Tamil political activity, mirroring its economic and cultural dominance over the rest of the north-east.[133] The activities of the JYC and the ACTC were concentrated mainly in the Northern Province and specifically the Jaffna peninsula. In contrast, the FP sought explicitly to build a support and organisational base that incorporated the north-east as a whole. Its electoral campaigns as well as its mass protests were organised on this regional scale. The eastern port town of Trincomalee was declared as the putative capital of a federal Tamil state[134] and N. R. Rajavarothiam, the FP MP for Trincomalee, was named the party's vice president at its inauguration in 1949.[135] The FP's first convention in 1951 was held in Trincomalee and was staged as something of a spectacle as party members organised processions from Jaffna and Batticaloa to converge at the convention site, their route physically tracing the geography of Tamil national claims.[136] The 1956 sit-down protest in front of parliament organised by the FP included volunteers from the north as well as the east.[137] Similarly, the 1961 protests brought civil administration to a standstill across the north and the east. Although the FP's electoral base was far more consolidated in the Northern Province, through a combination of direct mobilisation and the co-option of existing important politicians, the FP was able to mobilise significant electoral support in the east, where it regularly polled an average of 40 per cent of the vote in constituencies with Tamil majorities.[138]

The escalation of the Tamil–Sinhala conflict was therefore a matter of ideology and political process. The Tamil and Sinhala conceptions of national identity, national interest and the ideal orderings of the island's ethnic pluralism are mutually incompatible. This is in contrast to the Dravidian and Indian nationalist conceptions. This ideological antagonism is also not a simple case of identity always being formed in opposition to an oppositional other. Tamil nationalism and Sinhala Buddhist nationalism can both be traced to the late-nineteenth-century Tamil/Saivite and Buddhist revivals respectively. As discussed in Chapter 3, these movements did not develop in opposition to each other but rather in response to the intellectual, social and cultural changes associated with colonial rule. In the post-independence period, however, the rapid Sinhala Buddhist transformation of the Sri Lankan state, economy and social life was associated with a countervailing Tamil nationalist project. The escalating conflict is an expression of the ideological contradictions between the two projects rather than an outcome of their mere existence as separate bases for identities. Muslim political leaders have, for example, accepted and worked within the ideological framework of Sinhala Buddhist nationalism.

Conclusion

By 1977 two mutually incompatible conceptions of national identity and national interest had become firmly established as organising principles of the island's political life: the Sinhala Buddhist conception was reproduced by political parties and the activities of the state, whilst the Tamil conception was reproduced through political parties and later armed movements opposed to the state's project. The rise to political dominance of these two contrasting conceptions cannot be explained through temporally static variables—such as ethnic demography—or indeed the proximate interests and motivations that might have been served through their ascendance. Rather, the dominance of these two conceptions is a matter of political process that can be traced to the absence of engaged and temporally sustained work to establish a pan-ethnic conception of the nation from the late nineteenth century. As a consequence, mass electoral contestation on the island began in the absence of a shared understanding of how the island's ethnic pluralism could be reconciled with the need for a unified sense of national identity and national interest. Electoral contestation instead established two competing conceptions of reconciling ethnic pluralism and national identity: the hierarchical conception of Sinhala Buddhism, and the 'two equal collectives' conception of Tamil nationalism.

Furthermore, this escalation of conflict is not just a matter of the relative extremism or moderation of political leaders, but rather of the logic and political success of the respective national frameworks within which they operated. S. W. R. D. Bandaranaike, having led his SLFP to power on a Sinhala nationalist platform, sought to reach an accommodation with the Tamil parties, but was prevented from doing so by growing opposition— including from the UNP—framed in Sinhala Buddhist terms. Then in 1965, when UNP leaders sought to accommodate FP demands for territorial autonomy and language rights, they met stiff resistance both from their own backbenchers and from opposition parties, led by the SLFP. Similarly, the Tamil FP on two occasions—in 1956 and again in 1965—agreed to proposals that clearly fell short of its demands for federal autonomy, but nevertheless failed to prevent the inexorable centralisation and Sinhala nationalisation of the Sri Lankan state.[139] Finally the TULF, despite the strident rhetoric of its 1977 election manifesto demanding an independent Tamil state, came to an agreement with J. R. Jayewardene, the UNP president, on proposals to establish District Development Councils with limited autonomy in the Tamil-speaking areas.[140] Jayewardene's efforts were thwarted by a number of factors: notably resistance from the cabinet, his own ambivalence, steadily escalating clashes between Tamil insurgents and the military and finally growing collective violence against Tamils and other minorities that culminated in the 1983 anti-Tamil violence. All of these factors are, however, subordinate to the larger political problem: notably that between the Sinhala Buddhist hierarchical and centralised conception of order on the one hand, and the Tamil conception of equal nations on the other, there is very little overlapping space in which agreement can be found. Violently clashing political projects, rather than violence per se, have subsequently come to define Sri Lanka's Tamil–Sinhala politics and the still unresolved national question.

The following chapter traces the rapid escalation and internationalisation of Sri Lanka's ethnic conflict from the early 1980s onwards into a fully-fledged and bitterly fought civil war. The Jayewardene government's eager and rapid adoption of neo-liberal reforms and pro-Western tilt, abandoning previous support for the non-aligned movement, prompted equally enthusiastic Western backing—organised under the rubric of anti-communism—to bolster reform and strengthen Sri Lanka's then ongoing campaign against Tamil militants, quickly labelled terrorists. The growing ties between Sri Lanka and the West were viewed with suspicion in Delhi, where they led to fears of undue Western 'intrusion' into India's 'sphere of influence' and triggered the Indian intervention. Part Two discusses these events and explains why powerful international interventions failed to secure their stated ends—liberal reform for the West and regional primacy for India—and instead fuelled the escalation of the conflict that strengthened the Sri Lankan state, whilst entrenching its Sinhala Buddhist character, but also gave rise to renewed Tamil nationalist mobilisation now linked to armed struggle.

PART TWO

6

SRI LANKA'S CIVIL WAR

THE BEGINNING

Introduction

This chapter and the next trace the processes of Sinhala Buddhist and Tamil nationalist mobilisation and contestation through Sri Lanka's protracted armed conflict, from its emergence in the late 1970s to its end in 2009. They situate these within an international context and argue that the West-led processes of liberal order-making shaped, often decisively, the relative capacity of Sinhala Buddhist and Tamil nationalist actors to pursue their projects, for the most part strengthening the former at the expense of the latter. Sri Lanka's national and ethnic politics have of course always been embedded within global processes. The modern Sri Lankan state emerged through the twinned expansion of British colonial rule and capitalism, and the subsequent development of national and ethnic politics was shaped by the events and processes leading to the end of British Empire and, after independence, by the Cold War. However, from the late 1970s onwards and simultaneous with the onset of Sri Lanka's civil war, international actors, processes and mechanisms became internal to the dynamics of the conflict critically shaping both Sinhala and Tamil nationalist mobilisation. The analysis that follows shows how the escalation, development and ending of Sri Lanka's armed conflict as well as subsequent post-war developments are entangled within West-led and US-centred efforts since the Second World War to establish a global pacific order based on liberal democracy and market economics—or the liberal peace, as it has come to be known.[1] As the previous chapters have shown, Sinhala Buddhist and Tamil nationalisms emerged out of contingent and relatively autonomous political processes. But as this and subsequent chapters will show, from the onset of the civil war the conflict between them has been played out amidst international efforts to secure a lasting, and liberal, peace on the island. The increasing entanglement of international and domestic processes has led, from the moment the war ended, to the decisive relocation of Sri Lanka's nationalist contestations on a transnational plane, where the issue of accountability for atrocities that occurred in the final stages of the war (ending in May 2009) has become the central axis of conflict. The international–national configurations of the conflict have shifted in the post-war era, such that the Sri Lankan state and Sinhala opposition leaders found themselves resisting demands for accountability from a coalition of international and Tamil actors, the latter including Tamils in Sri Lanka, Tamil Nadu and the West-based Sri Lankan Tamil Diaspora. While post-war dynamics are discussed in Chapter 8, this chapter and the next discuss Sinhala Buddhist and Tamil nationalist politics in the context of the armed conflict, and their integral links with international processes during and after the Cold War. This chapter focuses on the first half of the armed conflict, from 1977 to 1994; and the next chapter on the second half, up to 2009.

The term 'liberal peace' is used here to refer to the reformist project of global order that brings together an array of loosely coordinated, rather than centrally planned, activities—including development, strengthening state military capacity, economic liberalisation and reform, democracy promotion and human rights protection, amongst others—undertaken by expanding 'strategic complexes' of multilateral, state and non-state actors.[2] The liberal peace is thus a directionality of international processes and activities. Not all of the myriad state and non-state actors engaged in activities such as conflict management, peace-building, democracy promotion or human rights advocacy necessarily explicitly recognise or endorse the overall objective of a global pacific order of liberal democratic states. Nevertheless the short-term tactical objectives they pursue in specific locales—for example specific projects aimed at promoting democracy or economic reform in Sri Lanka—are linked by funding streams and other institutional mechanisms, to the broad directionality of this project. While the liberal peace has been pursued since the Second World War, there was a marked shift in its emphasis from the Cold War to the post-Cold War eras, which in turn produced changing sets of opportunities and constraints for Sinhala Buddhist and Tamil nationalist politics. During the Cold War this US-led project was organised around containing the Soviet Union and expanding capitalist order by providing military, political and economic support for free market forces across the world. The processes and resources of anti-communism and capitalist expansion became embroiled in Sri Lanka's conflict from 1977 with the election of the pro-market and West-leaning government of J. R. Jayewardene. Western support led to a rapid expansion of Sri Lanka's military capacity, and violence more generally, whilst also prompting India's military and political intervention, which in turn dominated the island's politics throughout the 1980s. These interventions, which defined the last decade of the Cold War, substantively changed the structures and processes of Tamil and Sinhala Buddhist nationalist mobilisation, the former more radically than the latter.

Liberal peace efforts in the post-Cold War era had a more expansive set of transformative objectives. The demise of the Soviet Union was heralded by Western states and liberal actors as presaging the inevitability of a pacific global order based on the historically triumphant principles of liberal democracy and market economics.[3] This optimism was fused with a growing focus on 'internal conflicts', particularly ethnic conflicts, as key obstacles to liberal order and thus priorities for international intervention. The outbreak of ethnic and armed conflict in the former Yugoslavia, Rwanda and elsewhere in the immediate post-Cold War years led to a securitisation of 'internal conflict' as engendering a host of problems such as mass atrocities, refugee flows, terrorism, and the spread of disease that threatened international peace and stability.[4] International actors' efforts to build liberal peace in turn drew upon new and increasingly influential scholarly analysis that linked civil war, and in particular the emergence of armed non-state actors, to the erosion of state authority and opportunities for predatory economic activity.[5] Armed non-state actors were thus detached from political contestations and understood primarily as violent, economic agents self-interested in perpetuating conflict.[6] Thus the liberal peace response to armed conflict, in Sri Lanka as elsewhere, turns on containing these actors and their capacity for violence—that is, reinforcing the state—whilst simultaneously seeking to ameliorate conflict and prevent its recurrence by establishing a market-orientated, liberal–democratic state and society.[7] The election of President Kumaratunga in 1994 ushered this post-Cold War modality of liberal peace-making into Sri Lanka's war.

This chapter and the next analyse the dynamics of Sinhala Buddhist and Tamil nationalist politics amidst these shifting patterns of liberal order-making to explore two key puzzles. First, they explain why international involvement in the armed conflict over several decades failed to reach its stated goal, namely an ethnically plural, constitutionally liberal, market democracy, and instead entrenched Sinhala Buddhist majoritarianism in Sri Lanka's state and society, whilst also strengthening Tamil nationalist mobilisation against this. It shows how consistent and largely unqualified liberal peace support for the Sri Lankan state in its military campaigns against its Tamil adversaries, principally the LTTE, turned on and produced a radical disjuncture between Sri Lanka's international conduct and its domestic politics. In its international relations, Sri Lanka engaged the liberal peace on its own terms and accepted the principles of West-led liberal order. But its domestic policies remained firmly wedded to the principles of Sinhala Buddhist nationalism. This contradiction between Sri Lanka's international position and its domestic politics, which facilitated the internationally-assisted Sinhala Buddhist consolidation of Sri Lanka's state, was held in in abeyance while the LTTE remained a military threat. Since the end of the war, however, the contradiction has come to the fore and explains Sinhala state elites' difficulty in managing international demands for liberal reform alongside their domestic commitments to Sinhala Buddhist order.

For the second key puzzle, this chapter and the next explain how a Tamil national identity grounded in a territorial homeland in the island's north-east has endured as the foundation of Tamil politics despite several decades of intensely adverse conditions marked by both violent state repression[8] and hostile international interventions. In the past four decades, in contrast to the relative stability and continuity of Sinhala Buddhist politics, there have been radical changes in the configuration of Tamil politics. Nonetheless, amidst the tumult of rapid change from parliamentary politics to armed struggle, internecine strife and the rise and destruction of the LTTE and its de facto state, the principle of territorialised self-rule has persisted, whether Tamil demands are articulated as independent statehood (Tamil Eelam), federalism, 'devolution', or 'power-sharing'. While three decades of Federal Party mobilisation installed territorialised nationhood as the central pillar of Tamil politics,[9] the subsequent armed conflict and powerful international interventions in it fragmented the political unity of the TULF's 1977 electoral victory, but not the recurrent centrality of this principle. For example in 1985, the major Tamil armed groups and TULF insisted, to Delhi's anger, that territorial nationhood should form the basis for negotiations in Indian-mediated talks with the Sri Lankan government.[10] The armed struggle, which became synonymous with the LTTE that had emerged dominant from internecine clashes and Indian military efforts to end the insurgency, centred on giving material form to territorialised nationhood by militarily securing as much of the Tamil homeland as possible and establishing the structures of a de facto state there. At the turn of the century, the LTTE's resurgent military and political presence and the associated anticipation of a negotiated solution through Norwegian facilitation produced a renewed Tamil convergence on territorial nationhood, as the fragmented parliamentary groups came together to form the Tamil National Alliance (TNA). They negotiated a common manifesto that endorsed the Tamils' claims to territorial nationhood as the basis for negotiations and the LTTE as the sole Tamil representative in the Norwegian-led peace process. The manifesto received mass endorsement in the TNA's sweeping parliamentary victories in 2001 and 2004, echoing the TULF's victory in 1977. The analysis below examines the patterns of political organisation and mobilisation that sustained territorial nationhood as the foundation of Tamil politics through three decades of armed conflict against a well-armed and hostile Sri Lankan state with strong international political, economic and military support. It shows how international liberal peace hostility to Tamil nationalist politics was generative of political practices that combined nationalist demands with international engagement, creating a globally distributed set of capacities and orientations that, despite the LTTE's destruction, advance the nationalist project amid the changing international alignments since the end of the war.

The chapter examines the impact of Cold War anti-Communism and the Indian intervention from the escalation into armed conflict in the late 1970s to the election of President Kumaratunga in 1994. The next chapter focuses on the post-Cold War era and shows how international intervention to pursue liberal peace in Sri Lanka, including through the Norwegian Peace Process, led to an internationally mandated war against the LTTE that culminated in the mass atrocities of 2009 and the violent entrenchment of militarised Sinhala Buddhist rule in the Tamil-speaking areas.

Anti-Communism and the Indian intervention

This section focuses on the seventeen years of UNP rule from 1977 to 1994. Following the UNP's landslide election victory in 1977, its leader, J. R. Jayewardene, initiated a series of dramatic transformations in Sri Lanka's domestic and international politics. In a radical break with extant policies of state-led and state-controlled development, the government enthusiastically embraced free-market economics with an aggressive programme of trade liberalisation and cuts to welfare subsidies.[11] This in turn drew the enthusiastic support of the World Bank and other donors, and aid inflows soon 'became a veritable flood, making the country in per capita terms the world's leading aid recipient'.[12] This support continued through the early 1980s as ethnic tensions deepened, anti-Tamil rioting continued to escalate, and low-level and sporadic Tamil insurgency turned into a full-scale armed conflict. The government also earned strong backing from the United States, as the Reagan administration embarked on an intensified anti-Communist drive across the world.[13] In turn Sri Lanka abandoned previous governments' commitments to the Non-Aligned Movement (NAM) and turned decidedly to the West. This period marked the beginning of the radical disjuncture between Sri Lanka's international presentation of self and its domestic politics. While in the international realm, Sri Lanka adopted the universalist principles of free markets and anticommunism; in the domestic realm, the Sinhala Buddhist character of state and society deepened amidst repeated and escalating bouts of anti-Tamil violence, an expanding military campaign against Tamil militants and increasingly authoritarian forms of governance.

In 1978 the UNP installed a new constitution that centralised power in a directly elected executive presidency—which Jayewardene assumed—while introducing a system of proportional representation. He subsequently won the first presidential polls handsomely, held two years before the end of his allotted six-year term in October 1982. UNP leaders had predicted that worsening international economic conditions, coupled with the economic and social dislocations caused by liberalisation, would make an election harder to win, and thus passed a constitutional amendment (the third) allowing for a presidential incumbent to call early polls. While liberalisation had produced real economic benefits (per capita income rose by 6 per cent between 1977 and 1982, compared to 3.5 per cent for the period 1970–77), it also set in train a set of changes that produced unease amongst the core Sinhala Buddhist constituency. These included the closing of numerous public enterprises, privatisation, reductions in subsidies, a sense of increasing 'Westernisation' due to the impact of television, consumerism and tourism, the rapid expansion of labour migration to the Gulf states, as well as the growing success of Tamil enterprises, no longer hampered by the controls of the 'state-led' development model that had previously privileged Sinhalese business.[14] Jayewardene secured an impressive 53 per cent of the votes, 12 points ahead of his SLFP rival, aided by a divided opposition that was further constrained by the legal restrictions that the UNP had placed on the SLFP leader, Mrs Bandaranaike, preventing her from contesting. Soon afterwards, and conscious of the uneven popularity of UNP parliamentarians, Jayewardene had the UNP-dominated parliament pass an ordinance extending the life of parliament for a further six years—citing as one reason an alleged SLFP-led and Naxalite-inspired plot against his life.[15] The extension of parliament's term was subsequently endorsed in a referendum 'marred by force and fraud'.[16]

At the same time the ethnic conflict also deepened. Upon coming to power and in response to the growing Tamil insurgency, Jayewardene ordered troops to the Tamil north to 'wipe out' the 'terrorists',[17] and in 1978 the government passed the Prevention of Terrorism Act (PTA), reportedly modelled on South Africa's draconian law.[18] The cyclical violence of insurgency and counter-insurgency fermented a febrile anti-Tamil atmosphere that was sharpened by the effects of economic liberalisation which advantaged Tamil business interests at the expense of Sinhala Buddhist ones, fuelling bouts of anti-Tamil violence.[19] The period after 1977 was 'one of incessant ethnic rioting'[20] culminating in the July 1983 pogrom, which illustrated '*systematic* patterns of *organised* violence in which government actors played a central role'.[21] The violence targeted and destroyed a significant proportion of the Tamil economic base and also triggered a refugee flight, which began to swell the small diaspora to produce significant Tamil population concentrations in Europe, North America and Australia.[22] Senior government ministers legitimised and condoned the anti-Tamil logic of the violence, pointing to Tamils' alleged disproportionate share in the economy and the need to make room for the Sinhalese.[23] It also passed a constitutional amendment (the sixth) which proscribed advocacy of secession, forcing the TULF to forfeit its seats in parliament. For its part, the TULF was unable either to bring about a halt to the anti-Tamil violence and state repression, or to translate its electoral mandate of territorialised nationhood into a viable political project. In this context of drift and crisis in Tamil politics, militancy began to grow with the emergence of several groups whose ranks expanded rapidly after the 1983 pogrom, and a high-intensity armed conflict ensued. However, none of these developments deterred Western states and donors, who continued with their political, military and economic support to bolster the Sri Lankan state and neo-liberal development in the service of stability and liberal peace.[24]

However, the most powerful international intervention in Sri Lanka, dominating the 1980s, was by India. Sri Lanka's growing links with the US and the West were viewed with suspicion by Indira Gandhi's government, which interpreted these as unwelcome intrusion in India's 'sphere of influence'. In an effort to bring the wayward Jayewardene regime to heel, the Indian government began covertly funding and training several Tamil militant groups, who in turn stepped up attacks against Sri Lankan military and civilian targets, in close coordination with Indian officials.[25] At the same time the Indian government also began overtly and forcefully offering its 'assistance' in mediating a solution, arguing that India's own stability was at stake with the separatist strife in Sri Lanka threatening to 'spill over' into Tamil Nadu, where sympathy and support for the Sri Lankan Tamil cause was becoming increasingly vocal and widespread. Sri Lanka reluctantly acquiesced to India's pressure and in 1985 agreed to Indian-mediated talks with a coalition comprising the main Tamil armed groups and the TULF. The negotiations, held in Thimpu, Bhutan, ended in acrimonious failure following a military massacre of Tamil civilians, and the war resumed with Sri Lankan forces laying siege to the Jaffna peninsula, now controlled by the militant groups. The ensuing humanitarian crisis provided the context for direct Indian military intervention, which began in 1987 when the air force violated Sri Lankan airspace with a symbolic drop of food supplies over Jaffna. Sri Lanka halted its offensive and the two counties signed the Indo-Sri Lanka Accord, the high point of Indian intervention.[26]

The Accord set out the terms through which the two states bilaterally (that is, without the Tamil groups' participation) would resolve the ethnic conflict. Sri Lanka agreed to adopt an Indian-guided constitutional amendment (the thirteenth) that distributed administrative power between the centre and newly created provincial councils. Importantly, the Accord also merged the Tamil speaking northern and eastern provinces (subject to a referendum in the eastern province) to create a contiguous Tamil speaking political unit that was recognised as the 'areas of historic habitation of the Tamil speaking people.' Sri Lanka also agreed to release all Tamil political prisoners, reduce the military's presence in Tamil areas and halt state-backed Sinhala colonisation. Conversely, the Accord affirmed Sri Lanka's 'territorial integrity', a firm rejection of Tamil demands for sovereign statehood, and authorised the induction of an Indian Peace Keeping Force to ensure the surrender of the Tamil groups' weapons. The agreement unravelled when the Sri Lankan state and the LTTE (now the dominant group, and the only one not allied with Indian policy) refused to play ball and eventually conspired with each other to defeat Indian purposes whilst pursuing their own incompatible ends. Pointing to India's apparent inability or unwillingness to ensure that Sri Lanka met its side of the agreement—in relation to political prisoners, colonisation and de-militarisation—the LTTE declared its opposition to the Accord. The IPKF's efforts, supported by the remnants of other Tamil groups, to disarm the LTTE quickly and forcibly expanded into a protracted and ultimately abortive counter-insurgency campaign that ended with the IPKF's withdrawal from late 1989 at the formal request of the newly elected President Ranasinghe Premadasa, also of the UNP.

Premadasa's campaign for presidential elections fought against the backdrop of widespread Sinhalese fury at the Indian intervention that was fuelling a second and violent JVP insurgency (1987–9), centred on ejecting the Indian presence.[27] On coming to power in early 1989—and in an ironic reversal of earlier Indian actions—Premadasa began covertly assisting the LTTE with weapons and intelligence in its war against the IPKF. He also deployed Sri Lanka's military in a vicious counter-insurgency in the island's south that crushed the JVP, with widespread rights abuses and massacres by the military and government death squads in which 100,000 Sinhalese were killed.[28] In a high-profile demonstration of their shared rejection of the Accord, the LTTE and the Premadasa government also began new negotiations. Meanwhile, the newly elected coalition government in Delhi, keen to abandon a now discredited foreign policy adventure associated with the defeated Congress party, quickly agreed to Premadasa's demand for the IPKF's withdrawal. The Premadasa–LTTE cooperation collapsed shortly afterwards and the conflict resumed in 1990 with greater intensity, continuing until talks began with the newly elected government of President Kumaratunga in 1994, but not before the LTTE assassinated Premadasa in 1993.

As discussed in Chapters 3 and 5, even before the onset of the separate Western and Indian interventions, Sinhala Buddhist nationalist principles had become firmly entrenched in Sri Lanka's state and social order, while Tamil nationalist counter-mobilisation had culminated in territorial nationhood as its core organising principle and independent statehood as its goal. However, in the decade and a half from 1977, these international interventions had powerful impacts in different ways on the two nationalist projects, which are considered in turn below.

Sinhala Buddhist nationalism

This period marked a significant development in the evolution of Sinhala Buddhist nationalism. Deepening international engagement with the steadily escalating ethnic conflict opened up a gap between Sri Lanka's international posture and the Sinhala Buddhist nationalism that dominated domestic politics and the state—but at the same time also made the advancement of the Sinhala Buddhist project against the threat posed by Tamil militancy critically dependent on international financial, political and military backing. Sinhala state elites sought legitimacy and material support from Western states and allied international institutions on the basis of their commitment to neo-liberal reforms and anti-communism, portraying the campaign against Tamil militants in ethnically neutral—and internationally resonant—terms as a struggle against terrorism. International support further advanced and entrenched the Sinhala Buddhist character of state and society, but crucially also assured the relative stability and continuity of Sinhala Buddhist nationalism and its state amidst significant global shifts, including the expansion of a neo-liberal economic order and the associated decline of the norm of sovereign autonomy.

The UNP's successful 1977 electoral campaign drew extensively on Buddhist themes and focused on creating a 'dharmadista' or righteous society. J. R. Jayewardene's personal piety was an important part of the UNP's appeal, and he styled himself on the Buddhist king Asoka.[29] After the election and in a highly symbolic move, Jayewardene made his first speech from the Temple of the Tooth in Kandy, a venerated Buddhist site in the seat of the last Sinhala kingdom to fall to colonial rule. Addressing the nation, he observed that as '70 per cent of our country are Buddhists ... we shall lead our lives according to the sacred words of the Buddha'.[30] The Mahavamsa, the Buddhist chronicle that has been used to establish a Sinhala Buddhist narrative of the island in which Tamils are seen as perpetual threats repeatedly invading and destroying the pristine Sinhala Buddhist civilisation,[31] was also important to the government's presentation of self. The new government sponsored the updating of the Mahavamsa to cover events up to the inauguration of the new constitution in 1978, and Jayewardene often referred to the 'golden threads' that tied his government to the ancient Sinhala kings.[32] In a memorable refrain, he referred to himself as Sri Lanka's 193rd head of state, invoking continuity with the Sinhala rulers of the Mahavamsa and thereby reasserting the Sinhala Buddhist claim to the present.[33] However, this was not mere rhetoric alone. The two most important areas of government activity during this and subsequent periods—development and national security,[34] or the war against Tamil militants—both expanded and entrenched the Sinhala Buddhist character of state and society but were also crucially dependent on international processes and flows.

The sharp rise in Western aid to Sri Lanka was intended to support 'trade liberalisation and a balanced programme of public investment', but the government had other priorities, focused on 'the promotion of an economic expression of a resurgent Sinhalese nationalism, and support for favoured business and bureaucratic elites'.[35] In particular, a substantial proportion of the new aid flows—about 45 per cent between 1979 and 1981—went towards the government's signature development programme, the Mahavelli irrigation scheme.[36] The project used the waters of the Mahavelli to generate hydroelectricity and irrigate 390,000 acres of agricultural land in the dry zones of the island through a series of new dams and channels. Although the development rationale of the project was couched in the ethnically neutral terms of generating employment and easing landlessness through opening up new land for agricultural production, its domestic legitimisation and implementation expanded the Sinhala Buddhist project and also added a new dimension to the ethnic conflict.

The political rituals that formally inaugurated the dams, power stations and new colonies celebrated their Sinhala Buddhist identity;[37] and Gamini Dissanayake, the minister in charge of the scheme, praised the new irrigation systems it produced as 'testimony to the glorious past of the Sinhalese Buddhist civilization'.[38] The vast majority (just over 80 per cent)[39] of the new families settled in the new colonies were Sinhalese, and as many of the colonies overlapped with the predominantly Tamil-speaking regions, the colonisation and control of land became an increasingly militarised and violent site of the escalating conflict. In the context of rising Tamil militancy, the new Sinhala settlements were often strategically placed to disrupt the geographical and demographic continuity of the Tamil-speaking regions, and thereby undermine Tamil militants' claims to a Tamil homeland.[40] Strategically placed Tamil villages, such as those in Manal Aru at the nexus of the northern and eastern provinces, were forcibly evacuated by the security forces to make way for Sinhala settlers; Manal Aru was subsequently renamed in Sinhalese as Weli Oya.[41] The Sinhalese settlements were often armed and formed into vigilante groups called 'home-guards' to defend against frequent attacks by Tamil militants in which settlers were indiscriminately massacred. The home-guards themselves also became implicated in counter-massacres, participating in attacks by Sri Lankan security forces on Tamil villagers.[42]

The expansion of Sri Lanka's security forces and the increasing militarisation of the war against Tamil militants were likewise propelled by an interweaving of local and international dynamics that furthered the Sinhala Buddhist character of the state whilst embedding it in international efforts to secure a global liberal order. An important aspect of this interweaving was Sri

Lanka's use of the resonant label of terrorism to position its own military campaign within the US-led drive to confront global communism by supporting pro-market states and right-wing insurgencies against their enemies. The label of terrorism separated Tamil militancy from its origins in the contestation between Sinhala and Tamil nationalist projects, and transferred it, shorn of political content, to an international plane of opprobrium and illegitimacy, where it added urgency to the military support extended to Sri Lanka in securing stability and peace.[43] Sri Lanka's military quickly became embedded in the transnational networks of military force that were integral to Cold War anti-communism.[44] Sri Lankan officers were trained at military academies in the UK (Sandhurst) and US (West Point) and broader military assistance—material, training and advice—was delivered by Western allies Israel, Pakistan and South Africa, as well as private military contractors.[45]

Although embedded in the global anti-communist crusade, at home Sri Lanka's quest for national security was explicitly about defending the Sinhala Buddhist order against the threat of Tamil separatism. The war escalated at a moment of heightened anti-Tamil sentiment that was punctuated by repeated riots when political elites openly aired anti-Tamil views. Most startling was Jayewardene's claim in the weeks before the July 1983 pogrom that he could not think about the lives or opinions of the Tamil people and that if he were to 'starve the Tamils out, the Sinhala people will be happy'.[46] The ethnic character of the war was apparent in the military. The rapid expansion of the security forces in this period maintained the 'Sinhala only' recruitment policy that was instituted after the 1962 coup;[47] between 1985 and the end of the war the Sri Lankan armed forces expanded by an astonishing 650 per cent, but not a single Tamil was employed.[48] New units were named after Sinhala kings famed in nationalist narratives for defeating Tamil opponents; Buddhist rituals were integrated into military ones; and the Buddhist clergy and military command developed a close and naturalised relationship, signifying the equivalence of protecting the state and protecting Buddhism as enshrined in the constitution.[49] At the same time the campaign against Tamil militants was not just about combating terrorism qua political violence, but a broader campaign against Tamil separatism that was conceptualised in Buddhist terms as a 'just war'.[50] The terms 'terrorism' and 'Tamil separatism' became largely synonymous, and since the late 1970s the label of terrorism has been applied to Tamil nationalists as a whole, as well as to Tamil and non-Tamil critics of increasingly systematic rights violations and abuses by the security forces.

However, the reproduction of Sinhala Buddhist nationalism during this era was not just a matter of state policy and practice; it was also advanced by mobilisation against the state. The key point of contestation was the UNP's acceptance, albeit reluctant, of the Indo-Lanka Accord which, in the Sinhala Buddhist framework, recklessly acquiesced to Tamil demands for autonomy. Opposition to the Accord was led by the Muvbima Surakime Vyaparaya (MSV, or movement to protect the motherland), an umbrella organisation that brought together lay and clerical Buddhist groups, including the SLFP and a front organisation for the then proscribed JVP. The MSV became a mass movement holding a series of spectacular rallies and processions to oppose the Indo-Lanka Accord's threatened 'division' of the country. Its rallying cries of 'unity' and 'sovereignty' spoke to the core of Sinhala Buddhist nationalism, linking the very existence and flourishing of the Sinhala Buddhist people to their continued and unhindered control over the entire territory of the island.[51] The proposed devolution of powers in the Indo-Lanka Accord and the induction of Indian troops that it entailed were therefore held as vital threats to Sinhala Buddhist identity, not least because India serves in Sinhala Buddhist myths and narratives as the origin of the foremost foreign threats, with the island's Tamils as the vestiges of past invasions and occupations.[52] The MSV's climactic rally, on the eve of the official signing of the Indo-Lanka Accord, ended in a riot as police and protesters attacked each other in violence that left nineteen dead. The signing of the Accord itself then triggered the JVP's second insurgency (1987–9), which was only crushed by a high-intensity and murderous counter-insurgency.

The UNP government's vicious counter-insurgency generated widespread revulsion amongst the Sinhala populace, which propelled the SLFP led by Chandrika Kumaratunga to power in the 1994 parliamentary and presidential elections, thus ending seventeen years of UNP rule. The change in government represented therefore a rejection of the UNP's violent rule, rather than a popular turn away from Sinhala Buddhist nationalism. In other words, in the tumultuous post-1977 period, the substance and modalities of Sinhala Buddhist nationalism were unchanged by the escalation of inter-ethnic strife and the outbreak of armed conflict with Tamil militants, as well as the brutal intra-Sinhala conflict of the JVP uprising. This consensus amongst key Sinhala actors informed a shared commitment to violent methods of putting down Tamil militancy and rejecting Tamil demands for political autonomy, as well as support for nationalist transformative measures such as state-backed Sinhala colonisation of Tamil-speaking areas. While pursuing an explicitly majoritarian and ethnically hierarchical form of order-making domestically, in the international arena Sri Lankan elites and state officials emphasised commitment to liberalism and democracy. This meant that until the defeat of the LTTE, Sinhala nationalist actors did not need to rationalise or justify this profound contradiction. By contrast, Tamil nationalist actors, particularly the armed LTTE, were compelled from the outset to legitimise their claims and demands, and to mobilise support amidst intense international hostility and antipathy. The remainder of this chapter examines the dynamics of Tamil nationalist mobilisation.

Tamil nationalism: context

The outbreak of armed conflict and Indian intervention changed the configurations of Tamil politics beyond measure. Between the late 1970s and the mid-1990s, armed struggle replaced parliamentary politics as the modality of nationalist contestation and mobilisation; the LTTE rose to dominance amongst the armed groups and expanded into a powerful military and political organisation; guerrilla war turned into territorialised governance through structures of a de facto state; and nationalist struggle expanded to link diaspora locales with the north-east, producing a transnational form of organisation and mobilisation. The era of Tamil parliamentary politics reached its apogee with the TULF's sweeping victory in the 1977 elections, a moment of leadership and unity that it has never since regained. Yet those moments of close alignment between major Tamil actors—for example, during the 1985 negotiations in Thimpu or the Norwegian-led peace process in the early 2000s—have rested on advancing territorialised nationhood as the basis for addressing Tamil grievances. This was neither inevitable nor easily sustained. Apart from the fragmentation and often violent contestations amongst Tamil actors, the thrust of protracted and violent efforts by the Sri Lankan state and Sinhala nationalists on the one hand, and international liberal peace efforts on the other, has been to replace notions of Tamil nationhood and territorialised self-rule with de-territorialised alternatives: majority/minority hierarchy for the former, multi-ethnic liberal citizenship for the latter. The analysis below shows how territorialised nationhood, having become central to Tamil politics through three decades of non-violent mobilisation, has endured through four decades of high-intensity war, mass displacement and violent state repression, as well as the powerful international interventions outlined above.

Sri Lanka's domestic politics during the period from 1977 to the outbreak of all-out armed conflict in 1983 were marked by incessant and escalating anti-Tamil rioting and programmes (in 1977 and, the worst, in 1983), militarised state repression ('counter-terrorism') in the Tamil-speaking areas[53] and the consolidation and entrenchment of Sinhala Buddhist nationalism in the further centralised state. Having won a convincing electoral mandate, the TULF appeared immobilised by the anti-Tamil violence and state repression that followed the elections, and its efforts to negotiate concessions from the UNP government proved a feeble response to the latter's hostility and intransigence.[54] It is in this context that calls began to grow for armed struggle to realise the mandate of the Vaddukoddai Resolution, that is, for independent statehood. Emerging out of the youth and student movements integral to the mass mobilisation that generated the Resolution and the TULF's electoral victory, dozens of Tamil armed groups initially formed. These coalesced into five major armed groups: the LTTE, the Tamil Eelam Liberation Organisation (TELO), the People's Liberation Organisation of Tamil Eelam (PLOTE), the Eelam People's Revolutionary Liberation Front (EPRLF), and the Eelam Revolutionary Organisation of Students (EROS), the last being much less consequential.[55]

The nascent Tamil insurgency soon drew unofficial, but barely disguised, support from the Indian government in the form not only of arms and training, but also bases in Tamil Nadu and political support abroad. For example, the Indian High Commission in London assisted some militant groups' propaganda campaigns, while Indian media close to the government, such as *The Hindu* newspaper, gave sympathetic coverage to the insurgency. However, geared towards the primary goal of disciplining the West-leaning Jayewardene government, Indian military patronage was carefully calibrated to strengthen those groups more amenable to Indian direction and control—that is, the PLOTE, TELO and EPRLF, as opposed to the LTTE,[56] which sought logistical independence by seeking its own international networks and links (including, for example, with the African National Congress). In particular, whilst all Tamil groups developed links with the Tamil diaspora, this was core to the LTTE's strategy. Indian involvement deepened after all-out armed conflict erupted in late 1983 following the July pogrom, and Western support for Sri Lanka's counter-insurgency escalated. As the militants battled a rapidly expanding Sri Lankan military, Indian assistance also grew, and soon Indian military and intelligence officials were directly involved in operations by their favoured Tamil groups.

However, the fragmentation of the Tamil insurgency was organisational, rather than ideological. Whilst some groups espoused communist or socialist principles more than others, they all agreed on territorial nationhood, and independent statehood, as the basis for their liberation struggle. This was exemplified in the 1985 Indian-mediated talks in Thimpu, Bhutan. At the behest of the LTTE, the five groups and the TULF advanced as the basis for their negotiation a joint declaration which became known as the Thimpu Principles. These were, in effect, a condensed version of the Vaddukoddai resolution, asserting Tamils' national status, homeland and right to self-determination, as well as restoration of citizenship rights to Upcountry Tamils of Indian origin. Sri Lanka rejected outright the first three principles and the talks collapsed. Infuriated, the Indian government promptly expelled the LTTE from Tamil Nadu and, in a hugely consequential move, encouraged the other armed groups to eliminate the LTTE as part of their armed struggle. Vicious internecine war erupted in 1986, with the unintended outcome of the LTTE largely destroying the EPRLF, TELO and PLOTE. At the same time, the intensifying armed conflict precipitated a humanitarian crisis that triggered India's direct military intervention in 1987. When the LTTE refused to disarm, rejecting the Indo-Sri Lanka Accord, the Indian Peace-Keeping Force (IPKF) launched a protracted military campaign (involving 100,000 troops at its peak).[57] Abandoning their struggle for independence, the other three armed groups joined the Indian counter-insurgency. They also registered as political parties. In elections held amid the high-intensity fighting and marred by rigging, Indian-allied groups secured the majority of seats to the newly formed Northeast Provincial Council in 1988 and in 1989 the majority of parliamentary seats in the north-east (the TULF contested in alliance with EPRLF and TELO; the PLOTE separately).[58] When the IPKF pulled out in 1989–90 and armed conflict resumed, the other Tamil armed groups, and splinter groups, joined the Sri Lankan counter-insurgency, which continued until the end of the 1990s. They reconsolidated again as the Norwegian peace process began, and the major fragments from the EPRLF, TELO and TULF, along with the ACTC, united to form the Tamil National Alliance (TNA) and won the 2001 elections on a platform of territorial nationhood and backing for the LTTE as the sole Tamil representative in the talks.

This outline of developments from 1977 to the mid-1990s demonstrates the adverse conditions under which the principle of territorialised nationhood had to be sustained as the central pillar of Tamil national politics.[59] Unquestionably key to this was the LTTE. From the onset of armed conflict, the LTTE expanded steadily, growing from a few dozen fighters in 1983 to 10,000 fighters and cadres at the moment of the IPKF's withdrawal; they took control of large parts of the north-east, including the Jaffna peninsula where the LTTE set up a de facto state, running it from 1990 to 1995. Yet, from the moment the shooting war with the IPKF began, the LTTE was internationally isolated. It immediately lost its 'rear base' in Tamil Nadu, which it had earlier used to train and rehabilitate wounded cadres, and had to face the powerful Sri Lankan and Indian military forces. At the same time, from the 1970s onwards the international climate had turned decisively against armed struggle and the politics of national liberation. This international hostility to armed non-state actors worsened in the post-Cold War era of liberal peace and what later became formalised as the 'Global War on Terror'.

The LTTE's ability to maintain and expand political support for the project of territorial nationhood was not merely a self-evident consequence of its military success (a variant of Charles Tilly's 'war makes states' thesis).[60] Another related line of analysis attributes the LTTE's growth to trade in drugs and other illicit activities and/or coercive extraction, especially from the Tamil diaspora. While a full picture of the LTTE's financial flows is yet to emerge, accounts of illicit trade and smuggling rest on asserted and unsubstantiated claims while 'evidence implicating the LTTE in illegal activities is inconclusive and lacking'.[61] This is not to assert that the LTTE was not involved in illicit trade, but to argue this is a poor explanation for the expansion of the LTTE's war-fighting and state-building capacity, especially without concrete evidence that would contrast its impact with what is considered here: the complex effort of mobilising people, their resources and their activities, across time and space, to sustain a protracted war in hostile international conditions.

A similar problem is inherent to explanatory reliance on coercion. The LTTE certainly had a history of violently targeting prominent Tamil opponents and critics, notably including Neelan Thiruchelvam, the TULF MP, and Rajini Thiranagama, the Jaffna University lecturer and human rights activist. There is also evidence of coercive fundraising, in the island and abroad.[62] But coercion is a very partial explanation that cannot account for the persistence of nationalist mobilisation in inhospitable conditions. For one thing, coercion and violence went both ways. Throughout the conflict, actual and suspected LTTE members, supporters and political allies (including journalists, lawyers, politicians, etc.) were targeted by the Sri Lankan armed forces, the IPKF and allied Tamil paramilitaries. Notable examples were murders of the politicians Kumar Ponnamblam and Joseph Pararajasingham and the journalist Dharmaratnam Sivaram. Extrajudicial killings, 'disappearances' and torture, including sexual torture, generated an overarching climate of state-led terror under which Tamil nationalist mobilisation and politics had to take place, and which, having emerged in the early 1980s, persists to this day with a brief interlude of 18 months during the Norwegian peace process.[63] Moreover, the civil administration of the LTTE-run de facto state employed large numbers of people (LTTE members were unpaid) and included large welfare and public goods institutions.[64] Meanwhile, in diaspora centres, the LTTE built its extensive networks of mobilisation under close surveillance by host governments assisting Sri Lanka and, from the late 1990s, direct proscriptions under their anti-terrorism laws.[65] Yet, as even accounts foregrounding coercion acknowledge, over a quarter-century of war, the LTTE raised considerable willing donations from expatriate Tamils, through networks and institutions of unpaid volunteers. The poverty of coercion-based explanations for the LTTE's support was laid bare in the final months of the war by the sudden and unexpected nationalist mass mobilisation and protests in diaspora centres, even as the LTTE faced certain defeat.[66] As the following chapters illustrate, in the years since the LTTE's destruction, not only has this surge in mobilisation generated a range of powerful diaspora-based organisations and networks pursuing nationalist goals; but also the LTTE continues to be a touchstone of political legitimacy amongst Tamils in the diaspora and the island—for example, in contesting the 2013 elections for the Northern Provincial Council, the TNA placed a picture of the deceased LTTE leader, Vellupillai Pirapaharan, on election publications.[67] In short, while coercion and violence were part of the LTTE's repertoire, they existed alongside other and, it is argued here, much more potent forms of mobilisation and persuasion that secured and sustained its dominant position in Tamil politics, as well as its ongoing legacy.

Tamil nationalism: the LTTE's practices

The LTTE's growth is inextricably linked to successful nationalist mobilisation that rests on two key poles of activity. First, it set out a simple and clear message that was consistently taken to Tamils in the island and the diaspora, as well as the international community.[68] The core of the message was simply an elaboration of the Vaddukoddai Resolution along with a justification for the LTTE's claim to the sole or 'authentic' leadership of the Tamil nation and its struggle. The justification of armed resistance and struggle for independent statehood turned on demonstrating the Sri Lankan state's efforts to deny and violently undermine the Tamils' status as a nation equal to the Sinhalese. As with the Vaddukoddai Resolution and the Federal Party before that, the LTTE reiterated the Sinhala-dominated state's history of anti-Tamil violence and discrimination, but now also emphasised the widespread suffering and destruction wrought by the Sinhala-dominated military's repeated offensives into the

Tamil-speaking areas. The LTTE positioned itself as a national liberation movement, synonymous with the military and political struggle it was leading, and invoked the sacrifices made by its fighters in service of the nation as the basis for its legitimacy. This recurrent narrative of Sinhala state oppression and Tamil national resistance has since come to dominate Tamil nationalist historiography and generate a pattern of nationalist political practice that is centred on defying and resisting the Sinhala state in defence of the Tamil nation.

Second, the LTTE established an organisational infrastructure that proved capable of penetrating deep into Tamil society and reaching individual Tamils to act in support of its cause.[69] It could not, at this stage, co-opt the support of powerful institutions and figures, though this became integral to its efforts from the turn of the century. Most of the social, cultural and political institutions of Tamil society (such as the remnants of the TULF, schools, temples, churches and media) were variously ambivalent about or categorically opposed to the LTTE's political programme, its social reformist agenda (see below) or use of armed force. At the same time, the anti-Tamil violence and pogroms, followed by a decade of armed conflict, had done much to disrupt the continuity of patronage networks—whether of landowners, business interests or professional groups, such as lawyers and doctors. Thus where Hindu or Christian priests, teachers and lecturers, journalists, doctors or businesspeople acted in support of the LTTE or its political project, they did so as individuals, rather than organised interests. The LTTE therefore had to establish its own channels and structures to reach the population in the island and in the diaspora. The practices by which these were undertaken are discussed next, but it is worth reiterating how crucial these were to the LTTE's survival, let alone growth, given its isolation internationally.

To begin with, the themes of the LTTE message were constantly reasserted and elaborated by the LTTE and allied actors through a variety of media. From the outset, therefore, the LTTE prioritised the establishment of its own media outlets, including a clandestine radio service, the Voice of Tigers (VoT), and newspapers such as *Viduthalai Puligal*; from the late 1990s, the LTTE increasingly used the internet and satellite television channels. Articles and programmes sought to explain and rationalise the LTTE's major decisions, for example to enter into or break off from peace talks. They also carried regular updates of battlefront developments, civilian casualties, displacement, as well as the suffering and destruction resulting from Sri Lankan military offensives and government blockades on food, medicine and essential supplies into LTTE-controlled areas. The LTTE also expended considerable effort in disseminating material to mainstream and international media, and especially those in the diaspora. The LTTE's regular press releases, however, comprised a fraction of the material generated in Tamil and English—and even, albeit to a much lesser extent, Sinhala (the VoT ran a regular Sinhala broadcast). Such was the importance the LTTE attached to information dissemination that from the outset its infrastructure included a specialised media unit, which included writers, photographers and videographers who were routinely embedded, often with fatal consequences, with fighters on the frontline; they also invested heavily in satellite access and broadcast and other media equipment. The point here is not that LTTE's material was uncritically received by audiences responding like dupes, but that it could consistently challenge and undermine the claims, accounts and narratives of the Sri Lankan state and other opponents with those of its own, and, just as importantly, constantly reinforce the themes of resistance to state oppression and territorial nationhood. (In this sense, the LTTE early on adopted the principles of 'information warfare' that have since the Cold War become integral, if not central, to Western and other states' military operations.)

Relatedly, the LTTE was also adept at using culturally resonant poetry, artwork, images, icons and performances to communicate the themes of its political message. Along with news and analysis, LTTE media routinely carried poetry that was variously heroic and poignant, as well as illustrations, some vivid, others muted and impressionistic, by LTTE cadres and civilians depicting the experiences and conditions of the war zone.[70] Importantly, the LTTE also promoted the distinctive Tiger flag as a symbol of both Tamil national identity and resistance to state oppression. Similarly, the LTTE's Heroes' Day (27 November, the day when the first LTTE cadre—Shankar—fell in combat), having begun as internal to the organisation, was hosted publicly from the late 1990s. Heroes' Day events—themed as 'celebrations'—included rituals of public and collective mourning as well as the performance of songs and dramas that celebrated heroism and sacrifice, depicted suffering and loss, and celebrated the natural beauty of the 'homeland'. Heroes' Day soon became established as the single most important event in the nationalist calendar.[71] This was in no small part because, amongst the emotion, there were also important politics: the event was the occasion for the annual speech by Pirapaharan which responded to key political developments, international and local, and set out major policy decisions for the year to come, as well as signalling the LTTE's orientation on important issues. The speech in Tamil was broadcast live from LTTE headquarters at precisely 6.05 p.m. (the moment of Shankar's death) and received at mass rallies across the diaspora, thereby also serving as an annual transnational moment of 'nation-ness'. Amid the LTTE's military and political significance, the speech also commanded the attention of the international community, and the much anticipated text was released in Tamil and English to local and international media as Pirapaharan finished speaking.

The social penetration and spatial expansion of the LTTE's political agenda relied on an organisational infrastructure comprising four sets of institutions that came together under the LTTE's apex leadership: its military, its political wing, the de facto state[72] and an international network that organised and coordinated activities in the diaspora. The military comprised an army, a formidable navy and, from the mid-2000s, a fledgling air force. Notably, the LTTE raised separate male and female fighting units (infantry, artillery, etc.), as well as separate Sea Tiger forces, giving concrete form to a key plank of its political and social agenda, gender equality (discussed below).[73] From early on, the LTTE built an extensive and sophisticated intelligence network, which gathered information not only to support warfighting but, just as importantly, on political developments, actors and figures. The LTTE's Political Wing, whose activities included recruitment and media operations, was responsible for popular mobilisation (its activities are discussed in the next section, which considers the era of the Norwegian-led peace process, when the Political Wing became crucial). The LTTE began to establish institutions of territorial governance in 1990 after it took over substantial tracts of the north-east with the IPKF's withdrawal. Organised into a de facto state structure, these were headquartered in the Jaffna peninsula until 1995, when a major Sri Lankan military offensive forced their relocation to the Vanni region. The arms of the de facto state included a police force, judiciary, health services, border control, customs, rehabilitation and development, and a central bank.[74] The de facto state was at once a system of civil administration in its controlled areas; a vehicle for the pursuit of its social reform agenda (see below); and, just as importantly, a political project that gave tangible form to the aspiration for national self-determination and sovereign statehood. (The LTTE's practices in the diaspora are discussed in the next chapter.)

Key to both the LTTE's operational success and its claim to national political leadership was its emphasis on the principles of competition, merit and efficiency. Individuals progressed through the ranks on the basis of their ability to deliver results in their areas of responsibility. As became well recognised by supporters and detractors alike, these principles earned the LTTE, its institutions and members a strong reputation as disciplined, not corrupt and efficient, which also served as an essential aspect of its claim to political leadership and legitimacy of governance.[75] At the same time, important skills, capacities and procedures were carefully fostered to build redundancy and resilience into its organisational processes. These aspects became evident during the period of the Norwegian-led peace process and, especially, in the aftermath of the 2004 tsunami, when the LTTE's ability to manage post-disaster recovery and development became increasingly, if begrudgingly, recognised by international donors and INGOs.[76]

While reproduction of the principle of territorialised nationhood and the LTTE's growth were mutually dependent and inextricably linked, the LTTE faced considerable difficulties in building a national movement. These included cleavages and hierarchies within the Tamil-speaking population, including those based on caste, gender and, in particular, between Tamil and Muslim identities, as well as difficulties in expanding its reach effectively into the east. From the outset, the LTTE's political programme included a commitment to social reform, particularly in relation to effacing entrenched caste and gender differences. The LTTE was better able to pursue its reformist agenda within its own structures than within wider society. Indeed, the latter efforts often produced strong resistance that translated into opposition to its wider political agenda, the LTTE itself, or both. Consequently, the LTTE's reformist efforts focused primarily on enabling equality of opportunity, rather than a radical or wholesale transformation of Tamil social and cultural practices.[77] For example, as noted above, the LTTE established all-female units in its military and political arms as a means of encouraging women's participation in ways uninhibited by male prejudices, without attempting systematically to challenge those prejudices. All-female infantry, artillery and other regiments, and Sea Tiger units were comparably armed and equipped to the all-male units, and performed equally in combat, and women commanders rose to join the LTTE's apex leadership. Despite resistance, there were also attempts at broader societal reform. For example, while the LTTE could not eliminate the widespread practice of brides being given in marriage with dowries, it did introduce legislation in the de facto state that made dowry exclusively the woman's property, rather than her husband's.[78] The LTTE's focus on gender-based reform may not have revolutionised Tamil society, but it did have distinctly positive effects. For example, it was widely recognised that under LTTE rule, Jaffna became a 'crime free society',[79] and an important aspect of this was how, in sharp contrast to government-controlled areas, women could feel secure in public spaces, even at night.[80] Moreover, given the Sri Lankan military's widespread and still ongoing sexual abuse of detainees, ex-combatants and civilians,[81] strikingly few incidents of sexual violence are attributed to LTTE cadres, either against civilians or other cadres. Recent analysis explains this 'puzzle' in terms of both the LTTE's nationalist ideology and its organisational discipline.[82]

In confronting caste hierarchies, the LTTE adopted practices of positive discrimination within its own institutions and those of the de facto state, though these were implicit and centred on merit-based progress, rather than overt and quota driven.[83] Its efforts to tackle caste in wider society eventually became focused on conflict management rather than social reform per se. For example, a persistent source of caste conflict related to temple festivals and competing claims over the rights and privileges of participation, itself a mark of collective social status. Lower-caste groups' demands to take turns at pulling the temple chariot were often vehemently resisted by upper-caste groups; the LTTE's response was to assign each group a specific day or a particular portion of the chariot's circuit, a solution guaranteed by threat of more forceful sanctions.[84] Importantly, the LTTE's attempts to address caste were also not linked to an explicit anti-Hindu philosophy, as with the Dravidian movement. Many LTTE cadres did have personal commitments to the Dravidian philosophy, for example opting to have Self-Respect as opposed to religious marriages. However, this was a personal rather than organisational matter (the LTTE leader married in the early 1980s, in India, according to the Tamil Hindu rites). This ameliorative, rather than radically transformative, approach to caste hierarchy was in large part continuous with those of earlier periods of Tamil nationalist politics.

While the LTTE was able to manage caste and gender differences sufficiently in forging a cohesive Tamil-speaking political identity, the dynamics of armed conflict in the east led to a permanent political divide between Tamils and Muslims, such that the ideal of a cohesive Tamil-speaking political identity became impossible.[85] Tamil nationalist politics and mobilisation even in the Federal Party era only weakly extended amongst Tamil-speaking Muslims, for reasons that are discussed in Chapters 3 and 5. Muslim elites in this period generally worked to secure their constituents' interests through cooperation with ruling Sinhalese elites of either the UNP or the SLFP, whilst not challenging the fundamental Sinhala Buddhist character of the state.[86] Nonetheless, in its early years, the LTTE drew both support and volunteers from Muslim communities in the east. However, an outbreak of Tamil–Muslim rioting in 1985 was quickly and skilfully exploited by the UNP government. Apart from recruiting Muslims to the armed forces and intelligence services, the government set up Muslim paramilitary groups—'home-guards'—'which it utilised to fuel communal violence and open a third front in the bloody war'.[87] Tamil–Muslim clashes drew in LTTE and Muslim paramilitaries, resulting in escalating tit-for-tat massacres and Tamils and Muslims being driven out of their villages. The resumption of the LTTE–Sri Lanka war after the IPKF's withdrawal in 1990 produced a particularly vicious period of fighting in the east, with escalating massacres of Tamil and Muslim civilians. The most consequential event in this cycle was the decision by the LTTE to expel the Muslim community forcibly from Jaffna, Mannar, Mullaitivu and Kilinochchi in October 1990, forcing them to abandon their homes and businesses within hours. By September 1992 an estimated 150,000 Muslims had been ethnically cleansed out of the Northern Province.[88] This act consolidated Muslims' collective mistrust and antipathy towards the LTTE and Tamil nationalist politics more broadly.[89] In 2002, the LTTE formally apologised for the expulsion and in 2003 LTTE leader Pirapaharan signed an accord with SLMC leader Rauf Hakeem (also one of the government negotiators in the Norwegian-led peace process). Nonetheless, efforts by the LTTE and the TNA to forge a common Tamil-speaking front have been largely unsuccessful, as the SLMC and other Muslim elites have continued to prioritise relations with ruling Sinhala elites and the state.

The LTTE expansion in the east was not as robust as it was in the north or in the diaspora (see below). From the late 1970s to 1995, Jaffna was the centre of Tamil nationalist politics, more generally, and later the LTTE's key base area from which control radiated outwards. The LTTE's structures in the eastern areas of the putative homeland (Trincomalee and Batticaloa districts) were weaker than in the north, from which they were separated by large tracts of military-controlled territory, and also had a great deal of autonomy from the centre. The difficulties in maintaining communication and transport links with the north were made worse by many areas regularly changing hands between the LTTE and the government forces and paramilitaries, all of which severely hampered integration into the cross-cutting institutions of military control, political mobilisation and civil administration of the de facto state centred in Jaffna, and later Vanni. Nonetheless the LTTE did mobilise support and recruits from amongst the Tamil population in the past. The LTTE's platform of armed struggle for national liberation resonated and drew recruits in the conditions of violence and state repression replete with atrocities and counter-atrocities by the government forces and the LTTE, as well as other armed actors including army-backed Tamil paramilitaries and Sinhala and

Muslim 'home-guards' and the consequent forced displacement as well as state-backed colonisation. East-derived units such as the Jeyanthan Brigade were an important component of the LTTE's fighting formations and earned a reputation for military proficiency. Importantly, however, the principle of territorialised nationhood has always been in tension with the complex local exigencies of Tamil–Muslim enmity and conflict, and the mixed ethnic demography of the east.

In contrast to the relative stability of Sinhala Buddhist nationalism, the configurations of Tamil nationalist politics changed beyond measure during this era. Armed struggle organised on the basis of territorialised nationhood and self-determination replaced parliamentary politics as the principal mode of politics. The LTTE established its dominance through bitter internecine strife and subsequently a mode of organisation and mobilisation focused on setting out a clear message and directly reaching individual Tamils to mobilise support. There was also a shift in the orientation of politics. While the Federal Party had mostly sought to persuade and pressure Sinhala elites to share power, the LTTE was focused on persuading a hostile and sceptical international audience of the legitimacy of its demands. Crucially however, and in contrast to the Sri Lankan state's practices, the LTTE's international and domestic messages were aligned. For example, the LTTE leader's annual Heroes' Day speech, the text of which was released simultaneously in Tamil and English, at once addressed the Tamil people and the international community together, using a single set of rhetorical constructs, arguments and rationales in framing the legitimacy of Tamil demands and the illegitimacy of the Sri Lankan state. These drew directly on liberal principles. Sri Lanka was argued to violate constitutional and democratic norms in violent and systematic efforts to destroy the Tamils' collective national status and identity ('genocide'), and the demand for national self-determination and turn to armed struggle were argued as the inevitable resistance to this process of state oppression and necessary means of preserving Tamils' legitimate rights.[90] While these efforts bore little fruit in terms of materially undermining international support for Sri Lanka, they were nonetheless productive of the practices, orientations and capacities in the Tamil nationalist project that sustained it after the demise of the LTTE (see Chapter 8).

Conclusion

The powerful international interventions in Sri Lanka between 1977 and 1994 radically militarised the ethnic conflict, drawing it irreversibly into the international processes and dynamics of liberal order-making. These interventions inadvertently further consolidated the Sinhala Buddhist dominance of Sri Lanka's state and society whilst also fuelling Tamil nationalist mobilisation against it. Western processes reinforced the state and its war against Tamil militants. India's intervention at first supported Tamil militancy and then turned against it, but even while Indian troops fought Tamil militants, their very presence and the prospect of Tamil autonomy that the Indo-Lanka Accord implied galvanised Sinhala Buddhist nationalism's popular base. Western support for Sri Lanka was centred on advancing liberal market democracy as an integral part of global liberal order-making. India's shifting pattern of intervention was centred on arresting Sri Lanka's turn to the West and ensuring its docile acceptance of Indian regional hegemony. In that sense, both failed utterly.

Nonetheless, engagement with the international sphere became unavoidable for both Sinhala Buddhist and Tamil nationalist projects. For the former, this entailed separate internal (ethnic majoritarianism) and external (liberal peace) discourses, the contradictions between which were masked by linking the suppression of Tamil rebellion to global frameworks of anti-communism, anti-terrorism and liberal order-making. For the latter, the twinned militarisation and internationalisation of the conflict produced a shift to armed struggle with the LTTE emerging as the dominant Tamil nationalist actor leading an increasingly transnational movement centred on the claims to territorial nationhood and self-determination.

In 1994, Western support for Sri Lanka transferred smoothly to newly elected President Kumaratunga's administration, but now informed a more penetrative pattern of liberal peace intervention characteristic of the post-Cold War era. At the same time, India, chastened by its abortive military intervention, and outflanked by the radically changed geopolitical context in the aftermath of the Soviet Union's collapse, withdrew from direct engagement with the island's crisis. The next chapter examines the period between 1994 and 2009 and considers how the processes of the ongoing nationalist conflict became interwoven with the post-Cold War imperatives of liberal order-making, leading first to an escalation of the war and then to its final cataclysmic end in May 2009.

7

SRI LANKA'S CIVIL WAR

THE ENDING

Introduction

International intervention to end Sri Lanka's armed conflict and fashion an ethnically inclusive, liberal market democracy began in earnest with the election in 1994 of President Chandrika Kumaratunga. In an important shift from the Cold War period, a growing consensus held liberal peace to rest not only on ending the war, but also on addressing Tamil demands through a limited form of territorial autonomy. This is not to say, however, that international actors recognised a Tamil political collective in Sri Lanka, but rather that power-sharing, advocated first as 'devolution' and later as 'federalism', was intended to apply equally to Tamil and Sinhala majority provinces as a means of checking the over-centralisation of the Sri Lankan state and improving liberal governance in an ethnically neutral way. This prevailing international consensus was recognised by both Sinhala state and political elites and by Tamil nationalist actors, and deeply conditioned their activities. From 1994 to the end of the war, Kumaratunga and other Sinhala leaders consistently stated the need for and pledged to pursue some form of devolution, and generally 'expressed themselves with greater restraint on the ethnic issue'.[1] Tamil nationalist activity centred on establishing the insincerity of these pledges, the depth of Sinhala nationalism as an obstacle to inclusive peace, whilst also mobilising and demonstrating Tamil popular support for territorial nationhood as the basis for power-sharing. This chapter traces Sinhala Buddhist

191

nationalist and, especially, Tamil nationalist mobilisations amid expansive and penetrative international efforts to generate liberal peace in Sri Lanka.

Influential post-Cold War scholarly analysis on civil wars and ethnic conflict held that the key to lasting peace and stability was ending violence and ensuring state stability, on the one hand, and fostering liberal governance, on the other; therefore international efforts in Sri Lanka positioned the LTTE as the primary obstacle to liberal progress in Sri Lanka.[2] It was viewed as implacably committed to self-serving armed violence; consequently its insistence on Tamil territorial nationhood, self-determination and independent statehood was dismissed as a manifestation of a reactionary ethno-nationalism that was blind to, and on the wrong side of, history and globalisation.[3] International efforts to contain and marginalise the LTTE proceeded on the unquestioned and often stated assumption that the Tamils on the whole rejected the LTTE and its 'extremist' demands and were satisfied to remain within the Sri Lankan constitutional framework, provided their demands for devolution, development and good governance were met. This view was also enthusiastically promoted by Sinhala ruling elites, as well as by some Tamil leaders and actors, who argued that in the LTTE's absence all Sri Lankans, Tamils, Sinhalese and Muslims alike could together fashion a new and ethnically inclusive future.

Conversely, the international community viewed the Sri Lankan state as a promising, if flawed, liberal market democracy held back by 'conflict', and the menace of LTTE terrorism. International actors were open and unequivocal in their support for the Sri Lankan government and their condemnation of the LTTE. For example, at a press conference in Washington to discuss the still ongoing Norwegian peace process and the rising levels of violence that presaged the final war (2006–9), Nicholas Burns, the US Under Secretary of State, made clear his government's partisan position on the conflict. He stated that 'in the case of Sri Lanka ... we support the government. We have a good relationship with the government. We believe the government has a right to try and protect the territorial integrity of the country.' Moving to the LTTE, he stated: 'We also believe that that the Tamil Tigers, the LTTE, is a terrorist group responsible for massive bloodshed in the country and we hold the Tamil Tigers responsible for much of what has gone wrong in the country. We are not neutral in this respect.'[4]

This Manichean framing of the armed conflict and its protagonists produced, inevitably, a pattern of support for the Sri Lankan state's campaign against the LTTE that unfolded under the rubric of a 'war for peace'. The slogan became the hallmark of President Kumaratunga's government and succinctly captured the shared logic that to secure a lasting peace, Sri Lanka had to wage war against the LTTE to destroy or curtail its capacity for violent disruption of the process of liberal reform. The discourse of 'war for peace' encompassed that of 'counter-terrorism' which framed joint Sri Lankan and international efforts to marginalise and defeat the LTTE and politically allied actors, but which, for international actors at least, was folded into the larger project of transforming Sri Lanka into an ethnically inclusive market democracy. The international–local war for peace against the LTTE took place in two phases: the first under President Kumaratunga (1994–2002), the second under President Mahinda Rajapaksa (2006–9). They were separated by the Norwegian-led peace process (2002–6), which provided a momentary respite from war but also represented an intensified international effort to contain the LTTE—through political rather than just military means—and advance liberal peace.[5] This chapter first sets out an overview of events between 1994 and the end of the war in 2009, before examining in turn the dynamics of Sinhala Buddhist and Tamil nationalist politics in this period.

Overview: 1994–2009

The first phase of the 'war for peace' began in early 1995 after short-lived talks between the government of newly elected President Kumaratunga and the LTTE broke down over mutual recriminations of bad faith.[6] Enthusiastically supported by the international community, Kumaratunga's military strategy, as with Jayewardene's a decade earlier, centred on recapturing the Jaffna peninsula, destroying the LTTE and dismantling its de facto state.[7] Just before the offensive began, the government finally unveiled a promised set of devolution proposals. 'The package', as it became commonly known, was drafted by TULF stalwart Neelan Tiruchelvam, and framed in emblematic terms of liberal governance. Although rejected by the Tamil political parties as disregarding many Tamil demands,[8] and subsequently watered down in the face of fierce Sinhala nationalist opposition, the package was an essential element of Sri Lanka's new West-derived doctrine of counter-insurgency, whereby a political offer to win over 'moderate' Tamils was twinned with militarily confronting the 'extremist' LTTE. In a related vein, after Jaffna was recaptured, albeit without successfully destroying the LTTE, which retreated to the Vanni region in the south, international actors rushed to assist Sri Lanka in consolidating the military victory with a dramatic inflow of development aid intended to win Tamil 'hearts and minds'[9]—while the LTTE-controlled

Vanni was placed under a crushing economic and humanitarian embargo.[10] In another integral aspect of the 'war for peace', in 1997 the United States banned the LTTE as a terrorist organisation, as did the UK in February 2001.

However, the initial euphoria was soon replaced by mounting international concern. New offensives to destroy the LTTE in Vanni made initial progress, but slowed to a grinding pace; and the war expanded to undermine the general economy. At the same time, the constitutional reform process stalled amid intensifying Sinhala nationalist resistance. Donors also became increasingly frustrated at the 'disconnect' between their high levels of aid provision and the lack of developmental progress, and the growing signs that funds were being diverted to pro-government paramilitaries in Jaffna.[11] Frustration turned to alarm in late 1999 when the war turned with a massive LTTE counter-offensive that reversed in a matter of days the military's territorial gains of the preceding eighteen months, before going on to destroy the strategically significant military base complex at Elephant Pass in April 2000. With the LTTE advancing on Jaffna itself, Sri Lanka urgently sought military reinforcement: they secured powerful new artillery systems from the Czech Republic and jet fighter-bombers from Israel.[12] At the same time the Norwegian government had also been engaged in a behind-the-scenes effort to initiate dialogue between the government and the LTTE. Kumaratunga was initially supportive of these efforts, but became more hostile as the LTTE's threat to Jaffna ebbed and the arrival of new military hardware after the Elephant Pass debacle began to build confidence in the possibility of a fresh and decisive offensive by the armed forces. In the October 2000 parliamentary elections she promised a 'no-holds-barred' military campaign against the LTTE.[13] Following a meeting with Norwegian diplomats in Vanni, the LTTE announced a unilateral ceasefire in late 2000 and called on the government to reciprocate. Kumaratunga rejected the truce, and in April 2001 the military launched a fresh offensive which also failed. In July the LTTE launched a devastating attack on Sri Lanka's international airport in Colombo, which also serves as the main airbase. The high-profile attack, which destroyed several military planes and helicopters as well as five airlines of the national carrier, dominated world headlines for three days and sent the economy into freefall.

Amid Kumaratunga's continuing belligerence, the international community, through Norway, began to explore the possibility of talks between the LTTE and a new government headed by the main opposition UNP. The two sides came to an agreement whereby, were the UNP to come to power, it would hold talks with the LTTE, the basis of which would be an interim administration for the war-shattered north-east that would ensure the reset-tlement and rehabilitation of hundreds of thousands of displaced Tamils and otherwise restore normality. Discussion of a constitutional settlement, it was also agreed, would be deferred until this had advanced. Meanwhile, the vari-ous Tamil political parties, including some whose paramilitary wings were active in Sri Lanka's counter-insurgency, began to explore the idea of a coali-tion which would jointly advocate Tamil demands. The Tamil National Alliance (TNA) formed in late 2001, comprising the TULF, ACTC and the political factions of the EPRLF and TELO. In late 2001 Kumaratunga lost her parliamentary majority amid defections to the opposition, prompting early elections. The closely fought campaign produced a slim parliamentary majority for a UNP-led coalition which included Muslim and Upcountry Tamil parties and which LTTE openly encouraged Tamil voters outside the north-east to back. The TNA, contesting separately, swept the north-east (elections were not held in LTTE-controlled areas). In December the LTTE again announced a unilateral ceasefire, which the UNP government recipro-cated. The temporary truce was formalised into a Norwegian-mediated Ceasefire Agreement (CFA) signed in February 2002 by LTTE leader V. Pirapaharan and Prime Minister Ranil Wickremesinghe. Kumaratunga was unsupportive, but amid international plaudits could do little at this stage. Supervised by international monitors from several European countries, the CFA paved the way for the expansive peace process that followed.

Despite the emphasis on Norwegian-facilitated negotiations between the Wickremesinghe government and the LTTE, the internationally driven peace process was simply a continuation of extant Western patterns of involvement in Sri Lanka, but now in a more expanded, explicitly coordinated and high-profile way.[14] Overseen by a powerful quartet—the 'Co-Chairs'—of the United States, European Union, Japan and Norway (India was formally kept updated, but was largely not included), this intensified intervention com-prised several strands besides the formal talks: aggressive neo-liberal reform, development, rehabilitation, ending under-age recruitment, gender-related reform, and so on. The focus of attention, however, was inevitably on the six rounds of negotiations between the government and the LTTE, held in vari-ous international locations between September 2002 and March 2003, where the drama of peace played out through various 'breakthroughs' and 'setbacks'. However, the negotiations took place within an overarching liberal peace directionality that translated into securing and strengthening the UNP gov-ernment, and the state more broadly, as the key partner in the liberal peace transformation of Sri Lanka. First, the international community worked to reconstruct and substantially expand Sri Lanka's battle-worn military, pointedly overlooking its mono-ethnic character and rejecting the LTTE's argument that only military 'parity' between the two sides could sustain the stability of the peace process.[15] Second, the international community moved swiftly to stabilise and revive the war-shattered economy.[16] No sooner had the CFA been signed than donor aid began to flow in, turning into a flood after a landmark donor conference in Tokyo in June 2003 at which $4.5 billion was pledged, despite the talks having broken down two months earlier.[17]

Donors justified the massive aid inflow as necessary to generate a 'peace dividend' that would help sustain popular support for the peace process. The context, however, was the faltering of the UNP's electoral base amid intensifying Sinhala nationalist mobilisation, and anger at the soon felt pain of neo-liberal reform. As such, 'the bulk of the aid went into management of the economy and revival of the normal development process' and, except for a handful of projects, 'large-scale donor support did not materialize' for the north-east, where the war had largely been fought.[18] In great part this was due to a determination on the part of donors and development agencies that the LTTE and its de facto state structures should not be allowed to benefit from aid flowing into LTTE-controlled areas. While there was more flexibility after the December 2004 Indian Ocean tsunami devastated the island's northern, eastern and southern coastlines, particularly in relation to humanitarian assistance, this overriding concern continued to govern donors' developmental activity.

The Norwegian peace process was therefore driven in large part by international actors' conviction that the LTTE was uncommitted to 'peace' and therefore had to be prevented—coercively if necessary—from following its 'natural' instincts and returning to war.[19] This meant that 'progress' in the peace process came to be equated with the containment of the LTTE or the extent of its 'transformation' and was largely decoupled from the pressing need to address the existential problems of militarisation, large scale displacement and war related impoverishment in the Tamil speaking regions. In April 2003 the LTTE 'temporarily suspended' its participation, citing the government's continuing non-implementation of agreements reached in earlier rounds in the talks, as well as obligations set out in the CFA on demilitarisation of vast tracts of Tamil villages and the related resettlement of hundreds of thousands of displaced people, and disarming of pro-government paramilitaries.[20] At the same time, the LTTE reiterated its commitment to the ceasefire and argued that the basis for renewed talks should be, as agreed with the UNP in 2001, an interim administration for the north-east. Amid intensifying Sinhala nationalist agitation, in October 2003 the LTTE put forward its proposal for an Interim Self-Governing Authority (ISGA). The UNP agreed to renewed talks based on the ISGA, but Kumaratunga promptly exercised her presidential powers to seize control of several key ministries, crippling the government and the peace process; the Norwegians consequently suspended their facilitation.

In the 2004 parliamentary elections, the UNP government was toppled by an SLFP-led coalition of Sinhala nationalist parties that campaigned on explicit opposition to the peace process. With elections including LTTE-held areas, the TNA increased its number of parliamentary seats from fourteen to twenty-two. Just ahead of the elections, the LTTE's Eastern Commander, Colonel Karuna, split from the movement, and although the rebellion was put down after the elections, Karuna escaped to Colombo where his loyalists joined other paramilitaries working with the army. Although Norway resumed its shuttle diplomacy between the LTTE and the new government, a simmering 'shadow' war between the intelligence services of both sides began to intensify rapidly, with the paramilitaries targeting LTTE members, particular political cadres permitted under the CFA to work in government-controlled areas, and the LTTE targeting members of paramilitary groups and their political wings. Although the LTTE and the government continued to reiterate commitment to the CFA, the cycle of killings expanded to include Tamil nationalist activists, journalists and several TNA parliamentarians. International frustration was directed, however, solely at the LTTE, turning to outrage after the assassination of Sri Lankan Foreign Minister Lakshman Kadirgamar. In late 2005, presidential elections pitted UNP leader Wickremesinghe against the SLFP's Mahinda Rajapaksa (Kumaratunga's two terms were up). The LTTE, which had helped mobilise Tamil electoral support in favour of the UNP in the 2001 and 2004 parliamentary elections, declared its disenchantment with the UNP and called a boycott which it enforced in the Tamil-speaking areas. This further inflamed international hostility towards the LTTE, which was blamed for Rajapaksa's victory and Wickramasinghe's defeat.

Although Rajapaksa affirmed his support for the CFA, the 'shadow war' sharply escalated, and the now vastly expanded Sri Lankan military[21] prepared an all-out offensive against the LTTE. Another round of Norwegian-facilitated talks in February 2006 went nowhere. Three months later, Canada and the European Union both banned the LTTE as a terrorist organisation. The proscriptions were widely interpreted as a 'green light'[22] for the government to launch its military campaign, which began soon after. As Kumaratunga had done in the mid-1990s, Rajapaksa twinned the military offensive with a pledge to seek a constitutional solution and set up an All Party Representative Committee (APRC) to formulate one; the TNA, however, was not invited.[23] By the end of 2007, the military had recaptured LTTE-held areas in the east. As with the capture of Jaffna in 1995, the international community responded with developmental aid to consolidate the 'peace'.[24] Meanwhile, the military launched a massive offensive into LTTE-held Vanni. In a fairly predictable rerun of the 1990s' 'war for peace', initial international enthusiasm turned to alarm as it became clear that the war against the LTTE was turning into a mass slaughter of Tamil civilians. Despite the international community's repeated calls for restraint and the protection of civilians, as well as diplomatic efforts by Britain, France and the United States to bring about a temporary humanitarian ceasefire, the offensive and the mass killings continued. At the same time, Rajapaksa's earlier interest in constitutional models of ethnic accommodation quickly evaporated and was replaced by the assertion that with the defeat of the LTTE, there were no longer any minorities and therefore no more ethnic conflict to resolve.[25] The war ended in May 2009 with the destruction of the LTTE. As became increasingly clear since, at least 40,000 civilians were massacred in the final months.[26]

Sinhala Buddhist nationalism

Despite the powerful international efforts, in close cooperation with the state, to transform Sri Lanka into a liberal market democracy, the period from 1994 to the resumption of the war in 2006 saw both sustained Sinhala Buddhist nationalist mobilisation and further consolidation of Sinhala Buddhist order. This outcome rested on two interrelated tendencies. First, in Sri Lanka as elsewhere, the international community treated nationalist projects and sentiments as self-evidently marginal to mainstream politics and the preserve of 'fringe' actors: in the Tamil nationalist case, the LTTE; and in the Sinhala nationalist case, the JVP, and other small movements. The enduring and rarely questioned, let alone tested, assumption was that 'most' Sinhalese, Tamils and Muslims were desirous of a united, multi-ethnic and pluralist market democracy. Second, as discussed in Chapter 6, Sri Lanka's ruling and state elites simultaneously pursued politics along two contradictory tracks. In their international engagements they presented themselves as committed liberals, keen to advance the principles and modalities of the liberal peace and on this basis were thus treated by international actors as trusted partners in the process of liberal reform. Their domestic practices, however, were firmly governed by principles and politics of Sinhala majoritarianism. Key to deferring the inevitable confrontation between the liberal peace and Sinhala Buddhist nationalist projects was their separate but overlapping focuses on defeating the LTTE and ending the armed conflict. Yet, the explicit international demand for some measure of Tamil autonomy—through devolution of federalism—inevitably sustained ongoing Sinhala nationalist counter-mobilisation.[27] This manifested at key moments in vacillations on liberal reform by mainstream Sinhala leaders; powerful political interventions by the Buddhist clergy; mass protests and agitation; the rise of explicitly nationalist parties such as the JVP and newly formed JHU (Jathika Hela Urumaya); and a growing popular hostility towards the (Western) international community.[28]

Whilst largely ignored or discounted by the international community, the tension between liberal peace and Sinhala nationalism was readily apparent from the mid-1990s. There was fierce Sinhala nationalist resistance to Kumaratunga's devolution package, even though it was twinned with a military onslaught in the Tamil-speaking areas. The UNP opposed it; the Buddhist clergy denounced it, with two senior monks writing to every Sinhala Buddhist parliamentarian urging them to oppose 'handing over the country to minorities'; and mass protests erupted.[29] Indeed, the period from 1995 throughout the Norwegian-led peace process to the 2006 start of President Rajapapksa's renewed war against the LTTE was one of incessant Sinhala nationalist agitation and mass protests, often led by large numbers of Buddhist monks. The protests were against, variously, the 1995 devolution package, the 2002 Ceasefire Agreement, the 2002 Oslo Declaration, the LTTE's ISGA proposal in 2003, the 2005 LTTE–GoSL post-tsunami aid-sharing agreement (PTOMS), the Norwegian peace facilitators, and so on. These episodes of mass mobilisation against power-sharing, 'concessions' to Tamil demands, especially from the LTTE, and international peace intervention generally were reinforced by the related criticisms and warnings from Sri Lanka's powerful Buddhist orders, who are key underwriters of Sinhala political legitimacy.[30] An important dimension of the Sinhala nationalist mobilisation, especially with the advent of Norwegian facilitation and the peace process itself, was a growing hostility to the (largely Western) international community, which manifested most in vicious and at times histrionic denouncements of Norway, but also of international NGOs, especially those working on peace-building (for example, the Berghof Foundation), as well as their local allies (for example, the Centre for Policy Alternatives).[31]

The growth of Sinhala nationalist mobilisation in the late 1990s and during the peace process is exemplified in the electoral growth of the JVP, which had transformed itself into a political party following the violent crushing of its second insurgency (1987–9): in its first election in 1994 the JVP secured just one seat, but in 2000 secured ten seats, sixteen in 2001, and forty in 2004. The 2004 tally resulted in part from the JVP's alliance with the victorious SLFP on a joint platform of explicit opposition to the peace process.[32] In mid-2005 the JVP quit the ruling coalition in protest at the government's signing, at the international community's behest, the PTOMS aid-sharing agreement with the LTTE. The JVP also filed a Supreme Court challenge to the PTOMS, which rendered the agreement inoperative even before it was ruled illegal, and later that year threw its weight behind Rajapaksa's successful campaign for the presidency. Similarly, in early 2004, a new radical party the JHU (led by Buddhist monks) was formed, and in the election just two months later, the JHU secured nine seats and 6 per cent of the vote.[33]

Nonetheless, the intensity of Sinhala nationalist mobilisation against the peace process, the notion of power-sharing, and international liberal peace actors did not undermine international confidence in the possibility of exter-nally-assisted, state-led liberal reform or its efficacy in addressing Tamil 'griev-ances'. This was in great part because the international community could always find Sinhala and Tamil political elites who were willing both to engage in the modalities of liberal peace-building, deploying the ethnically neutral discourses of liberalism, democracy and development, and to reassure the international community of the actuality of a multi-ethnic majority desirous of this end. This was particularly marked in the first years after 1994. Although Kumaratunga's government, along with an emergent host of 'local' donor-funded, liberal peace-themed NGOs, championed Sri Lanka's 'vibrant' and 'ethnically inclusive' democracy whilst deriding the LTTE's 'ethno-national-ism' and its aspiration for a 'mono-ethnic' state, they projected Sinhala nation-alism as both the preserve of the political fringe and yet, at the same time, as another constraint (besides the LTTE and its violence) on the process of lib-eral peace reform. International confidence in Kumaratunga's, and later Wickremesinghe's governments was also fuelled by the support they received from Tamil political parties. In competing with the LTTE for the political leadership of the Tamils, these parties, including the TULF and the former militant groups, projected themselves as the 'moderate', 'democratically elected' and thus authentic/legitimate representatives (see below), and gave vital assurances to the international community—often in private rather than in public—of their confidence in Kumaratunga's and successive Sinhala elites' sincerity in seeking an equitable solution to the Tamil question.

Yet, the brittleness of Sinhala political elites' commitments to liberal peace was evidenced by the ease with which they entered into or abandoned such commitments when political circumstances changed. For example, the Kumaratunga government's devolution proposals, unveiled just after the talks with the LTTE broke down, were intended to 'redefine the constitutional foundation of a plural society',[34] and indeed in her international forays, the President spoke of her commitment to a 'wide devolution of power' as well as the principles of 'unity, equality and brotherhood'.[35] Yet even before the package was formally released, the President and the Justice Minister visited the Maha Nayakas of Asgiriya and Malwatte, the high-priests of the two most influential chapters of the Sangha, to reassure them of its contents and that it would not be implemented until the war against the LTTE was completed.[36] Having successfully captured the Jaffna peninsula from the LTTE in late 1995, Kumaratunga participated in a 'medieval' victory ceremony that was broadcast live on state television, in which she received a scroll from her deputy defence minister that was dated 'full moon day of the month of Uduwap in the year 2939 in the Buddhist era' and congratulating her on the extension of her rule to 'Yapa Putunua', the name for Jaffna used in Sinhala Buddhist chronicles.[37] The devolution proposals were watered down to appease Sinhala nationalist sentiment and finally discarded after they failed to secure parliamentary approval in August 2000. When the UNP took power in late 2001, Kumaratunga became a brooding and malevolent shadow over the unfolding peace process, and eschewing her earlier persona as a champion of liberal peace, adopted that of defender of Sinhala Buddhist order, exemplified in her surprise 2003 'coup' that crippled the UNP government and paved the way for her nationalist coalition (with the JVP) to regain power in 2004.

For its part, the UNP contributed to the Sinhala nationalist resistance which led to the watering down[38] of Kumaratunga's devolution proposals, but sensing international disillusionment with Kumaratunga and an opportunity to return to government, embraced a platform of peace and negotiations with the LTTE in campaigning for the 2001 elections.[39] After the UNP also lost the 2005 presidential elections, several of its parliamentarians, including, G. L. Peiris and Milinda Moragoda, its two lead negotiators in the Norwegian-mediated talks with the LTTE defected to Rajapaksa's SLFP-led government in 2006 and 2007. Pieris and Moragoda were widely celebrated by international actors, and their commitment to the liberal project was unquestioned.

Pieris in particular was heralded for his role in securing the Oslo Declaration with the LTTE, which committed both parties to 'exploring federalism' as a solution to the ethnic conflict. However, upon defecting to the Rajapaksa government, Pieris soon became a vocal opponent of federalism and power-sharing whilst advocating the military defeat of the LTTE. In 2010 Rajapaksa appointed him External Affairs Minister, a role in which he fronted Sri Lanka's diplomatic resistance to post-war liberal peace demands for account-ability for the wartime mass atrocities, demilitarisation of the north-east and a political solution to the Tamil question. The UNP's position on these key issues has also not been that different to that of the Rajapaksa administration. From the onset of the war it was silent on the unfolding mass atrocities and humanitarian crises that marked the offensive into LTTE-controlled areas, and did not protest at the post-war mass internment and abuse of Tamil civil-ians in military-run camps. Since the end of the war it has also not supported growing Tamil and international demands for demilitarisation of the north-east, whilst opposing calls for a credible investigation and accountability mechanism for wartime atrocities.[40]

Sinhala leaders' varying commitments to liberal reform and an equitable solution to the Tamil question were directly linked to the asymmetry in inter-national interventions that focused on the LTTE as the primary obstacle to liberal progress. Consequently, so long as the war was ongoing and the LTTE remained powerful, Sinhala leaders did not have to translate their liberal pledges—for example, on devolution or demilitarisation—into concrete action. For example, the LTTE's rejection of Kumaratunga's devolution pack-age need not have precluded in any way its implementation. Furthermore, the LTTE's rejection aside, the proposals were substantially watered down because of Sinhala nationalist resistance. The absence of any substantial move towards ethnically inclusive constitutional and political reform in the post-LTTE era[41] lays bare the real, if rarely discussed, obstacle to liberal reform: the long estab-lished and politically dominant Sinhala Buddhist antipathy to any form of autonomy for the Tamils as a vital threat to the Sinhala Buddhists' identity and their historically granted right to dominate the island's state and society. Thus while Kumaratunga's electoral victory in 1994 and Wickremesinghe's in 2001 were widely claimed as indicative of a popular desire for a liberal, multi-ethnic peace, the explanation for these results lies elsewhere. The 1994 result repre-sented a Sinhala turn away from the authoritarianism of seventeen years of UNP rule, and especially the savage brutality of Premadasa's counter-insur-gency against the JVP. The UNP's slim parliamentary majority in 2001 relied on coalitions with Muslim and Upcountry Tamil parties and, crucially, a split in the Sinhala vote between the hard-line SLFP and JVP. In sum, Sinhala Buddhist nationalist mobilisation was largely untrammelled by international interventions and from the mid-1990s inexorably expanded through electoral politics and mass mobilisation that systematically undermined and thwarted all attempts to advance the liberal peace, with the exception of some neo-liberal economic reforms.

Tamil nationalism

The post-Cold War era posed particularly hostile conditions for Tamil nationalist politics. Centred on the territorial state as the foundational container, and vehicle, for liberal reform, the liberal peace aggressively opposed demands for (sub-state) territorial nationhood as manifestations of exclusivist ethnonationalism, and armed non-state challengers to the state as the foremost threats to the progress, if not possibility, of liberal reform. In Sri Lanka, these came together in powerful international efforts to confront both the LTTE ('terrorism') and 'its' political project of territorial nationhood and independent statehood (that is, a 'mono-ethnic' state). Yet, the post-Cold War period has been one of dramatic expansion of both Tamil nationalist politics and, until the final phase of the war, the LTTE. Key to this were the LTTE's dramatic military success at the turn of the century and the ensuing Norwegian-led peace process, which together radically transformed the domestic and international contexts in which Tamil nationalist mobilisation took place. First, they propelled the LTTE firmly to the front of both Tamil politics and international efforts to manage Sri Lanka's crisis. Second, the peace process provided crucial, albeit temporary, respite from the high-intensity war ravaging the Tamil-speaking areas and opened up space for a range of mobilising processes in the island and in the diaspora, as well as the expansion of connections between them.

This is not to suggest that Tamil nationalism was some latent or innate tendency unleashed by the cessation of hostilities. Nor did the LTTE's military success or its prominent role in the Norwegian-led peace process spontaneously produce nationalist mobilisation. Rather, it is to argue that the peace process opened up space, albeit with powerful constraints and obstacles, in which the LTTE and diverse other Tamil actors pursued a range of practices and processes, or poles of activity, that effectively reproduced a Tamil national identity and generated a broad nationalist movement spanning the north-east and diaspora centres and focused on the principle of territorial nationhood. These interwoven clusters of activity, discussed briefly below, included: the growth of web-based and broadcast media in Tamil and English; the expanding structures and services of the LTTE-run de facto state; the 'Pongu Thamil' mass rallies; and the unification of fragmented political parties into the Tamil Nationalist Alliance (TNA). It is important to note that except for the de facto state, these clusters of activity were not critically dependent on the LTTE and its material resources, nor were they connected to the LTTE by clear command-and-control relations or simple extensions of its overlapping state-building/war-fighting networks. Rather, the momentum of nationalist mobilisation relied on the actions of diverse Tamil actors at various removes from the LTTE, and were closely tied to and heavily conditioned by specific social and political dynamics in various parts of the north-east and diaspora centres.

Media and the national public space

The 'war for peace' was not only a question of material violence, but also a struggle for representation, not only of battlefield events, but of the wider politics of the ethnic question. From the outset of its military campaign, the Kumaratunga administration, more effectively than its predecessors, restricted media access to the war zones and LTTE-controlled areas. All international media—including the news agencies, Reuters, Associated Press, Agence France Press, etc.—were either established in or operated from the capital, Colombo. The government also had effective control over local media, both the expansive state media and private media. When this later proved insufficient, the government imposed formal censorship, with all war-related copy having to be first submitted for the military's approval.[42] Nonetheless, the government, and the state more generally, enjoyed both a great deal of international credibility and considerable ease in projecting its messages to international audiences. Consequently, reporting on the war and related politics drew more or less explicitly on, and reproduced, dominant academic and policy tropes of the liberal peace, with the LTTE and its armed struggle framed exclusively in depoliticised and decontextualised terms of ruthless violence, suicide bombings, child soldiers, and so on, and the government as striving to pursue liberal reform and ethnic accommodation. The government was also able to direct and shape reporting in key Tamil diaspora outlets. For example, the news on the lone Tamil radio broadcast in London in the mid-1990s, a slot on the popular multi-lingual *Sunrise Radio*, came direct from the paramilitary PLOTE's offices in northern Sri Lanka, and the *Tamil Times* monthly, then the sole English language diaspora publication, took an actively anti-LTTE editorial line and was funded by advertisements from businesses with ties to the Sri Lankan state.

However, from the mid-1990s, Tamil nationalists in the diaspora sought to establish Tamil-language radio and satellite television stations, as well as Tamil- and English-language publications and websites that gradually became able to provide near instantaneous alternative coverage of political and military developments in the north-east. Global technological developments, such as the emergence of relatively low-cost satellite communications and, especially, the rapid expansion of the World Wide Web, provided novel opportunities, but Tamil nationalists actively sought these out in an explicit, and successful, bid to overcome and disrupt what they perceived as Sri Lanka's domination of information flows and the detrimental effects this was having on their efforts to mobilise Tamil and international support. In London, for example, diaspora Tamils, working more or less closely with the LTTE's International Secretariat, launched the IBC radio station, the TTN satellite channel and publications such as the *Tamil Guardian*. These were later joined by a range of commercially-motivated diaspora-based media enterprises. The predominantly Tamil-language websites, radio and television stations that appeared during this period drew on material directly from a variety of sources in both government and LTTE-controlled areas in the north-east, and transmitted via satellite phones and email. The advent of the ceasefire and peace process greatly opened up access and connections to the homeland, enabling daily coverage of political developments and major issues of concern. At the same time, the improved security climate following the ceasefire, the lifting of censorship and the de-proscription of the LTTE encouraged independent Tamil media in Sri Lanka—such as the *Uthayan* and *Virakesari* newspapers— to be more critical of the government and report freely on Tamil nationalist politics, including covering the LTTE's views. The cumulative effect of these diverse media was both to cater to and to create a new 'national' public space in which developments relating to the LTTE, its de facto state institutions, the TNA and other Tamil nationalist actors had prominence.

Arguably the most important outlet for Tamil media throughout the war and its aftermath was TamilNet, an English language news website launched in mid-1997.[43] Envisioned from the outset as a news agency, and updating throughout the day with prompt and detailed reports by a network of correspondents working at considerable risk 'on the ground', TamilNet successfully cut through Sri Lanka's censorship and other restrictions and brought to the fore the conditions of violent state repression, high-intensity conflict and mass displacement in the north-east[44] that contrasted sharply with the government's narrative of development, peace and progress in areas 'cleared' of the LTTE. Easily accessible, especially to second-generation diaspora members who were not reached by the Tamil-language media, TamilNet also soon drew an international audience, including the liberal peace policy nexus around Sri Lanka, while also becoming a key source for much of the rest of the diaspora media. This agenda-setting information flow not only responded immediately to military, political and other developments in Sri Lanka, thereby undermining the government-led narratives, but also—implicitly, rather than explicitly—framed the conflict in terms of state oppression and Tamil national resistance. Although widely denounced as 'pro-LTTE', TamilNet was nevertheless widely and avidly read, in great part because it soon earned a reputation for accuracy.[45] The 24-hour information flow by proliferating and competing diaspora-based media also connected Tamils in the various diaspora centres to the north-east, which, as the following section discusses, proved crucial to the mass mobilisation in the final months of the war.

Pongu Thamil: the return of mass action

A crucial modality of popular Tamil nationalist mobilisation during the peace process was the 'Pongu Thamil' mass rally. For the first time since the Indian intervention and public protests against the Indo-Sri Lanka Accord, there were Tamil nationalist mass demonstrations across the north-east, and later in all major diaspora centres. Occurring in waves and sometimes alone, and held in every district in the north-east as well as every major diaspora centre, these mass public events steadily grew in scale and political significance, with each event building momentum into the next. Hundreds of thousands of Tamils across the north-east, and similar numbers across the diaspora, attended the rallies, which were organised by Tamil student and political activists, and later LTTE political cadres, as well as, significantly, by a broad range of societal groups such as trader associations, teachers' unions, fishermen's societies, churches, etc., which in past eras had kept a distance from nationalist politics and the LTTE. Tying together a range of specific and local grievances (for example, the continued military occupation of vast tracts of residential and farming land, restrictions on fishing, discrimination in state employment, human rights abuses, etc.) with broader demands related to the peace process (for example, demands for an interim administration in the north-east, the disarming of army-backed paramilitaries, etc.), and framing these in terms of state oppression and Tamil national resistance, the rallies also explicitly affirmed territorial nationhood as the foundation for resolving the ethnic question.

The first Pongu Thamil event was organised in Jaffna in early 2001, amid the ongoing war, by Jaffna University students and other civil society activists, who coined the name (literally, 'Tamil Upsurge'), thereby pointedly framing the planned rally as an act of popular resistance to the military occupation.[46] The principal aim of the rally was to demand that the government reciprocate the LTTE's unilateral ceasefire, but in doing so it also reaffirmed the principles of Tamil nation, homeland and self-determination. Despite military threats, arrests and disruptions, the event on 17 January drew an astounding ten thousand participants. Though envisaged as a singular event, it prompted Tamil students in Batticaloa and Vavuniya to stage their own, albeit smaller, rallies in February. The demonstrated political potency of the event—and the name—was not missed by Tamil nationalists, and by following the CFA, Pongu Thamil rallies became a key way of intensifying mass mobilisation. (For example, in Jaffna, subsequent Pongu Thamil events drew 60,000 people in 2002, 150,000 in 2003 and 200,000 in 2005.)[47] Staged in sequence across each district in the Tamil homeland, and later each major diaspora centre, the Pongu Thamil rallies in and of themselves became markers of national identity and territorial nationhood.[48] Extensively covered by Tamil media in Sri Lanka and the diaspora—although absent from international media coverage—the events were endorsed by Tamil societal figures, such as university and school heads, senior church leaders, etc. and provided indispensable public platforms both in the north-east and in the diaspora for the TNA and the LTTE's Political Wing, amidst nationalist-themed cultural performances and speeches by local campaigners and figures. Meanwhile, quite apart from the spectacular rallies themselves, the organising of each event was productive of nationalist mobilisation. At each location, the collective efforts of student and political activists, LTTE political cadres (permitted to work in government-controlled areas under the CFA), Tamil politicians, civil servants and, in particular, a range of societal groups generated networks of activism that reached deep and wide into the public, while also generating localised struggle against the military authorities. While many of these activists were subsequently assassinated during the 'shadow war' of 2005–6 in an attempt to eliminate the threat of mass protest and rallies in the north-east, the processes of mobilisation entailed in the Pongu Thamil continue to have effects in the post-war era.

With their polemical speeches, cultural performances, slogans and nationalist livery, later including outsized cut-outs of LTTE leader V. Pirapaharan, the mass and emotive nationalism of Pongu Thamil was clearly at odds with the cosmopolitan ideals and individualist ethos of liberal peace. Thus, although organised and widely understood by participants as demonstrations to the international community of popular Tamil sentiment, and despite their growing scale and political significance, the rallies were derided and dismissed by international actors and Sri Lankan officials as being coercively engineered by the LTTE and not an authentic expression of Tamil sentiment. Yet, this sneering did not alter the growing momentum of Tamil nationalist mobilisation, and moreover it forcefully underscored international actors' blindness to the stark disconnect between the 'high politics' of negotiation, federalism and Norwegian mediation 'progress', on the one hand, and, on the other, the enduring day-to-day crises of mass displacement, military repression and government restrictions on livelihoods, which were mobilising mass attendances. As such, whilst failing to move international attitudes or policies, by foregrounding clear and enduring political messages, successfully generating high levels of mass participation and at the same time, co-opting a diverse array of Tamil societal groups, actors and figures, Pongu Thamil was successful at building and projecting a sense of 'nation-ness' and a national public space in which Tamil politics became inescapably located.

TNA: unity and ambiguity

The moment of possibility and heightened expectation of a negotiated solution that followed the LTTE's military successes and Norway's formal entry as peace facilitator at the turn of the century brought about a consolidation of Tamil parliamentary politics and a fresh sense of purpose and direction that had not been seen since the heyday of the late 1970s and the formation of the TULF. In the run-up to the 2001 parliamentary elections, the need for a common electoral platform to articulate Tamil demands and aspirations began to be openly discussed by Tamil journalists, activists and some of the parties. Fractious talks began amongst some of the groups, including the TULF, the older ACTC and political wings of some paramilitary groups. All of the groups, except the ACTC, had hitherto been hostile to the LTTE and supportive of Kumaratunga's government and the 'war for peace'. While the paramilitary groups were integral to the military's lethal counter-insurgency, their political wings and the TULF supported the government in parliament and had long provided invaluable endorsement of its liberal, pluralist claims. Yet, tellingly, none of the groups had publicly renounced their core Tamil nationalist commitments, nor changed their names to remove references to Eelam or the liberation struggle. Instead, they justified their opposition to the LTTE on the basis of its continued adherence to armed struggle and the eminent possibility of a lasting solution through negotiations between Tamil leaders (themselves) and Sinhalese leaders. However, the LTTE's dramatic military comeback and its emerging role as the key Tamil actor in internationally mediated negotiations, along with simmering anger at the military repression inherent to the 'war for peace', had created a palpably growing momentum in the Tamil electorate for unity behind the LTTE which was difficult to ignore.

The negotiations led to the formation of the TNA in late 2001, as a joint vehicle to contest the upcoming elections, comprising the TULF, the ACTC and politically dominant factions of the EPRLF and TELO. (The other factions of the two and the other paramilitary groups opted to ally implicitly or explicitly with Kumaratunga.) The alliance's common manifesto endorsed the LTTE as the sole representative of the Tamil people, set out a series of Tamil demands, and reiterated territorial nationhood and self-determination as the basis of an acceptable negotiated solution.[49] The TNA's subsequent sweeping victory in the north-east was, however, no foregone conclusion, not least as the utility of Tamil representation in Sri Lanka's parliament had since become questionable. Instead, the campaigning positioned the TNA as an embodiment of Tamil nationalist sentiment and urged voters to telegraph to the international community their clear endorsement of the manifesto. The campaign was supported by the Tamil media, the LTTE and a range of other Tamil nationalist activists and organisations. This was crucial as the TNA's own organisation infrastructure was weak, patchy and fragmented: on their own, each of its constituents could generate localised pockets of support that were tied to individual leaders and their personal networks of loyalty and patronage. In contrast to the Federal Party in the pre-militancy era of Tamil nationalist politics, none of the party machines could extend across the north-east and they were incapable of generating mass participation either singly or even collectively. Yet the TNA's electoral victory, repeated in 2004, was significant as, for the first time since 1977, Tamils across the north-east endorsed one unified nationalist party, and one that made explicit its support for the LTTE.

Despite its historic significance in unifying Tamil parliamentary politics, the TNA played an ambiguous role during the peace process. The widespread expectation, and assumption, was that the TNA's overwhelming electoral success would reinforce the LTTE's international credibility and strengthen its hand in the negotiations. Certainly this was the message which the TNA repeatedly asserted on election platforms and other public fora. However, in their interactions with the international community, many of its leaders routinely expressed misgivings and criticisms of the LTTE.[50] A gap between public commitments and private positions is, of course, a normal part of successful mass movements that pull together diverse actors with a variety of motivations.[51] However, amid the ongoing international efforts to marginalise the LTTE, the TNA leaders' privately expressed views to international actors were hugely consequential. Given their sweeping mandate from the Tamil electorate, the TNA had enormous credibility in the liberal peace nexus around Sri Lanka, and its senior leaders were taken seriously by international actors. Yet the message of unity on Tamil nationalist principles and the LTTE that made up this mandate was repeatedly contradicted by the TNA leadership's routine drawing of a contrast between themselves as democratically elected 'moderates', and the LTTE as armed 'extremists', critically undermining both the LTTE and the Tamil nationalist project. In the aftermath of the war, many in the TNA and in the international community assumed it would replace the LTTE as the apex of Tamil leadership. However, as the following section discusses, post-LTTE politics has developed in unexpected ways and the TNA is perhaps more constrained by the legacy of the LTTE-led mobilisation than it was by the LTTE itself.

LTTE's de facto state: connecting the nation

The LTTE's de facto state institutions expanded rapidly following the ceasefire agreement of 2002 and the advent of the Norwegian-led peace process.[52] As noted above, the de facto state was at once a system of civil administration, a vehicle for the LTTE's social reform agenda and, equally importantly, a political project that gave tangible form to the aspiration for national self-determination and sovereign statehood. This is exemplified in how from 2002 the processes and practices of state-building and governance in Vanni mobilised large numbers of diaspora Tamils in the routine provision of a range of public works, and in so doing advanced the consolidation of a new 'national' public space.[53]

For much of the twentieth century the fairly nondescript towns and villages of the Vanni were marginal to Tamil nationalist politics, but from the turn of the century they became central. The LTTE's headquarters and the administrative centre of the de facto state were located in Kilinochchi, the region's sole large town (with much of the rest of the population located in a wide network of villages centred on Mullaitivu township). The epicentre of the war for five years, and ravaged by economic blockade and mass displacement, the region's humanitarian needs were enormous in 2002, and made much worse by the tsunami in December 2004. The brief interlude in the armed conflict created by the ceasefire and the peace process opened up Vanni and space for diaspora engagement in diverse efforts to provide humanitarian relief and public goods, such as health, development, rehabilitation, education, vocational (including computer skills) training and so on, as well as employment in these projects. From 2002 large numbers of expatriates either travelled to Vanni to undertake public works directly, often establishing local institutions, or provided funding, expertise and organisational support through an expanding array of diaspora-based charitable and professional organisations. Many of these institutions were long established and already involved in supporting schools, villages, orphanages, clinics and so on, especially in Jaffna (from where many first-generation diaspora members originate), but also other parts of the north-east. After 2002, many of these began to prioritise the Vanni in their projects, as the expanding diaspora media, catering to a Tamil 'national' public, routinely covered both the needs there and other diaspora efforts to alleviate them. At the same time, the LTTE institutions and affiliated organisations in the diaspora actively sought to encourage Tamil expatriate participation, through public appeals and logistical assistance.

Whilst these diaspora activities were undertaken under the aegis of the LTTE's de facto state, what is notable is how the latter institutions sought to foster and facilitate, rather than manage, the various diaspora interventions. The cumulative effect, therefore, was to connect Tamils abroad with Tamils 'on the ground' through myriad autonomous activities that came to constitute both state-building and governance on the one hand, and the constitution of a Tamil national identity on the other. This was exemplified in how diaspora charities, in deciding where to direct their energies, prioritised where homeland Tamils' needs were greater, rather than, as in the past, simply focusing on specific locales to which they had ancestral connections. In that sense, a key aspect of the diaspora–local connections during the peace process was participation of second-generation diaspora members. For many young Tamils who travelled to the north-east to participate in humanitarian work, for ideological reasons or simply out of curiosity, their first connection or reconnection to the homeland was framed by a national space, wherein Kilinochchi and Mullaitivu had as much significance as Jaffna had to an earlier generation of young Tamils. Meanwhile the media-driven emergence during the peace process of a 'national' public space in which the LTTE, its de facto state institutions, the TNA and other Tamil nationalist actors were central, gave them a standing and visibility that soon rivalled and exceeded that of established cultural, religious and professional associations and figures in the diaspora. Consequently, for the latter (temples, Tamil schools, professional associations, past pupil associations, etc.), active and visible participation in the 'national' project became essential to retaining their standing in this new Tamil public space. Thus, while diaspora contributions to humanitarian and developmental work in the Vanni had important material consequences, they also had equally important, more intangible consequences, including instilling a deep-seated nationalist sensibility that has survived the violent destruction of the LTTE and the de facto state to give powerful shape to Tamil diaspora politics in the post-war era.

Conclusion

The post-Cold War period of armed conflict in Sri Lanka was characterised by both intensified and protracted interventions to generate liberal peace in the country, and yet the steady expansion of the Sinhala Buddhist and Tamil nationalist projects. The failure of the liberal peace project can be traced to international actors' tendency to reduce the persistence of ethnic crisis in Sri Lanka to the LTTE and its armed struggle and, simultaneously, to treat nationalism as a politically marginal phenomenon and the preserve of fringe actors, such as the LTTE and the JVP. The ideal of a multi-ethnic majority desirous of an inclusive and equitable liberal state underpinned the international community's confidence that the surest route to the liberal peace was through processes that would strengthen the Sri Lankan state whilst containing or destroying the LTTE. Sinhala and Tamil leaders recognised these prevailing international logics and for different reasons sustained international confidence in a multi-ethnic majority as well as the imminent possibility of liberal reform once the threat of 'extremist' nationalist actors was contained. Yet, both sets of elites remained reliant on increasingly nationalist publics for their continued political legitimacy, leading to persistent contradictions, ambiguity and vacillations between their expressed commitments to liberal principles on the one hand, and nationalist ones on the other. Moreover, as in the Cold War era, both Sinhala Buddhist and Tamil nationalist mobilisations were deeply shaped and conditioned by liberal peace interventions themselves.

Sinhala Buddhist mobilisation between 1994 and 2009 was centred on defending the majoritarian state and social order against international pressure for the accommodation of Tamils. It generated a powerful popular base that propelled Mahinda Rajapaksa to political power and legitimised his authoritarian, militarist and nationalist government. These events have consolidated a Sinhala electoral majority that is hostile to Tamil autonomy and supportive of ongoing militarisation and repression as a legitimate means of keeping Tamil political mobilisation in check. Meanwhile Tamil nationalist mobilisation centred on seeking international support for the principles of territorialised nationhood and national self-determination (as opposed to ethnically neutral territorial power-sharing). Although it failed to secure its objectives, it generated a deep-seated national identity which has become the touchstone of political legitimacy, as well as new capacities, practices and orientations that have made possible an intensified engagement between the Tamil nationalist project and the global complexes of liberal peace in the post-war era. The wider context for this, as the next chapter discusses, is the rapid coming to the fore, following the destruction of the LTTE, of the radical disjuncture between liberal peace and Sri Lanka's Sinhala Buddhist nationalist state and social order.

8

TAMIL NATIONALISM TODAY

Introduction

Since the end of Sri Lanka's war, there have been three interrelated and historically significant shifts in the international politics of the island's ongoing ethnic conflict. First, with the defeat and destruction of the LTTE, Tamil nationalism has lost its long-standing link with a single and dominant apex organisation, which began six decades previously with the Federal Party, and has become instead a globalised movement with a centre of gravity in the West-based diaspora. Tamil nationalist identity is now sustained by a transnational network of organisations that are bound by an overarching directionality, rather than a centralised decision-making body. Second, and for the first time since Sri Lanka's independence and certainly since the armed conflict began, Tamil nationalists are finding themselves loosely aligned with, rather than against, the forces and processes of international liberal order-making. This important realignment first emerged in the final months of the war when the long-standing contradiction between the Sinhala Buddhist order and international demands for liberal reform came to the fore and international opinion began to turn decisively against Sri Lanka and its treatment of the Tamils. The Sri Lankan state is no longer the trusted agent and partner of liberal reform, and a powerful nexus of international actors have sought to mobilise international support for more forceful intervention to secure an ethnically inclusive liberal state (reconciliation) and justice for wartime atrocities (accountability). Third, in a unique development in the post-independence history of the two Tamil-speaking regions, Tamil Nadu actors have worked independently of, and at odds with, Indian foreign policy to mobilise international action in support of Sri Lankan Tamil nationalist demands. But, importantly, this growing conflict over foreign policy has not unsettled political relations between Tamil Nadu and the Indian state; indeed, Tamil Nadu actors make demands of Delhi in the firm expectation that Indian policy should be accountable to them as Indians. It is therefore the maturity and stability of Tamil accommodation in India that allows Tamil Nadu to play an active role in Sri Lanka's conflict, just as relations in the island between the state and the Tamil population have been reduced to brute force alone. These various shifts have together transported Sri Lanka's ethnic conflict onto an internationalised plane of contestation, which now unavoidably includes the Tamil diaspora and Tamil Nadu.

This chapter discusses these important developments as the contemporary dynamics of a century-long processes of political contestation and identity formation on both sides of the Palk Strait. The first section details the growing contradictions and conflicts between continuing international pursuit of liberal reform and the reality of Sri Lanka's Sinhala Buddhist domestic order: the very context that has spurred the internationalisation of Sri Lanka's ethnic conflict and the growing prominence in it of the Tamil diaspora and Tamil Nadu. The second section discusses the networked form of Sri Lankan Tamil nationalism that has emerged since the end of the war and shows how it has become embedded in the capillaries of liberal peace engagement in Sri Lanka. It links this to the patterns and processes of Tamil nationalist politics that were established during the armed conflict and also discusses the awkward positioning of the Tamil National Alliance (TNA) on this new international plane of contestation. The final section examines the dynamics of Tamil Nadu's now prominent role in Sri Lanka's ethnic conflict.

Post-war Sri Lanka and liberal peace

The contradiction between Sinhala Buddhist nationalism and the liberal peace began to emerge in the final months of the war as Sri Lanka continued its high-intensity assault on the remaining enclaves of LTTE-controlled territory even after it became clear that the LTTE no longer posed a plausible military threat. From late 2008, after the military had recaptured Kilinochchi, the capital of the de facto state, the international community began to press for restraint and a negotiated surrender to end the war, and also a political solution to the ethnic question. Rejecting these calls, Sri Lanka instead stepped up its offensive. International concern turned to alarm as the war against the LTTE turned in early 2009 into the relentless artillery and aerial bombardment of an ever-shrinking territory packed with Tamil civilians. Even the 'no fire zones' declared by the government as sanctuaries for civilians became targets of sustained bombardment, while international calls for humanitarian access and a temporary ceasefire were bluntly rejected.[1] Amid growing international media coverage of large-scale civilian casualties and attacks on hospitals and food distribution centres, Western states became more vocal. First US Secretary of State Hillary Clinton and then newly elected President Barack Obama called for an end to attacks on civilians. The foreign ministers of Britain and France travelled to Sri Lanka to appeal to the Rajapaksa government directly. Sri Lanka furiously rebuffed these demands and vigorously continued its offensive. When the war finally ended on 18 May, Sri Lanka's long-standing allies in the war against the LTTE expressed relief rather than jubilation, and prioritised the quick rehabilitation and resettlement of the shattered Vanni population. At the same time, international rights groups began demanding an investigation into the mass-scale killing of civilians, the beginning of what would inexorably become the defining fault line between Sri Lanka and the Western international community. As such, though the significance would only become clear later, the events of early 2009 marked the beginning of a decisive break between international liberal order-making and the Sinhala Buddhist project, wherein long-held international assumptions about Sri Lanka as basically a 'good' liberal state confronting an implacable terrorist threat broke down.[2]

In the immediate aftermath of the war, Sri Lanka rebuffed international calls for rapid rehabilitation and resettlement, and interned the entire surviving Vanni population in military-run camps to which international aid agencies had restricted and supervised access. The government defended the mass internment as necessary to identify and capture LTTE cadres, but persistent accounts soon began to appear of squalid overcrowding, disappearances, torture and rape. The UN refused to continue funding for the camps, and after sustained international pressure, in late 2009 the government began gradually releasing the population. But international attitudes had begun to harden. For example, in early 2010 the EU reluctantly suspended Sri Lanka's preferential access to trade concessions, citing post-war rights abuses. In the following years, quite apart from the question of accountability for the wartime mass atrocities, the contradiction between Sinhala Buddhist nationalism and the construction of a liberal order and peace has manifested itself over post-war issues. The international community envisioned the post-war period as necessarily one that prioritised resettlement, rehabilitation and development, with a focus on reviving the former war zones as well as a political solution that provided political autonomy for the Tamil-speaking areas. In stark contrast to these expectations of liberal reform, Sri Lanka has actually pursued an expansive strategy of militarisation and state-sponsored Sinhalisation[3] in the Tamil-speaking regions, while ignoring the TNA's persistent pleas for talks.

Despite the end of the war, the defence budget has increased each year sustaining the mono-ethnic military, the bulk of which is deployed in the north-east, dominating civil administration, economic activity and, through an expansive system of surveillance spreading fear and mistrust in social and political life.[4] Whilst constraining political and civil society activism and the possibility of popular mobilisation through its blanket presence, the military and allied business interests have embarked on a range of economic activities (in tourism, food retail, farming and fishing) thereby undermining Tamil commerce.[5] Relatedly, the military has continued to occupy vast tracts of residential and farming land taken over in wartime offensives since the 1980s, preventing the resettlement of hundreds of thousands of Tamils, and has initiated expansive programmes of seizure of private lands through legal instruments.[6] While some of the land is used by the military for its own extensive basing and entrepreneurial activities, parcels are also given over to Sinhala businesses and settlements and used to build large numbers of Buddhist temples. Meanwhile, declaring the ethnic problem over with the destruction of the LTTE, the government has resisted international pressure for it to negotiate a political solution with the Tamil National Alliance. Although talks have been mooted or occasionally started at moments of particular pressure, there have been no negotiations. Interestingly, while throughout the war Sri Lankan governments have responded to international pressure for progress on power-sharing by proposing 'implementation' of the thirteenth amendment to the constitution, amid post-war international pressure on precisely this, the government has refused to accede to even the limited police and land powers associated with the provincial councils.

The overarching context of these government policies is the strident wave of Sinhala nationalist triumphalism that began in 2008 with the imminent and decisive defeat of the LTTE and has since the end of the war become the mainstay of the authoritarian but hugely popular Rajapaksa government; the 2010 presidential polls handed him a resounding victory over his main rival,

Lt. Gen. (retd) Sarath Fonseka, the wartime army commander, backed by the UNP, the JVP and, in a controversial move, even the TNA. Thus, while international hostility has increasingly come to focus on the Rajapaksa government, Sinhala opposition to international pressure over matters related to Sri Lanka's ethnic question is widespread and deep-rooted. Although the UNP and JVP have criticised the government over the rising cost of living, corruption and its repression against Sinhala opponents, they are more or less openly supportive of the government's resistance to international pressure over accountability for wartime atrocities, demilitarisation and a halt to ethnic reengineering.[7] Defending the military victory as a nationalist triumph and pressing forward the militarised Sinhalisation of the north-east has thus become the driving thrust of Sinhala nationalist politics in the post-war era; an evolution of the post-independence insistence on ensuring the Sinhalese 'their rightful place' in Sri Lanka's state and society.

But while victory over the LTTE has strengthened and rejuvenated Sinhala Buddhist nationalism, it has also made international demands for liberal reform more insistent. So long as the LTTE remained a potent military threat, Sinhala leaders could promise liberal reform and ethnic inclusion without having to disrupt the Sinhala Buddhist order. This is no longer the case, and the government's uncompromising stance on the Tamil question and its broader retreat from liberal peace have led to more forceful international action, particularly in relation to an investigation into and accountability for wartime atrocities. This turn in international opinion is uneven and far from complete. The US has taken the lead in pushing for an international investigation, a goal sought since 2009 by an expanding international NGO advocacy campaign. In late 2013, the UK abandoned its 'quiet diplomacy' with the Rajapaksa government to back this position unequivocally. However, Japan (one of the four co-chairs of the peace process) and Australia have prioritised good relations with Sri Lanka, explicitly disregarding the Tamil question. Importantly, the Congress-led government in India generally supported Sri Lanka in diffusing international pressure, whilst extending development aid for the north-east and encouraging Sri Lanka to negotiate with the TNA.[8]

Despite this unevenness, there has been a growing momentum behind interventions for liberal peace. In 2010, following the EU withdrawal of its preferential reduced trading tariffs for Sri Lanka's garment exports, and as evidence of wartime atrocities began to proliferate, the UN Secretary General acceded to international pressure and appointed a panel of experts to examine the events in the final months of the war. Sri Lanka refused to cooperate and barred access to the panel. In 2011, the panel issued its report, setting out a damning indictment of the conduct of the war, terming it 'a grave assault on the entire regime of international law' which 'constituted persecution of the population of the Vanni'.[9] It estimated that over 40,000 civilians had been killed, and placed overwhelming responsibility on government forces, while also accusing the LTTE of war crimes. Sri Lanka rejected the report, but it invigorated international action on accountability which took the form of a series of US-sponsored resolutions against Sri Lanka at the United Nations Human Rights Commission (UNHRC). The third resolution, passed in March 2014, mandated the Office of the High Commissioner for Human Rights (OHCHR) to conduct an independent investigation of wartime abuses in the period 2002–9. Sri Lanka has rejected all three resolutions and declared that it will not cooperate with the OHCHR probe.

Sri Lanka has responded to the hardening international climate in contradictory ways, reflecting the difficulty in navigating the deep-seated incompatibility between Sinhala Buddhist state order and international demands for reconciliation and accountability. The government has sought to build an anti-Western alliance on the basis of defending sovereignty by pursuing strong relations with China as well as other Asian, African and Latin American states. This effort has had limited purchase in a post-Cold War era where sovereignty is no longer a 'trumps all' norm. Moreover, while Sri Lanka's new allies can provide support in fora such as the UNHRC, they do not constitute an alternative international space in which Sri Lanka can secure itself from demands for liberal reform or the consequences of not fulfilling these. Sri Lanka's turn to China has been materially significant.[10] However, these investments do not subsidise and support Sinhala Buddhist order-making in the integrated way that Western backing arguably did throughout the three decades of armed conflict, and those before.[11] These investments primarily comprise loans (at near commercial rates) for large infrastructure projects with construction work undertaken by Chinese firms.[12] Despite the government's gloss, Sri Lanka's finances are characterised by deepening indebtedness, with debt repayments now exceeding state revenue.[13] At the same time, Sri Lanka's exports remain heavily reliant on Europe and the US.[14]

Thus, whilst rejecting US-led demands for accountability and reconciliation by seeking an anti-Western alliance, Sri Lanka also tried in various ways to turn back the tide of Western hostility. For example, it has hired UK- and US-based public relations firms, at some expense, in an attempt to shape public and political opinion in those states;[15] and simultaneously has produced publicity material that seeks to counter and challenge the growing evidence of wartime and post-war abuses, whilst offering evidence of progress on resettlement and rehabilitation of former LTTE cadres.[16] However, these efforts have run aground against the more forceful counter-mobilisation by the Tamil diaspora and allied liberal peace campaigners, and, at base, they are unavoidably hampered by the unwillingness of the government to move towards liberal reform.[17] Relatedly, Sri Lanka has sought to blame these difficulties on the activities of the Tamil diaspora.[18] It has become a common trope in post-war Sri Lanka, reproduced by Sinhala nationalists and government officials from the president down, to attribute international pursuit of accountability and power-sharing primarily to the orchestrations of the diaspora, seeking to 'revive' the LTTE and Tamil separatism by using its financial resources to influence Western media and politicians, with the latter supposedly beholden to a Tamil vote base. In short, after the war, 'the diaspora' has replaced the LTTE as the malevolent new force of Tamil nationalism threatening the Sinhala Buddhist order, and therefore 'terrorist' by definition. Since the war's end, apart from demanding international action under anti-terror laws—on the basis that leading diaspora actors are part of, or fronts for, the now apparently still existing LTTE—the government has warned Tamils in the island against contacts and links with the diaspora. This rhetoric escalated significantly during the March 2014 UNHRC session, when Sri Lanka claimed to have uncovered a diaspora-inspired 'plot' to resurrect the LTTE, and launched a man-hunt for alleged LTTE operatives, arrested prominent human rights activists, reintroduced sweeping wartime restrictions on fishing and resumed the once frequent cordon-and-search operations. Nonetheless the UNHRC resolution was passed successfully, whereafter Sri Lanka proscribed almost all major Tamil diaspora organisations and over 400 individuals, citing UN anti-terrorism instruments obliging cooperation from other member states. However, the US, UK, Canada and Australia rejected the proscriptions.

Tamil diaspora: renewed struggle

Since the end of the war, the West-based Tamil diaspora has become the base of a globalised Tamil nationalist movement which sustains the Tamil national identity whilst actively pursuing Tamil nationalist goals through the processes and categories of liberal order.[19] The Tamil national identity is reproduced through mass participation events, as well as in more routine ways, such as cultural and sporting events and popular cultural practices. Annual public commemorations on 27 November (Heroes' Day) and 18 May (marking the mass atrocities of 2009), and demonstrations at crucial moments when Sri Lanka becomes an international issue, draw thousands or tens of thousands of participants amid the ubiquitous presence of the red and yellow 'Tiger flag'.[20] At the same time, a well-connected network of diaspora organisations and activists pursue Tamil nationalist interests by establishing links with Western political parties, policy officials, media organisations and advocacy groups, and over time they have become embedded within the capillaries of the liberal peace policy nexus. Foregrounding Sri Lanka's past and ongoing abuses and persecution, diaspora campaigners, acting in isolation or in concert, seek to shift international policy to thwart the Sinhala Buddhist project whilst advancing the claim for Tamil national rights. In the five years after the war's end, these efforts have converged on securing an international investigation into wartime atrocities, and leading diaspora organisations have played a visible and important role in mobilising support for the successive US-sponsored resolutions at the UNHRC. This post-LTTE networked Tamil politics builds on practices of international engagement, capacity for mass mobilisation, developed broadcast and web-based media and daily flows of information with the 'homeland', all of which emerged during the armed conflict but continues without an organising centre or leadership.

This new wave of Tamil nationalism first came to the fore in the final months of the war, when an intense wave of mass demonstrations and protests spread across global diaspora centres demanding immediate international action to halt Sri Lanka's offensive into the Vanni. The protests were unprecedented in their scale and depth: in Toronto and London large crowds blocked traffic on main city centre thoroughfares, and London's Parliament Square became the site of a continuous 72-day protest, with crowds varying from several hundred to over 15,000. A month after the war ended, 100,000 people marched through London on 16 June.[21] These momentous events expressed and consolidated a renewed nationalist mobilisation centred on the recurrent themes of Sri Lankan state oppression and Tamil national resistance. The slogans, banners and images of the protests brought together outrage at Sri Lanka's 'slaughter' of Tamil civilians with a defiant assertion of Tamil national identity and recognition of the LTTE. Whilst unsuccessful in their stated goal—securing international action to stop the war—the protests generated new activist groups and organisations and dramatically raised the diaspora's political profile in the calculations of both international actors and the Sri Lankan state at a crucial moment when the new global alignments around the island's ethnic conflict began to emerge.

The key nodes in the 2009 explosion in nationalist political activity were the Tamil- and English-language diaspora media (broadcast and web-based) and diaspora activists and organisations, at various removes from the LTTE, already active in Tamil politics. However, they were soon joined and later supplanted by new actors and networks which emerged through the mass gatherings themselves. Well before the international media began covering unfolding events in the Vanni, the Tamil diaspora media provided daily coverage, accompanied by images and commentary from the ground, of the magnitude of civilian suffering caused by relentless and high-intensity bombardment and blockades on food and medicine. The broadcast media marked the singularity of the unfolding events by suspending their normal schedules to make way for round-the-clock coverage and 'call in' programmes which allowed viewers and listeners from across the world to share their outrage and despair, and debate what could be done. As the reports from Vanni became ever bleaker, Tamil activists and organisation representatives appeared on the media to call for public support at unfolding protests and demonstrations. At the same time, they intensified their efforts to lobby Western politicians, officials and media organisations. Apart from the immediate policy interactions and media appearances they produced, these efforts established a pattern of diaspora engagement with centres of power and influence in Western states that has subsequently become extensive and routine.[22] Meanwhile, the highly visible mass events unsettled and broke down the perception of criminalisation and threat that had characterised the Tamil diaspora as a result of host state attempts to marginalise the LTTE through anti-terror legislation.[23] Staged in city centres and in front of key political buildings, and openly displaying nationalist images such as the Tiger Flag that were liable to invite punitive sanctions associated with anti-terror measures, the continuous and often raucous protests forcefully inserted Tamil nationalist politics into the public realms of Western states. Daily interactions with law enforcement officers, journalists and politicians at the protest sites both raised the profile of Tamil nationalism and began to normalise it. The protesters came from the broad canvas of long-settled diaspora membership, including large numbers of second-generation Tamils fluent in national or official languages, and demanding action on the basis of their citizenship.[24]

Tamil diaspora politics in the post-LTTE era is organisationally fragmented but politically unified, a pattern that reflects nationalist political activity during the armed conflict which expanded the base of Tamil nationalist sentiment and activity without a centralised bureaucratic structure outside the

LTTE. With the demise of the LTTE, these overlapping but autonomous spaces of Tamil nationalist activity could not and did not congeal around a single centre of authority—despite notable efforts to produce pan-diaspora apex structures (see below). But they operate in concert, sometimes amicably and at other times fractiously, to advance Tamil nationalist demands.[25] The extensive and centralised structures through which the LTTE had raised funds and organised political activity continue, but these have declined and fractured amid the diffuse network form of post-war nationalist political activity in the diaspora.[26] However, these structures remain unmatched in organising and coordinating large-scale or transnational events such as the 27 November and 18 May commemorations, even though the very large crowds these draw are more an effect of the diffuse expansion of Tamil nationalist sentiment than of this organisational reach itself. The two diaspora organisations that aspire to be apex or umbrella bodies—the Global Tamil Forum and the Transnational Government of Tamil Eelam—both have international reach, but neither has, nor claims, exhaustive or exclusive global representativeness. Both were formed in 2010: the GTF through an association of organisations already active in Western states, the TGTE through direct elections held across the major diaspora centres and organised by the former LTTE networks. But since its inaugural elections, the TGTE leadership and the networks that helped bring it about have not been able to agree terms, each insisting on its authority over the other. There is an alternative set of country-level diaspora councils that were formed in some diaspora centres through elections, also held with the assistance of former LTTE networks. The relationship between the Country Councils and the LTTE networks remains close and cooperative, but even where they are set up, the councils are by no means the dominant organisations. Finally, there is a set of well-organised and adept organisations of varying sizes and specialisations (some of which are members of the GTF) which are at the forefront of diaspora advocacy and lobbying campaigns.[27]

But this organisational fragmentation is bound by unity on the core principles of Tamil nationalism; that is, Tamils' national status and the demand for self-rule in their homeland.[28] The principles are no longer tied to a single representative organisation, as in the eras of the Federal Party and the LTTE, but constitute the 'ground' on which all actors operate and compete for prominence, popular support and to define the direction of Tamil political activity.[29] As such the various diaspora organisations agree on the existence of the Tamil nation and the need to secure its political autonomy from the Sri

Lankan state, but disagree, often bitterly, on how best this might or ought to be done. For example, some prioritise the pursuit of accountability for mass atrocities, while others prioritise the pursuit of international recognition for Tamils' national status. Consequently there have been heated disagreements, for example on whether or not to welcome the various UNHRC resolutions against Sri Lanka, given their ethnically neutral language. These contestations are often intertwined with more prosaic and personal differences that can further accentuate the disputes. But these conflicts are meaningful (that is, mutually intelligible) precisely because they are based on shared nationalist goals that are reproduced and consolidated by the very disputes over how they should best be pursued.[30] In effect, Tamil territorial nationhood has become the banal and taken-for-granted field on which significant diaspora organisations operate, and it thus links them to Tamil political activity in Sri Lanka and in Tamil Nadu.

The central component of diaspora political activity is to develop relationships with international liberal peace actors to advance demands for more forceful international intervention in Sri Lanka. Consequently diaspora organisations have been important in collating and publicising primary evidence of wartime and ongoing abuses from witnesses and survivors and channelling it to Western officials, media and advocacy groups who in turn have disseminated these more widely. They have organised high-profile international meetings and conferences that include Tamils from Sri Lanka and Tamil Nadu, along with senior Western politicians and international advocacy groups. They have also engaged in international diplomacy. For example, delegations from some of the key diaspora organisations have worked at UNHRC sessions to lobby member states to support the US-sponsored resolutions against Sri Lanka, coordinating their efforts with US and other Western officials and advocacy organisations, as well as Tamil political and civil society leaders from Sri Lanka. In an interesting development, diaspora organisations also sent delegations to UNHRC members' capitals in Africa, Asia and Latin America to lobby those governments directly.

These established relations between Tamil nationalist actors and liberal peace actors do not, however, entail a shared understanding of the problem in Sri Lanka or the contours of an acceptable solution. Tamil actors situate the demand for accountability within a wider narrative of Sinhala state oppression and Tamil national resistance, and thus insist on Tamil national rights as foundational for a solution. The prevalent use of the term 'genocide' by many Tamil organisations—in Sri Lanka, the diaspora and in Tamil Nadu—to describe the pattern of Sri Lanka's anti-Tamil violence and persecution is intimately tied to this national status. But international actors overwhelmingly remain committed to an ethnically inclusive state, and see accountability as a means to that end. They are generally unsympathetic or even hostile to Tamil demands for 'national' rights. Crucially, however, Tamil actors do not conceal these nationalist commitments in their international dealings. During the armed conflict such positions were summarily dismissed as 'extremist' or simply ignored as marginal amid prevailing faith in Sinhala state elites and their Tamil and Muslim counterparts. The new alignments of the post-war era have opened up the space for a more collaborative engagement as Tamil actors pursue their nationalist goals alongside international actors pursuing liberal peace.

TNA: ambiguity and disunity

Meanwhile, the end of the war presented the Tamil National Alliance (TNA) with both an opportunity long sought by some of its leaders, and a crisis. On the one hand, the TNA was widely expected by many international and Tamil actors to become the LTTE's successor as the sole Tamil representative. On the other hand, the destruction of the LTTE not only put paid to the Sri Lankan government's willingness to negotiate, but exposed the TNA's inability independently to compel the government to talk or advance the Tamil nationalist principles on which it had resoundingly won elections in 2001 and 2004. In a replay of the TULF's difficulties after its landmark 1977 victory, in attempting to navigate the post-war landscape, the TNA has come to play an ambiguous and contested role in Tamil politics.

The Sinhala nationalist triumphalism that engulfed the country with the defeat of the LTTE presented an implacably hostile and threatening climate in which to articulate Tamil demands, which worsened as the Tamil diaspora and international actors began to forcefully pursue accountability for the wartime atrocities. Amidst the international shifts and uncertainty of the immediate post-war years, the TNA focused on seeking negotiations with the government on a political solution and, to this end, avoided drawing nationalist ire. This meant backing away from growing Tamil and international demands for accountability, but also distancing itself from Tamil nationalist principles.[31] In their parliamentary speeches and English-language statements, the TNA set out an alternative political position: denouncing the LTTE, rejecting independence and seeking a solution based on a 'united, undivided country'.[32] But the TNA's electorate remains wedded to the core principles of

Tamil nationhood, homeland and self-determination, and this necessitated a countervailing set of practices in which Tamil nationalist principles, and even the LTTE's legacy of struggle, are invoked. For example, the TNA's manifesto for the first elections since the late 1980s to the Northern Provincial Council had on its cover a photograph of the deceased LTTE leader V. Pirapaharan,[33] and the theme for its 2014 May Day rally was self-determination.[34] Maintaining these contradictory postures has produced persistent vacillation and, inevitably, a perception amongst both Tamils and Sinhalese of the TNA as Janus-faced.

TNA leaders' attempts to pursue a strategy of compromise and negotiation with the Sri Lankan state, independent of sentiments in its electorate and the Tamil diaspora, faced several constraints. Quite apart from the Rajapaksa government's lack of interest in negotiations—except at moments when the appearance of talks can help undermine international pressure—the post-war era saw continued military repression and occupation of Tamil residential and farm lands, state-sponsored Sinhala colonisation, persisting displacement, etc. As a consequence, the strategy of compromise and patient and incremental progress is difficult to sell to the Tamil electorate, let alone the diaspora. This is compounded by the organisational weakness of the coalition itself. The TNA's infrastructure and autonomous capacity to mobilise support are limited and cannot compare to those of the old Federal Party or the LTTE. The TNA is therefore unable to set out a clear political alternative to Tamil nationalism and then secure popular support by direct mobilisation and co-option of social institutions. At the same time, it is dependent on the already consolidated Tamil nationalism of its electorate for its continuing electoral success. Conversely, the Tamil electorate have no alternative at present through which to collectively express nationalist sentiments.[35] Just as the ongoing conditions of repression fuel resentment against the TNA leadership's tepid advocacy of Tamil interests, they also assure it of near unqualified support as a means of expressing a unified national identity.[36] Nonetheless, the TNA is habitually secretive about its moves regarding a political solution. For example, from January 2011 to May 2012 the TNA doggedly pursued negotiations with the government, but would not make public the proposals it had submitted, or the substance of the talks.[37]

Apart from occasional eruptions of public anger[38] and persistent critical questioning in the diaspora media, the TNA's ambivalence has also produced differences and disputes within its own ranks. In early 2010, one TNA leader, Gajen Ponnambalam of the ACTC, and two MPs quit in protest after R.

Sampanthan and the other leaders decided to back former army commander Lt. Gen. (retd) Sarath Fonseka in his unsuccessful presidential campaign against Rajapaksa. Although there have been no further splits since then, differences amongst the TNA leaders surface regularly in public and media fora. For example, while the leadership the leadership has wavered in support of the international campaign for accountability, other sections of the TNA, in particular the newly elected Northern Provincial Council, have been more forthright and clearly aligned with the diaspora and Tamil Nadu on the need for an international investigation. In February 2015, for example, the NPC passed a resolution stating that Tamils in Sri Lanka had been subject to genocidal attacks since independence and calling on the UN to investigate these claims.[39] In contrast, Sampanthan and his close associates have characterised the armed conflict as a civil war in which the Sri Lankan state and the LTTE were equally culpable and all ethnicities were equally victimised[40] (eschewing the TNA leadership's earlier denouncing of state violence as 'genocide').[41] As such, rather than a recognised and apex Tamil leadership, the TNA has instead become an important site of struggle between those seeking more forceful international intervention in Sri Lanka and those who seek to foreclose it.

Without an autonomous and non-nationalist Tamil support base, the TNA leadership is also unable to assert its authority against the diaspora and the latter's prominent nationalist advocacy in the international arena. In the early years of the post-war era, when the international momentum for accountability was still emergent and the diaspora's advocacy mechanisms were not well established, the TNA asserted the primacy of its leadership and its sole competence to decide in the best interests of the Tamil people.[42] Amid intensifying diaspora campaigning for an international accountability mechanism, the TNA instead pursued negotiations with a clearly reluctant and half-hearted Rajapaksa administration.[43] It also refused to send a delegation to Geneva for the March 2012 UNHRC session where the first US resolution on Sri Lanka was being discussed, and some TNA figures said that the party supported an internal rather than international investigation.[44] Since then, however, there has been a marked shift as both the international campaign for accountability and diaspora advocacy have gathered momentum. In February 2013 Sampanthan attended a GTF-organised conference, held in the UK Houses of Parliament and addressed by senior British politicians, which was dominated by the theme of accountability.[45] TNA delegates were also prominent in Geneva during the March 2014 UNHRC session and worked with Tamil diaspora actors to lobby support for the US-sponsored resolution authorising an OHCHR investigation. But along with such cooperation, there is often discord. When Tamil diaspora, Tamil Nadu and a range of international actors united in urging Commonwealth leaders to boycott the 2013 summit in Colombo, the TNA was noticeably ambivalent. Soon after the 2014 UNHRC resolution and the Sri Lankan government's proscription of several diaspora organisations, TNA leaders unexpectedly announced that they would be travelling to South Africa to discuss the possibility of mediated talks with the government. They were, however, characteristically 'tight-lipped' about the substance of their discussions in a context where the South African initiative was being described in Sri Lankan media as offering the government a possible 'way out' of the impending UN investigation.[46]

The TNA has thus emerged as a complex and internally differentiated actor on the international stage of Sri Lanka's ethnic politics. It was forged in a moment of Tamil nationalist anticipation in the wake of the LTTE's military successes at the turn of the century which brought together a disparate array of Tamil parliamentary and former paramilitary groups; they continue to be held together by circumstance, self-interest and the dominance of a nationalist identity amongst the electorate. The demise of the LTTE has not, however, returned Tamil politics to the earlier era of parliamentary manoeuvres. At the same time the high politics of Sri Lanka's ethnic conflict have moved decisively away from Colombo's elite drawing rooms to an international plane, where an active and organised set of Tamil diaspora organisations is unwilling simply to hand the mantle of leadership to the TNA.[47]

Tamil Nadu: a new consensus

Tamil Nadu today plays a prominent role in the international politics of Sri Lanka's ethnic conflict which is significant and important but also autonomous of Delhi. Yet this is a historically novel rather than inevitable development. Tamil Nadu's role in Sri Lanka's conflict has changed over time, but for most of the post-independence era has largely been aligned with Indian foreign policy, which in turn has prioritised good bilateral relations with Sri Lanka—except for the brief period of support for Tamil militants in the early 1980s—and limiting external involvement in the region.[48] However, since the end of war, Tamil Nadu has become an important component of the international mobilisation for forceful intervention that has constrained Delhi's ability to support Colombo, both bilaterally and at international fora such as the UNHRC and Commonwealth. This is driven by a powerful consensus that has become established in Tamil Nadu on the primacy of securing Sri Lankan Tamil political rights and accountability for war time atrocities.[49] But, importantly, this divergence between Tamil Nadu and Delhi on foreign policy objectives in Sri Lanka rests on a long settled and taken for granted accommodation between Tamil and national identities in India.

The emergence of today's Tamil Nadu consensus on securing Sri Lankan Tamil interests can be traced to the widespread public outrage and mass protests that erupted across the state from the mid-2000s in response to growing awareness of civilian casualties and suffering generated by Sri Lanka's resumed war against the LTTE. The protests, directed in the main against Delhi's support for Sri Lanka's offensive, were unsuccessful in shifting Indian policy during the war. But they were nonetheless significant: they were the first mass protests in support of Sri Lankan Tamils since those triggered by the island's July 1983 pogrom.[50] However, while the post-July 1983 protests were in alignment with Indian foreign policy, this new wave was diametrically opposed, and set in train a gathering wave of public sentiment that would in time form a novel and significant break between Tamil Nadu's main political parties and the central government.

The Congress and Dravidian parties that ruled Tamil Nadu paid little attention to the post-independence escalation of anti-Tamil discrimination and violence in Sri Lanka, despite the centrality of Tamil rights and interests in their political platforms.[51] During the early 1980s the Dravidian parties did outbid each other to support Tamil militants in Sri Lanka, but did so amid a prevailing context of India's decision to do the same. The mainstream Tamil Nadu press, both Tamil and English, began to give extensive coverage to Sri Lankan state violence and atrocities against the Tamils, whilst being broadly sympathetic to the militants and their demands. In this atmosphere of growing public awareness and political attention in Tamil Nadu, the 1983 pogrom triggered widespread protests and demonstrations across the state, drawing support from students, the hugely influential film industry and all the major political parties.

Indian policy on Sri Lanka reversed with the Indo-Sri Lanka Accord, and became consolidated by the high intensity IPKF intervention. India proscribed the LTTE following the assassination of former premier Rajiv Gandhi in May 1991, and from the mid-1990s sought to rebuild cordial relations with Sri Lanka, setting aside the thorny issue of the Tamil question. In 1998 the two countries signed a bilateral free trade agreement that led to a significant increase in Indian investment in Sri Lanka and an expansion of trade.[52] As the war escalated, the policy of non-interference in the ethnic conflict turned into one of active support for Sri Lanka's war against the LTTE. This was spurred in part by the emergence of a challenge to a central plank of Indian foreign policy, namely preventing extra-regional powers' entry into India's 'backyard'. These came in the form of powerful liberal peace interventions, most significantly in the form of the Norwegian peace initiative backed by the US and other Western states, Sri Lanka's growing military ties with Pakistan and China, and Chinese investments. India responded with intensified efforts to strengthen and deepen ties to Sri Lanka. When the LTTE reversed Sri Lankan military gains in 2000, India became actively involved, facilitating critical arms purchases from Israel, and reportedly offering to evacuate Sri Lankan troops trapped by the LTTE's advance. Diplomatic and military ties deepened following President Kumaratunga's 2003 'coup' against the pro-West UNP government. Her successor, Mahinda Rajapaksa, received robust military, political and economic support, especially when Sri Lanka resumed a determined military onslaught against the LTTE in 2006.[53]

The Dravidian parties largely followed this Indian foreign policy direction and visibly backed away from the Sri Lankan Tamil issue, particularly after the assassination of Rajiv Gandhi. The ADMK in particular was overtly hostile to the LTTE and to the Sri Lankan Tamil cause more generally, but the DMK also at various times prosecuted Tamil Nadu groups and individuals charged with supporting the LTTE. Throughout most of the 1990s, explicit support for the LTTE and the demand for Tamil Eelam came mainly from small parties and organisations such as the MDMK, the PMK and Pazha Nedumaran, a former Congressman turned Tamil nationalist activist. Meanwhile, Tamil Nadu media coverage in the mainstream English and Tamil press was hostile to the LTTE, focusing on LTTE attacks against civilians and abuses of the population in its territory whilst largely ignoring the overarching conditions of state repression in Sri Lanka. This pattern continued well into the new millennium. In 2002, when the LTTE called on India to host the forthcoming Norwegian-facilitated negotiations in Tamil Nadu, the then ruling ADMK vociferously objected, citing the risk of LTTE infiltration into the state.[54] Meanwhile, throughout the war and its attendant massacres, the DMK has been a key member of successive coalition governments in Delhi, and while it often publicly denounced casualties amongst Tamil civilians, it did nothing more.[55] Thus, the Dravidian parties' strident stance on the Sri Lankan Tamil issue and their willingness to break with and challenge Delhi's foreign policy priorities is historically novel. What is crucial is that the Dravidian parties' now strident support for Sri Lankan Tamils has been led—and in many ways forced—by the expansion of popular sentiment in support of the Sri Lankan Tamils, which has grown rapidly from the mid-2000s, soon becoming mainstream. The Dravidian parties have thus followed rather than led the change in popular sentiment, which in turn has been led by groups and spaces outside party political structures and competition.

Key to this was growing awareness of and access to Sri Lankan Tamil nationalist publications and media. The LTTE's print publications had a clandestine circulation in Tamil Nadu throughout the 1990s, but this was small and limited. During the Norwegian peace process however, the LTTE considerably expanded the reach and transmission of its broadcast media such that these could be received in Tamil Nadu.[56] At the same the time news and information circulated through diaspora-run English- and Tamil-language news websites, such as TamilNet, reached a new and growing internet-connected demographic which was socially and politically conscious, but outside the party political system. The output of this professionally managed and sophisticated media framed Sri Lanka's ethnic crisis in Tamil nationalist terms, but also invoked the liberal tropes of human rights, humanitarian protection and rules of war that resonated with this new demographic. While the LTTE-produced printed and broadcast material reached those in rural areas and literate primarily in Tamil, the websites began reaching those in urban areas and literate in English. These avenues were important in the early stages of the mobilisation, as the mainstream Indian and Tamil Nadu media largely ignored Sri Lankan military attacks against civilians. In short, a fuller account of ongoing events in Sri Lanka was available to Tamil Nadu audiences than was available either through mainstream media or the Indian and Tamil Nadu governments.

When Sri Lanka's war resumed, reports of attendant Tamil civilian casualties triggered spontaneous demonstrations and protest marches, which became incessant and widespread across the state.[57] The intensity of Sri Lanka's offensive established a clear narrative of massive state violence and civilian suffering that was increasingly labelled as genocide. Each fresh wave of Tamil casualties and displacement triggered demonstrations, blockades, strikes and 'human chain' protests.[58] While long-standing supporters of the Tamil Eelam cause such as the PMK, MDMK and Pazha Nedumaran continued to be active, new forces began to join them. For example, Communist parties that had previously been cool or overtly hostile to the LTTE also became actively involved, and the issue was raised in a demonstration in Delhi by the All India

Students Federation in November 2008, which was otherwise focused exclusively on education issues.[59] But the qualitative shift in this new phase of growing mobilisation was the participation of wide sections of society who had previously little if any involvement in the Sri Lankan Tamil issue and party politics more broadly. Students from rural high schools to colleges in Chennai and Madras University, as well as lawyers, film industry associations and IT workers, all began to organise and actively campaign.[60] Whilst protests were often spontaneous, there was also widespread and coordinated agitation. For example, in late 2008 traders' unions organised a strike (*bandh*) that drew in street vendors and major retailers and led to a comprehensive shutdown of commercial activities across the state.[61] Amid the increasingly charged atmosphere, there were occasional self-immolations. The mainstream Tamil and English media responded to the popular mobilisation, and started covering events in Sri Lanka sympathetically. Opinion polls commissioned by the *Indian Express* and the populist Tamil-language *Ananda Vikadan* showed growing public support for the LTTE and the demand for Tamil Eelam.[62]

It is in this context of a popular turn to active support for the Sri Lankan Tamils that the Dravidian parties also hardened their positions. The first indication came in late 2005 when newly elected President Rajapaksa visited India. A proposed meeting with Chief Minister Jayalalitha fell through when she failed to schedule it (Rajapaksa instead visited a temple in Kerala).[63] Although no reason was given, just days earlier pro-government paramilitaries had gunned down TNA parliamentarian Joseph Pararajasingham during Christmas Mass at a church in his Batticaloa constituency. Soon after all-out war resumed in 2006, the Sri Lankan Air Force bombed a children's home in LTTE-controlled territory, killing sixty-one girls. This led to the first mass protests in Tamil Nadu. The state assembly passed a resolution condemning the attack, with the DMK and ADMK putting aside their normally acrimonious differences to provide unanimous support.[64] These dynamics—of growing popular sentiment in support of the Sri Lankan Tamils and the LTTE, as well as Tamil Nadu parties diverging from Delhi's support for Sri Lanka—intensified as the war continued. In the run-up to the April 2009 Lok Sabha elections, the force of sentiments was such that Karunanidhi, whose DMK was in India's ruling coalition, undertook a token fast to demand a ceasefire.[65] Jayalalitha had also openly changed her position, unequivocally condemning the ongoing mass atrocities and also stating that Tamil Eelam was the only solution.[66] The ADMK subsequently campaigned for the 2011 state assembly elections on a platform that foregrounded the need to secure justice and political rights for the Sri Lankan Tamils. Having won an impressive victory, it then moved a series of resolutions in the state assembly—which were passed unanimously— demanding that India impose sanctions on Sri Lanka, actively participate in UN-led efforts on war crimes, and work for a UN-mandated referendum on Eelam.[67] This last demand was also included in both the DMK and ADMK resolutions in their manifestos for the April 2014 parliamentary elections.

These developments have also raised Tamil Nadu's profile in the international politics of Sri Lanka's ethnic conflict and made it an important node in US-led efforts to mobilise international action against Sri Lanka. This was underlined in July 2011 when US Secretary of State Hillary Clinton travelled to Chennai as part of her official visit to India and met Jayalalitha, recently re-elected as Chief Minister. Amongst the subjects they discussed were US efforts to find 'innovative and creative ideas to break the impasse' in Sri Lanka over the Tamil issue.[68] But at the same time the growing alignment between Tamil Nadu and international liberal peace efforts has also brought to the fore the contradictions between these and Delhi's efforts to secure regional dominance by supporting the Sri Lankan state. Despite improved ties in the post-Cold War era, US and Indian objectives in Sri Lanka, as elsewhere in the region, have not been aligned. This was not problematic during the armed conflict, as both states supported Sri Lanka against the LTTE, but with the end of the war, India has been out of step with the growing international campaign to secure accountability for Sri Lanka's wartime atrocities. The key constraint on India's ability to support Sri Lanka has been Tamil Nadu.

The multiple pressures acting on India's Sri Lanka policy have thus pulled it in different and often inconsistent directions. In 2009, and in line with its policy of maintaining good bilateral relations, India supported a UNHRC resolution that welcomed Sri Lanka's recent military victory, characterising it as a humanitarian operation to rescue Tamil civilians whilst making no mention of the mass atrocities.[69] But in 2012 and 2013, India changed tack and backed US-sponsored resolutions that demanded Sri Lanka take steps to investigate allegations of mass atrocities. In late 2013 the contradiction became inescapable, when the Commonwealth Summit was held in Colombo. Amid vehement demands from Tamil Nadu for Prime Minister Manmohan Singh to boycott the event, the government vacillated. Matters came to a head when Canada confirmed, as earlier warned, that Prime Minister Stephen Harper was boycotting the summit over Sri Lanka's human rights record. Ultimately Singh did not go, but sent Rajapaksa a letter expressing 'regret'.[70] At the 2014 UNHRC session, at which another resolution was passed mandating an

OHCHR investigation into Sri Lanka's wartime atrocities, India abstained; but not before supporting last-minute efforts by Pakistan, China and others to derail the US-led initiative. While it remains to be seen what Indian foreign policy on Sri Lanka will be, it is now widely recognised, both within Sri Lanka and internationally, that Tamil Nadu will be an important factor in constraining the extent to which India can pursue a policy of building bi-lateral relations with Colombo whilst overlooking the still ongoing ethnic conflict. More specifically and in the near term, any Indian efforts to support Sri Lanka ward off growing international pressure for genuine political reforms and a credible process of accountability for wartime abuses will continue to have to contend with countervailing pressure from Tamil Nadu.[71]

As noted earlier, these are historically novel developments. For the first time since independence, Tamil Nadu has become an active and important site of popular and political support for the Sri Lankan Tamil nationalist project. Nonetheless, the core dynamics of Sri Lankan and Indian Tamil politics remain distinct in their orientations, substance and conditions of operation. Tamil Nadu's position within the Indian nation-state framework is taken for granted and bound by a shared consensus on the promotion of Tamil interests and identity, as established during the colonial period. The Dravidian parties make their demands for Indian government action and the cause of Tamil Eelam secure in their Indian identity. This was evident in the DMK's leaders' terse response to a provocation from the then Sri Lankan Defence Secretary Gothabaya Rajapaksa. The latter, exasperated by the former's vocal demands for Tamil Eelam, asked why he (Karunanidhi) did not ask for Tamil Eelam in India, to which Karunanidhi responded that it was because 'unlike the Sri Lankan government the Indian government is not persecuting Tamils and is allowing them to live peacefully, therefore there is no reason for us (Tamils) to separate from India'.[72]

CONCLUSION

The politics of national identity are at the centre of the stark differences between the Tamil-speaking regions of Sri Lanka and south India. Sri Lanka's militarised domination of the Tamil-speaking areas, its attendant repression, economic exclusion and violent ethnic re-engineering are driven by the logic of expanding the ethnically hierarchical Sinhala Buddhist order across the Tamil-speaking population and territory. In contrast, the relative prosperity and stability of Tamil Nadu have been facilitated by the inclusion of Tamil identity and interests as valued components of the Indian nation-state framework. National identity is therefore materially productive, and in the era of popular sovereignty the conceptual centre of political life. It is the taken-for-granted ground on which all politics happen; it determines the boundaries of political community, the terms on which ethnic groups are included in the national whole and the basis on which public goods and resources should be distributed. The nation is the people for whom the state exists and should act. Therefore unless protagonists share a conception of national identity and its terms of ethnic inclusion, they cannot engage in agonistic politics about how best to pursue shared objectives and ideals. In the absence of a broad but shared conception of national identity and national interest, politics become the antagonistic—and often violent—pursuit of mutually incompatible goals.

The historical and comparative survey presented here shows that the emergence of more or less inclusive conceptions of national identity is a matter of long-run patterns of political activity through which national identities are first asserted, then contested and more or less securely established. These outcomes were far from inevitable and could not be predicted from temporally static variables such as ethnic demography, the patterns of material interests or political institutions. The very different relationships between national and

Tamil identities in India and Sri Lanka emerged amidst comparable conditions and historical experiences. The range of significant ethnic and nationalist movements that were evident in the early decades of the twentieth century were also similar and in many instances connected. The Sinhala Buddhist and Hindu nationalist movements were ethnically hierarchical in near identical ways and both drew on the Aryan idea. At the same time there were also pan-ethnic movements in both states. Tamil politics in Sri Lanka, far from being secessionist, was orientated towards securing Tamil-Sinhala equality within a unified state and was influenced by the Indian nationalist strand of Tamil cultural revivalism. In contrast, Tamil politics in south India were strongly influenced by the Dravidian movement that attacked Hinduism and Indian nationalism as antithetical to Tamil identity and interests. By the late 1970s, however, the patterns of national and ethnic politics had taken definite and contrasting shapes. In Sri Lanka, Sinhala Buddhist nationalism was dominant and was hostile to Tamil demands for collective Tamil–Sinhala equality; the contradiction triggered a three-decade civil war and underlies the present dynamics of Sinhala occupation and Tamil resentment. In contrast in India, the post-independence framework has been shaped by the Congress movement's pan-ethnic nationalism, which is able to accommodate Dravidian demands for the cultivation of Tamil cultural and economic interests.

The national identities that came to dominate India and Sri Lanka are therefore those that are linked to powerful and successful political movements. The pan-ethnic movements that emerged in colonial Sri Lanka were weak and transient, easily overwhelmed by the more expansive and sustained mobilisation of Sinhala Buddhist nationalism. In contrast, the pan-ethnic Congress movement successfully brought together activities of setting out a conception of national identity, directly mobilising support and co-opting the support of existing social and political actors. The unevenness of Congress's pan-ethnic nationalism—un-problematically including Tamils but less so Muslims—was also a matter of process. It was able to mobilise support in the Tamil-speaking regions because it was organisationally and ideologically Tamil; it operated through the Tamil language, adopted culturally resonant forms and incorporated core Tamil political demands as Indian ones. In contrast, and although Congress's pan-ethnic nationalism was theoretically equally capable of incorporating Muslims, the regional Congress structures in the areas with substantial Muslim populations were dominated by Hindu nationalists who were ideologically opposed to incorporating Muslim identity and interests. The political dominance of Sinhala Buddhist nationalism is also not simply the brute translation of ethnic demography, but has required the political and organisational incorporation of intra-Sinhala caste, regional and ethnic differences.

Likewise, the important differences between Sri Lankan and Indian Tamil identities also reveal their political and historically constituted character. There continue to be strong and ongoing religious and cultural links between south Indian and Sri Lankan Tamils, on the island and in the diaspora. However, the content of their politics is importantly different and, for the most part of the period studied in this book, largely unconnected. The Dravidian idea has an been an important influence in south Indian Tamil politics, creating a Tamil identity that is focused on asserting a Tamil language and culture distinct from north-Indian Hinduism and Sanskrit as well as challenging caste hierarchies. The Dravidian idea has not been anywhere near as important in Sri Lankan Tamil politics, which has instead come to be organised on challenging Sinhala Buddhist dominance by asserting Tamils' equal national status to the Sinhalese and demanding self-rule. South Indian and Sri Lankan Tamil politics have also operated with the presumption that the two populations constitute distinct and separate political communities with different trajectories and interests. For example, and until quite recently, the major Dravidian parties had followed Indian foreign policy on the Sri Lankan Tamil issue and refrained from taking up Sri Lankan Tamil rights independently of the government in Delhi. Tamil Nadu's recent and strident advocacy on Tamil rights in Sri Lanka, contravening Delhi's foreign policy priorities, is linked to the radical internationalisation of Sri Lanka's ethnic conflict and has focused on shifting Indian foreign policy to support the growing momentum for more forceful international intervention. Crucially, therefore, Tamil Nadu demands are directed at the Indian government, which is thereby reaffirmed as the legitimate and appropriate actor in the international realm, but also one that can be moved by the force of moral persuasion. In contrast, Tamil mobilisation in Sri Lanka has long been directed at the international community as a means of constraining the state. The processes of politics have thus produced unexpected outcomes. In the early twentieth century the Dravidian movement sought independence from India, whilst Sri Lankan Tamils sought equality in a unified state. But under a hundred years later, the accommodation between Tamil and Indian identity is so assured and taken for granted that Dravidian parties can demand independence for Sri Lankan Tamils without it raising hackles about the threat of irredentism. Dravidian separatism has become a historical curiosity, whilst the historically unexpected demand for Tamil Eelam has become commonplace.

This analysis of ethnic accommodation and ethnic conflict has important implications for ongoing international attempts to establish an ethnically inclusive liberal state in Sri Lanka. These efforts have focused largely on securing institutional and constitution reform, ignoring the politics of national identity. Since President Jayewardene's Westward and neo-liberal turn in 1977, successive Sinhala leaders have endorsed and accepted liberal principles in their international postures, whilst continuing to advance the Sinhala Buddhist project in their domestic politics. As a consequence, throughout the armed conflict, the institutional forces pursuing the liberal peace backed Sri Lankan state elites—along with their Tamil and Muslim allies—as the preferred partner in liberal reform, without any regard for their organisational capacity and political willingness to deliver the promised reform. Whilst the pervasive and all-encompassing force of Sinhala Buddhist nationalism was overlooked and characterised as the preserve of small and fringe actors such as the JVP and JHU, Tamil nationalism was exclusively associated with the 'extremist' LTTE. The vast majority of Tamils were therefore held to be 'moderate' and seeking inclusion within an inclusive multi-ethnic state; whilst the LTTE claims that the Sri Lankan state was unwilling to reform were ignored and it was dammed as an inherently illiberal actor atavistically committed to a mono-ethnic Tamil Eelam. The consequence of these efforts has been to strengthen and entrench the Sinhala Buddhist character of the state whilst facilitating its eventual military defeat of the LTTE amidst mass atrocities and a post-war wave of Sinhala Buddhist euphoria in which the militarised domination of the north-east is normalised. At the same time the escalation of the war, intensified state repression and mass displacement have also facilitated the rise of a globalised Tamil nationalist movement which is increasingly embedded in the structures and processes of an ever-advancing liberal order. But liberal peace actors remain committed to the possibility of a unified and ethnically plural Sri Lanka, believing that underneath it all Sinhalese, Tamils and Muslims can be persuaded to live together amicably and share power.

The example of south India is instructive and shows that stable and long-lasting ethnic accommodation is a matter of political mobilisation and ideological overlap rather than constitutional reform or indeed the fostering of accommodative and amicable sentiments through various 'peace-building' programmes. It was not the federal provisions of the Indian constitution, but rather sustained Congress mobilisation within the Tamil-speaking areas that incorporated core Dravidian demands within the Indian nation-state framework. Indian pluralism, where it works, does so by incorporating mobilised identities rather than erasing them. A robust and stable multi-ethnic state in Sri Lanka would therefore require a deep-seated and powerful multi-ethnic nationalist movement that could undermine the political salience of the existing Sinhala Buddhist and Tamil ones. However, the crucial insight from this study is that politically dominant identities emerge through sustained patterns of activity by individuals pursuing a variety of ends; an outcome that relies crucially on agency and choice—by individuals who could always do otherwise—and is therefore difficult to engineer or consciously facilitate. In the absence of a robust pan-ethnic sense of national identity, the efforts to secure compromise within a Sinhala Buddhist-dominated framework are inevitably brittle and short-lived. During the armed conflict, international confidence in the possibility of liberal reform was bolstered by the faith that many Tamil political leaders expressed, often privately, in the willingness of Sinhala leaders to cede to Tamil demands for autonomy. However, in the post-war era this faith has been put to the test and Tamil political leaders have been unable to deliver any form of meaningful reform despite their repeated and expressed willingness to work within the Sri Lankan framework and disavowal of separatism. Meanwhile, although there was close cooperation between the Muslims and the Sri Lankan state during the campaign against the LTTE, with Muslims working as intelligence agents and paramilitaries, in the post-war era Muslim political leaders have been unable to stem the rise in anti-Muslim violence, despite being members of the ruling coalition government.

Sri Lanka's deep-seated ethnic crisis is not, however, an inevitable state of affairs. The ideologically incompatible national identities that sustain it are not set in stone and ultimately dependent on human agency: the daily and ongoing patterns of political activity that reproduce them. But while Sinhala Buddhist and Tamil nationalisms are indeed constructed, they are also deep-seated and not easily overridden. At the same time the conflict between these two nationalisms is also not an internal one; it has always been embedded in international processes. The Sri Lankan state emerged amidst the processes of British colonial rule, and British officials were important in shaping the ethnic dimensions of independence. Liberal peace actors and processes were also intimately involved in the armed conflict. Liberal order-making has therefore been hugely consequential to shaping Sri Lanka's ethnic conflict and continues to be so in foregrounding accountability for wartime abuses as key to producing an ethnically inclusive state. The UNHRC's mandating of an investigation independent of Sri Lanka, against broad-ranging Sinhala Buddhist opposition, is therefore an important departure from the past patterns of international intervention. At the very least the investigation will establish an authoritative account of events at the end of the war and identify direct culpability: outcomes that both the Sri Lankan state and its Tamil nationalist opponents will be unable to avoid or ignore. However, accountability alone is not going to create a broad-ranging pan-ethnic nationalism, or indeed create an ideological overlap between Sinhala Buddhist and Tamil nationalists.

The example of south Indian Tamil identity shows that an ethnically inclusive nationalism is not simply a default position that miraculously appears in the absence of ethnic conflict. Rather it is a positive political outcome that in south India emerged through hard-fought and sustained processes of mobilisation and incorporation. Sri Lanka's ethnic conflict is not therefore the unfortunate eruption of ethnicity into a potentially ethnically neutral politics, but rather the result of an absence of a shared understanding of national identity. While considerable, the full range of liberal peace sanctions and incentives cannot engineer an inclusive ethnic identity, but can change the conditions and possibilities of both Sinhala Buddhist and Tamil nationalist politics. Key to this are steps such as de-militarisation, the repeal of punitive anti-terror legislation and creating the space for rehabilitation and development in the north-east that is outside Sinhala majoritarian control. It is only under these conditions, which will have to be guaranteed by external sanction, that Sinhala Buddhist politics will have to turn away from majoritarian expansion and look to other objectives. At the same time Tamil nationalism can equally move from oppositional mobilisation to the more multifarious problems of governance. These shifts alone will not resolve Sri Lanka's ethnic conflict but will certainly produce new problems and therefore new patterns of political activity, which are crucial to moving beyond the current impasse of violent state repression and seething Tamil resentment.

APPENDICES

APPENDIX 1

POPULATION STATISTICS

Table 1: India 1891

Total population	287, 223, 431
Madras	35, 630, 440
Tamil speakers	15, 229, 759
Hindu	187, 937, 450
Muslim	50, 121, 585
Christian	1, 862, 634

Source: *Census of India, 1891* (Government of India, 1892).

Table 2: India 1921

Total population	318, 942, 480
Madras	42, 794, 155
Tamil speakers	18, 780, 000
Hindu	216, 735, 000
Muslim	68, 735, 000
Christian	4, 754, 000
Indo-European language speakers	
(Hindi, Hindustani, Bengali, Gujarati, Marathi, Urdu, Maithili)	232, 846, 549
Dravidian language speakers	
(Tamil, Telugu, Kandadam, Malayalam)	64, 128, 052

Source: *Census of India, 1921* (Government of India, 1922).

Table 3: Distribution of Indian Muslim population in 1921

Province	Muslim population	Muslim population as per cent of total provincial population	Muslim population as per cent of total Indian Muslim population
Bengal	25, 210, 810	54.00	43
United Provinces	6, 481, 032	14.25	11
Punjab	11, 444, 321	55.33	20

- Figures taken from Mushirul Hasan, *Nationalism and Communal Politics in India, 1885–1930* (New Delhi: Manohar Publications, 1991), p10.
- While these three provinces contained 84 per cent of the population, the remaining 16 per cent were distributed across Madras, Bombay, Central Provinces and the Princely States.

Table 4: Sri Lanka 1891

Total population	3, 007, 789
Sinhalese	2, 041, 158
Tamil	723, 853
Muslims	197, 166
Malays	10, 133

Source: *Census of Ceylon, 1891* (Government of Ceylon, 1892).

Table 5: Sri Lanka 1921

Total population	4, 498, 605
Sinhalese	3, 016, 154
• Low country	1, 927, 057
• Kandyan	1, 089, 097
Sri Lankan Tamils	517, 623
Indian Tamils	602, 735
Others (mainly other Indians, burghers and Europeans)	77, 426
Muslims	284, 964
Buddhists	2,743,702
Hindus	964,927
Christians	443, 043

- The religious composition of the low country Sinhalese was majority Buddhist (86.26 per cent) and minority Christian (13.69 per cent).
- The religious composition of the Kandyan Sinhalese was overwhelmingly Buddhist (99.26 per cent).
- The religious composition of the Sri Lankan Tamils was majority Hindu (83.01 per cent) and minority Christian (15.79 per cent).

APPENDIX 1

- The religious composition of the Indian Tamils was majority Hindu (89.01 per cent) and minority Christian (8.21 per cent).
- The ethnic composition of the Christian population was as follows: Low country Sinhalese (59.49 per cent), Sri Lankan Tamil (18.42 per cent), Indian Tamils (11.16 per cent) and others—mainly burghers and Europeans (14.93 per cent).
- Figures taken from the *Census of Ceylon, 1921* (Government of Ceylon,1923).

APPENDIX 2

SRI LANKA ELECTORAL STATISTICS

Northern and Eastern Provinces/FP (TULF in 1977) per cent share of the votes polled

		1952	1956	Mar 1960	Jul 1960	1965	1970	1977
Eastern Province	Batticaloa	00.00	51.22	46.86	51.81	42.76	32.66	24.33
	Batticaloa 2			00.00	4.3	00.00	00.00	20.49
	Kalkudah	00.00	00.00	47.83	58.39	34.93	37.77	42.70
	Padiruppu	00.00	49.14	61.82	66.05	51.14	48.52	48.80
	Trincomalee	45.32	56.62	70.70	64.32	59.87	47.83	45.65

		1952	1956	Mar 1960	Jul 1960	1965	1970	1977
Northern Province	Chavakachcheri	27.45	64.23	64.73	85.33	68.77	54.33	63.08
	Jaffna Town	39.36	32.34	29.19	31.26	30.71	35.48	56.43
	Kankesanthurai	42.44	53.75	66.79	87.98	57.62	44.09	84.90
	Kayts	6.42	70.61	56.07	81.11	69.37	53.14	63.83
	Kilinochchi			41.21	71.78	44.31	46.39	73.22
	Kopay	44.29	53.15	47.84	66.94	51.15	55.50	76.86
	Manipay							83.48
	Mannar	00.00	52.69	46.93	55.49	39.25	48.70	51.44

Northern Province							
Mullaitivu							52.16
Nallur			48.95	64.92	44.88	44.47	89.05
Point Pedro		20.47	39.91	66.75	45.98	48.28	55.59
Udupiddy			18.02	37.91	32.67	46.24	63.18
Uduvil	00.00	00.00	43.62	62.45	48.04	49.07	
Vavuniya	00.00	00.00	00.00	42.08	24.87	42.80	58.82
Vaddukoddai	18.96	57.12	52.81	71.05	60.09	50.17	71.21
FP seats won out of total available	2 out of 13	8 out of 13	14 out of 18	14 out of 18	12 out of 18	12 out of 18	17 out of 19
Average FP vote	15.79	43.03	43.52	59.44	44.89	43.63	59.22

• Figures collated from G. P. S. Harischandra De Silva, *A Statistical Survey of Elections to the Legislatures of Sri Lanka, 1911–1977* (Colombo: Marga Institute, 1979).

• New constituencies were created through fresh boundary delimitations in 1960 and 1977. The 1977 changes eliminated the Uduvil Constituency. In the 1960 changes, Batticaloa was made into a two-member constituency, each registered voter was given two votes and the two highest-scoring candidates were elected.

• In 1977 the FP led a coalition of Tamil parties (including the ACTC), called the TULF.

• In the Northern Province constituencies, the bulk of the non-FP vote went to the All Ceylon Tamil Congress (ACTC). In the Eastern Province it was won mainly by UNP candidates or independents. The percentage share of 'non Tamil parties' (i.e. other than the FP or ACTC) was a high of 25.1 per cent in 1952 but a low of 14 per cent in 1960. In the Northern Province the non-Tamil vote went to Marxist parties, while in the Eastern Province it went to the UNP or independents. James Jupp, *Sri Lanka: Third World Democracy* (London: Frank Cass, 1978), p. 139.

• Where a zero is shown, the FP did not contest.

NOTES

INTRODUCTION

1. Until 1972 Sri Lanka was known as Ceylon. For convenience this book will use Sri Lanka throughout.
2. Tamil Nadu's economic and human development outcomes are good relative to other Indian states. In 2012–13 it had the third highest domestic output per capita of all the major Indian states (after Haryana and Maharashtra). See Government of India, *Economic Survey 2014–15*, Statistical Appendix, A19. It also has the third highest score on the human development index. For details, see Jean Drèze and Reetika Khera, 'Regional patterns of human and child deprivation in India', *Economic and Political Weekly* 57 (2012), pp. 42–9.

    The Tamil-speaking regions of Sri Lanka were relatively prosperous as well as productive during the colonial era and up to the beginning of the war in 1981. For the Dutch and British colonial eras, see Sinnappah Arasaratnam, 'Social history of a dominant caste society; the Vellalar of north Ceylon (Sri Lanka)', *Indian Economic and Social History Review* 18.3–4 (1981); also Murugar Gunasingam, *Sri Lankan Tamil Nationalism: a study of its origins* (Sydney: MV Publications, 1999). During the colonial era Tamils were relatively well represented in the administrative services, and the agricultural production of these areas was also fairly efficient; but in the decades following, there was a distinct economic decline as the policies of majoritarian preference had an impact (for details, see Chapter 1). However, even as late as 1981 the Northern Province still contributed the second largest share of total GDP; but the impact of the war has been devastating and it now ranks last. Figures taken from Bhavani Fonseka and Mirak Raheem, 'Land in the Northern Province: post-war practices, policy and practices', Centre for Policy Alternatives, December 2011, p. 119, available at http://www.cpalanka.org/land-issues-in-the-northern-province-post-war-politics-policy-and-practices/, last accessed May 2015. Economic reconstruction after the war remains severely constrained by the intense militarisation of these areas; for details, see International Crisis Group, *Sri Lanka's North II: rebuilding under the military*, Asia Report 220 (2012).

3. Marguerite Ross Barnett, *The Politics of Cultural Nationalism in South India* (Princeton, NJ: Princeton University Press, 1976), p. 133.

4. Narendra Subramanian, *Ethnicity and Populist Mobilization: political parties, citizens, and democracy in South India* (Delhi: Oxford University Press, 1999), p. 301.

5. See Chapters 3 and 5.

6. Christophe Jaffrelot, *The Hindu Nationalist Movement and Indian Politics, 1925 to the 1990s: strategies of identity building, implantation and mobilisation (with special reference to central India)* (London: Hurst & Co., 1996); Thomas B. Hansen and Christophe Jaffrelot, *The BJP and the Compulsions of Politics in India* (New Delhi: Oxford University Press, 2001).

7. A. K. Verma, Beg Mizra Asmer and Kumar Sudhir, 'A saffron sweep in Uttar Pradesh', *The Hindu*, 23 May 2014, http://www.thehindu.com/opinion/op-ed/a-saffron-sweep-in-uttar-pradesh/article6037683.ece?homepage=true, last accessed 30 May 2014; Sanjay Kumar, 'Bihar: interpreting the massive mandate', *The Hindu*, 23 May 2014, http://www.thehindu.com/opinion/op-ed/bihar-interpreting-the-massive-mandate/article6037680.ece?homepage=true, last accessed 30 May 2014.

8. Hugo Gorringe, *Untouchable Citizens: Dalit movements and democratization in Tamil Nadu* (Delhi: Sage Publications India, 2005).

9. Sujit Sivasundaram, *Islanded: Britain, Sri Lanka, and the bounds of an Indian Ocean colony* (Chicago, IL: University of Chicago Press, 2013).

10. See Chapter 3.

11. Sankaran Krishna, *Postcolonial Insecurities: India, Sri Lanka, and the question of nationhood* (Minneapolis: University of Minnesota Press, 1999).

12. See Chapter 8.

13. For the connections between popular sovereignty and nationalism, see Bernard Yack, 'Popular Sovereignty and Nationalism', *Political Theory* 29.4 (2001), pp. 517–36; and Connor Walker, 'Nationalism and political illegitimacy', in Conversi, Daniele, ed., *Ethnonationalism in the contemporary world: Walker Connor and the study of nationalism* (London: Routledge, 2004), pp. 24–47.

14. Michael Billig, *Banal Nationalism* (London: Sage, 1995), p. 29.

15. Ibid., ch. 4 and 5.

16. Andreas Wimmer, *Nationalist Exclusion and Ethnic Conflict: shadows of modernity* (Cambridge: Cambridge University Press, 2002), p. 1.

17. For critical analyses of the civic–ethnic dichotomy, see Rogers Brubaker, *Ethnicity without Groups* (Cambridge, MA: Harvard University Press, 2004), ch. 6; and Bernard Yack, 'The myth of the civic nation', *Critical Review* 10.2 (1996), pp. 193–211.

18. Jawaharlal Nehru, *The Discovery of India* (London: Meridian Books, 1969), p. 49.

19. See Chapter 2.

20. J. R. Jayewardene, *Daily News*, 12 June 1987, Colombo, p. 1, quoted in Krishna, *Postcolonial Insecurities*, p. 41.

21. See Chapter 5.

22. Stewart Bell, 'Inside Sri Lanka: A life given over to war', *National Post*, 23 September 2008, available at http://www.nationalpost.com/Inside+Lanka+life+given+o ver/832374/story.html, last accessed April 2015.

23. John Breuilly, *Nationalism and the State* (Manchester: Manchester University Press, 1993), p. 93.

24. Rogers Brubaker, 'Ethnicity, race, and nationalism', *Annual Review of Sociology* 35 (2009), p. 21.

25. Ibid., p. 28.

26. For key examples, see Brueilly, 'Nationalism and the State'; Billig, 'Banal Nationalism'; and Wimmer, 'Nationalist Exclusion'.

27. Alfred Stepan, Juan J. Linz and Yogendra Yadav, *Crafting State-Nations: India and other multinational democracies* (Baltimore, MD: John Hopkins University Press, 2011).

28. Krishna, 'Postcolonial Insecurities'.

29. Kristian Stokke, 'Sinhalese and Tamil nationalism as post-colonial political projects from "above", 1948–1983', *Political Geography* 17.1 (1998), pp. 83–113.

30. David A. Washbrook, *The Emergence of Provincial Politics: the Madras Presidency, 1870–1920* (Cambridge: University of Cambridge, Centre of South Asian Studies, 1976); Christopher J. Baker, *The Politics of South India, 1920–1937* (Cambridge: Cambridge University Press, 1976).

31. Paul R. Brass, *Language, Religion and Politics in North India* (Lincoln, NE: iUniverse, 2005).

32. Kanchan Chandra, *Why Ethnic Parties Succeed: patronage and ethnic head counts in India* (Cambridge: Cambridge University Press, 2007).

33. Sumantra Bose, *States, Nations, Sovereignty: Sri Lanka, India, and the Tamil Eelam movement* (New Delhi: Sage Publications, 1994); Neil DeVotta, *Blowback: linguistic nationalism, institutional decay, and ethnic conflict in Sri Lanka* (Stanford, CA: Stanford University Press, 2004).

34. Kenneth Bush, *The Intra-Group Dimensions of Ethnic Conflict in Sri Lanka* (London: Palgrave Macmillan, 2003).

35. Chapter 3.

36. Ross Barnett, *The Politics of Cultural Nationalism in South India*.

37. Subramanian, *Ethnicity and Populist Mobilization*.

38. James Manor, 'The Failure of Political Integration in Sri Lanka (Ceylon)', *Commonwealth and Comparative Politics* 17.1 (1979), pp. 21–47; Katharine Adeney and Andrew Wyatt, 'Democracy in South Asia: getting beyond the structure–agency dichotomy', *Political Studies* 52.1 (2004), pp. 1–18.

39. Sumit Sarkar, 'Indian democracy: the historical inheritance', in Kohli, Atul, ed., *The Success of India's Democracy* (Cambridge: Cambridge University Press, 2001).

40. Ashutosh Varshney, *Ethnic Conflict and Civic Life: Hindus and Muslims in India* (New Haven, CT: Yale University Press, 2003).
41. Steven Wilkinson, *Votes and Violence: electoral competition and ethnic riots in India* (Cambridge: Cambridge University Press, 2006).
42. Varshney, *Ethnic Conflict and Civic Life*, p. 11.
43. Chapter 6.
44. For reports of the violence, see 'Fear, shock among Sri Lankan Muslims in the aftermath of Buddhist mob violence', CNN News, http://edition.cnn.com/2014/06/19/world/asia/sri-lanka-muslim-aluthgama/, last accessed April 2015; '"Fascists" in saffron robes: the rise of Sri Lanka's Buddhist ultra-nationalists', CNN News, http://edition.cnn.com/2014/07/17/world/asia/sri-lanka-bodu-bala-sena-profile/index.html, last accessed April 2015; International Crisis Group, *Crisis Watch Database*, Sri Lanka, 1 July 2014, http://www.crisisgroup.org/en/publication-type/crisiswatch/crisiswatch-database.aspx?CountryIDs=%7bE3AEAB0F-4DC7-4926-9510-3165AA4F182B%7d#results, last accessed April 2015.
    For Muslim ministers' inability to prevent or halt the rising tide of anti-Muslim violence and rhetoric from Buddhist organisations in the post-2009 era, see A. Ali, 'The End of the Road', *South Asia Journal* 9 (2013).
45. 'Disillusioned kingmakers: Sri Lanka's Muslims may choose opposition', *The Hindu*, http://www.thehindu.com/news/international/south-asia/disillusioned-kingmakers-sri-lankan-muslims-may-choose-opposition/article6749341.ece?topicpage=true&topicId=1820, last accessed April 2015.
46. 'As riot hit Muzzafarnagar votes, religious divide favours Modi', Reuters, http://in.reuters.com/article/2014/04/10/election-muzaffarnagar-bjp-congress-modi-idINDEEA3903W20140410, last accessed April 2015; '"Jats and Muslims in Muzzafarnagar are victims of a devilish design", Seema Mustafa', Tehelka, http://www.tehelka.com/jats-and-muslims-in-muzaffarnagar-are-victims-of-a-devilish-design-seema-mustafa/, last accessed April 2015.
47. For the previous decline in violence, see Wilkinson, *Votes and Violence*, pp. 160–71; and for the return of Hindu–Muslim violence, see Badri Narayan, 'Communal riots in Uttar Pradesh', *Economic and Political Weekly* 49.37 (2014), pp. 29–32.
48. Stepan, Linz and Yadav, *Crafting State-nations*.
49. James Manor, 'Center-state relations', in Kohli, Atul, ed., *The Success of India's Democracy* (Cambridge: Cambridge University Press, 2001), pp. 78–102.
50. Brass, *Language, Religion and Politics*, pp. 17–19.
51. Chapter 2.
52. Chapter 4.
53. Chapter 1.
54. Nicholas B. Dirks, *Castes of Mind: colonialism and the making of modern India* (Princeton, NJ: Princeton University Press, 2011).
55. Nira Wickramasinghe, *Sri Lanka in the Modern Age: a history* (London: Hurst & Co., 2014).

56. Krishna, *Post-colonial Insecurities*.
57. Sumathi Ramaswamy, *Passions of the Tongue: language devotion in Tamil India, 1891–1970* (Berkeley, CA: University of California Press, 1997).
58. John D. Rogers, 'Caste as a social category and identity in colonial Lanka', *Indian Economic and Social History Review* 41.5 (2004), pp. 51–77.
59. Dirks, *Castes of Mind*, p. 275.

1. THE ORIGINS

1. For a discussion of the transformations associated with British rule in India, see Manu Goswami, *Producing India: from colonial economy to national space* (Chicago, IL: University of Chicago Press, 2004); and David A. Washbrook, 'South India 1770–1840: the colonial transition', *Modern Asian Studies* 38.3 (2004,) p. 37. For Sri Lanka, see ch. 18–23 in K. M. De Silva, *A History of Sri Lanka* (New Delhi: Penguin, 2005); Donald R. Snodgrass, *Ceylon: an export economy in transition,* (Homewood, Ill: Irwin, 1966); and Lennox A. Mills, *Ceylon under British rule, 1795–1932, with an account of the East India Company's embassies to Kandy, 1762–1795* (London: Frank Cass, 1964).
2. Christopher A. Bayly, *Indian Society and the Making of the British Empire* (Cambridge: Cambridge University Press, 1988).
3. Bayly, *Indian Society*.
4. Michael N. Pearson, *The Portuguese in India* (Cambridge: Cambridge University Press, 1987).
5. De Silva, *A History of Sri Lanka*.
6. The discussion of the eighteenth-century British transition from trade to empire in India draws on Bayly, *Indian Society* and P. J. Marshall, *The Making and Unmaking of Empires: Britain, India, and America c.1750–1783* (Oxford: Oxford University Press, 2005).
7. John S. Galbraith, 'The "Turbulent Frontier" as a factor in British expansion', *Comparative Studies in Society and History* 2.2 (1960), pp. 150–60.
8. Government of India, *Census of India 1891*, 1892.
9. Ibid.
10. Goswami, *Producing India*.
11. Washbrook, 'South India 1770–1840'.
12. Bayly, *Indian Society*.
13. 'In the last years of the eighteenth century at least 2 million men circulated in India's "military market place" looking for mercenary employment in the armies of its regional potentates': David A. Washbrook, 'India, 1818–1860: the two faces of Colonialism', in A. Porter, ed., *The Oxford History of the British Empire: The Nineteenth Century (Volume III)* (Oxford: Oxford University Press, 1999), p. 405. Figure taken from D. H. A. Kolff, *Naukar, Rajput and Sepoy: the ethno-history of*

the military labour market in Hindustan, 1450–1850 (Cambridge: Cambridge University Press, 1990), pp. 110–16.

14. Washbrook, 'South India 1770–1840', pp. 507–8.
15. Dharma Kumar, *Land and Caste in South Asia: agricultural labour in the Madras Presidency during the nineteenth century* (Cambridge: Cambridge University Press, 1965).
16. This account is taken from Mills, *Ceylon under British Rule*; C. J. Jeffries, *Ceylon: the path to independence* (London: Pall Mall Press, 1962); and De Silva, *A History of Sri Lanka*.
17. Jeffries, *Ceylon*, pp. 14–15.
18. This reflected parliament's growing insistence on controlling distant territorial possessions (Marshall, *The Making and Unmaking of Empires*).
19. For a history of the rise of low country Sinhalese commercial groups, see Michael Roberts, *Caste Conflict and Elite Formation: the rise of a Karava elite in Sri Lanka, 1500–1931* (Cambridge: Cambridge University Press, 1982).
20. K. Indrapala, *The Evolution of an Ethnic Identity: the Tamils in Sri Lanka c.300 BCE to c.1200 CE* (Colombo: Vijitha Yapa, 2007).
21. Colonial Office, *Census of Ceylon 1891* (Colombo: Government Printer, 1892).
22. The 1891 Census did not distinguish between the two. Indian Tamil labour migration at this time was to a substantial extent cyclical and also unregulated. As tea plantations replaced coffee plantations, the demand for labour became less seasonal and the labourers became more settled on the island. The 1921 Census did distinguish between the two populations. It shows that the total Tamil population of 1,120,358 consisted of 602,735 Indian Tamils (54 per cent) and 517,623 Sri Lankan Tamils (46 per cent). See Table 5.
23. Thomas R. Metcalf, *Ideologies of the Raj* (Cambridge: Cambridge University Press, 1994), p. 28.
24. Eric Stokes, *The English Utilitarians and India* (Oxford: Clarendon Press, 1959).
25. Quoted in Cyril Henry Phillips, *The Evolution of India and Pakistan, 1858–1947: select documents* (Oxford, Oxford University Press, 1962), p. 10.
26. Quoted in G. C. Mendis, *The Colebroke–Cameron papers: documents on British colonial policy in Ceylon, 1796–1833* (Oxford: University Press, 1956), p. 152.
27. Quoted in Metcalfe, *Ideologies of the Raj*, p. 34.
28. Quoted in Mendis, *The Colebroke–Cameron Papers*, p. 54.
29. For British official attitudes towards India from the mid nineteenth century, see Sarvepalli Gopal, *British Policy in India, 1858–1905* (Cambridge: Cambridge University Press, 1965); and Thomas R. Metcalf, *The Aftermath of revolt: India, 1857–1870* (London: Oxford University Press, 1965).
     For Sri Lanka, see Lennox A. Mills, *Ceylon under British Rule, 1795–1932, with an account of the East India Company's embassies to Kandy, 1762–1795* (London: Frank Cass, 1964); and Nira Wickramasinghe, *Ethnic Politics in Colonial Sri Lanka, 1927–1947* (New Delhi: Vikas, 1995).

30. S. R. Mehrotra, *Emergence of the Indian National Congress* (New Delhi: Vikas, 1971).

31. Michael Roberts, 'Stimulants and ingredients in the awakening of latter day nationalism', in Roberts, Michael, ed., *Sri Lanka: collective identities revisited* (Colombo: Marga Institute, 1997).

32. Anil Seal, *The Emergence of Indian Nationalism: competition and collaboration in the later nineteenth century* (Cambridge: Cambridge University Press, 1968).

33. Sumit Sarkar, *Modern India: 1885–1947* (Basingstoke: Macmillan, 1989).

34. Michael Billig, *Banal Nationalism* (London: Sage, 1995), p. 29.

35. Quoted in Gopal, *British Policy in India*, p. 175.

36. Peter Hardy, *The Muslims of British India* (Cambridge: Cambridge University Press, 1972).

37. Eleanor Zelliot, 'Congress and the Untouchables, 1917–1950', in Sission, Richard and Stanley Wolpert, eds, *Congress and Indian Nationalism: the pre-independence phase* (Berkeley, CA: University of California Press, 1988).

38. Wickramasinghe, *Ethnic Politics*.

39. As in India, there was greater change at the level of local government: during the 1860s, municipal councils were established for Galle, Colombo and Kandy, with an electorate based on a restricted franchise that included Sri Lankans (Mills, *Ceylon under British Rule*).

40. This account is taken from De Silva, *A History of Sri Lanka*; Nira Wickramasinghe, *Sri Lanka in the Modern Age: a history of contested identities* (London: Hurst & Co., 2006); and Jane Russell, *Communal Politics under the Donoughmore Constitution, 1931–1947* (Dehiwala, Sri Lanka: Tisara Prakasakayo, 1982).

41. In India the franchise was extended to 6.5 million people out of a total population of 306 million (Sarkar, *Modern India*, pp. 36, 337). In Sri Lanka the franchise was extended in 1921 to just over 53,000 out of a total population of just under 4.5 million (G. P. S. Harischandra De Silva, *A Statistical Survey of Elections to the Legislatures of Sri Lanka, 1911–1977*, Colombo: Marga Institute, 1979, pp. 79–82).

42. Shahid Amin, 'Gandhi as Mahatma: Gorakhpur District, Eastern UP, 1921–2', in Guha, R., ed., *Subaltern Studies, Volume III* (Oxford: Oxford University Press, 1984).

43. For India, see David A. Washbrook, *The Emergence of Provincial Politics: the Madras Presidency, 1870–1920* (University of Cambridge: Centre of South Asian Studies, 1976); and Baker, *The Politics of South India*. For Sri Lanka, see Russell, *Communal Politics*.

44. There is a large literature on the social classifications of colonial rule, particularly in relation to India. Examples include Bernard S. Cohn, *Colonialism and its Forms of Knowledge: the British in India* (Princeton, NJ: Princeton University Press, 1996); Nicholas B. Dirks, *Castes of Mind: colonialism and the making of modern*

India (Princeton, NJ: Princeton University Press, 2001); Richard King, *Orientalism and Religion: post-colonial theory, India and 'the mystic East'* (London: Routledge, 1999); and Gyanendra Pandey, *The Construction of Communalism in Colonial North India* (Delhi: Oxford University Press, 1990).

For Sri Lanka, see Wickramasinghe, *Sri Lanka in the Modern Age*; John D. Rogers, 'Caste as a social category and identity in colonial Lanka', *Indian Economic and Social History Review* 41.5 (2004), pp. 51–77; and David Scott, *Refashioning Futures: criticism after postcoloniality* (Princeton, NJ: Princeton University Press, 1999).

45. For contrasting accounts of the impact of British colonialism on the caste system, see Dirks, *Castes of Mind*; and Susan Bayly, *Caste, Society and Politics in India from the Eighteenth Century to the Modern Age* (New York: Cambridge University Press, 1999). Similarly for contrasting accounts of the impact of British colonialism on religiously motivated collective violence, see Christopher A. Bayly, 'The Pre-History of "Communalism"? Religious conflict in India, 1700–1860', *Modern Asian Studies* 19.2 (1985), pp. 177–203; and Pandey, *The Construction of Communalism*.

46. Ernst Gellner, *Nations and Nationalism* (Oxford: Blackwell, 1983).

47. For a discussion of the importance of revivalist activities and particularly nationalism in diffusing modern administrative categories and processes amongst non-elite sections of colonial society, see David Rampton, '"Deeper hegemony"; the politics of Sinhala nationalist authenticity and power-sharing in Sri Lanka', *Comparative and Commonwealth Politics* 49.2 (2011), pp. 245–73.

48. Thomas R. Trautmann, *Aryans and British India* (Delhi: Yoda Press, 2004).

49. For details, see Trautmann, *Aryans*, ch. 5, 6.

50. Ibid., pp. 145–53.

51. For accounts of the Aryan narrative of Indian history, see Goswami, *Producing India*; Peter Van der Veer, *Imperial Encounters: religion and modernity in India and Britain* (Princeton, NJ: Princeton University Press, 2001), and Trautmann, *Aryans*.

52. V. Ravindran, 'Discourses of empowerment: missionary Orientalism in the development of Dravidian nationalism', in Brook, Timothy and André Schmid, eds, *Nation Work: Asian elites and national identities* (Ann Arbor, MI: University of Michigan Press, 2000); Thomas R. Trautmann, *Languages and Nations: the Dravidian proof in colonial Madras* (Berkeley and London: University of California Press, 2006).

53. John D. Rogers, 'Historical images in the British Period', in Spencer, Jonathan, ed., *Sri Lanka: history and the roots of conflict* (London: Routledge, 1990); K. N. O. Dharmadasa, *Language, Religion, and Ethnic Assertiveness: the growth of Sinhalese nationalism in Sri Lanka* (Ann Arbor, MI: University of Michigan Press, 1992); Marisa Angell, 'Understanding the Aryan Theory', in Tiruchelvam, Mithran

and C. S. Dattathreya, eds, *Culture and Politics of Identity in Sri Lanka* (Colombo: International Centre for Ethnic Studies, 1998).

54. This account of caste is taken from Bayly, *Caste*, pp. 1–24.
55. John C. B. Webster, 'Who is a Dalit?' in Michael, S. M, ed., *Untouchable: Dalits in modern India* (Boulder, CO: Lynne Rienner, 1999).
56. For discussions of these competing approaches to caste, see Dirks, *Castes of Mind*; Bayly, *Caste*; and M. S. S. Pandian, *Brahmin and non-Brahmin: genealogies of the Tamil political present* (Delhi: Permanent Black, 2007).
57. As Baker notes, the '1891 Census in Madras set out to catalogue subcastes defined by interdining and intermarriage: it counted up to 25, 000 before giving up and admitting that the list was far from complete'. *The Politics of South India, 1920–1937* (Cambridge: Cambridge University Press, 1976), p. 4.
58. Bayly, *Caste*.
59. Baker, *The Politics of South India*, p. 29.
60. Dirks, *Castes of Mind*.
61. K. Nambi Arooran, *Tamil Renaissance and Dravidian Nationalism 1905–1944* (Madurai: Koodal Publishers, 1980), p. 31; Dirks, *Castes of Mind*, p. 223.
62. Wickramasinghe, *Sri Lanka in the Modern Age*, p. 140.
63. Ross Barnett, *The Politics of Cultural Nationalism in South India*, 1976), pp. 15–17; Bayly, *Caste*, p. 32.
64. Ravindran, 'Discourses of empowerment'; Trautmann, *Languages and Nations*.
65. Donald L. Horowitz, *Ethnic Groups in Conflict* (Berkeley, CA: University of California Press, 1985), p. 37.
66. D. Denis Hudson, 'Tamil Hindu responses to Protestants: nineteenth-century literati in Jaffna and Tinnevelly', in Kaplan, Steven, ed., *Indigenous Responses to Western Christianity* (New York and London: New York University Press, 1995); Pandian, *Brahmin and non-Brahmin*.
67. R. Suntharalingam, *Politics and Nationalist Awakening in South India, 1852–1891* (Tucson, AZ: University of Arizona Press, 1974).
68. J. B. P. More, *The Political Evolution of Muslims in Tamilnadu and Madras, 1930–1947* (Hyderabad: Orient Longman, 1997); J. B. P. More, *Muslim Identity, Print Culture and the Dravidian Factor in Tamil Nadu* (London: Orient Longman, 2004).
69. Hansen and Jaffrelot, *The BJP and the Compulsions of Politics in India*.
70. For contrasting views on this issue, see articles by John Harriss, 'Whatever Happened to Cultural Nationalism in Tamil Nadu? A reading of current events and the recent literature on Tamil politics', *Commonwealth and Comparative Politics* 40.3 (2002), pp. 97–117; and S. V. Rajadurai and V. Geetha, 'A Response to John Harriss', *Commonwealth and Comparative Politics* 40.3 (2002), pp. 118–24.
71. For the commercial rise of the Karava, see Roberts, *Caste Conflict*; see also De Silva, *A History of Sri Lanka*, p. 428.

72. Wickramasinghe, *Ethnic Politics*, p. 31.

73. Nicholapillai Maria Saveri, *A Catholic–Hindu Encounter: relations between Roman Catholics and Hindus in Jaffna, Sri Lanka, 1900–1926* (Jaffna, Sri Lanka: Centre for Performing Arts, 1993).

2. BECOMING NATIONAL: TAMILS, MUSLIMS AND CONGRESS IN COLONIAL INDIA

1. Christopher J. Baker, *The Politics of South India, 1920–1937* (Cambridge: Cambridge University Press, 1976), p. 211.

2. Sumit Sarkar, *Modern India: 1885–1947* (Basingstoke: Macmillan, 1989), p. 349.

3. For the importance of patronage networks in south India, see Baker, *Politics of South India*, p. 35; and for Muslim politics, see Ayesha Jalal, *The Sole Spokesman: Jinnah, the Muslim League, and the demand for Pakistan* (New Delhi: Cambridge University Press, 1994), pp. 138–73.

4. Table 3.

5. For the Hindu nationalist orientation of the Bengal Congress, see Joya Chatterji, *Bengal Divided: Hindu communalism and partition, 1932–1947* (Cambridge: Cambridge University Press, 1994); for the Congress in Punjab, see Norman G. Barrier, 'The Arya Samaj and Congress Politics in the Punjab, 1894–1908', *Journal of Asian Studies* 26.3 (1967), pp. 363–79; and for UP, see Richard Gordon, 'The Hindu Mahasabha and the Indian National Congress, 1915 to 1926', *Modern Asian Studies* 9.2 (1975), pp. 145–203.

6. Baker suggests that about two-thirds of the newly elected Congress candidates in the 1937 Madras provincial legislature were local power-holders who had no previous affiliation to the Congress (*Politics of South India*, p. 313). Some established magnates withdrew from the electoral contest when confronted by the prospect of a well organised electoral campaign (ibid., pp. 267, 303), whilst others simply switched their allegiance to the Congress (ibid., pp. 268, 313). In UP, Jalal argues that Congress's 'rural activism' during the Civil Disobedience movement persuaded Hindu landlords to accept the Congress ticket (Jalal, *Sole Spokesman*, p. 31).

7. In the 1937 elections, the League secured only 4.4 per cent of the total Muslim votes cast (Jalal, *Sole Spokesman*, pp. 32, 171). In the 1946 elections, however, it won 75 per cent of the total Muslim votes cast (ibid., p. 171). In the 1937 elections, most Muslim votes went to large landlords or other candidates able to command the allegiance of significant vote banks (ibid., ch. 1).

8. Quoted in S. R. Mehrotra, *Emergence of the Indian National Congress* (New Delhi: Vikas, 1971), p. 600.

9. See Mehrotra, *Emergence*, p. 12; and Anil Seal, *The Emergence of Indian Nationalism: competition and collaboration in the later nineteenth century* (Cambridge: Cambridge University Press, 1968), p. 245.

10. See Seal, *Emergence*, ch. 4; Sarvepalli Gopal, *British Policy in India, 1858–1905*

(Cambridge: Cambridge University Press, 1965), ch. 2 and 3; and Mehrotra, *Emergence*, ch. 5 and 6.

11. Seal, *Emergence*, ch. 6.
12. Quoted in ibid., p. 586.
13. Seal, *Emergence*, p. 267.
14. Mehrotra, *Emergence*, p. 592.
15. The drain of wealth argument was in circulation in upper Indian cities between 1806 and 1818: Christopher A. Bayly, *Indian Society and the Making of the British Empire* (Cambridge: Cambridge University Press, 1988), p. 196.
16. Manu Goswami, *Producing India: from colonial economy to national space* (Chicago, IL: University of Chicago Press, 2004), pp. 215–24.
17. John R. McLane, 'The early Congress, Hindu populism and the wider society', in Sisson, Rishard and Stanley Wolpert, eds, *Congress and Indian Nationalism: the pre-independence phase* (Berkeley, CA: University of California Press, 1988), p. 53.
18. Quoted in Goswami, *Producing India*, p. 222.
19. Quoted in ibid., p. 224.
20. Ibid., p. 225.
21. Indian National Congress and A. M. Zaidi, *A Tryst with Destiny: a study of economic policy resolutions of INC passed during the last 100 years* (New Delhi: Indian Institute of Applied Political Research, Publication Dept, 1985).
22. John R. McLane, *Indian Nationalism and the Early Congress* (Princeton, NJ: Princeton University Press, 1977), p. 144.
23. Goswami, *Producing India*, p. 212.
24. Sarkar, *Modern India*, pp. 111–37.
25. For examples, see Sarkar, *Modern India*, p. 22; Seal, *Emergence*, p. 165; Gopal, *British Policy in India*, pp. 36–8; and Mehrotra, *Emergence*, pp. 494–7.
26. Seal, *Emergence*, pp. 137–43, 163–5.
27. Mrinalini Sinha, *Colonial Masculinity: the 'manly Englishman' and the 'effeminate Bengali' in the late nineteenth century* (Manchester: Manchester University Press, 1995), ch. 2, p. 162.
28. See Chapter 4.
29. Sarkar, *Modern India*, p. 29.
30. Ibid., p. 329.
31. See Chapter 4.
32. Quoted in Mehrotra, *Emergence*, p. 576.
33. Sarkar, *Modern India*.
34. Chapter 1 and Trautmann (2004).
35. Peter Van der Veer, 'Hindus: a superior race', *Nations and Nationalism* 5.3 (1999), pp. 419–30.
36. Goswami, *Producing India*, p. 183.
37. Ibid., ch. 6.

38. Christophe Jaffrelot, *The Hindu Nationalist Movement and Indian Politics, 1925 to the 1990s: strategies of identity building, implantation and mobilisation (with special reference to central India)* (London: Hurst & Co., 1996); Van der Veer, 'Hindus', p. 429; Goswami, *Producing India*, p. 267.

39. Kenneth W. Jones, 'Communalism in the Punjab: The Arya Samaj Contribution', *Journal of Asian Studies* 28.1 (1968), p. 43; Peter Van der Veer, *Imperial Encounters: religion and modernity in India and Britain* (Princeton, NJ: Princeton University Press, 2001), pp. 49–52.

40. Jones, 'Communalism in the Punjab'; Van der Veer, 'Hindus'.

41. Sarkar, *Modern India*, p. 74.

42. Van der Veer, *Imperial Encounters*, p. 52.

43. Barrier, 'Arya Samaj'.

44. William Gould, *Hindu Nationalism and the Language of Politics in Late Colonial India* (Cambridge: Cambridge University Press, 2004), ch. 4.

45. Jones, 'Communalism in the Punjab'.

46. Krishna Kumar, 'Hindu Revivalism and Education in North-Central India', *Social Scientist* 18.10 (1990), pp. 4–26; Richard D. King, *Nehru and the Language Politics of India* (Delhi: Oxford University Press, 1999), pp. 74–91.

47. Oliver Mendelsohn and Marika Vicziany, *The Untouchables: subordination, poverty and the state in modern India* (Cambridge: Cambridge University Press, 1988), p. 96.

48. R. Suntharalingam, *Politics and Nationalist Awakening in South India, 1852–1891* (Tucson, AZ: University of Arizona Press, 1974), pp. 290–311.

49. Ibid., p. 303.

50. Ibid., p. 295.

51. Ibid., pp. 298, 303.

52. Washbrook, *Madras Presidency*, p. 290; M. S. S. Pandian, *Brahmin and non-Brahmin: genealogies of the Tamil political present* (Delhi: Permanent Black, 2007), p. 36.

53. Mehrotra, *Emergence*, p. 561.

54. Washbrook, *Madras Presidency*, pp. 238, 239.

55. Ibid., pp. 245–8, 289.

56. Peter Van der Veer characterises Theosophy, and the broader Spiritualist movement of which it was a part, as oppositional movements that contested the late-nineteenth-century hegemonic alliance of Evangelical Christianity and Imperialism (*Imperial Encounters*, pp. 58–66). He situates Annie Besant's biography within the sociological dynamics and intellectual currents of this movement (*Imperial Encounters*, p. 63).

57. Seal, *Emergence*, p. 300.

58. Peter Hardy, *The Muslims of British India* (Cambridge: Cambridge University Press, 1972), pp. 50–60.

59. Hardy, *Muslims*, p. 59.
60. Ibid., pp. 56, 58.
61. Ibid., p. 59.
62. Ibid., pp. 81–5.
63. Ibid., p. 31.
64. Mehrotra, *Emergence*, pp. 368–9.
65. Hardy, *Muslims*, p. 125.
66. Ibid., p. 96.
67. Seal, *Emergence*, pp. 318–19.
68. Ibid., pp. 309, 310.
69. Ibid., pp. 312–13.
70. See for example Pandian, *Brahmin and non-Brahmin*; and Sumathi Ramaswamy, *Passions of the Tongue: language devotion in Tamil India, 1891–1970* (Berkeley, CA: University of California Press, 1997).
71. Chapter 1.
72. Chapter 1.
73. There were multiple and often conflicting uses of the Dravidian idea. While some used it to revive and reform Saivism, the south Indian tradition of worship and theology (Ramaswamy, *Passions of the Tongue*, pp. 24–34), others used it to attack religion as a whole and sought to reform south Indian society by appealing to universally applicable humanist principles (M. S. S. Pandian, '"Nation" from its margins: notes on E. V. Ramaswamy's "impossible" nation', in Bhargava R., A. K. Bagchi and R. Sudarshan, eds, *Multiculturalism, Liberalism and Democracy* (Calcutta: Oxford University Press, 1999)).
74. Baker, 'Introduction'; Ramaswamy, *Passions of the Tongue*, pp. 46–62.
75. Pandian, *Brahmin and non-Brahmin*, pp. 52–5.
76. K. Nambi Arooran, *Tamil Renaissance and Dravidian Nationalism 1905–1944* (Madurai: Koodal Publishers, 1980), p. 61.
77. V. Ravindran, 'Discourses of empowerment: missionary Orientalism in the development of Dravidian nationalism', in Brook, Timothy and André Schmid, eds, *Nation Work: Asian elites and national identities* (Ann Arbor, MI: University of Michigan Press, 2000).
78. Pandian, *Brahmin and non-Brahmin*, pp. 121–41.
79. Ramaswamy, *Passions of the Tongue*, pp. 25–9.
80. Ravindran, 'Discourses of empowerment'.
81. Pandian, *Brahmin and non-Brahmin*, pp. 121–41; Ravindran, 'Discourses of empowerment'.
82. E. V. Ramaswamy, the founder of the Self-Respect Movement, described his political creed as 'no god, no religion, no Gandhi, no Congress, and no Brahmins' (Pandian, '"Nation"', p. 289).
83. Baker, 'Introduction', p. 15; Ramaswamy, *Passions of the Tongue*, pp. 46–56.

NOTES

84. Ravindran, 'Discourses of empowerment'.
85. Not all Tamil Congress activists were committed to social reform; see Pandian, *Brahmin and non-Brahmin*, p. 93.
86. For example, the poet C. Subramania Bharathi (1882–1921) condemned the practice of untouchability, but worked very much within a Hindu or Saivite devotional idiom to promote Indian nationalism (Nambi Aroonan, *Tamil Renaissance*, pp. 60–62). In the late-nineteenth-century debates on the issue of child marriage and widow remarriage, both south Indian conservatives and social reformers appealed to the authority of the Sanskrit texts (Suntharalingam, *Politics and Nationalist Awakening*, pp. 83, 311–37). For discussions of the sociological assumptions driving social reform efforts within the Indian nationalist movement, see Susan Bayly, *Caste, Society and Politics in India from the Eighteenth Century to the Modern Age* (New York: Cambridge University Press, 1999), ch. 5, 6; and Dirks, *Castes of Mind*, ch. 11.
87. By 1902 only 40 of the 1,067 officers of the elite Indian Civil Service were Indians (McLane, *Indian Nationalism*, p. 24). A 1924 Royal Commission envisaged a 50 per cent Indianisation of the civil service after 15 years (Sarkar, *Modern India*, p. 237).
88. Direct elections to the provincial legislatures were only introduced with the 1919 Montague–Chelmsford Reforms and for the Central Legislature only with the 1935 reforms.
89. In 1896 the Indian Government, under pressure from London, imposed excise taxes on Indian textiles that were beginning to compete with Lancashire cotton (McLane, *Indian Nationalism*, p. 134). Indian business interests continued to express frustration at government policy and alleged discrimination in favour of European firms in the 1920s and up to the 1940s (Sarkar, *Modern India*, pp. 238, 23).
90. See Chapter 3.
91. For a list of the different cities, see: http://www.congress.org.in/new/congress-sessions.php
92. Seal, *Emergence*, pp. 315, 324.
93. Ibid., p. 333.
94. Suntharalingam, *Politics and Nationalist Awakening*, pp. 289, 315.
95. Sarkar, *Modern India*, p. 71.
96. Goswami, *Producing India*, p. 232.
97. Suntharalingam, *Politics and Nationalist Awakening*, p. 288; Goswami, *Producing India*, p. 232.
98. The number of Muslim delegates at the Congress sessions grew during its early years: 2 in 1885, 33 in 1886, 79 in 1887 and 222 in 1888. Seal, *Emergence*, pp. 329, 331.
99. McLane, 'The early Congress', p. 53.

100. M. S. Khan, *Tilak and Gokhale: a comparative study of their socio-political-economic programmes of reconstruction* (New Delhi: Ashish Publishing House, 1992), p. 161.

101. McLane, *Indian Nationalism*, pp. 98, 99.

102. Milton Israel, *Communications and Power: propaganda and the press in the Indian nationalist struggle* (Cambridge: Cambridge University Press, 1994), p. 163.

103. Seal, *Emergence*, p. 279.

104. McLane, *Indian Nationalism*, pp. 140, 146.

105. Gopal, *British Policy in India*, p. 267.

106. Sarkar, *Modern India*, pp. 89–100.

107. Ibid., 111–37; David Arnold, *The Congress in Tamilnad: nationalist politics in South India, 1919–1937* (London: Curzon Press, 1977), p. 26.

108. McLane, *Indian Nationalism*, pp. 366–8.

109. Sarkar, *Modern India*, p. 137.

110. Arnold, *Congress in Tamilnad*, p. 27

111. David Arnold, *Gandhi* (New York: Longman, 2001), p. 106.

112. Baker, *Politics of South India*, pp. 20–21.

113. Sarkar, *Modern India*, p. 150.

114. Sarkar, *Modern India*, p. 151.

115. Irschick, *Politics*, pp. 89–96; Baker, *Politics of South India*, p. 22.

116. Sarkar, *Modern India*, p. 194.

117. Baker, *Politics of South India*, p. 32; Arnold, *Congress in Tamilnad*, pp. 29–32.

118. In April 1919, police fired into an unarmed peaceful crowd at Jallianwala Bagh (Punjab), under the orders of General Dyer, killing 379 people according to official estimates, but unofficial figures were higher (Sarkar, *Modern India*, p. 191). The incident produced outrage across India, and the Bengali poet Rabindranath Tagore resigned his knighthood in protest (ibid., p. 194). The official commission appointed to investigate the incident published its report in May 1920, which was condemned by Gandhi as a 'whitewash' (ibid., p. 196). In the same month as the report, the terms of the peace treaty with Turkey were also published and condemned by Indian pan-Islamists (ibid.).

119. Ibid., p. 197.

120. Gopal Krishna, 'The Development of the Indian National Congress as a Mass Organisation, 1918–1923', *Journal of Asian Studies* 25.3 (1966), pp. 413–30.

121. Arnold, *Congress in Tamilnad*, p. 47.

122. Krishna, 'The Development of the Indian National Congress', p. 415.

123. Ibid., p. 419.

124. For a discussion of the diverse and autonomous (of Congress) movements that propelled these campaigns—often exceeding the limits of Congress's official programme—see Sarkar, *Modern India*.

125. Arnold, *Congress in Tamilnad*, p. 65.

126. Baker, *Politics of South India*, pp. 169–200.
127. 'The Non–cooperation campaign was initiated by Gandhi and by politicians who had been disappointed by the reforms; the agitations which contributed to the campaign in the southern province, however, were scattered and sporadic and had little to do with the politicians' stated aim of driving the British into the Indian Ocean. Liquor manufacturers registered a protest against the new excise rules and taxes and helped to give weight to the temperance campaign. Cattle graziers and forest tribesmen, objecting to new regulation of the forests and to new taxes on forest produce, raised an agitation which temporarily undercut the tenuous hold of law and order in the forest tracts.' (Baker, *Politics of South India*, p. 21)
128. By giving concrete expression to the discontents created by the Depression, Congress claimed for itself the role of representing popular grievance against government policy and repression. In 1934 Tamil Nadu Congressmen argued that other parties should withdraw from the elections so that 'Congress could demonstrate the strength of public opposition to Government repression'. David Arnold, 'The Politics of Coalescence: the Congress in Tamilnad, 1930–1937', in D. A. Low, ed., *Congress and the Raj: facets of the Indian struggle 1917–1947* (Oxford: Oxford University Press, 2004), p. 278.
129. The initial phase of the Civil Disobedience movement led to the famous face-to-face talks between Gandhi and the Viceroy Lord Irwin in early 1931. Although the talks were largely unproductive in moving the Congress agenda forward (Arnold, *Gandhi*, p. 152), they were nevertheless symbolically important. 'Gandhi met the Viceroy, face-to-face, as the sole representative of the Congress, and carried on discussions as if they were the commanders of two opposing but unbeaten armies' (ibid.).
130. Arnold, *Gandhi*, pp. 146–7.
131. For south India, see Baker, *Politics of South India*, pp. 37, 72.
132. Baker, *Politics of South India*, p. 261.
133. Jalal, *Sole Spokesman*, p. 146.
134. Mehrotra, *Emergence*, p. 591.
135. Nambi Aroonan, *Tamil Renaissance*; Ramaswamy, *Passions of the Tongue*; Pandian, *Brahmin and non-Brahmin*.
136. Baker, *Politics of South India*, pp. 162, 163.
137. Ibid., p. 312.
138. S. Theodore Baskaran, *The Message Bearers: the nationalist politics and the entertainment media in South India, 1880–1945* (Madras: Cre-A, 1981), pp. 29–42; Ramaswamy, *Passions of the Tongue*, pp. 46–62.
139. Ravindran, 'Discourses of empowerment'; Pandian, *Brahmin and non-Brahmin*, pp. 125–36.
140. Ramaswamy, *Passions of the Tongue*, p. 238; Pandian, '"Nation"', pp. 297–9.

141. Nambi Aroonan, *Tamil Renaissance*, pp. 160–69.
142. Washbrook, *Madras Presidency*, pp. 245, 246; Arnold, *Congress in Tamilnad*, p. 27; Nambi Aroonan, *Tamil Renaissance*, p. 64.
143. King, *Nehru*, p. 63.
144. Nambi Arooran, *Tamil Renaissance*, pp. 59–62.
145. Arnold, *Gandhi*, p. 179.
146. Bayly, *Caste*, p. 269.
147. Irschick, *Politics*, p. 35.
148. Ibid., p. 37.
149. Ibid., pp. 37, 63.
150. Arnold, *Congress in Tamilnad*, p. 23.
151. Irschick, *Politics*, p. 47.
152. Ibid., p. 48.
153. Ibid., pp. 358–67.
154. Ibid., p. 51.
155. Nambi Aroonan, *Tamil Renaissance*, pp. 49, 50.
156. Washbrook, *Madras Presidency*, ch. 3.
157. Baker, *Politics of South India*, pp. 90, 95.
158. Washbrook, *Madras Presidency*, pp. 145, 198.
159. Baker, *Politics of South India*, pp. 48–51; Washbrook, *Madras Presidency*, p. 276.
160. Irschick, *Politics*, pp. 275–85.
161. Ibid., p. 61.
162. It was disbanded in early 1920, once the final forms of the Montague–Chelmsford reforms had been settled; its members joined either Justice or Congress (Irschick, *Politics*, p. 166).
163. Baker, *Politics of South India*, pp. 155–66.
164. Ibid., pp. 37, 48, 64–71, 76, 77.
165. Washbrook, *Madras Presidency*, p. 277.
166. Baker, *Politics of South India*, p. 241.
167. For details of the Non-Cooperation movement in the Tamil-speaking areas, see Baker, *Politics of South India*, p. 21; Arnold, *Congress in Tamilnad*, pp. 46–77; and Irschick, *Politics*, pp. 193–201.
168. For details of Civil Disobedience in the Tamil-speaking areas, see Arnold, *Congress in Tamilnad*, pp. 118–40; Arnold, 'The Politics of Coalescence'; and Baker, *Politics of South India*, pp. 211–24.
169. Irschick, *Politics*, pp. 285–9.
170. Ibid.; Baker, 'Introduction', p. 15.
171. Ibid., p. 14.
172. Baskaran, *The Message Bearers*, pp. 29–42.
173. Ibid.
174. Irschick, *Politics*, pp. 182–3, 315.

175. Srividya Natarajan, 'Another stage in the life of the nation: Sadir, Bharathanatyam, feminist theory', PhD Dissertation, School of Humanities, University of Hyderabad, 1997; Lakshmi Subramanian, 'The reinvention of a tradition: nationalism, Carnatic music and the Madras Music Academy, 1900–1947', *Indian Economic and Social History Review* 36.2 (1999), pp. 131–63.
176. Although the Dravidian category in theory applied to all four south Indian languages (Tamil, Telugu, Kannadam and Malayalam), the Self-Respect movement's activities were confined to the Tamil-speaking districts as its founder, E. V. Ramaswami, worked in Tamil and English (Irschick, *Politics*, p. 334).
177. For a political biography of E. V. Ramaswami Naicker (1879–1973), see Irschick, *Politics*, pp. 330–50; Nambi Aroonan, *Tamil Renaissance*, pp. 152–85; and Pandian, '"Nation"'.
178. Nambi Aroonan, *Tamil Renaissance*, pp. 160–69.
179. E. S. Visswanathan, *The Political Career of E. V. Ramasami Naicker: a study in the politics of Tamil Nadu 1920–1949* (Madras: Ravi and Vasanth, 1983).
180. Narendra, Subramanian, *Ethnicity and Populist Mobilization: political parties, citizens, and democracy in South India* (Delhi and New York: Oxford University Press, 1999), p. 120. In many ways Ramaswamy shared his indifference to political power with Gandhi. As Nicholas Dirks notes:

'Except for a brief moment in his early career, his interest was far less in the representation of non-Brahmins in numerical terms than in the representation of non-Brahmins in symbolic terms; non Brahmins were to be seen both as the majority and as the principal modality of social value. Indeed E.V.R. shared a great deal with Gandhi—in his reliance, for example, on the symbolic character of politics, on the necessity of social reform, and in his overriding interest in ideology rather than political process' (*Castes of Mind*, pp. 263–4).

'Ramaswami's hostility to the political process, including his refusal to participate in electoral contestation, eventually led to a split with his principal lieutenant, C. N. Annadurai, who subsequently went on to form the Dravida Munnetra Kalzaham, the party that displaced Congress from power in Tamil Nadu in 1967.' Marguerite Ross Barnett, *The Politics of Cultural Nationalism in South India* (Princeton, NJ: Princeton University Press, 1976), ch. 7.
181. Sarkar, *Modern India*, pp. 336–8.
182. Quoted in Arnold, *Congress in Tamilnad*, p. 172.
183. For a description of the Congress campaign tactics, see Arnold, *Congress in Tamilnad*, pp. 160–74; and Baker, *Politics of South India*, pp. 263, 278, 279, 283, 299, 302.
184. 'The conditions for being accepted as a Congress candidate were simple: one had to sign the Congress pledge, a formula in which the signatory promised allegiance to the Congress programme and goals. There was rarely any close scrutiny of the political antecedents of candidates. It was evident that the Congress was

primarily interested in winning and the door to the organisation had been opened as wide as possible to ensure victory.' Baker, *Politics of South India*, p. 276; see also 297, 301.

185. Ibid., pp. 282–93.
186. Ibid., pp. 301, 303.
187. Arnold, *Congress in Tamilnad*, p. 143.
188. Baker, *Politics of South India*, p. 303.
189. Y. Vincent Kumaradoss, 'Kamaraj Remembered', *Economic and Political Weekly* 39.17 (2004), pp. 1655–7.
190. Nambi Aroonan, *Tamil Renaissance*, pp. 195–215.
191. Barnett, *Politics of Cultural Nationalism*, pp. 49, 52.
192. Nambi Aroonan, *Tamil Renaissance*, pp. 243–5, 227–8.
193. Barnett, *Politics of Cultural Nationalism*, p. 77.
194. Mushirul Hasan, *Nationalism and Communal Politics in India, 1885–1930* (New Delhi: Manohar Publications, 1991), pp. 66–7.
195. An organisation that was formed in 1906 in Dhaka; for details, see Hardy, *Muslims*, p. 164.
196. Sarkar, *Modern India*, pp. 150, 235.
197. Jalal, *Sole Spokesman*, pp. 10, 13, 44, 121.
198. Ibid., pp. 19–34.
199. Ibid., pp. 171–2.
200. For the calculations in Punjab, see ibid., pp. 143, 144; and for Bengal, see ibid., pp. 151–63.
201. David Gilmartin, 'A magnificent gift: Muslim nationalism and the election process in colonial Punjab', *Comparative Studies in Society and History* 40.3 (1998), pp. 415–36.
202. Jalal, *Sole Spokesman*, p. 151.
203. Ibid., pp. 57–60. Ayesha Jalal argues that while Jinnah took a public position on maximum provincial autonomy, he always intended to use this as a bargaining chip. The provincial autonomy position was moreover important to Muslims in the Muslim majority provinces, particularly Punjab. What Jinnah actually hoped to secure was adequate Muslim representation at a strong centre for which he would concede provincial autonomy. Jinnah himself had no base in provincial politics and always operated at the national level (ibid., pp. 10, 57–60).
204. Ibid., pp. 175, 188.
205. Barrier, 'Arya Samaj'.
206. Chatterji, *Bengal Divided*, ch. 2, 3.
207. Gordon, 'The Hindu Mahasabha'.
208. Gould, *Hindu Nationalism*.
209. Hasan, *Nationalism*, pp. 127–32, 220.
210. Gould, *Hindu Nationalism*, ch. 2, 3.
211. Jalal, *Sole Spokesman*, p. 30.

212. Hasan, *Nationalism*, pp. 46–52.

213. Sarkar, *Modern India*, pp. 411, 421.

214. Gordon, 'The Hindu Mahasabha', p. 151; McLane, *Indian Nationalism*, p. 283.

215. Jalal, *Sole Spokesman*.

216. Hasan, *Nationalism*, p. 42.

217. McLane, *Indian Nationalism*, p. 113.

218. In 1933 the Hindu Mahasabha called for the defence of Hindus as well as the capitalists and landlords as a class (Sarkar, *Modern India*, p. 332). Similarly interethnic parties representing landlord interests dominated electoral politics in the Punjab till the elections of 1945 (Jalal, *Sole Spokesman*, pp. 21, 22) and in the United Provinces until 1937 (Ibid., pp. 29, 30). See also Mushirul Hasan, 'The Muslim mass contacts campaign: analysis of a strategy of political mobilisation', in Sisson, Rishard and Stanley Wolpert, eds, *Congress and Indian Nationalism: the pre-independence phase* (Berkeley, CA: University of California Press, 1988), p. 210. Finally there was also from the late 1920s onwards an emergent Communist movement which from the late 1930s was contained (covertly) as the Congress Socialist Party (CSP) (Sarkar, *Modern India*, pp. 247–51).

The impact of the 1930s depression led to widespread peasant or Kisan movements in Bihar, Andhra Pradesh and Bengal. These movements cut across the Hindu–Muslim barrier. The Kisan movements also led often violent demonstrations and protests against Congress-led ministries. However, neither the Congress nor the League, including Congress Socialists like Nehru and Bose, were willing to make peasant mobilisation a core component of their programme or structure. This is primarily because in the late 1930s the Congress in particular was building a base amongst richer or dominant peasant groups, whose interests were very different from marginal peasants and landless labourers (Sarkar, *Modern India*, pp. 363–5).

219. Hasan, 'The Muslim mass contacts campaign', p. 209.

220. Jalal, *Sole Spokesman*, p. 43.

221. Hasan, 'The Muslim mass contacts campaign', pp. 213–15.

222. Jalal, *Sole Spokesman*, p. 44.

223. Sarkar, *Modern India*, pp. 432–9.

224. Steven Wilkinson, *Votes and Violence: electoral competition and ethnic violence in India* (Cambridge and New York: Cambridge University Press, 2004), p. 12.

225. Christophe Jaffrelot, *The Hindu Nationalist Movement and Indian Politics, 1925 to the 1990s*.

3. BECOMING NATIONAL: TAMILS AND SINHALESE IN COLONIAL SRI LANKA

1. According to Nira Wickramasinghe, Senanayake was the 'prime initiator' of moves which led to the formation of a United National Party in April 1946. The party was

nicknamed the 'Until New Parliament' party. Wickramasinghe, *Ethnic Politics in Colonial Sri Lanka, 1927–1947* (New Delhi: Vikas, 1995), p. 223.

2. For Senanayake's increasingly prominent role from 1942 onwards, see Jane Russell, *Communal Politics under the Donoughmore Constitution, 1931–1947* (Dehiwala, Sri Lanka: Tisara Prakasakayo, 1982), pp. 302–4; and K. M. De Silva, *A History of Sri Lanka* (New Delhi: Penguin, 2005), p. 554. For Senanayake's close links to Sinhala Buddhist revivalism, see ibid., p. 464; and also K. N. O. Dharmadasa, *Language, Religion, and Ethnic Assertiveness: the growth of Sinhalese nationalism in Sri Lanka* (Ann Arbor, MI: University of Michigan Press, 1992), pp. 230, 332–3.

3. V. Nalliah, a Tamil representative from the Eastern Province, stated during a debate on constitutional reform in November 1945: 'I am not going to differ from the majority of the Sinhalese. I am prepared to accept what today seems to be the majority decision of the majority community, because on them rests the responsibility for taking a correct decision' (Debates in the State Council of Ceylon, 8 November 1945; Col 6995). The following day, Mr A. R. A. Razik a Muslim representative, referred to the forthcoming constitutional reforms as an 'hour of triumph' for 'the Sinhalese Community' (Debates in the State Council of Ceylon, 9 November 1945; Col 7064).

4. Russell, *Communal Politics*; Wickramasinghe, *Ethnic Politics*.

5. Stanley J. Tambiah, *Leveling Crowds: ethno-nationalist conflicts and collective violence in South Asia* (Berkeley, CA: University of California Press, 1997), p. 39.

6. H. L. Seneviratne, *The Work of Kings: the new Buddhism in Sri Lanka* (Chicago, IL: University of Chicago Press, 1999). For a discussion of the role of Tamils in Buddhist revivalist narratives, see Dharmadasa, *Language*, pp. 7–14, 120, 138.

7. Dharmadasa, *Language*, p. 19.

8. Tambiah, *Leveling Crowds*, p. 43.

9. John D. Rogers, 'Historical images in the British period', in Spencer, Jonathan, ed., *Sri Lanka: history and the roots of conflict* (London: Routledge, 1990); M. Angell, 'Understanding the Aryan Theory', in Tiruchelvam, M. and C. S. Dattathreya, eds, *Culture and Politics of Identity in Sri Lanka*, Colombo, International Centre for Ethnic Studies, 1998.

10. Dharmadasa, *Language*, p. 3.

11. Rogers, 'Historical images'.

12. Bertram H. Farmer, *Pioneer Peasant Colonization in Ceylon: a study in Asian agrarian problems* (Oxford: Oxford University Press, 1957), p. 15.

13. Dharmadasa, *Language*, pp. 47, 79, 139.

14. Ibid., p. 112.

15. For a brief discussion of colonial archaeology, see Dharmadasa, *Language*, p. 112; for a discussion of British and Sinhala Buddhist approaches to the sites, see Rogers, 'Historical images', p. 100; and for examples of official patronage and support for

Sinhala Buddhist revival activities, specifically in relation to historical sites and relics in the late nineteenth century, see De Silva, *A History*, p. 432; and in the early twentieth century, see Wickramasinghe, *Ethnic Politics*, p. 120.

16. Nira Wickramasinghe, *Sri Lanka in the Modern Age: a history of contested identities* (London: Hurst & Co., 2006), p. 87.
17. Wickramasinghe, *Sri Lanka*, p. 88; see also Rogers, 'Historical images', p. 87.
18. Dharmadasa, *Language*, pp. 79, 106.
19. Tambiah, *Leveling Crowds*, p. 39. Peter Van der Veer suggests that the Theosophists had a much more important role in the Buddhist revival than the Hindu movement in India. 'The role of Olcott and the Theosophical society in the creation of a particular anti-colonial Hindu nationalism was minor compared to their role in creating Buddhist nationalism' (*Imperial Encounters*, p. 75).
20. Stanley J. Tambiah, *Buddhism Betrayed? Religion, politics, and violence in Sri Lanka* (Chicago and London: University of Chicago Press, 1992), p. 6.
21. Dharmadasa, *Language*, pp. 107–8.
22. Tambiah, *Buddhism Betrayed*, pp. 7–8.
23. Van der Veer, *Imperial Encounters*.
24. See Chapter 1 for a discussion of the historical origins of the differences between low country and Kandyan Sinhalese. The 1921 Census showed that the Low Country and Kandyan Sinhalese constituted 64 per cent and 36 per cent respectively of the total Sinhalese population (Table 5).
25. Michael Roberts, 'Elite formation and elites: 1832–1921', in Roberts, Michael, ed., *Sri Lanka: collective identities revisited* (Colombo: Marga Institute, 1997); De Silva, *A History*, pp. 421–5.
26. De Silva, *A History*, p. 432.
27. Christophe Jaffrelot, *The Hindu Nationalist Movement and Indian politics, 1925 to the 1990s: strategies of identity building, implantation and mobilisation* (London: Hurst & Co., 1996).
28. Dagmar Hellmann-Rajanayagam, 'The politics of the Tamil past', in Spencer, J. ed., *Sri Lanka: history and the roots of conflict* (London, Routledge, 1990).
29. Hellmann-Rajanayagam suggests that amongst the recurring themes of Tamil uses of history is the 'assumed linguistic, cultural, religious and "racial" difference between the Sinhala and the Tamils' that is always made the 'basis of the argument, whether for an autonomous Jaffna or for a united, multi-ethnic Sri Lanka' ('The politics of the Tamil past', p. 118).
30. The Dravidian idea was often invoked, particularly during the 1930s (Russell, *Communal Politics*, pp. 148–9). However, it did not have the same anti-Hindu meanings associated with the Dravidian idea in south India. Instead in Sri Lankan Tamil politics the Dravidian idea was often invoked alongside the idea of India as the Tamils' spiritual and cultural home. The Tamil politician R. Sri Pathmanathan stated for example that all 'of us Tamils owe allegiance to India and are thankful

to her for her spiritual gifts and privileges which she gave us'. He went on to identify the Tamils as Dravidians, stating 'we, Dravidians, have a pre-Aryan culture extending to the time of Mohenjodaro' (Russell, *Communal Politics*, p. 149). Similarly the 1926 history *Ancient Tamils*, written by C. Rasanayagam, describes the history of the island as a whole as linked to 'Tamil–Hindu or Dravidian history' (Hellman-Rajanayagam, 'The politics of the Tamil past', p. 111). The Dravidian idea in Sri Lankan Tamil politics was also not tied to the need for radical social reform—including the rejection of Hinduism—as it was with the Self-Respect movement in south India. Instead social reform in Sri Lankan Tamil politics was closer to the Gandhian and Congress conception of reform that worked within rather than against the framework of Hindu norms. Finally the Dravidian idea in Ceylon Tamil politics did not become associated with sustained social or political activity.

31. Dagmar Hellmann-Rajanayagam, 'Arumuka Navalar: religious reformer or national leader of Eelam', *Indian Economic and Social History Review* 29.2 (1989), pp. 234–57, 250.
32. D. Denis Hudson, 'Arumuga Navalar and the Hindu Renaissance among the Tamils', in Jones, K.W., ed., *Religious Controversy in British India: dialogues in South Asian languages* (Albany, NY: State University of New York Press, 1992), p. 35.
33. Murugar Gunasingam, *Sri Lankan Tamil Nationalism: a study of its origins* (Sydney: MV Publications, 1999), p. 126.
34. Discussions of Navalar's religious and educational activities as well as contributions to Tamil literary developments can be found in Hellmann-Rajanayagam, 'Arumuka Navalar'; Hudson, 'Arumuga Navalar'; Bernard Bate, 'Arumuga Navalar, saivite sermons, and the delimitation of religion, c.1850', *Indian Economic and Social History Review* 42.4 (2005); and Gunasingam, *Sri Lankan Tamil Nationalism*, pp. 113–58.
35. Peter Van der Veer argues that a modern public sphere or public culture emerged in early-nineteenth-century south India through the three tiered contests between missionaries, the East India Company and the south Indian associations that emerged to meet the missionary challenge to existing beliefs and practices (*Imperial Encounters*, pp. 20–21). See also M. S. S. Pandian, *Brahmin and non-Brahmin: genealogies of the Tamil political present* (Delhi: Permanent Black, 2007), pp. 22–3. For the expansion of education and print culture in the Tamil-speaking areas of Sri Lanka, see Gunasingam, *Sri Lankan Tamil Nationalism*, pp. 103–8, 121, 124–36.
36. Navalar promoted Saivism primarily as a means of salvation: 'Human birth is rare to obtain, even more so birth in this meritorious land of Bharatha (South Asia) where the Vedas and Agamas, the true books are esteemed. Birth among those who perform asceticism is even rarer. And most rare of all is birth amongst the lin-

273

eage of Shaivas' (quoted in Hudson, 'Arumuga Navalar', p. 42). In Navalar's think-
ing, it is not that Tamils 'owned' Saivism or had a special 'national' obligation to
protect Saivism; rather, for those born as Tamils, Saivism was the ideal means of
salvation.

Similarly one of Navalar's disciples, Kopay Sapapathy Navalar (1844–1903),
differentiated religious 'consciousness' from other types of affiliation: '... there are
several types of consciousness such as caste consciousness and patriotism that are
valued by human beings... Caste consciousness, patriotism and language consciousness are aspects of knowledge that one displays in relation to the world outside oneself. (But religious consciousness is not like this.) Therefore, human beings
should show the greatest regard for religious consciousness above all other types
of consciousness.' Quoted in Gunasingam, *Sri Lankan Tamil Nationalism*,
pp. 130–31.

37. Gunasingam, *Sri Lankan Tamil Nationalism*, pp. 150–51.
38. The study of Tamil literary and religious texts and the production of reliable printed
editions of these works became an important locus of concern for Christians and
Saivites. See Hellmann-Rajanayagam, 'Arumuka Navalar', pp. 243–5; Hudson,
'Arumuga Navalar'; D. Denis Hudson, 'Tamil Hindu Responses to Protestants:
nineteenth-century literati in Jaffna and Tinnevelly', in Kaplan, Steven, ed.,
Indigenous Responses to Western Christianity (New York and London: New York
University Press, 1995); Gunasingam, *Sri Lankan Tamil Nationalism*, pp. 103,
143. This eventually led to the promotion and cultivation of Tamil language and
literature being a shared concern between Hindus and Christians. See Russell,
Communal Politics, p. 122; Nicholapillai Maria Saveri, *A Catholic–Hindu
Encounter: relations between Roman Catholics and Hindus in Jaffna, Sri Lanka,
1900–1926* (Jaffna, Sri Lanka: Centre for Performing Arts, 1993), pp. 152, 331;
Gunasingam, *Sri Lankan Tamil Nationalism*, p. 152. Christians and Hindus were
also jointly involved in the promotion of Carnatic music and Bharathanatyam
(Russell, *Communal Politics*, pp. 69, 121). However, theological disputes between
Christians and Hindus continued and there was ongoing, often violent, conflict
between the two over funding for schools and the social status and rights of low-
caste Christians. See S. Kadirgamar, 'The Jaffna Youth Congress', in *Handy
Perinbanayagam, a memorial volume: the Jaffna Youth Congress and selections from
his writings and speeches* (Chunnakam, Jaffna: H. P. C. Society, Thirumakal Press,
1980), pp. 14, 35–8, 43, 62–3; Saveri, *A Catholic–Hindu Encounter*. For the ongoing importance of religious and caste affiliations in Tamil politics, see Russell,
Communal Politics, pp. 41, 76, 81, 101.
39. S. Arasaratnam, 'Social history of a dominant caste society; the Vellalar of north
Ceylon (Sri Lanka)', *Indian Economic and Social History Review* 18.3&4 (1981),
pp. 377–91.
40. Gunasingam, *Sri Lankan Tamil Nationalism*, pp. 40–113.

41. Ibid., pp. 132, 140–41.
42. Ibid., p. 171.
43. Saveri, *A Catholic–Hindu Encounter*, pp. 257–313.
44. Russell, *Communal Politics*, pp. 37–8; K.M. De Silva, 'Resistance movements in nineteenth century Sri Lanka', in Roberts, Michael, ed., *Sri Lanka: collective identities revisited* (Colombo, Marga Institute, 1997).
45. Kadirgamar, 'The Jaffna Youth Congress'; Michael Roberts, 'Stimulants and ingredients in the awakening of latter day nationalism', in Roberts, Michael, ed., *Sri Lanka*, pp. 279–80.
46. The total size of the electorate for the 'educated' Ceylonese seat and the conditions for the franchise are given in De Silva, G. P. S. Harischandra, *A Statistical Survey of Elections to the Legislatures of Sri Lanka, 1911–1977* (Colombo: Marga Institute, 1979), pp. 3, 4, 79. The population figure for 1912 is given in Colonial Office, *Ceylon: Report of the Special Commission on the Constitution*, 1928, p. 13.
47. See De Silva, *A Statistical Survey*, p. 5, for franchise conditions; and Colonial Office, *Ceylon*, 1928, p. 82, for electorate and voting figures.
48. Table 5.
49. Russell, *Communal Politics*, p. 23.
50. Roberts, 'Elite formation', p. 231.
51. P. Ramanathan also had a career in the public service and served as Solicitor General (1892–4; 1894–6) and once as Acting Attorney General (1896–1907). See A. Jeyaratnam Wilson, *Sri Lankan Tamil Nationalism: its origins and development in the nineteenth and twentieth centuries* (London: Hurst & Co., 2000), p. 45.
52. M. Vythilingam, *The Life of Sir Ponnambalam Ramanathan* (Jaffna: Thirumakal Press, 1971), pp. 544–52; Saveri, *A Catholic–Hindu Encounter*, pp. 52–3, 247.
53. De Silva, *A History*, p. 464. Don Spater Senanayake (1848–1907) was father of Don Stephen Senanayake (1884–1951) and grandfather of Dudley Shelton Senanayake (1911–73). Don Stephen Senanayake entered the legislative council in 1924 and became the first Prime Minister of independent Sri Lanka. Dudley Shelton entered the State Council (as it was known in the period of the Donoughmore Constitution) in 1936 and was appointed Prime Minister after his father's death in 1953. He resigned in 1953 following food riots and served again as Prime Minister between 1965 and 1970.
54. Roberts, 'Elite formation', p. 207.
55. Russell, *Communal Politics*, pp. 72–6, 90–103.
56. Vythilingam, *Sir Ponnambalam Ramanathan*, p. 394.
57. K. M. De Silva, 'Resistance movements', p. 161.
58. Gunasingam, *Sri Lankan Tamil Nationalism*, pp. 211–13.
59. K. M. De Silva, 'Resistance movements', p. 161.
60. The CNA submitted a memorandum, drafted by Ramanathan, calling for very

moderate constitutional reforms in 1890 (Vythilingam, *Sir Ponnambalam Ramanathan*, p. 586) and was briefly active again in 1915 following the ethnic violence between Sinhalese and Muslims (Gunasingam, *Sri Lankan Tamil Nationalism*, p. 211).

61. Kadirgamar, 'The Jaffna Youth Congress', pp. 11, 71–5; Roberts, 'Stimulants', pp. 273–84; Gunasingam, *Sri Lankan Tamil Nationalism*, pp. 199–203.
62. De Silva, 'Resistance movements', p. 162.
63. Ibid., p. 156.
64. Gunasingam, *Sri Lankan Tamil Nationalism*, p. 192.
65. Ibid., pp. 165–8.
66. The brother of P. Ramanathan, P. Arunachalam entered the civil service in 1875 and retired in 1913 as Registrar General. Like his brother, he had wanted to become a Supreme Court judge. (Wilson, *Sri Lankan Tamil Nationalism*, p. 49).
67. Gunasingam, *Sri Lankan Tamil Nationalism*, pp. 205, 212–13.
68. Ibid., p. 214.
69. Russell, *Communal Politics*, p. 109.
70. Wickramasinghe, *Ethnic Politics*, p. 43; Gunasingam, *Sri Lankan Tamil Nationalism*, pp. 212–13.
71. The 1921 Census shows that the majority (88 per cent) of the total population of Sri Lankan Tamils (just over half a million) lived in the Tamil-speaking northern and eastern provinces. Of the population that lived outside these provinces, just under 40 per cent lived in the Western Province: figures taken from Colonial Office, *Ceylon*, 1928, pp. 63, 122, 165. Many of the Sri Lankan Tamils living outside the north-east had white-collar employment either in the administrative services or in the private sector (Roberts, 'Elite formation', pp. 229–30).
72. Gunasingam, *Sri Lankan Tamil Nationalism*, pp. 214–15.
73. De Silva, *A History*, p. 486.
74. Gunasingam, *Sri Lankan Tamil Nationalism*, p. 212.
75. Tambiah, *Leveling Crowds*, pp. 48–56.
76. Wickramasinghe, *Sri Lanka*, pp. 117–18. Wickramasinghe notes that although 'Tamils were the largest non-Sinhala community living in Anuradhapura, the campaign led by Buddhist leaders in the early twentieth century against the modern town that had emerged next to the ruins was not directed against them. The targets were the colonial administration, the Christians and later the moors' (*Sri Lanka*, p. 118).
77. De Silva, 'Resistance movements', pp. 155–63.
78. De Silva, *A History*, pp. 453–7.
79. Saveri, *A Catholic-Hindu Encounter*, ch. 5.
80. Gunasingam, *Sri Lankan Tamil Nationalism*, p. 193.
81. V. Samaraweera, 'The Muslim revivalist movement 1880–1915', in Roberts, Michael, ed., *Sri Lanka: collective identities revisited* (Colombo: Marga Institute, 1997), pp. 308–9.

82. Tambiah, *Leveling Crowds*, pp. 56–81.
83. Ibid., p. 70.
84. Dharmadasa, *Language*, p. 138; Wickramasinghe, *Sri Lanka*, p. 90.
85. Tambiah, *Leveling Crowds*, pp. 62–8, 72.
86. Vythilingam, *Sir Ponnambalam Ramanathan*, p. 482.
87. Ibid., p. 476.
88. Saveri, *A Catholic–Hindu Encounter*, p. 53.
89. De Silva, *A History*, pp. 475–9.
90. Ibid., p. 497.
91. Wickramasinghe, *Ethnic Politics*, p. 33; Wilson, *Sri Lankan Tamil Nationalism*, p. 48.
92. Quoted in Dharmadasa, *Language*, p. 149.
93. Ibid., p. 224.
94. Wickramasinghe, *Sri Lanka*, pp. 103–11.
95. Dharmadasa, *Language*, p. 139.
96. Quoted in ibid., p. 140.
97. Ibid., p. 136.
98. Wilson, *Sri Lankan Tamil Nationalism*, pp. 48, 54, 56.
99. Gunasingam, *Sri Lankan Tamil Nationalism*, p. 214.
100. Ibid., p. 217.
101. Quoted in ibid., p. 205.
102. Kadirgamar, 'The Jaffna Youth Congress', pp. 15, 39; Russell, *Communal Politics*, pp. 69, 83, 200.
103. The Tamil Mahajana Sabhai (founded 1921) and the All Ceylon Tamil League (founded 1923) (Gunasingam, *Sri Lankan Tamil Nationalism*, pp. 216–17) did not become established, and new organisations were formed in the 1920s and 1930s. See also Russell, *Communal Politics*, pp. 219–21, for the fissiparous and fleeting nature of many associations.
104. Colonial Office, *Ceylon: Report of the Commission on Constitutional Reform*, 1945.
105. Colonial Office, *Ceylon*, 1945, p. 53.
106. The report notes that hopes for 'political programmes that would turn attention from communal to party politics ... have not yet been realised' (Colonial Office, *Ceylon*, 1945, p. 33).
107. See Colonial Office, *Ceylon*, 1945, pp. 7–32, for a summary of constitutional developments from the onset of British rule to 1945.
108. For a discussion of the influence of the Indian National Congress on Ceylon politics see Russell, *Communal Politics*, pp. 42–3, 157; and Roberts, 'Stimulants', pp. 284–5.
109. The 1927 Commission (under the chairmanship of Lord Donoughmore) had been appointed to recommend constitutional reforms and advocated universal

manhood suffrage and territorial as opposed to communal electorates. The recommendation of universal franchise was not supported by most of the associations and politicians it met—even those who advocated self-government (Colonial Office, *Ceylon: Report of the Special Commission on the Constitution*, 1928, pp. 82–3). For a discussion of the wide array of demands and proposals put before the Commission, see Wickramasinghe, *Ethnic Politics*, pp. 60–77.

110. 'D. S. Senanayake emerged as the self-proclaimed representative of a moderate strand of Ceylonese nationalism and it was not long before he was eagerly appointed as a privileged *compagnon de route* by the Governor and the Colonial Office on the road leading to independence.... The complex nature of the Ceylonese polity seems to have been deliberately overlooked by the colonial rulers and faith was placed in the vision of unity and reason projected by a man who, after all, was hardly representative of anyone besides himself' (Wickramasinghe, *Ethnic Politics*, p. 184).

111. From the late nineteenth century, British officials increasingly saw the island as essentially Sinhala Buddhist in history and character; see Rogers, 'Historical images' and C. J. Jeffries, *Ceylon: the path to independence* (London: Pall Mall Press, 1962), p. 3. The introductory pages of the Donoughmore Report reproduced the modern 'Mahavamsa' narrative of flourishing Sinhalese Buddhist colonisation and Tamil invasion precipitating decline (Colonial Office, *Ceylon*, 1928, pp. 5–6). While the Donoughmore Commissioners derided the 'communalism' they found rampant in the island's politics (ibid., pp. 31, 41), they nevertheless noted that the Ceylon Tamils for 'various reasons, wholly admirable' have 'obtained political influence somewhat disproportionate to their numerical strength' (ibid., p. 92). The Commissioners also noted that the advocates for full self-government were always from 'the larger communities' who if freed 'from external control would be able to impose their will on all who dissented from them' (ibid., p. 31). Meanwhile the minorities 'though united in no other respect, are solid in their opposition to the proposal' (ibid., p. 31). The Commissioners set as their objective the development of a 'free, united and democratic nation' (ibid., p. 91) and argued that only the abolition of communal representation would foster the 'various communities to develop together to a true national identity' (ibid., p. 99).

Similarly the Soulbury Report spoke of the majority as being 'entitled' to a 'proportionate share in all aspects of Government activity' (Colonial Office, *Ceylon: Report of the Commission on Constitutional Reform*, 1945, p. 53). The Commission characterised ethnic harmony as one of good behaviour by the majority. One the one hand, it warned sternly that it 'will behove the Sinhalese majority to take the utmost care to avoid giving cause for any suspicion of unfairness or partiality' (ibid., p. 50). On the other hand, the Commission also expressed confidence that 'the Government of Ceylon (presumably a Sinhalese government) is fully aware that the contentment of the minorities is essential not only to their own well-being but to the well-being of the Island as a whole' (ibid., p. 50, comments added).

112. Wickramasinghe, *Ethnic Politics*, p. 42.
113. Ibid., pp. 67–9.
114. Colonial Office, *Ceylon*, 1945, p. 56.
115. De Silva, *A History*, p. 349.
116. Ibid., pp. 385–7.
117. Roberts, 'Elite formation', pp. 229–30.
118. Russell, *Communal Politics*, p. 23.
119. Wickramasinghe, *Ethnic Politics*, p. 84.
120. Colonial Office, *Ceylon*, 1928, pp. 83, 86.
121. Colonial Office, *Ceylon*, 1945, p. 13; Wickramasinghe, *Ethnic Politics*, p. 85.
122. Wickramasinghe, *Sri Lanka*, pp. 77–9, 89.
123. Ibid., pp. 81, 93.
124. Wickramasinghe, *Ethnic Politics*, p. 134.
125. Russell, *Communal Politics*, pp. 249–50; Wickramasinghe, *Sri Lanka*, pp. 130–35.
126. Russell, *Communal Politics*, p. 191; Wickramasinghe, *Ethnic Politics*, p. 69.
127. Russell, *Communal Politics*, pp. 142, 236; Wickramasinghe, *Ethnic Politics*, pp. 170–71.
128. Quoted in Russell, *Communal Politics*, p. 157.
129. Wickramasinghe, *Ethnic Politics*, p. 175.
130. G. G. Ponnambalam was a barrister who entered the State Council in 1934. By the late 1930s he had established a position as the unofficial spokesperson of the Northern Province of Sri Lankan Tamils (Russell, *Communal Politics*, p. 297), although his position was heavily criticised by the Jaffna press (ibid., pp. 291–3). In 1944 he, along with others, founded the All Ceylon Tamil Congress, which was the largest Tamil political party until it was eclipsed by the Federal Party in 1956.
131. Kadirgamar, 'The Jaffna Youth Congress'.
132. The Jaffna *Morning Star* newspaper summed up the differences between the two groups as a question of 'whether the Tamil community is to assume an attitude of defence towards the majority community in the island, and preventing it encroaching on our rights or misappropriating any share in the number of places we are entitled to in government service, or whether the attitude of the Tamil community should be one of unsuspicious and trustful co-operation' (6 July 1934, quoted in Russell, *Communal Politics*, pp. 74, 39).
133. Many well-known Sinhala politicians attended the JYC's annual sessions in Jaffna (Kadirgamar, 'The Jaffna Youth Congress', pp. 20, 39, 47; Russell, *Communal Politics*, p. 292). However, some of the early attendees, such as A. E. Goonesinha, often later adopted openly anti-Tamil stands (Russell, *Communal Politics*, p. 31; Wickramasinghe, *Ethnic Politics*, p. 135).

134. Russell, *Communal Politics*, pp. 66–7, 235–48.
135. Kadirgamar, 'The Jaffna Youth Congress', p. 13.
136. Ganapathipillai Gangaser Ponnambalam, *The Marathon Crusade for 'fifty, fifty' in the State Council, 1939: a commemorative publication* (Chennai, India: Manimekalai Prasuram, 2001), p. 5.
137. Kadirgamar, 'The Jaffna Youth Congress', 1980.
138. Russell, *Communal Politics*, p. 122.
139. The JYC was clearly rooted in Jaffna society and politics, although it forged links with Sinhalese and Indian politicians. All of the sessions, for example, were held in Jaffna.
140. Kadirgamar, 'The Jaffna Youth Congress', pp. 58–60, 72–82.
141. Ibid., p. 78.
142. The JYC gained this influence partly because of links with Indian politicians, who were popular and well known on the island, particularly the Jaffna peninsula. In particular the JYC was central to organising Gandhi's 1927 visit to the island, including his highly popular visit to Jaffna (Kadirgamar, 'The Jaffna Youth Congress', pp. 27–38). The JYC also engaged successfully in direct political mobilisation, giving the impression that it could mobilise popular opinion. As Jane Russell notes, 'The Jaffna Congress held its meetings in the villages, in the vernacular. The leaders who dressed in the verti and banian, talked freely with all, regardless of cast or social status, and were willing to enrol any person who wished to join' (*Communal Politics*, p. 28).
143. Russell, *Communal politics*, pp. 31, 33
144. H. A. P. Sandarasagara, a Sinhalese politician, interpreted the move as a form of Ulster Unionism, rather than pan-Island nationalism, stating: 'I'll make Jaffna an Ulster and I'll be its Lord Carson' (De Silva, *A History*, p. 528). The Governor also misinterpreted the boycott as stemming from the fact that the Tamils were unhappy with the level of representation they would obtain in the State Council (ibid., p. 528). The Soulbury Report similarly explained the boycott as a 'protest against the abolition of communal representation' (Colonial Office, *Ceylon*, 1945, p. 14).
145. The demand for balanced representation began to be consolidated from 1933 onwards (Russell, *Communal Politics*, pp. 67, 187, 250–52).
146. Wickramasinghe, *Ethnic Politics*, p. 242.
147. Russell, *Communal Politics*, p. 324.
148. Ibid. Ponnambalam gained over 70 per cent of the votes polled (De Silva, *A Statistical Survey*, p. 186). Mahadeva had won in that constituency in the previous elections held in 1934 and 1936 (De Silva, *A Statistical Survey*, p. 98).
149. D. S. Senanayake retained this post from 1931 until 1947 when he became Prime Minister. Following this his son, Dudley Senanayake, took over the post of Agriculture and Lands Minister until he in turn became Prime Minister in 1953 (Farmer, *Pioneer Peasant*, p. 144).

150. The Dry Zone comprises around 70 per cent of the land area (Farmer, *Pioneer Peasant*, p. 3) but contained only 25 per cent of the population (Colonial Office, *Ceylon*, 1928, p. 165). Land development policy until the 1920s had primarily relied on private enterprise, although between 1870 and 1890 there had been a vigorous policy of the government-sponsored restoration of irrigation tanks, including many in the Eastern Province. During the 1920s there was a noticeable shift in the emphasis of land policy from improving food production and generating government revenue to preserving the peasantry as an institution and relieving congestion in the over-crowded Wet Zone areas of the island. This was laid out explicitly in the report of the Land Commission published in 1929, which called for government support for colonists; the Commission included a number of Sinhalese as well as Tamil politicians. The Commission's recommendations were finally incorporated into a Land Development Ordinance that was passed by the State Council in 1935 (Farmer, *Pioneer Peasant*, pp. 103–27).
151. Ibid., p. 144.
152. The Land Development Ordinance was framed in such a way as to exclude Indian Tamils (Wickramasinghe, *Ethnic Politics*, pp. 191–2). Sri Lankan Tamils were not formally excluded, but complained that they were discriminated against through executive and administrative acts (Russell, *Communal Politics*, p. 168). From 1900 to 1931, the Northern and Eastern Provinces received almost 50 per cent of total expenditure on irrigation, but after 1931 the share fell to 19 per cent (ibid., p. 170).

In 1939 G. G. Ponnambalam complained: 'the scant attention paid to colonization and to the production of paddy and to food production both in the Northern and Eastern Provinces, the recent rejection of the scheme of the Director of Irrigation to spend Rs. 3,000,000 for food production in Kalmunai in the South of Batticaloa, the finest paddy-production district in Ceylon—these things alone, if any proof is needed, will justify the demands of the minorities' (Ponnambalam, *The Marathon Crusade*, p. 187).

Meanwhile as a result of the expenditure on irrigation works in Batticaloa during the nineteenth century, this province was able to export rice to Jaffna and other parts of the island (De Silva, *A History*, p. 385). Similarly the system of agriculture on the over-crowded Jaffna peninsula was—compared to other regions on the island—intensive and efficient (De Silva, *A History*, p. 387; Farmer, *Pioneer Peasant*, p. 50).
153. G. G. Ponnambalam asked for a colonisation scheme for the Jaffna peninsula in 1939 because of the rising levels of unemployment (Russell, *Communal Politics*, p. 24). The percentage of landless families in Jaffna (31.7 per cent) and Batticaloa (57.8 per cent) (Farmer, *Pioneer Peasant*, p. 66) was also comparable to the range of landlessness in the districts of the Wet Zone (from a low of 14.2 per cent in Colombo to a high of 41.8 per cent in Nuwara Eliya) (ibid., p. 89). (NB much

of the landless population in Nuwara Eliya may well have been the Tamil labourers in the plantation districts.)

154. Russell, *Communal Politics*, pp. 25, 169; Wickramasinghe, *Ethnic Politics*, pp. 150–51.
155. Russell, *Communal Politics*, pp. 286–7.
156. Colonial Office, *Ceylon*, 1945, pp. 33, 71.
157. Ibid., pp. 47–50.
158. 'After the Commission had finished its work in Ceylon, D. S. Senanayake was invited to England by the Secretary of State for discussions ... Interestingly, Senanayake had made it plain to the Governor that he was not prepared to sit around a table with G. G. Ponnambalam. Colonel Stanley decided not to provide representatives of any particular group with passage facilities and all delegations were received separately ... G.G. Ponnambalam saw the Secretary of State ... for half an hour ...' (Wickramasinghe, *Ethnic Politics*, pp. 202–3).
159. Jeffries, *Ceylon*, pp. 112–13.
160. Ibid., pp. 115–16.
161. Wickramasinghe, *Ethnic Politics*, p. 223.
162. Ibid., p. 242.
163. Ibid., p. 224.
164. Russell, *Communal Politics*, p. 42.

4. TAMILS IN THE NATION: POST-INDEPENDENCE INDIA

1. For the centrality of economic development to Congress's conceptions of national interest, see Granville Austin, *The Indian Constitution: cornerstone of a nation* (Bombay: Oxford University Press, 1972), ch. 2; Manu Goswami, *Producing India: from colonial economy to national space* (Chicago: University of Chicago Press, 2004), ch. 7; Partha Chatterjee, *Nationalist Thought and the Colonial World: a derivative discourse?* (London: Zed for the United Nations University, 1986), ch. 5; and Stuart Corbridge and John Harriss, *Reinventing India: liberalization, Hindu nationalism and popular democracy* (Malden, MA: Polity Press, 2000), ch. 2.
2. Sumit Sarkar, 'Indian democracy: the historical inheritance', in Kohli, A., ed., *The Success of India's Democracy* (Cambridge: Cambridge University Press, 2001).
3. The Congress retained its dominance from independence to 1967. During this period it won majorities in all of the elections to the national (or Union) legislature, and all but one (Kerala in 1957) of the elections in the sub-national (or state) legislatures. This period was described as the 'dominant party system', in which competitive party politics existed without a change in government at the Union level and in most states. See Rajni Kothari, *Politics in India* (New Delhi: Little, Brown, 1970).
4. In fact the DK leader E. V. Ramaswamy had declared the day of Indian independence (15 August 1947) a day of national mourning. C. N. Annaduria, Ramaswamy's

principal lieutenant, publicly disagreed with the DK leader on this point and went on to form the DMK. See Marguerite Ross Barnett, *The Politics of Cultural Nationalism in South India* (Princeton, NJ: Princeton University Press, 1976).

5. The constituent assembly was elected indirectly in July 1946 from the legislatures of the provincial councils (fresh provincial council elections had been held in the winter of 1945). Following independence and partition, the constituent assembly also functioned as the Union parliament; Congress held 82 per cent of the seats in the assembly (Austin, *The Indian Constitution*, pp. 10–11).

6. Sunil Sarkar, 'Indian democracy: the historical inheritance', in Kohli, Atul, ed., *The Success of India's Democracy* (Cambridge: Cambridge University Press, 2001).

7. The key figures that have been cited are Jawaharlal Nehru (1889–1964), Bhimrao Ramji Ambedkar (1891–1956), Rajendra Prasad (1884–1963), Vallabhbhai Patel (1874–1950) and Abul Kalam Azad (1888–1958). See Corbridge and Harriss, *Reinventing India*, p. 269; and Austin, *The Indian Constitution*, p. 18.

8. For a discussion of the differences between Vallabhbhai Patel and the others on land reform and the inviolability of private property, see Austin, *The Indian Constitution*, pp. 87–101; and Corbridge and Harriss, *Reinventing India*, pp. 45–9.

9. Austin, *The Indian Constitution*, pp. 21, 187–207.

10. This was particularly so as the debates took place in the context of independence and partition, and the large-scale ethnic violence that ensued. See Austin, *The Indian Constitution*, pp. 43–4; and for further examples, ibid., pp. 29, 140, 150, 189, 239, 273, 283.

11. For a discussion of the politics of language and the historical relations between Urdu (linked to Persian and Arabic), Hindi (linked to Sanskrit) and Hindustani (the *lingua franca* across much of north India), see Richard D. King, *Nehru and the Language Politics of India* (Delhi: Oxford University Press, 1998), pp. 74–81; and for the promotion of Sanskritised Hindi, see Krishna Kumar, 'Hindu Revivalism and Education in North-Central India', *Social Scientist* 18.10 (1990), pp. 4–26; as well Pritam Singh, 'Hindu bias in India's "secular" constitution: probing flaws in the instruments of governance', *Third World Quarterly* 26.6 (2005), pp. 909–26.

12. Singh, 'Hindu bias'.

13. Austin, *The Indian Constitution*, p. 275.

14. Goswami, *Producing India*, ch. 6; Singh, 'Hindu bias'.

15. Alfred Stepan, Juan J. Linz and Yogendra Yadav, *Crafting State-Nations: India and Other Multinational Democracies* (Baltimore, MD: Johns Hopkins University Press, 2001), ch. 2.

16. Austin, *The Indian Constitution*, pp. 144–55.

17. Susan Bayly, *Caste, Society and Politics in India from the Eighteenth Century to the Modern Age* (New York: Cambridge University Press, 1999), ch. 7.

18. Stepan, Linz and Yadav, *Crafting State-Nations*, p. 69.

19. Ibid., p. 69.
20. Austin, *The Indian Constitution*, p. 80.
21. Ibid., p. 64.
22. For a discussion of the battles between Hindu nationalists and 'unity in diversity' advocates on the national language and linguistic provinces issue, see Austin, *The Indian Constitution*, pp. 236–43, ch. 12; and King, *Nehru*, ch. 3.
23. Quoted in Austin, *The Indian Constitution*, p. 298.
24. King, *Nehru*, p. 131.
25. For a discussion of the Telugu movement and its importance in triggering the process of linguistic reorganisation, see Lisa Mitchell, *Language, Emotion, and Politics in South India: the making of a mother tongue* (Bloomington, IN: Indiana University Press, 2009).
26. King, *Nehru*, p. 64.
27. Quoted in Austin, *The Indian Constitution*, p. 239.
28. King, *Nehru*, ch. 4.
29. Quoted in Austin, *The Indian Constitution*, p. 242.
30. Ibid., p. 242.
31. Mitchell, *Language*.
32. King, *Nehru*, p. 12.
33. Sumathi Ramaswamy, *Passions of the Tongue: language devotion in Tamil India, 1891–1970* (Berkeley, CA: University of California Press, 1997), p. 157.
34. Quoted in Austin, *The Indian Constitution*, p. 188.
35. As Ayesha Jalal notes, the Congress was eventually happy to cede Pakistan in exchange for a strong centre and an early transition of power, something that Jinnah did not expect; in *The Sole Spokesman: Jinnah, the Muslim League, and the demand for Pakistan* (New Delhi: Cambridge University Press, 1994).
36. Narendra Subramanian, *Ethnicity and Populist Mobilization: political parties, citizens, and democracy in South India* (Delhi and New York: Oxford University Press, 1999), p. 40.
37. Subramanian, *Ethnicity*, p. 134.
38. Ibid., p. 145.
39. Barnett, *Politics of Cultural Nationalism*, p. 3.
40. David A. Washbrook, 'Caste, Class and Dominance in Modern Tamil Nadu: Non Brahminism, Dravidianism and Tamil Nationalism', in Frankel, F. and M. Rao, eds, *Dominance and State Power in Modern India: decline of a social order* (Delhi: Oxford University Press, 1989), p. 249.
41. Barnett, *Politics of Cultural Nationalism*, p. 133.
42. Subramanian, *Ethnicity*, p. 193.
43. For a discussion of the ideological content of the DMK, see Robert L. Hardgrave, *The Dravidian Movement* (Bombay: Popular Prakashan, 1965); and Barnett, *Politics of Cultural Nationalism*, ch. 5, 9, 10.

44. Austin, *The Indian Constitution*, pp. 41–3.
45. Subramanian, *Ethnicity*, p. 143.
46. Ramaswamy, *Passions of the Tongue*, pp. 161–78.
47. Arun Swamy, 'Parties, Political Identities and the Absence of Mass Political Violence in South India', in Basu, Amitra and Atul Kohli, eds, *Community Conflicts and the State in India* (New Delhi: Oxford University Press, 1998), p. 115; Corbridge and Harriss, *Reinventing India*, pp. 67–73; Subramanian, *Ethnicity*, pp. 191–8.
48. Subramanian, *Ethnicity*, p. 193; Swamy, 'Parties, Political Identities', p. 116.
49. Barnett, *Politics of Cultural Nationalism*, pp. 99–100.
50. Subramanian, *Ethnicity*, p. 139.
51. Bayly, *Caste*, ch. 7.
52. Bayly, *Caste*.
53. Yogendra Yadav, 'Reconfiguration in Indian politics: state assembly elections in 1993–1995', in Chatterjee, Partha, ed., *State and Politics in India* (Oxford: Oxford University Press, 1997).
54. Chatterjee, *Nationalist Thought*, ch. 5; M. S. S. Pandian, '"Nation" from its margins: notes on E. V. Ramaswamy's "impossible" nation', in Bhargava R., A. K. Bagchi and R. Sudarshan, eds, *Multiculturalism, Liberalism and Democracy* (Calcutta: Oxford University Press, 1999).
55. For a discussion of Congress government's responses to Sikh and Kashmiri movements, see Paul R. Brass, *The Politics of India since Independence* (Cambridge: Cambridge University Press, 1994).
56. For a discussion of the differences between the DK and the DMK and the events leading to the eventual split, see Hardgrave, *The Dravidian Movement*; Barnett, *Politics of Cultural Nationalism*; and Subramanian, *Ethnicity*.
57. Subramanian, *Ethnicity*, p. 291.
58. Swamy, 'Parties, Political Identities'.
59. Barnett, *Politics of Cultural Nationalism*, p. 269.
60. Nicholas B. Dirks, *Castes of Mind: colonialism and the making of modern India* (Princeton, NJ: Princeton University Press, 2001), p. 264.
61. Barnett, *Politics of Cultural Nationalism*, p. 291.
62. Ibid., p. 273.
63. Subramanian, *Ethnicity*, p. 232.
64. Pandian, '"Nation"'.
65. Barnett, *Politics of Cultural Nationalism*, pp. 242–8.
66. Ramaswamy, *Passions of the Tongue*, pp. 157, 161–78; Subramanian, *Ethnicity*, p. 222.
67. Subramanian, *Ethnicity*, p. 222.
68. Barnett, *Politics of Cultural Nationalism*, pp. 248–9.
69. King, *Nehru*, p. 114.

70. M. Rengaswamy, *Tamil Nationalism: political identity of the Tamil Arasu Kazhagam* (Chennai: Hema Publishers, 2006).
71. Rengaswamy, *Tamil Nationalism*; Interviews with Congress and Communist Party India (CPI) leaders and party activists, July–August 2007.
72. Disputes between Tamils and Telugus over the status of Madras city became significant in the months leading up to independence. Congress had included the linguistic reorganisation of provinces in its manifesto for the elections in late 1945/6 and most Tamil and Telugu Congress politicians expected that a new Congress government would work quickly to implement this promise (Mitchell, *Language*; Rengaswamy *Tamil Nationalism*).
73. The TAK's eventual ejection from Congress was due to the factional differences between Rajagopalachari and Kamraj (Rengaswamy, *Tamil Nationalism*).
74. 'Nehru ... knew, however, that the Tamils and Rajagopalachari would themselves fast to death rather than relinquish Madras City as their capital, now would they ever agree to a shared capital. That part of Sriramulu's demands Nehru could never have granted; it would have cost him far too dearly in Tamil support and made of Rajagopalachari an implacable enemy instead of an occasional headache' (King, *Nehru*, p. 114).
75. Ramaswamy, *Passions of the Tongue*, p. 161.
76. Barnett, *Politics of Cultural Nationalism*, p. 134; Subramanian, *Ethnicity*, p. 193.
77. Subramanian, *Ethnicity*, pp. 198–9.
78. Ibid., p. 301.
79. Philip, Spratt, *D.M.K. in Power* (Bombay: Nachiketa Publications, 1970); Y. Vincent Kumaradoss, 'Kamaraj Remembered', *Economic and Political Weekly* 39.17 (2004), pp. 1655–7.
80. Kumaradoss, 'Kamaraj Remembered'.
81. Robert L. Hardgrave, *Nadars of Tamilnad: the political culture of a community in change* (Bombay: Oxford University Press, 1969).
82. Kumaradoss, 'Kamaraj Remembered'.
83. Subramanian, *Ethnicity*, p. 219.
84. Ibid., pp. 150, 290–1.
85. Corbridge and Harriss, *Reinventing India*, p. 50.
86. Partha Chatterjee, 'Introduction: a political history of independent India', in Chatterjee, Partha, ed., *State and Politics in India* (Delhi: Oxford University Press, 1997), p. 15.
87. Non-Congress coalition governments—often fractious and unstable—were formed in Punjab, Haryana, Uttar Pradesh, Madhya Pradesh, Bihar, West Bengal, Orissa and Kerala (Ibid.).
88. Yadav, 'Reconfiguration in Indian politics'.
89. Quoted in Corbridge and Harriss, *Reinventing India*, p. 53.
90. These included for example the alliances that were formed by Ramaswamy with

Kamraj and then Rajagopalachari against the DMK. The DMK then formed an alliance with Indira Gandhi's Congress (R) against the Tamil Nadu Congress led by Kamraj.

91. Barnett, *Politics of Cultural Nationalism*, p. 141.
92. Ibid., p. 140.
93. Subramanian, *Ethnicity*, pp. 147, 172–4.
94. Ibid., p. 171.
95. Barnett, *Politics of Cultural Nationalism*, p. 138.
96. Karunanidhi assumed the leadership of the DMK after C. N. Annadurai's death in 1969; he continues to retain that post.
97. Subramanian, *Ethnicity*, p. 164.
98. Ibid., p. 145.
99. Ibid., p. 162.
100. S. Theodore Baskaran, *The Message Bearers: the nationalist politics and the entertainment media in South India, 1880–1945* (Madras: Cre-A, 1981).
101. Interviews with Congress party activists, July–August 2007.
102. Subramanian, *Ethnicity*, p. 165.
103. Ibid., p. 174.
104. Ibid., p. 209.
105. Corbridge and Harriss, *Reinventing India*, pp. 67–8.
106. Subramanian, *Ethnicity*, pp. 72–3.
107. Ibid., pp. 237–43.
108. Barnett, *Politics of Cultural Nationalism*, p. 298.
109. Interviews with Congress and DMK leaders and party activists, July–August 2007.
110. Barnett, *Politics of Cultural Nationalism*, pp. 109–10.
111. Ibid., p. 127.
112. Rengaswamy, *Tamil Nationalism*.
113. Ibid., pp. 64–7.
114. Subramanian, *Ethnicity*, p. 301.
115. Ibid., p. 300.

5. NATIONS APART: TAMILS AND SINHALESE IN POST-INDEPENDENCE SRI LANKA

1. For the rapid post-independence consolidation of Sinhala Buddhism and the UNP's role in that, see Sumantra Bose, *States, Nations, Sovereignty: Sri Lanka, India, and the Tamil Eelam movement* (New Delhi: Sage Publications, 1994); Sankaran Krishna, *Postcolonial Insecurities: India, Sri Lanka, and the question of nationhood* (Minneapolis: University of Minnesota Press, 1999).
2. See Appendix 2.
3. Tamil nationalism as a political movement had its base almost exclusively amongst

the Sri Lankan Tamils concentrated in the north-east. There were also other Tamil-speaking minorities—the Muslims and the Indian Tamils, primarily plantation workers who were mainly in the Central Province. However, these populations have not become part of the Tamil nationalist project. The Muslims speak Tamil but tend to 'identify themselves with the Sinhalese leadership in national politics' (Wilson, *Politics in Sri Lanka*, p. 48) and have not made demands for territorial autonomy or equality in terms of official recognition of Tamil. The Indian Tamils meanwhile have tended to be represented by the Ceylon Workers Congress (CWC) and the Democratic Workers Congress (DWC). These parties have generally worked with whichever party is in government (Ibid., pp. 155–6). Tamil nationalism as a political project has therefore been a Sri Lankan Tamil phenomenon. The term 'Tamil' is used here therefore to refer to the Sri Lankan Tamils.

4. As Mick Moore states, the 'use of state power for the benefit of the ordinary Sinhalese has been, and remains, the primary legitimation, implicit or explicit, of all governments elected since 1956 at least, and arguably, since 1931': *The State and Peasant Politics in Sri Lanka* (Cambridge: Cambridge University Press, 1985), p. 29.

5. Donald E. Smith, 'Religion, Politics and the Myth of Reconquest', in Fernando, Tissa, Robert N. Kearney and Nagalingam Balakrishnan, eds, *Modern Sri Lanka: a society in transition* (Syracuse, NY: Maxwell School of Citizenship and Public Affairs, 1979); Bose, *States, Nations, Sovereignty*; Krishna, *Postcolonial Insecurities*.

6. Neil DeVotta, *Blowback: linguistic nationalism, institutional decay, and ethnic conflict in Sri Lanka* (Stanford, CA: Stanford University Press, 2004), p. 6.

7. The figures are taken from Wilson, *Politics in Sri Lanka*, pp. 156–9.

8. Michael Billig, *Banal Nationalism* (London: Sage, 1995).

9. Ibid., p. 99.

10. Newton Gunasinghe, 'The Open Economy and its Impact on Ethnic Relations in Sri Lanka', in Winslow, Deborah W. and Michael D. Woost, eds, *Economy, Culture and Civil War in Sri Lanka* (Bloomington and Indianapolis: Indiana University Press, 2004), p. 100.

11. Quoted in Robert N. Kearney, *The Politics of Ceylon (Sri Lanka)* (London: Cornell University Press, 1973), p. 163.

12. James Manor, 'The Failure of Political Integration in Sri Lanka (Ceylon)', *Commonwealth and Comparative Politics* 17.1 (1979), pp. 21–47.

13. Moore, *Peasant Politics*, p. 226.

14. Ibid., pp. 226–7.

15. James Manor, *The Expedient Utopian: Bandaranaike and Ceylon* (Cambridge: Cambridge University Press, 1989), pp. 110–15.

16. Jane Russell, *Communal Politics under the Donoughmore Constitution, 1931–1947* (Dehiwala, Sri Lanka: Tisara Prakasakayo, 1982), p. 157.

17. Wilson, *Politics in Sri Lanka*, p. 101.

18. The schemes did not increase overall food production or returns on capital investment, and mainly functioned to establish beneficiaries with the status of 'landowners' (Farmer, *Pioneer Peasant Colonization*).
19. Moore, *Peasant Politics*, p. 46; Chelvaduri Manogaran, *Ethnic Conflict and Reconciliation in Sri Lanka* (Honolulu: University of Hawaii Press, 1987), ch. 3.
20. Manor, *Expedient Utopian*, pp. 227–53; DeVotta, *Blowback*, ch. 3.
21. Manor, *Expedient Utopian*.
22. Wilson, *Politics in Sri Lanka*, p. 125.
23. Quoted in Ponnambalam, *Sri Lanka*, p. 84.
24. Wilson, *Chelvanayakam*, p. 52.
25. Stanley J. Tambiah, *Buddhism Betrayed? Religion, politics, and violence in Sri Lanka* (Chicago and London: University of Chicago Press, 1992), ch. 5–7.
26. Manor, *Expedient Utopian*, pp. 229–30.
27. Wilson, *Chelvanayakam*, p. 52.
28. Ponnambalam, *Sri Lanka*, p. 94.
29. Wilson, *Chelvanayakam*, p. 59.
30. Jupp, *Sri Lanka*, p. 60.
31. Bose, *States, Nations*, p. 67.
32. Quoted in Ponnambalam, *Sri Lanka*, p. 164.
33. Ibid., pp. 197–8.
34. Moore, *Peasant Politics*, p. 219.
35. Janice Jiggins, *Caste and Family in the Politics of the Sinhalese, 1947–1976* (Cambridge: Cambridge University Press, 1979), p. 150.
36. Moore, *Peasant Politics*, p. 224.
37. Jiggins, *Caste and Family*, p. 154.
38. Kearney, *Politics of Ceylon*, p. 95. Furthermore from 1956, the pattern of electoral support in most constituencies in the Sinhala electorates was aligned with nationwide swings rather than dependent upon local peculiarities (Jupp, *Sri Lanka*, pp. 210–15). Political parties have thus come to dominate electoral politics, and in the 1970 general election 'all but two of the 151 parliamentary seats and 94 per cent of the popular votes were captured by parties that had been in existence for at least 19 years' (Kearney, *Politics of Ceylon*, p. 100).
39. Kearney, *Politics of Ceylon*, p. 103; Jupp, *Sri Lanka*, pp. 91–7.
40. Kearney, *Politics of Ceylon*, p. 185.
41. Wilson, *Politics in Sri Lanka*, p. 139.
42. Ibid., p. 149.
43. Ibid., p. 38.
44. Vaithianathan Navaratnam, *The Fall and Rise of the Tamil Nation: events leading to the Tamil war of independence and resumption of Eelam sovereignty* (Madras: Kaanthalakam, 1991).
45. Wilson, *Chelvanayakam*.

46. Wilson, 'Politics and Political Development', p. 302.
47. Jupp, *Sri Lanka*, p. 37.
48. Ibid., pp. 149–51.
49. Ibid., pp. 148–9.
50. Ibid., pp. 149–51.
51. Wilson, *Politics in Sri Lanka*, p. 46.
52. Kearney, *Politics of Ceylon*, p. 172.
53. In 1970, before these measures were introduced, 48 per cent of students in the Engineering and the Medicine and Dental faculties were Tamil. By 1983 this had fallen to 28 per cent for the Engineering faculty and 22 per cent for the Medicine and Dental faculty (Manogaran, *Ethnic Conflict*, p. 125).
54. Donald L. Horowitz, *Coup Theories and Officers' Motives: Sri Lanka in comparative perspective* (Princeton, NJ: Princeton University Press, 1980).
55. Brian Blodgett, *Sri Lanka's Military: the search for a mission (1949–2004)* (Aventine Press, 2004), p. 54.
56. Manogaran, *Ethnic Conflict*, p. 129.
57. For details see Bose, *States, Nations*; or Wilson, *Politics in Sri Lanka*.
58. Between 1956 and 1970, the proportion of Tamils employed in the elite Administrative Services fell from 30 to 5 per cent; in the Professional and Technical Services from 60 to 10 per cent; and in the Clerical Services from 50 to 5 per cent.
59. Gunasinghe, 'The Open Economy'.
60. Wilson, *Politics in Sri Lanka*, p. 11.
61. Horowitz, *Coup Theories*, p. 112.
62. Ibid., p. 113.
63. Ibid., p. 113.
64. Jupp, *Sri Lanka*, p. 24.
65. Wilson, *Politics in Sri Lanka*, pp. 22–31, 155–60.
66. Wilson, *Chelvanayakam*, pp. 107–11.
67. Ibid., p. 96.
68. Wilson, *Politics in Sri Lanka*, p. 11.
69. Gunasinghe, 'The Open Economy'.
70. Blodgett, *Sri Lanka's Military*, p. 62.
71. Manogaran, *Ethnic Conflict*, p. 129.
72. Ibid., pp. 88–114.
73. Moore, *Peasant Politics*, p. 46.
74. Bose, *States, Nations*; Krishna, *Postcolonial Insecurities*.
75. Jupp, *Sri Lanka*, p. 152.
76. Ibid., p. 153.
77. Ibid., p. 152.
78. Wilson, *Politics in Sri Lanka*, p. 48.
79. Ponnambalam, *Sri Lanka*, pp. 154–5.

80. Jupp, *Sri Lanka*, p. 140.
81. One FP MP defected in 1960 (Ponnambalam, *Sri Lanka*, p. 155) and two in 1977 (Jupp, *Sri Lanka*, p. 139).
82. Jupp, *Sri Lanka*, p. 138.
83. Quoted in Wilson, *Chelvanayakam*, p. 74.
84. See Dagmar Hellmann-Rajanayagam, 'The politics of the Tamil past', in Spencer, J., ed., *Sri Lanka: history and the roots of conflict* (London, Routledge, 1990).
85. Quoted in Wilson, *Chelvanayakam*, p. 54.
86. It contested 7 seats and won only 2; see Appendix 2.
87. Wilson, *Chelvanayakam*, p. 32.
88. Ibid., p. 25.
89. Ibid., p. 72.
90. For the events that led to Sir John Kotelawala's premiership, see Manor, *Expedient Utopian*, pp. 209–23.
91. Wilson, *Chelvanayakam*, p. 59.
92. Quoted in ibid., p. 70.
93. Ponnambalam, *Sri Lanka*, pp. 105–6.
94. Wilson, *Chelvanayakam*, p. 85.
95. Tambiah, *Buddhism Betrayed*, p. 49.
96. Wilson, *Chelvanayakam*, pp. 87–8.
97. For accounts of the violence, see Manor, *Expedient Utopian*, pp. 287–94; Tambiah, *Buddhism Betrayed*, pp. 51–7.
98. Manor, *Expedient Utopian*, p. 293.
99. Krishna, *Postcolonial Insecurities*, p. 54.
100. For details, see Wilson, *Chelvanayakam*, pp. 94–6; and also Navaratnam, *Fall and Rise of the Tamil Nation*.
101. Ponnambalam, *Sri Lanka*, p. 131.
102. Quoted in Wilson, *Chelvanayakam*, p. 96.
103. Appendix 2.
104. Wilson, *Chelvanayakam*, p. 102.
105. Ibid., p. 104.
106. Ponnambalam, *Sri Lanka*, p. 146.
107. Quoted in Wilson, *Chelvanayakam*, p. 110; see also Bryan Pfaffenberger, 'The Political Construction of Defensive Nationalism: the 1968 temple-entry crisis in northern Sri Lanka', *Journal of Asian Studies* 49.1 (1990), pp. 78–96, 92.
108. The SLFP won 90 out of the 150 seats and 60 per cent of the vote (Wilson, *Politics in Sri Lanka*, p. 159).
109. De Silva, *Statistical Survey*, p. 196.
110. Ponnambalam, *Sri Lanka*, p. 185.
111. Appendix 2.
112. Anton S. Balasingham, *War and Peace: armed struggle and peace efforts of the Liberation Tigers* (Mitcham, Surrey: Fairmax Publishing, 2004), pp. 21–6;

Brendan O' Duffy, 'LTTE: Liberation Tigers of Tamil Eelam, majoritarianism, self-determination, and military-to-political transition in Sri Lanka', in Marianne Heiberg, Brendan O'Leary and John J. Tirman, eds, *Terror, Insurgency and the State: ending protracted conflicts* (Philadelphia: University of Philadelphia Press, 2007).

113. Interviews with Tamil National Alliance (TNA) politicians, July 2007; and LTTE officials, October 2006.
114. Ponnambalam, *Sri Lanka*, p. 184.
115. Ibid., pp. 182–3.
116. Pfaffenberger, 'The Political Construction'.
117. Interviews with TNA politicians, July 2007.
118. De Silva, *Statistical Survey*, p. 241.
119. Ibid., p. 186.
120. Billig, *Banal Nationalism*.
121. Wilson, *Chelvanayakam*, p. 75.
122. Ibid., p. 50.
123. Ibid., p. 64.
124. V. Samaraweera, 'The Muslim revivalist movement 1880–1915', in Roberts, Michael, ed., *Sri Lanka: collective identities revisited* (Colombo: Marga Institute, 1997).
125. Wilson, *Chelvanayakam*, p. 74.
126. Jupp, *Sri Lanka*, p. 143; De Silva, *Statistical Survey*, pp. 241, 277.
127. Pfaffenberger, 'The Political Construction'.
128. Ponnambalam, *Sri Lanka*, p. 78.
129. Interviews with TNA politicians, July 2007.
130. Ibid.
131. Ibid.
132. Interviews with LTTE officials, October 2006; Bose, *States, Nations*, p. 105.
133. Moore, *Peasant Politics*, pp. 133–4.
134. Wilson, *Chelvanayakam*, p. 73.
135. Ibid., p. 32.
136. Navaratnam, *Fall and Rise of the Tamil Nation*.
137. Ibid.
138. Appendix 2.
139. For details of the agreements, see Navaratnam, *Fall and Rise of the Tamil Nation*.
140. Wilson, *The Break-up of Sri Lanka*.

6. SRI LANKA'S CIVIL WAR: THE BEGINNING

1. The literature on liberal order-making—or the liberal peace—as well as debates about the pacific character of liberal democratic states—or the democratic peace—are both extensive. See, for example, John G, Ikenberry, *Liberal Leviathan: the ori-*

gins, crisis and transformation of American world order (Princeton, NJ: Princeton University Press, 2012); Tarak Barkawi and Mark Laffey, eds, *Democracy, Liberalism, and War: rethinking the democratic peace debate* (Boulder, CO: Lynne Rienner, 2001); Mark Duffield, *Global Governance and the New Wars: the merging of development and security* (London: Zed Books, 2001); John M. Owen, *Liberal Peace, Liberal War: American politics and international security* (London: Cornell University Press, 1997); Roland Paris, *At War's End: peace building after civil conflict* (Cambridge: Cambridge University Press, 1997); Oliver P. Richmond, *The Transformation of Peace* (Basingstoke: Palgrave Macmillan, 2005).

2. The term 'liberal peace' thus captures the set of international processes, activities and principles linked to attempts to establish a pacific order of liberal democratic states. Advocates and critics of liberal order-making have used the terms 'liberal peace-building' or 'liberal peace' to capture this phenomenon. For an influential and broadly sympathetic account, see Paris, *At War's End*; see also Richmond, *The Transformation of Peace*. For a critical account, see Mark Duffield, *Global Governance* (who uses the term 'strategic complexes'). For overviews and recent debates of liberal peace-building between advocates and critics, see Roland Paris, 'Saving Liberal Peacebuilding', *Review of International Studies* 36.2 (2010), pp. 337–65; David Chandler, 'The uncritical critique of 'liberal peace', *Review of International Studies* 36.S1 (2010), pp. 137–55; as well as Neil Cooper, Mandy Turner and Michael Pugh, 'The end of history and the last liberal peace-builder: a reply to Roland Paris', *Review of International Studies* 37.4 (2011), pp. 1–13.

Importantly, the terms 'liberal peace-building' or 'liberal peace' have also now come to be extensively used in the literature on Sri Lanka that is focused on the dynamics of international intervention, particularly in the post-Cold War era. See, for example, Kristian Stokke and Uyangoda Jayadeva, eds, *Liberal Peace in Question: the politics of state and market reform in Sri Lanka* (London: Anthem Press, 2011); and Suthaharan Nadarajah and David Rampton, 'The limits of hybridity and the crisis of liberal peace', *Review of International Studies* 41.1 (2015), pp. 49–72.

3. Francis Fukuyama, *The End of History and the Last Man* (London: Penguin, 1992); Michael Mandelbaum, *The Ideas that Conquered the World: peace, democracy, and free markets in the twenty-first century* (New York: Public Affairs, 2002).

4. For an influential analysis that sets out a 'securitised' analysis of internal conflict as well as an account of liberal peace-building, see Paris, *At War's End*.

5. For a critical overview, see Lars-Erik Cederman, Kristian Skrede Gleditsch and Halvard Buhaug, *Inequality, Grievances, and Civil War* (Cambridge: Cambridge University Press, 2013).

6. Emblematic works include: Paul Collier and Anke Hoeffler, 'Greed and Grievance in Civil War', *Oxford Economic Papers* 56 (2004), pp. 563–95; Mary Kaldor, *New and Old Wars* (Cambridge: Polity, 2001).

7. For the impact of these policies on the armed conflicts in Nepal and Sri Lanka, see

Madurika Rasaratnam and Mara Malagodi, 'Eyes Wide Shut: persistent conflict and liberal peace building in Nepal and Sri Lanka', *Conflict, Security and Development* 12.3 (2012), pp. 299–327.

8. From the late 1970s onwards, successive Sri Lankan governments have used the Prevention of Terrorism Act and the rapidly expanding military to combat both Tamil militants but also to target and repress non-armed Tamil nationalist actors and to exercise control over Tamil politics and society more broadly. The abuses entailed in this approach have been systematic and continuous over time. They include the following: the regular use of torture, sexual abuse, extra-judicial executions, disappearances, extended detention without trial, massacres of civilians by Sri Lankan security force personnel and allied paramilitary forces, aerial bombardment of civilian targets (including the use of barrel bombs and cluster munitions), repression of press freedom (including through lethal targeting of media workers by the military and allied paramilitary groups) and the use of humanitarian as well as economic blockades as a tactic of warfare. The details of these practices and their consequences have been documented in detail over the decades by an array of international advocacy organisations, domestic and international media, as well as being the subject of academic analysis.

For details of systematic and continuous practices of torture, disappearances, extra-judicial executions and prolonged detention without charge and trial after the end of the war by the Sri Lankan security forces, see the following reports by Amnesty International: *Report of an Amnesty International Mission to Sri Lanka*, 1983; *Sri Lanka: current human rights concerns and evidence of extra-judicial killings*, 1984; *Disappearances*, 1986; *Sri Lanka: government's responses to widespread 'disappearances' in Jaffna*, 1997; *Sri Lanka: torture in custody*, 1999; and *Sri Lanka: twenty years of make-believe, Sri Lanka's Commissions of Inquiry*, 2009. See also Human Rights Watch, *Legal Limbo: the uncertain fate of detained LTTE suspects in Sri Lanka*, 2010; Channel Four, 'Who are Sri Lanka's disappeared?' 14 November 2013, http://www.channel4.com/news/sri-lanka-disappeared-white-vans-missing-people-warchogm, last accessed 18 April 2014; International Bar Association, *Justice in Retreat: Sri Lanka*, 2009. According to the UN, Sri Lanka has the second highest number of unresolved disappearances after Iraq; for details, see Channel Four, 'Who are Sri Lanka's disappeared?'

For the still ongoing patterns of sexual abuse by Sri Lankan security forces against Tamil civilians, ex-combatants and detainees, see Human Rights Watch, 'We will teach you a lesson: sexual violence against Tamils by Sri Lankan security forces', 2010; Yasmin Sooka, the Bar Human Rights Committee of England and Wales and the International Truth and Justice Project, Sri Lanka, 'An unfinished war: torture and sexual violence in Sri Lanka 2009–14', 2014, https://www.barhumanrights.org.uk/unfinished-war-torture-and-sexual-violence-sri-lanka-2009-2014, last accessed April 2015.

Media repression has also been linked to increasingly levels of violence and conflict in Sri Lanka and has been particularly targeted at the Tamil press. Sri Lanka is ranked 165 out of 180 countries on Reporters Without Borders Press Freedom Index, just below Saudi Arabia at 164 and just above Uzbekistan at 166. Reporters without Borders, 'Press Freedom Prize goes to Uzbek journalist and Sri Lankan daily', 27 November 2013, http://en.rsf.org/press-freedom-prize-goes-to-uzbek-27-11-2013,45522.html, last accessed April 2015.

Whilst lethal attacks against journalists and other media employees have become commonplace, the Tamil media have been disproportionately targeted. Of the 48 media workers killed between 2004 and 2013, 41 were Tamils. That is, Tamils constituted 87 per cent of victims of lethal violence against the media (primarily by the state and allied paramilitary groups) despite constituting only 12 per cent of the population. For details, see Tamils Against Genocide, 'Silencing the press: an analysis of violence against the media in Sri Lanka', 2013, http://www.tamilsagainst-genocide.org/read.aspx?storyid=123, last accessed November 2013.

The onset of the civil war in the early 1980s prompted the rapid militarisation of the Tamil-speaking regions. There has been a steadily and still ongoing expansion of military camps, checkpoints and high-security zones in majority Tamil districts. During the high-intensity periods of the war, areas not controlled by the military were also subject to often crippling economic embargoes of food and medicine alongside indiscriminate aerial bombardment, including the targeting of hospitals and other shelters such as temples and churches.

For examples of reports detailing the use of aerial bombardment against civilian targets, see the following: *Daily Telegraph*, 'Sri Lankans are just killing civilians at random', 13 September 1990 (which includes details of the use of barrel bombs and aerial showering of civilian areas with human and animal excrement); reports from the early 1990s also suggested that bombing of hospitals, power stations and transport infrastructure left the north-east 'virtually paralyzed' and contributed to 'near famine conditions in already strained refugee camps'; for details, see Human Rights Watch, 'Human Rights in Sri Lanka: an update', 12 March 1991, http://www.hrw.org/reports/pdfs/s/srilanka/srilanka913.pdf, last accessed April 2015 (quotes taken from p. 13).

Further details of the economic blockade are available at Tamil Information Centre, *Sri Lanka—Economic Blockade*, 1986. For analysis of Sri Lanka's blockages on food and medicines and whether or not these constituted abuses of humanitarian law, see Jordan J. Paust, 'The Human Rights to Food, Medicine and Medical Supplies, and Freedom from Arbitrary and Inhumane Detention and Controls in Sri Lanka', *Vanderbilt Journal of Transnational Law* 31 (1998), pp. 617–42.

For discussion and analysis of the targeting of civilians in the final stages of the civil war, see Human Rights Watch, 'Sri Lanka: repeated shelling of hospitals evidence of war crimes', 8 May 2009; United Nations, 'Report of the Secretary

General's Panel of Experts on Accountability in Sri Lanka', 31 March 2011, available at http://www.un.org/News/dh/infocus/Sri_Lanka/POE_Report_Full.pdf, last accessed 12 June 2012.

For more overarching discussions of the repressive relationship between the state, security forces and the Tamil population, see Nancy Murray, 'The state against the Tamils', *Race and Class* 26.1 (1984), pp. 97–109; Virginia A. Leary, *Ethnic Conflict and Violence in Sri Lanka*, International Commission of Jurists, 1981; Paul Sieghart, *Sri Lanka: A mounting tragedy of errors*, International Commission of Jurists, 1984; Walter Schwarz and Murray Dickson, *The Tamils of Sri Lanka* (London: Minority Rights Group, 1975); Walter Schwarz, *The Tamils of Sri Lanka* (London: Minority Rights Group, 1983); Tamil Information Centre, *Militarisation in Sri Lanka*, 1986; International Crisis Group, *Sri Lanka's North 1: the denial of minority rights*, Asia Report No. 219, 2012; International Crisis Group, *Sri Lanka's North II: rebuilding under the military*, Asia Report No. 220, 2012.

The charge that Sri Lanka's abuses against the Tamil population amount to genocide has also become increasingly asserted by Tamil actors from the northeast, from the Diaspora and from Tamil Nadu. For an exhaustive overview of Sri Lankan state crimes collated from primary and secondary sources and organised within a legal framework as prosecutable evidence, see Tamils Against Genocide, 'Grand jury indictment for genocide: proposed to the United States Department of Justice', 2009, http://www.tamilsagainstgenocide.org/Research.aspx, last accessed April 2015.

9. See Chapter 5.

10. Anton S. Balasingham, *War and Peace: armed struggle and peace efforts of the Liberation Tigers* (London: Fairmax Publishing, 2004).

11. See, for example, Newton Gunasinghe, 'The Open Economy and its Impact on Ethnic Relations in Sri Lanka', in Winslow, Deborah W. and Michael D. Woost, eds, *Economy, Culture and Civil War in Sri Lanka* (Bloomington and Indianapolis: Indiana University Press, 2004), pp. 99–114; Ronald J. Herring, 'Making Ethnic Conflict: the Civil War in Sri Lanka', in Esman, Milton J., and Ronald J. Herring, eds, *Carrots, Sticks and Ethnic Conflict: rethinking development assistance* (University of Michigan Press, 2001), pp. 140–74; Mick Moore, 'Economic Liberalisation versus Political Pluralism in Sri Lanka?' *Modern Asian Studies* 24.2 (1990), pp. 341–83.

12. Nisha Arunatilake, Sisira Jayasuriya and Saman Kelegama, 'The economic cost of the war in Sri Lanka', *World Development* 29.9 (2001), p. 1485. In concrete terms, aid flows in the period 1978–83 reached $3 billion, a threefold increase when compared to the previous five years. See Brian Levy, 'Foreign Aid in the Making of Economic Policy in Sri Lanka', *Policy Sciences* 22 (1989), pp. 437–61.

13. Odd Arne Westad, *The Global Cold War: third world interventions and the making of our times* (Cambridge: Cambridge University Press, 2005).

14. For a discussion of these factors, see C. R. De Silva, 'Plebiscitary democracy or creeping authoritarianism? The presidential election and referendum of 1982', in Manor, James, ed., *Sri Lanka in Change and Crisis* (London: Croom Helm, 1984), pp. 38–49; Newton Gunasinghe, 'The Open Economy and its Impact'.
15. C. R. De Silva, 'Plebiscitary democracy'.
16. Moore, 'Economic liberalization'.
17. Satchi Ponnambalam, *Sri Lanka: national conflict and the Tamil liberation struggle* (London: Zed Books, 1983), p. 203.
18. Virginia Leary, *Ethnic Conflict and Violence in Sri Lanka: report of a mission to Sri Lanka in July–August 1981 on behalf of the International Commission of Jurists* (1981), pp. 43–55.
19. Gunasinghe, 'The open economy'.
20. Ibid., p. 100.
21. Kenneth D. Bush, *The Intra-Group Dimensions of Ethnic Conflict in Sri Lanka: learning to read between the lines* (Basingstoke: Palgrave, 2003), p. 128 (emphasis in original).
22. 'The Wages of Envy', *The Economist*, 20 August 1983.
23. Ibid.
24. Diplomatic ties between Sri Lanka and its Western allies were largely unaffected by the 1983 anti-Tamil violence that was played out in full view of Colombo's diplomatic community and extensively covered in the international media. In September 1983 the US Defence Secretary Casper Weinberger made a short visit to Colombo, en route to Pakistan. For details see L. Piyadasa, *Sri Lanka: the holocaust and after* (London: Marram Books, 1984), p. 122. During the meeting the Sri Lankan government submitted its 'shopping list of military supplies', and Sri Lankan press reports from the same time also quoted the strong possibility of military supplies from the UK. For details, see E. M. Thornton and R. Niththyananthan, *Sri Lanka, Island of Terror* (London: Eelam Research Organisation, 1984), p. 98. In June the following year, the Sri Lankan President made an official visit to Washington, where he was hosted at a White House dinner by President Reagan. For details see *Sunday Times*, 'When Reagan hosted JR to a White House dinner', 13 February 2011, http://www.sundaytimes.lk/110213/Timestwo/t2_14.html, last accessed April 2015. For the continuation of donor support during this period, see Ronald J. Herring, 'Making ethnic conflict'.
25. Thomas A. Marks, 'Ideology of Insurgency: new ethnic focus or old Cold War distortions?' *Small Wars and Insurgencies* 15.1 (2004), pp. 107–28; Balasingham, *War and Peace*.
26. For discussion of events around the Indo-Sri Lanka Accord, see, for example, Sumantra Bose, 'Flawed Mediation, Chaotic Implementation: the 1987 Indo-Sri Lanka Peace Agreeement', in Stedman, John Stephen, Donald Rothchild and Elizabeth M. Cousens, eds, *Ending Civil Wars: the implementation of peace agree-*

ments (Boulder, CO: Lynne Rienner Publishers, 2002), pp. 631–62; for an account by the LTTE's Chief Negotiator, see Balasingham, *War and Peace*. For an account by India's High Commissioner to Sri Lanka, see Jyotindra Nath Dixit, *Assignment Colombo* (Delhi: Konark Publishers, 1998).

27. For a detailed study of the JVP, see David Rampton, "'Deeper hegemony'": the populist politics of Sinhala nationalist discontent and the JVP in Sri Lanka', doctoral dissertation, University of London, 2010.

28. David Rampton, "'Deeper hegemony'": the politics of Sinhala nationalist authenticity and the failures of power-sharing in Sri Lanka', *Commonwealth and Comparative Politics* 49.2 (2011), pp. 256–8.

29. For discussion, see Stephen Kemper, *The Presence of the Past: chronicles, politics and culture in Sinhala life* (Ithaca and London: Cornell University Press, 1991), pp. 161–93.

30. Ibid., pp. 173–4.

31. See Chapter 1.

32. Patrick Peebles, 'Colonization and Ethnic Conflict in the Dry Zone of Sri Lanka', *Journal of Asian Studies* 49. 1 (1990), pp. 30–55.

33. Kemper, *The Presence of the Past*, p. 170.

34. Serena N. Teenekoon, 'Rituals of development: the accelerated Mahaveli development program of Sri Lanka', *American Ethnologist* 15.2 (1988), p. 295.

35. Brian Levy, 'Foreign Aid', p. 438.

36. Ibid., p. 442.

37. Tennekoon, 'Rituals of development'.

38. Somapala Jayawardhana, *History of Maduru Oya* (Dehiwala, Sri Lanka, 1982), quoted in Peebles, 'Colonization and Ethnic Conflict', p. 44.

39. Ibid., p. 47.

40. For details, see Human Rights Watch, 'Playing the communal card: communal violence and human rights', 1 April 1995, http://www.hrw.org/reports/1995/04/01/playing-communal-card, last accessed April 2015; and M. H. Gunaratna, *For a Sovereign State* (Ratmalana: Sarvodaya Book Publishing Services, 1988).

41. R. Muggah, *Relocation Failures in Sri Lanka: a short history of internal displacement and resettlement* (London and New York: Zed Books, 2008), pp. 119–27.

42. 'By 1987 there were an estimated 11,000 home guards in the Northern and Eastern provinces': Human Rights Watch, 'Playing the communal card'.

43. Suthaharan Nadarajah and Dhananjayan Sriskandarajah, 'Liberation struggle or terrorism? The politics of naming the LTTE', *Third World Quarterly* 26.1 (2005), pp. 87–100.

44. Tarak Barkawi and Mark Laffey, 'The imperial peace: democracy, force and globalization', *European Journal of International Relations* 5.4 (1999), pp. 403–34; and Westad, *The Global Cold War*.

45. For examples, see Phil Miller, *Britain's Dirty War against the Tamil people: 1970–*

2009 (Bremen: International Human Rights Association, 2014), http://www. ptsrilanka.org/images/documents/britains_dirty_war.pdf, last accessed April 2015; Tamil Information Centre, 'The Mossad connection and state terrorism in Sri Lanka', 1986; and note 24 above.

46. *Daily Telegraph*, 11 July 1983, quoted in Fernando Jude Lal, 'The politics of representation of mass atrocity in Sri Lanka and human rights discourse: challenges to justice and recovery', in Admirand, Peter, ed., *Loss and Hope: global, interreligious and interdisciplinary perspectives* (London and New York: Bloomsbury Academic, 2014), p. 30.

47. See Chapter 5.

48. Alfred Stepan, Juan J. Linz and Yogendra Yadav, *Crafting State-Nations: India and Other Multinational Democracies* (Baltimore, MD: Johns Hopkins University Press, 2001), p. 165 ftn 56. At the end of the war the total strength of the Sri Lankan military (army, navy and air force) was 450,000. According to World Bank figures, Sri Lanka's population is almost 20.5 million, giving a military to civilian ration of 1:45. For the sake of comparison the equivalent figures for India and Pakistan are 1:455 and 1:192 respectively. If the Indian military were to be proportionately the same size as Sri Lanka's, it would have to grow from its present size of 2.7 million to 27 million; whereas the Pakistani military would have to grow from its present size of 947,800 to 4 million. Calculations made by author, figures taken from World Bank for 2013 (see http://data.worldbank.org/indicator/SP.POP.TOTL for population statistics and http://data.worldbank.org/indicator/MS.MIL.TOTL.P1 for size of armed forces personnel).

49. Tessa J. Bartholomeusz, *In Defence of Dharma: just-war ideology in Buddhist Sri Lanka* (Richmond: Curzon, 2002).

50. Ibid.

51. For a discussion of the MSV and the role of the Indo-Lanka Accord in galvanising opposition to the UNP government, see Stanley J. Tambiah, *Buddhism Betrayed? Religion, politics, and violence in Sri Lanka* (Chicago and London: University of Chicago Press, 1992).

52. For the role of India as the origin of the Tamil threat, see for example Krishna, *Postcolonial Insecurities*, p. 43; and Chapter 1. The nationalist narrative of a pristine hydraulic Sinhala Buddhist civilisation repeatedly destroyed by south Indian invasions was more recently reasserted by former President Chandrika Kumaratunga, who asserted in an interview with a media outlet that while 'people' in Sri Lanka are fond of India, they also have some 'fear' because in ancient times:

'Sri Lanka was invaded by south Indian kings 52 times. Invaders often destroyed our irrigation system leading to floods everywhere. And ours was an irrigation economy. People felt that Indians were not like us. The perception continued till the recent past... Indira Gandhi was very unwise... After Mrs Gandhi, every Indian government has sought to normalise relations.' Quoted in DNAIndia, '"Lankan

PM merely joked about shooting": Chandrika Kumaratunga', 17 April 2015, available at http://www.dnaindia.com/analysis/interview-lankan-pm-merely-joked-about-shooting-chandrika-kumaratunga-2078090, last accessed April 2015. Importantly, Kumaratunga links hostility to Indira Gandhi's policies—namely the Indian intervention—to the nationalist narrative.

53. See references in note 8 above.
54. A. Jeyaratnam Wilson, *The Break-up of Sri Lanka: the Sinhalese–Tamil conflict* (London: Hurst & Co., 1988).
55. For an analysis of the history and differing organisational structures of these groups see Paul Staniland, *Networks of Rebellion: explaining insurgent cohesion and collapse* (Ithaca, NY: Cornell University Press, 2014), pp. 141–81.
56. Krishna, *Postcolonial Insecurities*, p. 123; for a detailed account of Indian and Tamil Nadu governments' interaction with Tamil militancy, see Balasingham, *War and Peace*.
57. Bose, 'Flawed Mediation, Chaotic Implementation,' p. 632.
58. For details of these events, see Dagmar Hellmann-Rajanayagam, *The Tamil Tigers: armed struggle for identity* (Stuttgart: Franz Steiner Verlag, 1994), pp. 101–25.
59. Interestingly, even those Tamil groups which switched sides in the armed conflict, first to the IPKF and then to the Sri Lankan government, have continued to keep the names with which they began their armed struggles, including the foremost pro-government paramilitary group since the late 1990s, the Eelam People's Democratic Party (EPDP), which began as a splinter of the EPRLF.
60. Charles Tilly, 'War Making and State Making as Organized Crime,' in Peter Evans, Dietrich Rueschemeyer, and Theda Skocpol, eds, *Bringing the State Back In* (Cambridge: Cambridge University Press, 1985).
61. Kim Jordan and Myriam Denov, 'Birds of Freedom? Perspectives on female emancipation and Sri Lanka's Liberation Tigers of Tamil Eelam', *Journal of International Women's Studies* 9.1 (2007), p. 46.
62. Human Rights Watch, 'Funding the "Final War": LTTE intimidation and extortion in the Tamil Diaspora', 14 March 2006, http://www.hrw.org/publications/reports?topic=All&region=164, last accessed April 2015.
63. For details, see note 8 above.
64. For a detailed study of economic and welfare-related dynamics within the LTTE's de facto state in Jaffna between 1990 and 1995, see Meghan O'Sullivan, 'Household entitlements during wartime: the experience of Sri Lanka', *Oxford Development Studies* 25.1 (1997), pp. 95–121.
65. On proscriptions, see Nadarajah and Sriskandarajah, 'Liberation struggle or terrorism? The politics of naming the LTTE', pp. 87–100.
66. See Chapter 8.
67. *Tamil Guardian*, 'TNA sets out to win support of the masses', 18 September 2013, available at http://www.tamilguardian.com/article.asp?articleid=8750, last accessed 15 January 2015.

68. 'LTTE was supremely successful in getting its message across to the population via its papers, journals, magazines, pamphlets, books, songs, poems and plays. In this game other groups were left far behind.' Hellman-Rajanayagam, *The Tamil Tigers*, p. 49.

69. See also Paul Staniland, *Networks of Rebellion*, who likewise argues that the LTTE's growth was built on a combination of 'ideology, the pre-existing vanguard core, and Sri Lanka's brutal but incompetent repression', p. 158. He notes as a puzzle the LTTE's capacity to expand without building local alliances (co-option in the terminology used here, or local imposition), p. 177. The argument presented here is that expansion was dependent on a core ideology, consistently propagated through cohesive structure in activities that were continuous over space and time.

70. For a representative anthology of poetry in the Tamil liberation genre, see M. Neminathan, ed., *Tamil Eelam Literature* (Tamil Information Centre, 1996). For an analysis of the themes and concerns of this genre, see D. Hellman-Rajanayagam, 'And Heroes Die: poetry of the Tamil Liberation Movement in northern Sri Lanka', *South Asia: Journal of Asian Studies* 28.1 (2005), pp. 112–53.

71. For a description of Heroes' Day events in LTTE-held Vanni in 1998, see TamilNet, 'Great Heroes' Day celebrations in Vanni', 27 November 1998, available at http://www.tamilnet.com/art.html?catid=13&artid=2389, last accessed 15 January 2015.

72. For discussion of the LTTE's de facto state, see N. Malathy, *A Fleeting Moment in my Country: the last years of the LTTE de facto state* (Atlanta, GA: Clearday Books, 2012); O'Sullivan, 'Household entitlements'; Kristian Stokke, 'Building the Tamil Eelam State: emerging state institutions and forms of governance in LTTE-controlled areas in Sri Lanka', *Third World Quarterly* 27.6 (2006), pp. 1021–40; Zachariah Cherian Mampilly, *Rebel Rulers: insurgency governance and civilian life during war* (Ithaca, NY: Cornell University Press, 2011).

73. Jordan and Denov, 'Birds of Freedom?'

74. A. J. V. Chandrakanthan, 'Eelam Tamil nationalism: an inside view', in Wilson, A. Jeyaratnam, *Sri Lankan Tamil Nationalism: its origins and development in the nineteenth and twentieth centuries* (London: Hurst & Co., 2000), pp. 157–76.

75. 'The LTTE is in many key respects an outlier in the broader universe of armed groups in terms of its eventual fighting power, its capacity for governance, and its organizational control.' Paul Staniland, 'Networks of Rebellion', p. 149.

76. Needs reference

77. Jordan and Denov, 'Birds of Freedom?'

78. Ann Adele, *Unbroken Chains: explorations into the Jaffna dowry system* (Jaffna: Vasan Litho Printers, 1995), p. 50.

79. O'Sullivan, 'Household entitlements', p. 111.

80. See also N. Malathy, *A Fleeting Moment in my Country*, pp. 105–16.

81. See note 8 above.

82. Elizabeth Jean Wood, 'Armed Groups and Sexual Violence: when is wartime rape rare?' *Politics and Society* 37.1 (2009), pp. 131–61.
83. The well-known Indian journalist N. Ram, who became one of its fiercest critics, 'sarcastically describes the LTTE as an "equal opportunity (and one might add, affirmative-action) employer"'. Quoted in S. Bose, 'States, Nations, Sovereignty: Sri Lanka, India and the Tamil Eelam movement' (New Delhi: Sage Publications, 1994), p. 105.
84. Interviews with LTTE officials, October 2006.
85. For discussion of the deterioration in Tamil–Muslim relations in the east from the mid-1980s, see A. R. M. Imtiyaz, 'The Eastern Muslims of Sri Lanka: special problems and solutions', *Journal of Asian and African Studies* 44.4 (2009), pp. 407–27.
86. Imtiyaz, 'The Eastern Muslims'. See also A. Ali, 'The End of the Road', *South Asia Journal* 9 (2013).
87. Imtiyaz, 'The Eastern Muslims', pp. 411–12. For the escalation of Tamil–Muslim violence, see also Human Rights Watch, 'Playing the communal card: communal violence and human rights', 1 April 1995, http://www.hrw.org/reports/1995/04/01/playing-communal-card, last accessed April 2015.
88. Human Rights Watch, 'Playing the communal card'.
89. Ibid.
90. A key example of the LTTE's use of human rights norms and international law to make its case is a book titled *Indictment against Sri Lanka* (1993) which was produced by the Legal and Human Rights Division of its International Secretariat and published in London in 1993. It was widely circulated in the mid-1990s by the LTTE and allied Tamil nationalists and sets out a chronology of Sri Lankan state abuses, beginning with the disenfranchisement of the Indian Tamils and ending with human rights reports of the early 1990s. Crucially it relies almost entirely on quotes from Western newspapers, human rights reports by advocacy organisations and speeches by Western politicians. See also from the same era the LTTE leader's Maha Veerar Naal Address given on 27 November 1993: 'We are standing on a strong moral foundation. We are fighting a just cause. Our political objectives conform with international norms and principles.' Available at http://tamilnation.co/ltte/vp/mahaveerar/vp93.htm, last accessed 15 January 2015.

7. SRI LANKA'S CIVIL WAR: THE ENDING

1. Amita Shastri, 'An Open Economy in a Time of Intense Civil War: Sri Lanka, 1994–2000', in Winslow, Deborah W. and Michael D. Woost, eds, *Economy, Culture and Civil War in Sri Lanka* (Bloomington and Indianapolis: Indiana University Press, 2004), p. 88.
2. M. Rasaratnam and M. Malagodi, 'Eyes Wide Shut: persistent conflict and liberal

peace building in Nepal and Sri Lanka', *Conflict, Security and Development* 12.3 (2012), pp. 299–327.

3. See, for example, the landmark speech by the then US Ambassador: Ashley Wills, 'The US Stand on Sri Lanka's Conflict—Speech at Jaffna Public Library', 7 March 2001, http://www.tamilnation.co/intframe/us/01willis.htm, last accessed 30 May 2014.

4. Press conference on Tokyo donors conference, 21 November 2006, US Department of State Archive, http://2001-2009.state.gov/p/us/rm/2006/76483.htm, last accessed April 2015.

5. For a detailed discussion of the containment of the LTTE as a central problematic driving international actors engaged in the Norwegian peace process, see Suthaharan Nadarajah, 'Clash of Governmentalities: liberal peace, Tamil freedom and the 2001–2006 Peace Process in Sri Lanka', PhD Dissertation, University of London, 2010.

6. See a summary in Tamil Information Centre, 'Western nations to provide arms to Sri Lanka', 19 May 1995, available at: http://www.ticonline.org/images/publicationpdffiles/Western_nations_to_provide_arms_to_Sri_Lankan_94.pdf. For a detailed discussion of the talks by the LTTE's chief negotiator, including the correspondence between both sides, see Anton Balasingham, *The Politics of Duplicity* (Mitcham, Surrey: Fairmax Publishing, 2000).

7. Sri Lanka's military expenditure rose dramatically from just under 13 per cent of total government spending in 1994, to a high of just over 19 per cent in 1995 and 1996. It has subsequently remained at over 10 per cent of government expenditure (in line with regional averages, except for Pakistan). Figures from the Stockholm International Peace Research Institute, military expenditure database, http://www.sipri.org/research/armaments/milex/milex_database, last accessed April 2015.

8. Tamil Information Centre, 'The Killing of Neelan Tiruchelvam', 2 August 1999, available at http://www.ticonline.org/images/publicationpdffiles/Killing_of_Dr_Neelan_Tiruchelvam_116.pdf. For a detailed critique of the devolution proposals, see Tamil Information Centre, 'Sri Lanka Devolution Proposals, August 1995–January 1996 (London, 1996).

9. In 1995 Sri Lanka's donors pledged $850 million in concessional aid, and in 1996 this increased to $860 million: http://tamilnation.co/tamileelam/aid/index.htm#Structural Dependency

10. Jordan J. Paust, 'The Human Rights to Food, Medicine and Medical Supplies, and Freedom from Arbitrary and Inhumane Detention and Controls in Sri Lanka', *Vanderbilt Journal of Transnational Law* 31 (1998), pp. 617–42.

11. See comments by Mieko Nishimizu, Vice President for the World Bank's operations in South Asia, to the Sri Lanka Development Forum in 2004. TamilNet, 'Aid "disconnect" in Paris', 22 December 2000, available at http://www.tamilnet.com/art.html?catid=13&artid=5674.

12. Total arms exports to Sri Lanka jumped from $86 million in 1999 to its highest level of $298 million in 2000. This included arms transfers from China ($18 million), Czech Republic ($8 million), India ($16 million), Israel ($134 million), Pakistan ($3 million), Ukraine ($55 million), United Kingdom ($43 million) and the United States ($10 million). Figures are in 1990 prices and taken from the Stockholm International Peace Research Institute, Arms Transfers Database, http://www.sipri.org/databases/armstransfers, last accessed April 2015.
13. BBC, 'Tamil Tigers "serious about peace"', 2 November 2000, available at http://news.bbc.co.uk/1/hi/world/south_asia/1004145.stm, last accessed April 2015.
14. For detailed discussion of the peace process, see Nadarajah, 'Clash of Governmentalities'. See also the Norwegian government's review of its initiative in Jonathan Goodhand, Bart Klem and Gunnar Sørbø, 'Pawns of Peace: evaluation of Norwegian peace efforts in Sri Lanka, 1997–2009', commissioned by Norad Evaluation Department, Report 5/2011, 2011. For an account by the LTTE's chief negotiator, see Anton S. Balasingham, *War and Peace: armed struggle and peace efforts of the Liberation Tigers* (Mitcham, Surrey: Fairmax Publishing, 2004); and for an account by Sri Lanka's Defence Secretary, see Austin Fernando, *My Belly is White* (Colombo: Vijitha Yapa Publications, 2008). Generally, see also Kristian Stokke and Jayadeva Uyangoda, eds, *Liberal Peace in Question: politics of state and market reform in Sri Lanka* (London: Anthem Press, 2011).
15. Brian Blodgett, *Sri Lanka's Military: the search for a mission (1949–2004)* (Chula Vista, CA: Aventine Press, 2004); Jeffrey Lunstead, 'The United States' Role in Sri Lanka Peace Process, 2002–2006', Asia Foundation, 2007.
16. Sunil Bastian, 'The economic agenda and the peace process', Asia Foundation, 2005. Available at www.asiafoundation.org/resources/pdfs/SLEconomicsofPeace.pdf; Suthaharan Nadarajah, '"Conflict sensitive" Aid and Making Liberal Peace', in Duffield, Mark and Vernon Hewitt, eds, *Empire, Development and Colonialism: The Past in the Present* (Martleshm, Suffolk: James Currey, 2009), pp. 109–29.
17. BBC, 'Sri Lanka wins $4.5bn aid pledge', 10 June 2003, available at http://news.bbc.co.uk/1/hi/world/south_asia/2977230.stm, last accessed April 2015.
18. Bastian, 'The economic agenda', p. 8.
19. Senior government officials engaged in the peace process talked of the existence of an 'international safety net' that would deter the LTTE from returning to war. See for example Amaia Sánchez-Cacicedo, *Building States, Building Peace: global and regional involvement in Sri Lanka and Myanmar* (Basingstoke: Palgrave Macmillan, 2014), p. 219. The LTTE also cited the existence of a coercive 'international safety net' as a reason for deciding to suspend its participation in the formal negotiations of the peace process. See TamilNet, 'Pirapaharan's Heroes' Day address', 27 November 2003, https://www.tamilnet.com/art.html?catid=13&artid=10554, last accessed April 2015. During the negotiations, Norwegian facilitators made clear to LTTE leaders on several occasions that while the interna-

tional community trusted the government's willingness to pursue peace and reform, the LTTE had yet to prove its commitment (interviews with LTTE leaders, September 2006).

20. Interestingly, whilst the international community then dismissed these demands as excuses by the violent and separatist LTTE to evade committing to a political solution, several years after the war these same demands are being made of the government of President Mahinda Rajapaksa by the international community. See Chapter 8.

21. 'In 2005 when President Rajapaksa assumed charge the strength (of the armed forces) was 125,000. Between 2005 and 2009 the figure swelled to 450,000 out of which 300,000 is the strength of the Army.' Gotabaya Rajapaksa Defence Secretary (2005–15), quoted in V. K. Shashikumar, 'Winning wars: political will is the key—Defence Secretary', *Indian Defense Review* 24 (July–Sept 2009), also available at http://www.defence.lk/new.asp?fname=20100429_05, last accessed April 2015.

22. *Tamil Guardian*, 'International Mandate' Editorial, 13 December 2006, available at http://www.tamilguardian.com/article.asp?articleid=1027, last accessed April 2015.

23. TamilNet, 'APRC: how long you tolerate a farce, Suresh asks India and IC', 12 November 2008, available at http://www.tamilnet.com/art.html?catid=79& artid=27459

24. According to the ICG, more than $500 million was committed from 2007 onwards for the Eastern province, excluding already ongoing post-tsunami assistance programmes. For details, see International Crisis Group, 'Development assistance and the conflict in Sri Lanka: lessons from the Eastern Province', *Asia Report* 165, 16 April 2009, http://www.crisisgroup.org/en/regions/asia/south-asia/sri-lanka/165-development-assistance-and-conflict-in-sri-lanka-lessons-from-the-eastern-province.aspx

25. Mahinda Rajapaksa, 'Address by his Excellency President Mahinda Rajapaksa at the ceremonial opening of Parliament, Sri Jayawardhanapura, Kotte', 19 May 2009, available at http://www.priu.gov.lk/news_update/Current_Affairs/ca200905/20090519terrorism_defeated.htm, last accessed 16 January 2015.

26. United Nations, 'Report of the Secretary General's Panel of Experts on Accountability in Sri Lanka', 31 March 2011, available at http://www.un.org/News/dh/infocus/Sri_Lanka/POE_Report_Full.pdf, last accessed 12 June 2012.

27. For a discussion of Sinhala nationalist mobilisation in relation to the Norwegian-led peace process, see especially David Rampton and Asanga Welikala, *The Politics of the South* (Colombo: Asia Foundation, 2005); and also Neil DeVotta, *Sinhalese Buddhist Nationalist Ideology: implications for politics and conflict resolution in Sri Lanka* (Washington, DC: East–West Center, 2007).

28. Neil De Votta and Jason Stone, 'Jathika Hela Urumaya and Ethno-Religious Politics in Sri Lanka', *Pacific Affairs* 81.1 (2008), pp. 31–51.

29. Nirupama Subramanian, 'Back to the Freezer', *Frontline* 17 (19 Aug-1 Sept 2000), available at http://www.frontline.in/static/html/fl1717/17171100.htm, last accessed 16 January 2015.
30. See Rampton and Welikala *The Politics of the South*; and De Votta, *Sinhalese Buddhist Nationalist Ideology*.
31. DeVotta, *Sinhalese Buddhist Nationalist Ideology*, pp. 33–6.
32. Ibid., p. 25.
33. Neil DeVotta and Jason Stone, 'Jathika Hela Urumaya'.
34. Quoted in Rohan Edrisinha, 'Constitutionalism, pluralism, ethnic conflict', in Rotbert, R., ed., *Creating Peace in Sri Lanka: civil war and reconciliation* (Washington, DC: Brookings Institute Press, 19990, p. 175.
35. Chandrika Kumaratunga-Bandaranaike, *Profiles of Freedom, selected speeches by Chandrika Bandaranaike Kumaratunga* (Colombo: Government Information Department, 1996), pp. 40–50.
36. *Sunday Leader*, 'President Kumaratunga promises Buddhist High Priests "political package will not be finalized until war is over"', 6 August 1995.
37. *Time Magazine*, 'President Kumaratunga "conquers" Jaffna and holds a medieval victory ceremony', 18 December 1995.
38. *Sunday Times*, 'Government to water down devolution', 20 August 1995; and Edrisinha, 'Constitutionalism, pluralism, ethnic conflict'.
39. Balasingham, *War and Peace*.
40. *Tamil Guardian*, 'Silences between the shouts', 13 May 2014, available at http://www.tamilguardian.com/article.asp?articleid=10894, last accessed May 2015.
41. See Chapter 8.
42. Committee to Protect Journalists, 'CPJ denounces Sri Lankan censorship', 9 June 1998, https://cpj.org/news/1998/srilanka9june98.html, last accessed April 2015.
43. For a thoroughgoing discussion of TamilNet, see Mark P. Whitaker, 'Tamilnet.com: some reflections on popular anthropology, nationalism, and the internet', *Anthropological Quarterly* 77.3 (2004), pp. 469–98.
44. For a discussion of the conditions of state repression in the Tamil-speaking areas of the north-east that have been in place since the early late 1970s to early 1980s and continue to this day, see Chapter 6, note 8.
45. On this point, see discussion in Whitaker, 'Tamilnet.com', p. 478.
46. The word '*pongu*' or '*pongum*' in this context refers to the boiling over or effervescence of the sweet rice (*pongal*) traditionally made in the open air at sunrise in an earthenware pot to celebrate the Tamil harvest festival (Thai Pongal) in January.
47. See for example the TamilNet report on the Jaffna 2005 Pongu Thamil rally: 'Thousands attends Jaffna Pongu Thamil rally, seek Army withdrawal,' 30 September 2005, https://www.tamilnet.com/art.html?catid=13&artid=15986, last accessed April 2015.
48. According to the TamilNet report, by 2008 nearly 150,000 Tamils in North

America, Europe, Africa and Australia had participated in Pongu Thamil events: 'Grand finale for Pongku Thamizh in London', 13 July 2008, http://www.tamil-net.com/art.html?artid=26338&catid=79, last accessed April 2015. See also N. Malathy, *A Fleeting Moment in my Country: the last years of the LTTE de facto state* (Atlanta GA: Clearday Books, 2012), p. 53.

49. TNA, 'Our Election Manifesto, Tamil National Alliance, 2001', available at https://www.tamilnet.com/img/publish/2010/03/TNA_Election_Manifesto_2001.pdf, last accessed May 2015.

50. A notable exception was ACTC leader Gajan Ponnambalam. The ACTC, Sri Lanka's oldest Tamil party, is distinctive amongst Tamil parliamentary parties in the post-Cold War era in consistently asserting the primacy of Tamil territorial nationhood as the basis for addressing Tamil grievances, and in recognising the LTTE as the legitimate Tamil leadership. In 2010 Ponnambalam split from the TNA in protest at the other leaders' decision to support the former army commander, Lt. Gen. Sarath Fonseka, as presidential candidate.

51. See the Introduction on the components of successful political mobilisation; and also Chapter 2 on the consolidation of the Indian nationalist movement.

52. For discussion of the LTTE's de facto state, see N. Malathy *A Fleeting Moment*; O'Sullivan, 'Household entitlements'; Kristian Stokke, 'Building the Tamil Eelam State: emerging state institutions and forms of governance in LTTE-controlled areas in Sri Lanka', *Third World Quarterly* 27.6 (2006), pp. 1021–40; Zachariah Cherian Mampilly, *Rebel Rulers: insurgency, governance and civilian life during war* (Ithaca, NY: Cornell University Press, 2011).

53. Extant studies of Tamil diaspora relations with the LTTE have largely focused on financial contributions, voluntary or coerced, for its armed struggle. See, for example, Daniel Byman, Peter Chalk, Bruce Hoffman, William Rosenau and David Brannan, *Trends in Outside Support for Insurgent Movements* (Santa Monica, CA: Rand Corporation, 2001); Sarah Wayland, 'Ethno-nationalist Networks and Transnational Opportunities: the Sri Lankan Tamil diaspora', *Review of International Studies* 30.3 (2004), pp. 405–26. But see also C. Christine Fair, 'Diaspora involvement in insurgencies: insights from the Khalistan and Tamil Eelam movements', *Nationalism and Ethnic Politics* 11.1 (2005), pp. 125–56.

8. TAMIL NATIONALISM TODAY

1. For a detailed account of the final months of the war, see United Nations, 'Report of the Secretary General's Panel of Experts on Accountability in Sri Lanka', 31 March 2011, available at http://www.un.org/News/dh/infocus/Sri_Lanka/POE_Report_Full.pdf

2. See, for example, Amnesty International, 'Sri Lanka: twenty years of make-believe', June 2009, available at http://www.amnesty.org/en/library/asset/ASA37/005/2009/en/c41db308-7612-4ca7-946d-03ad209aa900/asa370052009eng.pdf

In January 2015 Presidential Elections, Mahinda Rajapaksa was defeated by Maithripala Sirisena, his former minister who unexpectedly defected from Rajapaksa's government in November 2014 to challenge Rajapaksa's re-election bid. Sirisena was backed by the opposition UNP and the former President Chandrika Kumaratunga. His campaign focused primarily on the themes of good governance, attacking the corruption and nepotism of the Rajapaksa era, but also sought to improve Sri Lanka's international image and rebuild ties with Sri Lanka's former allies, principally western states and India. In the August 2015 parliamentary elections, the UNP emerged as the largest party with 106 out of 225 seats, but failed to secure an outright majority. The TNA won sixteen out of 22 seats from the northeast. There were expectations that in the event that the UNP failed to secure an outright majority it might form a coalition with the TNA or indeed rely on TNA support to secure a majority. However, the UNP subsequently formed a national unity government with the SLFP and thus the possibility of a UNP-TNA parliamentary alliance forming the basis for a political solution seem at the time of writing (September 2015) to be unlikely. The new government, led by Prime Minister Ranil Wickremesinghe has reaffirmed President Sirisena's commitment to rebuilding relations with western states and India. It has also stated that it will pursue accountability through a credible domestic process and is committed to reconciliation, including meaningful devolution. These shifts have been broadly welcomed by the international community. At the time of writing, however, the new government's more accommodating stance towards the international community has not been translated into concrete proposals or material changes to the conditions of militarisation, repression and surveillance in the Tamil speaking regions.

3. International Crisis Group, *Sri Lanka's North I: the denial of minority rights*, Asia Report No. 219, 2012, pp. 17–22. See also International Crisis Group, 'Sri Lanka: Tamil Politics and the Quest for a Political Solution', 20 November 2012, available at: http://www.crisisgroup.org/en/publication-type/media-releases/2014/asia/reconciliation-and-accountability-in-sri-lanka.aspx; International Crisis Group, 'Sri Lanka's Potemkin Peace: Democracy Under Fire', 13 November 2013, available at http://www.crisisgroup.org/en/regions/asia/south-asia/sri-lanka/253-sri-lanka-s-potemkin-peace-democracy-under-fire.aspx

4. The military to civilian ration in the Northern Province is estimated to be one to five; for details see Correspondent, 'Notes on the military presence in Sri Lanka's Northern Province', *Economic and Political Weekly* 43.28, 14 July 2012. This is 'even higher than the ratio of military personnel to civilians found today in Kashmir, at the height of the second war in Chechnya or the conflict in Northern Ireland, during the surge in Iraq, or even during the French occupation of Algeria'; quoted in International Crisis Group, 'The forever war? Military control in Sri Lanka's north', In Pursuit of Peace Blog, 25 March 2014, available at http://blog.crisisgroup.org/asia/2014/03/25/the-forever-war-military-control-in-sri-lankas-north/, last

accessed April 2015. A retired Indian army colonel who served in Sri Lanka described the Sri Lankan military's posture in the north-east as one of 'operational readiness' rather than post-conflict repose. Quoted in *The Hindu*, 'Sri Lankan Army still has vast presence in North and East', 19 September 2012, available at http://www.thehindu.com/news/sri-lankan-army-still-has-vast-presence-in-north-east/article3915391.ece

5. For details of the military's economic activities, see International Crisis Group, *Sri Lanka's North II*, pp. 22–3; also *New York Times*, 'Sri Lanka's Tamil minority grows impatient with just promises', 15 March 2015.

6. The Northern Provincial Council (elected in September 2013) has stated that 65,000 acres of land are occupied by the military across the north as a whole; quoted in Journalists for Democracy in Sri Lanka, 'Sri Lanka IPD displeasure at 'release of land' on eve of presidential visit', 16 February 2015, available at http://www.jdslanka.org/index.php/news-features/politics-a-current-affairs/518-sri-lanka-idp-displeasure-at-release-of-land-on-eve-of-presidents-india-tour, last accessed May 2015.

The military occupies 18 per cent of the land area of the Jaffna peninsula, as quoted in *Sunday Times*, 'HSZ Row, story behind the story', 29 December 2002. In the post-war era, the government has sought to take legal ownership of occupied land. In 2013 the government issued acquisition orders for over 7,000 acres of military-occupied land in Jaffna high-security zones, estimated to have a commercial value of $2 billion. For details, see Sri Lanka Campaign for Peace and Justice, 'The Sri Lankan army is seizing land that could be worth $2billion', 30 May 2013, available at http://www.srilankacampaign.org/the-sri-lankan-army-is-seizing-land-that-could-be-worth-2bn/

7. See *Tamil Guardian*, 'Silences between the shouts', 13 May 2014, available at http://www.tamilguardian.com/article.asp?articleid=10894, last accessed May 2015.

8. The BJP government elected in April 2014 has largely continued with this approach.

9. United Nations, 'Report of the Secretary General's Panel of Experts on Accountability in Sri Lanka', p. ii.

10. In the period 2009–14 China financed projects worth nearly $5 billion in Sri Lanka. For details, see Tom Miller, 'The perils of leadership', *GavekalDragonomics*, Global Research, 14 April 2015. Since taking power in April 2015, President Sirisena has sought to move away from his predecessor's close alliance with China.

11. An important example of this institutional support was the increase in concessional lending to Sri Lanka from the late 1970s onwards. Sri Lanka's total government debt has increased from just under 20 per cent of GDP in 1950 to reach a high of around 102 per cent in 1989. For details, see Mahinda Pushpakumara, 'Dynamics of debt accumulation in Sri Lanka: impact of primary fiscal deficit,

GDP growth and interest rate', Sri Lanka Economic Research Conference, 2012, available at: http://archive.cmb.ac.lk/research/bitstream/70130/3763/1/Dynamics_of_Debt_Accumulation.PDF, last accessed May 2015. The debt to GDP ratio in 2014 was 75 per cent, see Central Bank of Sri Lanka, *Annual Report 2014*, Colombo, Sri Lanka, p. 151, available at: http://www.cbsl.gov.lk/htm/english/10_pub/p_1.html, last accessed May 2015. However, for much of this period the majority of the lending is categorised by the World Bank as concessional (that is, at lower than commercial interest rates and with a grant element of 25 per cent). Between 1986 and 2009, for example, concessional aid was more than 65 per cent of total lending (reaching a high of almost 80 per cent in 2004, during the Norwegian peace process and just after the 2003 Tokyo aid conference). Figures taken from World Bank, 'International Debt Statistics', 2014, available at http://data.worldbank.org/data-catalog/international-debt-statistics, last accessed May 2015. However, since 2009, the share of concessional loans in overall debt has steadily declined as Sri Lanka has sought alternative forms of finance, including infrastructure loans from China as well as sovereign bond issues. Concessional loans constituted half of all debt in 2012. See Dushini Weerakoon, 'Sri Lanka's external stability; foreign debt and exchange earnings', *Talking Economics, Institute of Policy Studies*, 14 May 2013, available at http://www.ips.lk/talkingeconomics/2013/05/14/sri-lankas-external-stability-foreign-debt-and-export-earnings/, last accessed May 2015.

12. According to Ravi Karunanayake, appointed finance minister in January 2015, Chinese loans and investments were on 'very, very commercial terms. Most of the loans are at about 6 per cent, but the highest is 8.8 per cent.' Quoted in Miller, 'The perils of leadership', p. 3. Multilateral lenders typically charge well under 2 per cent, ibid.

13. Nimal Sanderatne, 'How burdensome is the country's increasing indebtedness?' *Sunday Times*, 25 May 2014, available at http://www.sundaytimes.lk/140525/columns/how-burdensome-is-the-countrys-increasing-indebtedness-100319.html

14. In 2012, almost half of Sri Lanka's exports went to the EU and US. Less than 5 per cent of Sri Lanka's trade (and mainly imports) was with China. See European Commission, 'European Union Trade in goods with Sri Lanka', 16 April 2014, p. 9.

15. In 2010 it was reported that Sri Lanka was paying British PR firm Bell Pottinger £3 million a year to improve the country's post-war image. See BBC, 'Sri Lanka "pays PR firm £3 million to boost post-war image"', 22 October 2010, available at http://www.bbc.co.uk/news/world-south-asia-11606899. In February 2014, just before the vote at the UNHRC, Thomson Advisory Group, a US lobby firm hired by the Sri Lankan government, aired a 28-minute paid-for programme titled 'Sri Lanka: Reconciling and rebuilding' on the NBC network. The Central Bank was reported to have been paying the firm a fee of $66,000 a month. Reported in

DailyFT, 'Thirty minute infomercial on Lanka aired on US NBC network', 6 February 2014, available at http://www.ft.lk/2014/02/06/30-minute-infomercial-on-lanka-aired-on-us-nbc-network/, last accessed May 2015.

16. For example, in an effort to refute the series of high-profile Channel 4 documentaries on the mass atrocities that took place in the final months of the war—*Sri Lanka's Killing Fields* (2011), *Sri Lanka's Killing Fields: war crimes unpunished* (2012) and *No Fire Zone* (2013)—the Sri Lankan government has actively promoted a book called *Corrupted Journalism: Channel 4 and Sri Lanka*, written and produced by Engage Sri Lanka (2013), available at http://www.corruptedjournalism.com/book/Corrupted%20Journalism.pdf, last accessed May 2015. The book was included in the press pack given to all journalists attending the Commonwealth Heads of Government Meeting in Colombo, November 2013. For details see Channel 4, 'Sri Lanka, "Corrupted Journalism" and Channel 4 news', 9 November 2013, available at http://www.channel4.com/news/sri-lanka-corrupted-journalism-and-channel-4-news

17. For example, in response to the launch of the UN expert panel, the government launched its own 'Lessons Learned and Reconciliation Commission' tasked with investigating events leading to onset of war in 2006 and ensuing abuses. The LLRC's lengthy report, published in December 2011, seven months after the UN expert panel's, accepted that there had been 'considerable civilian casualties', but perhaps unsurprisingly exonerated government forces while blaming the LTTE. The report nevertheless made recommendations on devolution and de-militarisation which many liberal peace actors welcomed, not least as these ran counter to the post-war Sinhala Buddhist consensus; but Sri Lanka's continued failure to implement the recommendations of its own panel became an important justification in the campaign for an international investigation. See, variously, Human Rights Watch, 'Sri Lanka: report fails to advance accountability', 19 December 2011, available at http://www.hrw.org/news/2011/12/16/sri-lanka-report-fails-advance-accountability; International Crisis Group, 'Statement on the Report of Sri Lanka's Lessons Learnt and Reconciliation Commission', 22 December 2011, available at http://www.crisisgroup.org/en/publication-type/media-releases/2011/asia/statement-on-the-report-of-sri-lanka-s-lessons-learnt-and-reconciliation-commission.aspx; International Crisis Group, 'Briefing Note: Reconciliation and Accountability in Sri Lanka: UNHRC action remains crucial', 28 February 2014, available at http://www.crisisgroup.org/en/publication-type/media-releases/2014/asia/reconciliation-and-accountability-in-sri-lanka.aspx

18. See discussion in Suthaharan Nadarajah and Vicki Sentas, 'The Politics of State Crime and Resistance: Self-determination in Sri Lanka', in Elizabeth Stanley and Jude McCulloch, eds, *State Crime and Resistance* (Abingdon, Oxon: Routledge, 2013), pp. 68–83.

19. This section draws on several years of participant observation in Tamil diaspora

politics, beginning in the late 1990s. There is now a growing literature on Tamil diaspora politics; recent analysis includes: Luxshi Vimalarajah and R. Cheran, 'Empowering Diasporas: the politics of post-war transnational Tamil politics', Berghof Peace Support, Occasional Paper No. 31, 2010, available at: http://www.berghof-peacesupport.org/publications/SL_Empowering_Diasporas.pdf; International Crisis Group, *The Sri Lankan Tamil Diaspora after the LTTE*, Asia Report No. 186 (2010), available at http://www.crisisgroup.org/en/regions/asia/south-asia/sri-lanka/186-the-sri-lankan-tamil-diaspora-after-the-ltte.aspx; Vicki Sentas, 'One More Successful War? Tamil diaspora and counter-terrorism after the LTTE', in Poynting, S and D. Whyte, eds, *Counter-Terrorism and State Political Violence* (Abingdon, Oxon: Routledge, 2012); C. Orjuella, 'Diaspora Identities and Homeland Politics: lessons from the Sri Lanka/Tamil Eelam case', in Lyons, T. and P. Mandeville, eds, *Politics from Afar: transnational diasporas and networks* (London: Hurst & Co., 2012), pp. 91–116; Suthaharan Nadarajah and Vicki Sentas, 'The Politics of State Crime and Resistance: self-determination in Sri Lanka', in Stanley, Elizabeth and Jude McCulloch, eds, *State Crime and Resistance* (Abingdon, Oxon: Routledge, 2013), pp. 68–83.

20. For example, see the following for a round-up of Heroes' Day commemorations across the world: *Tamil Guardian*, 'Maaveerar Naal 2014 commemorated world-wide', 28 November 2014, available at http://www.tamilguardian.com/article.asp?articleid=12974, last accessed May 2015.

21. BBC, 'Tamil protest ends after 73 days', 16 June 2009, available at http://news.bbc.co.uk/1/hi/england/london/8105879.stm

22. These routine and behind the scenes forms of engagement establish the context in which more high-profile events take place, such as the meeting between the British Prime Minister and Tamil diaspora organisations in Downing Street just before the November 2013 Commonwealth Summit in Colombo. For details, see *Tamil Guardian*, 'British Tamils disappointed at Cameron's commitment to CHOGM, continue call for boycott', 7 November 2013, available at http://www.tamilguardian.com/article.asp?articleid=9109, last accessed May 2015.

23. See discussion in Suthaharan Nadarajah, 'Disciplining the Diaspora: Tamil self-determination and the politics of proscription', in Ingram, Alan and Klaus Dodds, eds, *Spaces of Security and Insecurity: geographies of the War on Terror* (Farnham, Surrey: Ashgate, 2009), pp. 109–30.

24. For example, all of the organisations that met with the Prime Minister explicitly positioned themselves as making demands on the basis of their British citizenship. Jan Jananayagam, representing Tamils Against Genocide, said at the meeting: 'Today's meeting was a significant step in deeper engagement between Tamils and *our* government' (emphasis added), quoted in *Tamil Guardian*, 'British Tamils disappointed', 7 November 2013.

25. This political unity is apparent at critical moments when an array of Tamil organ-

isations, from across the world, take a common stance and release joint statements. Importantly these statements are often addressed to the international audiences, rather than the Sri Lankan state. See for example the statement released in February 2015 calling on the UN Human Rights Commissioner not to delay releasing the report of the UN inquiry into Sri Lankan mass atrocities: *Tamil Guardian*, 'Diaspora orgs urge UN human rights chief to release Sri Lanka inquiry report', 15 February 2015, available at http://tamilguardian.com/article.asp?articleid= 13791, last accessed May 2015.

26. It is often assumed—and claimed by Sri Lanka—that these splits are over control of financial resources, but the actual disputes have been about tactics and strategies by which to pursue nationalist goals without the LTTE. The LTTE's funds were often spent as soon as, or even before, they were collected and primarily used to strengthen military and de facto state capacities. The fundraising networks held little by way of substantial assets beyond their well-developed organisational capacity. It is this capacity that has been weakened by disputes amongst its members over how it should be used: for example, whether to engage Western states and politicians for accountability or to be suspicious of international actors long allied with Sri Lanka and focus instead on asserting the claim for territorial nationhood.

27. These include, amongst many others, the British Tamil Forum (BTF), the Canadian Tamil Council (CTC), the United States Tamil Political Action Council (USTPAC), Tamils Against Genocide (TAG), etc.

28. In February 2015 the Northern Provincial Council passed a resolution stating that 'successive Sri Lankan governments have perpetrated genocide amongst the Tamils'. For details and full resolution, see Journalists for Democracy in Sri Lanka, 'NPC passes landmark resolution calling it a "genocide against Tamils"', 10 February 2015, available at http://www.jdslanka.org/index.php/news-features/politics-a-current-affairs/515-npc-passes-resolution-calling-it-a-genocide-against-tamils, last accessed May 2015. The resolution was promptly endorsed by a range of Tamil diaspora organisations across the world in a statement that also called for an international investigation into the allegations of genocide, demilitarisation of the Tamil 'homelands', as well as political autonomy and constitutional protections for Tamil language and culture. See *Tamil Guardian*, 'Tamil Diaspora orgs urge', 15 February 2015.

29. For a discussion of the nation as the 'ground' or 'rhetorical place' in which political contestation takes place, see Michael Billig, *Banal Nationalism* (London: Sage, 1995), pp. 95–9.

30. 'Rival politicians and opposing factions present their different visions of the nation to their national electorates. In order for the political argument to take place within the nation, there must be elements which are beyond argument. Different factions may argue about how "we" should think of "ourselves" and what is to be "our" national destiny. In so doing they will take for granted the reality of "us," the people in its national place.' Ibid., pp. 95–6.

31. US Embassy cable, 'Sri Lanka war-crimes accountability: the Tamil perspective', 15 January 2010, available at http://wikileaks.org/cable/2010/01/10COLOMBO 32.html

32. *Sunday Times*, 'Sampanthan says TNA stands for undivided Lanka', 17 January 2010, available at http://sundaytimes.lk/100117/News/nws_12.html

33. *Tamil Guardian*, 'TNA sets out to win support of the masses', 18 September 2013, available at http://www.tamilguardian.com/article.asp?articleid=8750, last accessed 15 January 2015.

34. *Tamil Guardian*, 'TNA calls for end to Sri Lankan state oppression at May Day', 2 May 2014, available at http://www.tamilguardian.com/article.asp?articleid=10805, last accessed May 2015.

35. The Tamil National People's Front (TNPF), formed by figures who split from the TNA, is yet to establish a pan-north-east presence.

36. This dynamic was again visible in the August 2015 parliamentary elections when the TNA won sixteen of the twenty two seats from the Tamil speaking north-east, but on a platform that sought support for Tamil self-rule and an international accountability process.

37. For the sequence of these negotiations, although not their substance, see this statement by the TNA leader R. Sampanthan: 'Response to G. L. Pieris in Geneva: it is necessary that the truth be stated', 13 March 2014, available at https://www.colombotelegraph.com/index.php/response-to-g-l-peiris-in-geneva-it-is-necessary-the-truth-be-stated/, last accessed May 2015.

38. *Tamil Guardian*, 'Video emerges of TNA leader facing Tamils protesting against disappearances', 23 November 2013, http://www.tamilguardian.com/article.asp?articleid=9319, last accessed 30 May 2014.

39. See Journalists for Democracy in Sri Lanka, 'NPC passes landmark resolution', 10 February, 2015.

40. M. A. Sumanthiran, 'Tamil people, where did we go wrong?' *Colombo Telegraph*, 7 December 2013, https://www.colombotelegraph.com/index.php/tamil-people-where-did-we-go-wrong/, last accessed 30 May 2014.

41. See, for example, TamilNet, 'Stop genocide against Tamils, TNA appeals to UN', 10 November 2006, available at http://www.tamilnet.com/art.html?catid=13&artid=20226; TamilNet, 'Sampanthan blames SL state for committing genocide, protests Budget speech', 6 November 2008, available at http://www.tamilnet.com/art.html?catid=13&artid=27407

42. See R. Sampanthan, 'Response to G. L. Pieris', *Colombo Telegraph*, 13 March 2014.

43. https://www.colombotelegraph.com/index.php/response-to-g-l-peiris-in-geneva-it-is-necessary-the-truth-be-stated/

44. BBC Sinhala Service 'Sri Lanka divided after the war, says cabinet minister', 14 February 2012, http://www.bbc.co.uk/sinhala/news/story/2012/02/printable/120214_llrc.shtml, last accessed 30 May 2014.

45. *Tamil Guardian*, 'GTF conference reaffirms calls for investigation', 28 February 2013, available at http://www.tamilguardian.com/article.asp?articleid=7154
46. *Tamil Guardian*, 'Enter South Africa?' 19 April 2014, available at http://www.tamilguardian.com/article.asp?articleid=10689; *Sunday Times*, 'South Africa mediation offers way out for Govt', 20 April 2014, available at http://www.sundaytimes.lk/140420/columns/south-africa-mediation-offers-way-out-for-govt-93065.html
47. TNA won handsomely in the August 2015 parliamentary elections—but again by competing on a solid Tamil nationalist platform emphasising its commitment to an international accountability process.
48. Sankaran Krishna, *Postcolonial Insecurities: India, Sri Lanka, and the question of nationhood* (Minneapolis: University of Minnesota Press, 1999), pp. 59–100; Brian Orland, 'India's Sri Lanka Policy: towards economic engagement', *Institute of Peace and Conflict Studies Research Papers* 16 (New Delhi: Institute of Peace and Conflict Studies, 2008).
49. This consensus can be gauged through opinion poll surveys from mid-2008, which showed growing sympathy for Sri Lankan Tamils and support for the LTTE amidst a wave of protests and demonstrations against Indian support for Sri Lanka's military campaign in the Tamil-speaking areas. For details, see *Tehelka*, 'Pirabhakaran "returns" to India' 5.43, 1 November 2008; and TamilNet, 'Indian Express survey shows Tamil Nadu support for LTTE', 12 October 2008, available at https://www.tamilnet.com/art.html?catid=13&artid=27173, last accessed May 2015. The consensus is also apparent in the political positions of the two major political parties, the DMK and AIADMK. The AIADMK's manifesto for the April 2014 parliamentary elections criticises the DMK's failure to prevent the 'genocide' of the Sri Lankan Tamils while it was in the governing coalition, while committing to supporting an international prosecution of Sri Lankan leaders accused of wartime abuses as well as securing international support for a UN mandated referendum amongst Sri Lankan Tamils on creating a separate state. For details, see Election Manifesto of the All India Anna Dravida Munnetra Kazhagam: Lok Sabha General Election 2014, available at http://aiadmk.com/documents/manifesto/2014/AIADMK-Election-Manifesto-LS-Elections-2014-English.pdf, last accessed May 2015. The DMK manifesto likewise committed the party to urging the Indian government to securing a UN mandate referendum amongst Sri Lankan Tamils to choose their own political future. For details, see the DMK Manifesto—Parliamentary Elections 2014, available at http://www.ndtv.com/elections-news/full-text-dmks-manifesto-for-2014-general-election-555262, last accessed May 2015.
50. M. Myilvaganam, 'The re-emergence of the Tamil Nadu factor in India's Sri Lanka policy', *Strategic Analysis* 31.6 (2007), pp. 943–64.
51. For the alignment of both the DMK and the ADMK with Indian policy on the Sri Lankan Tamil issue, see Krishna, *Postcolonial Insecurities*, pp. 93–4.

52. Orland, 'India's Sri Lanka Policy: towards economic engagement'.
53. See for details Sandra Destradi, 'Sri Lanka's civil war: the failure of regional conflict management in south Asia', *Asian Survey* 52.3 (2012), pp. 595–616. For further analysis of the close relationship between the Rajapaksa and Congress governments, as well as subsequent souring of relations, see DailyFT, 'Honeymoon with Modi', 29 May 2014, available at http://www.ft.lk/2014/05/29/honeymoon-with-modi/, last accessed May 2015.
54. Rediff, 'Talking with the Tigers', 22 January 2002, available at http://www.rediff.com/news/2002/jan/22spec.htm, last accessed May 2015.
55. The Sri Lankan Tamil issue was not at all important to the inner working of the Congress–DMK alliance during and after the war. In early 2011, when the DMK leader met with the then Prime Minister Manmohan Singh on what was effectively a courtesy call, the issue of the Sri Lankan Navy firing on Indian fishermen was raised purely for the consumption of Tamil Nadu audiences. In the more substantive meetings with Sonia Gandhi, the issue was not raised at all. For details, see The Caravan, 'The last year', 1 April 2011, available at http://www.caravan-magazine.in/reportage/last-lear?page=0,1, last accessed May 2015.
56. *Tehelka*, 'Pirabhakaran "returns" to India', 1 November 2008.
57. The first large protest followed the August 2006 Sri Lankan Air Force bombing of a children's home in LTTE-controlled areas in the Vanni. 'For the first time since the assassination of Rajiv Gandhi, perhaps, people cutting across political parties took to the streets to protest the Sri Lankan Air Force raids in northern and eastern Sri Lanka.' Mayilvaganam, 'The re-emergence of the Tamil Nadu factor', p. 949. Following this, there was a steady rise in protests and demonstrations that drew support from across the political spectrum; see for example TamilNet, 'Sign of the times in Tamil Nadu', 18 September 2007, available at http://www.tamilnet.com/art.html?catid=79&artid=23291. By early 2009, the protests were incessant and the atmosphere was febrile. The government temporarily shut down all colleges and hostels in the state to prevent demonstrations and protests from escalating; see for details DNAIndia, 'Lawyers join Tamil Nadu agitation for Lankan Tamils', 3 February 2009, available at http://www.dnaindia.com/india/report-lawyers-join-tamil-nadu-agitation-for-lankan-tamils-1227176, last accessed May 2015. Ranil Wickramasinghe, the then Sri Lankan opposition leader, was in Chennai en route to Colombo from Delhi when a state-wide protest by lawyers erupted; he was asked to stay in a secure room at the airport for his own safety and then put on the first flight to Colombo out of Chennai. For details, see *Sunday Times*, 'Tamil Nadu gripped by anti-Lanka tension', 22 February 2009.
58. For example, a 'human chain' protest in Chennai in late 2008 saw the participation of senior DMK and film industry figures as well as college students. For details, see *The Hindu*, 'Thousands take part in human chain despite rain', 25 October 2008, available at http://www.thehindu.com/todays-paper/thousands-take-part-in-human-chain-despite-rain/article1363555.ece, last accessed May 2015.

59. TamilNet, 'Youth of India voice for Eezham Tamils', 14 November 2008, available at https://www.tamilnet.com/art.html?catid=13&artid=27477, last accessed May 2015.

60. For the involvement of students and IT workers, see The Caravan, 'Vital Signs', 1 May 2013, available at http://www.caravanmagazine.in/perspectives/vital-signs, last accessed May 2015; see also DNAIndia, 'Lawyers join Tamil Nadu agitation', 3 February 2009; and for state-wide student protests in January 2009, see TamilNet, 'Tamil Nadu gears up for more protests', 23 January 2009, available at http://www.tamilnet.com/art.html?artid=28113&catid=13, last accessed May 2015. For an example of a protest by a film industry association, see TamilNet, 'Tamil Nadu film industry vows support to Eezham Tamils', 20 October 2008, available at https://www.tamilnet.com/art.html?catid=13&artid=27229, last accessed May 2015.

61. TamilNet, 'Tamil Nadu shuts down for traders' bandh on Eelam Tamil issue', 31 October 2008, http://www.tamilnet.com/art.html?catid=13&artid=27344, last accessed 30 May 2014.

62. See note 46 above; also TamilNet, 'Tamil Nadu opinion poll calls for independent Eezham', 2 August 2008, available at: http://www.tamilnet.com/art.html?catid=79&artid=26518, last accessed May 2015.

63. TamilNet, 'Tamil Nadu CM cancels Rajapaksa meeting', 29 December 2005, available at http://www.tamilnet.com/art.html?catid=13&artid=16689, last accessed May 2015.

64. See M. Myilvaganam, 'The re-emergence of the Tamil Nadu factor'; also Tehelka, 'Tamil Nadu at the crossroads', 23 September 2006.

65. Times of India, 'Karuna goes on sudden fast, ends it even faster', 28 April 2009, available at http://timesofindia.indiatimes.com/india/Karuna-goes-on-sudden-fast-ends-it-even-faster/articleshow/4453257.cms, last accessed May 2015.

66. The Hindu, 'Eelam is the only solution, avers Jayalalitha', 26 April 2009, available at http://www.thehindu.com/todays-paper/tp-national/tp-tamilnadu/eelam-the-only-solution-avers-jayalalithaa/article316092.ece, last accessed May 2015.

67. Tamil Guardian, 'Tamil Nadu Assembly adopts resolution seeking Eelam referendum', 27 March 2013, available at http://www.tamilguardian.com/article.asp?articleid=7427, last accessed May 205. See also Tamil Guardian, 'Tamil Nadu Assembly demands India pursue Sri Lankan war criminals', 9 June 2011, available at http://www.tamilguardian.com/article.asp?articleid=3226, last accessed May 2015.

68. The Hindu, 'U.S. looking at "creative ideas" to break impasse in Sri Lanka', 21 July 2011, available at http://www.thehindu.com/news/national/us-looking-at-creative-ideas-to-break-impasse-in-sri-lanka/article2277184.ece

69. Reuters, 'U.N. rights body backs Sri Lankan resolution on war', 27 May 2009, available at http://www.reuters.com/article/2009/05/27/us-srilanka-un-rights-idUSTRE54Q5XP20090527, last accessed May 2015.

70. Rediff, 'CHOGM summit: PM writes to Rajapaksa, expresses regret', 10 November 2013, available at http://www.rediff.com/news/report/chogm-summit-pm-writes-to-rajapaksa-expresses-regret/20131110.htm

71. The BJP government elected in April 2014 does not depend on coalition support from Tamil Parties and is therefore less directly susceptible to popular pressure from Tamil Nadu. Yet, if the BJP ignores Tamil Nadu sentiments completely it may also undermine its own more long term efforts to build electoral support in the state and therefore its attempts to pursue an autonomous (of Tamil Nadu) policy on Sri Lanka will have to be balanced with its desire to bring Tamil Nadu into the Hindu nationalist fold.

72. Dinamani Karunanidhi, 'We are not prepared for terrorism', 21 April 2012, http://www.dinamani.com/tamilnadu/article826482.ece, last accessed 31 May 2014.

BIBLIOGRAPHY

Adeney, Katharine and Andrew Wyatt, 'Democracy in South Asia: getting beyond the structure–agency dichotomy', *Political Studies* 52.1 (2004), pp. 1–18.

Ali, A., 'The End of the Road', *South Asia Journal* 9 (2013).

Angell, M., 'Understanding the Aryan Theory', in Tiruchelvam, M. and C. S. Dattathreya, eds, *Culture and Politics of Identity in Sri Lanka*, Colombo, International Centre for Ethnic Studies, 1998.

Amin, Shahid, 'Gandhi as Mahatma: Gorakhpur District, Eastern UP, 1921–2', in Guha, R., ed., *Subaltern Studies, Vol. III*, Oxford, Oxford University Press, 1984.

Amnesty International, *Report of an Amnesty International Mission to Sri Lanka*, New York, Amnesty International Publications, 1983.

———, *Sri Lanka: current human rights concerns and evidence of extra-judicial killings*, New York, Amnesty International Publications, 1984.

———, *Disappearances*, New York, Amnesty International Publications, 1986.

———, *Sri Lanka: government's responses to widespread 'disappearances' in Jaffna*, New York, Amnesty International Publications, 1997.

———, *Sri Lanka: torture in custody*, New York, Amnesty International Publications, 1999.

———, *Sri Lanka: rape in custody*, New York, Amnesty International Publications, 2002.

———, *Sri Lanka: twenty years of make-believe. Sri Lanka's Commissions of Inquiry*, New York, Amnesty International Publications, 2009.

Arasaratnam, Sinnappah, 'Social history of a dominant caste society; the Vellalar of north Ceylon (Sri Lanka)', *Indian Economic and Social History Review* 18.3–4 (1981).

Arbour, Louise, 'Let the UN unmask the criminals of Sri Lanka's war', *New York Times*, 28 February 2014, http://www.nytimes.com/2014/02/28/opinion/let-the-un-unmask-the-criminals-of-sri-lankas-war.html?_r=0, last accessed 30 May 2014.

Arnold, David, *The Congress in Tamilnad: nationalist politics in South India, 1919–1937*, London, Curzon Press, 1977.

————, 'The Politics of Coalescence: the Congress in Tamilnad, 1930–1937', in Low, D. A., ed., *Congress and the Raj: facets of the Indian struggle 1917–1947*, Oxford, Oxford University Press, 2004.

————, *Gandhi*, New York, Longman, 2001.

Austin, Granville, *The Indian Constitution: cornerstone of a nation*, Bombay, Oxford University Press, 1972.

Arunatilake, Nisha, Sisira Jayasuriya and Saman Kelegama, 'The economic cost of the war in Sri Lanka', *World Development* 29.9 (2001), pp. 1483–500.

Baker, Christopher J., *The Politics of South India, 1920–1937*, Cambridge, Cambridge University Press, 1976.

————, 'Introduction', in Baskaran, S. Theodore, *The Message Bearers: the nationalist politics and the entertainment media in south India 1880–1945*, Madras, Cre-A, 1981.

Balasingham, Anton S., *War and Peace: armed struggle and peace efforts of the Liberation Tigers*, Mitcham, Surrey, Fairmax Publishing, 2004.

Barkawi, Tarak and Mark Laffey, eds, *Democracy, Liberalism, and War: rethinking the democratic peace debate*, Boulder, CO, Lynne Rienner, 2001.

————, 'The imperial peace: democracy, force and globalization', *European Journal of International Relations* 5.4 (1999), pp. 403–4.

Barrier, Norman G., 'The Arya Samaj and Congress Politics in the Punjab, 1894–1908', *Journal of Asian Studies* 26.3 (1967), pp. 363–79.

Bartholomeusz, Tessa J., *In Defense of Dharma: just-war ideology in Buddhist Sri Lanka*, Richmond, Curzon, 2002.

Bartholomeusz, Tessa J. and Chandra Richard De Silva, *Buddhist Fundamentalism and Minority Identities in Sri Lanka*, Albany, NY, State University of New York Press, 1998.

Baskaran, S. Theodore, *The Message Bearers: the nationalist politics and the entertainment media in South India, 1880–1945*, Madras, Cre-A, 1981.

Bate, Bernard, 'Arumuga Navalar, saivite sermons, and the delimitation of religion, c.1850', *Indian Economic and Social History Review* 42.4 (2005), pp. 469–84.

Bayly, Christopher A., 'The Pre-History of "Communalism"? Religious conflict in India, 1700–1860', *Modern Asian Studies* 19.2 (1985), pp. 177–203.

————, *Indian Society and the Making of the British Empire*, Cambridge, Cambridge University Press, 1988.

Bayly, Susan, *Caste, Society and Politics in India from the Eighteenth Century to the Modern Age*, New York, Cambridge University Press, 1999.

BBC, 'Tamil Tigers "serious about peace"', 2 November 2000, available at http://news.bbc.co.uk/1/hi/world/south_asia/1004145.stm, last accessed April 2015.

————, 'Sri Lanka wins $4.5bn aid pledge', 10 June 2003, available at http://news.bbc.co.uk/1/hi/world/south_asia/2977230.stm, last accessed April 2015.

————, 'Tamil protest ends 73 days', 16 June 2009, available at http://news.bbc.co.uk/1/hi/england/london/8105879.stm, last accessed 20 June 2012.

Billig, Michael, *Banal Nationalism*, London, Sage, 1995.

Blodgett, Brian, *Sri Lanka's Military: the search for a mission (1949–2004)*, Chula Vista, CA: Aventine Press, 2004.

Bose, Sumantra, *States, Nations, Sovereignty: Sri Lanka, India, and the Tamil Eelam movement*, New Delhi, Sage Publications, 1994.

———, 'Flawed Mediation, Chaotic Implementation: The 1987 Indo-Sri Lanka Peace Agreeement', in Stedman, John Stephen, Donald Rothchild and Elizabeth M. Cousens, eds, *Ending Civil Wars: the implementation of peace agreements*, Boulder, CO, Lynne Rienner Publishers, 2002, pp. 631–62.

Brass, Paul R., 'Elite groups, symbol manipulation and ethnic identity among the Muslims of south Asia', in Taylor, David and Malcolm Yapp, eds, *Political Identity in South Asia*, London, Curzon, 1979.

———, *The Politics of India since Independence*, Cambridge, Cambridge University Press, 1994.

———, *Language, Religion and Politics in North India*, Lincoln, NE, iUniverse, 2005.

Breckenridge, Carol A. and Peter van der Veer, *Orientalism and the Postcolonial Predicament: perspectives on South Asia*, Philadelphia, University of Pennsylvania Press, 1993.

Breuilly, John, *Nationalism and the State*, Manchester, Manchester University Press, 1993.

Brubaker, Rogers, *Nationalism Reframed: nationhood and the national question in Europe*, Cambridge, Cambridge University Press, 1996.

———, *Ethnicity without Groups*, Cambridge, MA, Harvard University Press, 2004.

Bush, Kenneth D., *The Intra-Group Dimensions of Ethnic Conflict in Sri Lanka: learning to read between the lines*, Basingstoke, Palgrave, 2003.

Byman, Daniel, Peter Chalk, Bruce Hoffman, William Rosenau and David Brannan, *Trends in Outside Support for Insurgent Movements*, Santa Monica, CA, Rand Corporation, 2001.

Cederman, Lars-Erik, Kristian Skrede Gleditsch and Halvard Buhaug, *Inequality, Grievances, and Civil War*, Cambridge, Cambridge University Press, 2013.

Chandler, David, 'The uncritical critique of "liberal peace"', *Review of International Studies* 36.S1 (2010), pp. 137–55.

Chandra, Kanchan, *Why Ethnic Parties Succeed: patronage and ethnic headcounts in India*, Cambridge, Cambridge University Press, 2004.

———, 'Ethnic Parties and Democratic Stability', *Perspectives on Politics* 3.2 (2005), pp. 235–52.

Chandrakanthan, A. J. V., 'Eelam Tamil nationalism: an inside view', in Wilson, A. Jeyaratnam, *Sri Lankan Tamil Nationalism: its origins and development in the nineteenth and twentieth centuries*, London, Hurst & Co., 2000, pp. 157–76.

Channel Four, 'Who are Sri Lanka's disappeared?' 14 November 2013, http://www.channel4.com/news/sri-lanka-disappeared-white-vans-missing-people-war-chogm, last accessed 18 April 2014.

Chatterjee, Partha, *Nationalist Thought and the Colonial World: a derivative discourse?* London, Zed Books for the United Nations University, 1986.

———, 'Introduction: a political history of independent India', in Chatterjee, Partha, ed., *State and Politics in India*, Delhi, Oxford University Press, 1997.

Chatterji, Joya, *Bengal Divided: Hindu communalism and partition, 1932–1947*, Cambridge, Cambridge University Press, 1994.

Cohn, Bernard S., *Colonialism and its Forms of Knowledge: the British in India*, Princeton, NJ, Princeton University Press, 1996.

Collier, Paul and Anke Hoeffler, *Greed and Grievance in Civil War*, Oxford Economic Papers 56 (2004), pp. 563–95.

Colonial Office, *Census of Ceylon 1891*, Colombo, Government Printer, 1891.

———, *Ceylon: Report of the Special Commission on the Constitution*, 1928 (also known as the Donoughmore Report).

———, *Ceylon: Report of the Commission on Constitutional Reform*, 1945 (also known as the Soulbury Report).

Committee to Protect Journalists, 'CPJ denounces Sri Lankan censorship', 9 June 1998, https://cpj.org/news/1998/srilanka9june98.html, last accessed April 2015.

Connor, Walker, 'Nationalism and political illegitimacy', in Conversi, Daniele, ed., *Ethnonationalism in the Contemporary World: Walker Connor and the study of nationalism*, London, Routledge, 2004, pp. 24–47.

Cooper, Neil, Mandy Turner and Michael Pugh, 'The end of history and the last liberal peacebuilder: a reply to Roland Paris', *Review of International Studies* 37.4 (2011), pp. 1–13.

Corbridge, Stuart and John Harriss, *Reinventing India: liberalization, Hindu nationalism and popular democracy*, Malden, MA, Polity Press, 2000.

Correspondent, 'Notes on the military presence in Sri Lanka's Northern Province', *Economic and Political Weekly*, 43.28, 14 July 2012.

Cramer, Christopher, 'Homo Economicus Goes to War: methodological individualism, rational choice and the political economy of war', *World Development* 30.11 (2002), pp. 1845–64.

Daily Telegraph, 'Sri Lankans are just killing civilians at random', London, 13 September 1990.

De Silva, C. R., 'Plebiscitary democracy or creeping authoritarianism? The presidential election and referendum of 1982', in Manor, James, ed., *Sri Lanka in Change and Crisis*, London, Taylor & Francis, 1984, pp. 35–49.

De Silva, G. P. S. Harischandra, *A Statistical Survey of Elections to the Legislatures of Sri Lanka, 1911–1977*, Colombo, Marga Institute, 1979.

De Silva, K. M., 'Resistance movements in nineteenth century Sri Lanka', in Roberts, Michael, ed., *Sri Lanka: collective identities revisited*, Colombo, Marga Institute, 1997.

———, *A History of Sri Lanka*, New Delhi, Penguin, 2005.

Destradi, Sandra, 'Sri Lanka's civil war: the failure of regional conflict management in south Asia', *Asian Survey* 52.3 (2012), pp. 595–616.

DeVotta, Neil, *Blowback: linguistic nationalism, institutional decay, and ethnic conflict in Sri Lanka*, Stanford, CA, Stanford University Press, 2004.

———, *Sinhalese Buddhist Nationalist Ideology: implications for politics and conflict resolution in Sri Lanka*, Washington, DC, East–West Center, 2007.

DeVotta, Neil and Jason Stone, 'Jathika Hela Urumaya and Ethno-Religious Politics in Sri Lanka', *Pacific Affairs* 81.1 (2008), pp. 31–51.

Dharmadasa, K. N. O., *Language, Religion, and Ethnic Assertiveness: the growth of Sinhalese nationalism in Sri Lanka*, Ann Arbor, University of Michigan Press, 1992.

Dhavamony, Mariasusai, *Love of God According to Saiva Siddhanta*, Oxford, Oxford University Press, 1971.

Dinamani, '"We are not supporting terrorism": Karunanidhi', 21 April 2012, http://www.dinamani.com/tamilnadu/article826482.ece, last accessed 31 May 2014.

Dirks, Nicholas B., *Castes of Mind: colonialism and the making of modern India*, Princeton, NJ, Princeton University Press, 2001.

Dixit, Jyotindra Nath, *Assignment Colombo*, Delhi, Konark Publishers, 1998.

DNA India, '"Lankan PM merely joked about shooting": Chandrika Kumaratunga', 17 April 2015, available at http://www.dnaindia.com/analysis/interview-lankan-pm-merely-joked-about-shooting-chandrika-kumaratunga-2078090, last accessed April 2015.

Duffield, Mark, *Global Governance and the New Wars: the merging of development and security*, London, Zed Books, 2001.

Edrisinha, Rohan, 'Constitutionalism, pluralism, ethnic conflict', in Rotbert, R., ed., *Creating Peace in Sri Lanka: civil war and reconciliation*, Washington, DC, Brookings Institute Press, 1999, pp. 169–89.

Fair, C. Christine, 'Diaspora involvement in insurgencies: insights from the Khalistan and Tamil Eelam movements', *Nationalism and Ethnic Politics* 11.1 (2005), pp. 125–56.

Farmer, Bertram H., *Pioneer Peasant Colonization in Ceylon: a study in Asian agrarian problems*, Oxford: Oxford University Press, 1957.

Fearon, James D. and David D. Laitin, 'Ethnicity, insurgency and civil war', *American Political Science Review* 97.1 (2003), pp. 75–90.

Fernando Jude Lal, 'The politics of representation of mass atrocity in Sri Lanka and human rights discourse: challenges to justice and recovery', in Admirand, Peter, ed., *Loss and Hope: global, interreligious and interdisciplinary perspectives*, London and New York, Bloomsbury Academic, 2014.

Forrester, Duncan, 'Factions and filmstars: Tamil Nadu politics since 1971', *Asian Survey* 16.3 (1976), pp. 283–96.

Freitag, Sandria B., 'Sacred symbol as mobilizing identity: the north Indian search for a "Hindu" community', *Comparative Studies in Society and History* 22.4 (1980), pp. 597–625.

Fukuyama, Francis, *The End of History and the Last Man*, London, Penguin, 1992.

Galbraith, John S., 'The "Turbulent Frontier" as a factor in British expansion', *Comparative Studies in Society and History* 2. 2 (1960), pp. 150–60.

Gellner, Ernest, *Nations and Nationalism*, Oxford, Blackwell, 1983.

Gilmartin, David, 'A magnificent gift: Muslim nationalism and the election process in colonial Punjab', *Comparative Studies in Society and History* 40. 3 (1998), pp. 415–36.

Goodhand, Jonathan, Bart Klem and Gunnar Sørbø, *Pawns of Peace: evaluation of Norwegian peace efforts in Sri Lanka, 1997–2009*, commissioned by Norad Evaluation Department, Report 5/2011, 2011, available at http://www.norad.no/en/tools-and-publications/publications/evaluations/publication/_attachment/386345?_download=true&_ts=134128d5c39, last accessed 20 June 2012.

Gopal, Sarvepalli, *British Policy in India, 1858–1905*, Cambridge, Cambridge University Press, 1965.

Gordon, Richard, 'The Hindu Mahasabha and the Indian National Congress, 1915 to 1926', *Modern Asian Studies* 9.2 (1975), pp. 145–203.

Gorringe, Hugo, *Untouchable citizens: Dalit movements and democratization in Tamil Nadu*, Delhi, Sage Publications India, 2005.

Goswami, Manu, *Producing India: from colonial economy to national space*, Chicago, IL, University of Chicago Press, 2004.

Gould, William, *Hindu Nationalism and the Language of Politics in Late Colonial India*, Cambridge, Cambridge University Press, 2004.

Government of Ceylon, *Census of Ceylon 1891*, 1892.

Government of India, *Census of India 1922*, 1922.

Gunaratna, M. H., *For a Sovereign State*, Ratmalana, Sarvodaya Book Publishing Services, 1988.

Gunasingam, Murugar, *Sri Lankan Tamil Nationalism: a study of its origins*, Sydney, MV Publications, 1999.

Gunasinghe, Newton, 'The Open Economy and its Impact on Ethnic Relations in Sri Lanka', in Winslow, Deborah W. and Michael D. Woost, eds, *Economy, Culture and Civil War in Sri Lanka*, Bloomington and Indianapolis, Indiana University Press, 2004, pp. 99–114.

Hansen, Thomas B. and Christophe Jaffrelot, *The BJP and the Compulsions of Politics in India*, New Delhi and Oxford, Oxford University Press, 2001.

Hardgrave, Robert L., *The Dravidian Movement*, Bombay, Popular Prakashan, 1965.

———, *Nadars of Tamilnad: the political culture of a community in change*, Bombay, Oxford University Press, 1969.

Hardy, Peter, *The Muslims of British India*, Cambridge, Cambridge University Press 1972.

Harrison, Selig S., *India: the Most Dangerous Decades*, Princeton, NJ, Princeton University Press, 1960.

Hasan, Mushirul, 'The Muslim mass contacts campaign: analysis of a strategy of political mobilisation', in Sisson, Rishard and Stanley Wolpert, eds, *Congress and Indian Nationalism: the pre-independence phase*, Berkeley, University of California Press, 1988.

———, 'Indian Muslims since independence: in search of integration and identity', *Third World Quarterly* 10.2 (1988), pp. 818–42.

———, *Nationalism and Communal Politics in India, 1885–1930*, New Delhi, Manohar Publications, 1991.

Hellmann-Rajanayagam, Dagmar, 'Arumuka Navalar: religious reformer of national leader of Eelam', *Indian Economic and Social History Review* 29.2 (1989), pp. 234–57.

———, 'The politics of the Tamil past', in Spencer, Jonathan, ed., *Sri Lanka: history and the roots of conflict*, London, Routledge, 1990.

———, *The Tamil Tigers: armed struggle for identity*, Stuttgart, Franz Steiner Verlag, 1994.

———, 'And Heroes Die: poetry of the Tamil Liberation Movement in northern Sri Lanka', *South Asia: Journal of Asian Studies* 28.1 (2005).

Herring, Ronald J., 'Making Ethnic Conflict: the Civil War in Sri Lanka', in Esman, Milton J. and Ronald J. Herring, eds, *Carrots, Sticks and Ethnic Conflict: rethinking development assistance*, University of Michigan Press, 2001, pp. 140–74.

Hogg, Charu Lata, *Sri Lanka: prospects for reform and reconciliation*, Chatham House Asia Programme Paper ASP PP 2011/0, 2011, at http://www.chathamhouse.org/sites/default/files/1011pp_srilanka_0.pdf, last accessed 11 November 2011.

Horowitz, Donald L., *Coup Theories and Officers' Motives: Sri Lanka in comparative perspective*, Princeton, NJ, Princeton University Press, 1980.

———, *Ethnic Groups in Conflict*, Berkeley and Los Angeles, University of California Press, 1985.

Hudson, D. Denis, 'Arumuga Navalar and the Hindu Renaissance among the Tamils', in Jones, K. W., ed., *Religious Controversy in British India: dialogues in South Asian languages*, Albany, NY, State University of New York Press, 1992.

———, 'Tamil Hindu Responses to Protestants: nineteenth-century literati in Jaffna and Tinnevelly', in Kaplan, Steven, ed., *Indigenous Responses to Western Christianity*, New York and London, New York University Press, 1995.

Hutchinson, John, *Nations as Zones of Conflict*, London, Sage, 2005.

Human Rights Watch, 'Human Rights in Sri Lanka: an update', 12 March 1991, http://www.hrw.org/reports/pdfs/s/srilanka/srilanka913.pdf, last accessed April 2015.

———, 'Playing the communal card: communal violence and human rights', 1 April 1995, http://www.hrw.org/reports/1995/04/01/playing-communal-card, last accessed April 2015.

———, 'Funding the "Final War": LTTE intimidation and extortion in the Tamil

Diaspora', 14 March 2006, http://www.hrw.org/publications/reports?topic=All&region=164, last accessed April 2015.

———, 'Sri Lanka: repeated shelling of hospitals evidence of war crimes', 8 May 2009, New York.

———, 'Legal Limbo: the uncertain fate of detained LTTE suspects in Sri Lanka', 2010, New York.

———, 'We will teach you a lesson: sexual violence against Tamils by Sri Lankan security forces', 2010, New York.

———, *Blood and Belonging: journeys into the new nationalism*, London, Vintage, 1983.

Ikenberry, John G., 'Liberal internationalism 3.0: America and the dilemmas of liberal world order', *Perspectives on Politics* 7.1 (2009), pp. 71–87.

Imtiyaz, A. R. M., 'The Eastern Muslims of Sri Lanka: special problems and solutions', *Journal of Asian and African Studies* 44.4 (2009), pp. 407–27.

Indian Express, '"Tamil Nadu 1 in economy, power, roads and health" ASSOCHAN', 15 March 2015, http://www.newindianexpress.com/states/tamil_nadu/Tamil-Nadu-Number-1-in-Economy-Power-Roads-and-Health-Assocham/2015/03/15/article2714885.ece, last accessed 18 April 2015.

Indian National Congress and A. M. Zaidi, *A Tryst with Destiny: a study of economic policy resolutions of INC passed during the last 100 years*, New Delhi, Publication Dept, Indian Institute of Applied Political Research, 1985.

Indrapala, K., *The Evolution of an Ethnic Identity: the Tamils in Sri Lanka c.300 B.C.E to c.1200 CE*, Colombo, Vijitha Yapa, 2007.

International Bar Association, *Justice in Retreat: Sri Lanka*, London, 2009.

International Crisis Group, *Development Assistance and the Conflict in Sri Lanka: lessons from the Eastern Province*, Asia Report No. 165, 16 April 2009.

———, *Reconciliation in Sri Lanka: harder than ever*, Asia Report No. 209, 2011.

———, *Sri Lanka's North I: the denial of minority rights*, Asia Report No. 219, 2012.

———, *Sri Lanka's North II: rebuilding under the military*, Asia Report No. 220, 2012.

———, 'The forever war? Military control in Sri Lanka's north', In Pursuit of Peace Blog, 25 March 2014, available at http://blog.crisisgroup.org/asia/2014/03/25/the-forever-war-military-control-in-sri-lankas-north/, last accessed April 2015.

Irschick, Eugene F., *Politics and Social Conflict in South India: the Non-Brahman Movement and Tamil separatism, 1916–1929*, Berkeley, University of California Press, 1969.

———, *Tamil Revivalism in the 1930s*, Madras, Cre-A, 1986.

Israel, Milton, *Communications and Power: propaganda and the press in the Indian nationalist struggle*, Cambridge, Cambridge University Press, 1994.

Jaffrelot, Christophe, *The Hindu Nationalist Movement and Indian Politics, 1925 to the 1990s: strategies of identity building, implantation and mobilisation (with special reference to central India*, London, Hurst & Co., 1996.

Jalal, Ayesha, *The Sole Spokesman: Jinnah, the Muslim League, and the demand for Pakistan*, New Delhi, Cambridge University Press, 1994.

Jeffries, C. J., *Ceylon: the path to independence*, London, Pall Mall Press, 1962.

Jiggins, Janice, *Caste and Family in the Politics of the Sinhalese, 1947–1976*, Cambridge, Cambridge University Press, 1979.

Jones, Kenneth W., 'Communalism in the Punjab: the Arya Samaj contribution', *Journal of Asian Studies* 28.1 (1968), pp. 39–54.

Jordan, Kim and Myriam Denov, 'Birds of Freedom? Perspectives on female emancipation and Sri Lanka's Liberation Tigers of Tamil Eelam', *Journal of International Women's Studies* 9.1 (2007), p. 46.

Journalists for Democracy in Sri Lanka, 'Sri Lanka IPD displeasure at "release of land" on eve of presidential visit', 16 February 2015, available at http://www.jdslanka. org/index.php/news-features/politics-a-current-affairs/518-sri-lanka-idp-displeasure-at-release-of-land-on-eve-of-presidents-india-tour, last accessed May 2015.

Jupp, James, *Sri Lanka: Third World democracy*, London, Frank Cass, 1978.

Kadirgamar, S, 'The Jaffna Youth Congress', in *Handy Perinbanayagam, a memorial volume: the Jaffna Youth Congress and selections from his writings and speeches*, Jaffna, Thirumakal Press, 1980.

Kaldor, Mary, *New and Old Wars*, Cambridge, Polity, 2001.

Kalyvas, Stathis N., '"New" and "Old" Wars: A Valid Distinction?' *World Politics* 54.1 (2001), pp. 99–118.

Kapferer, Bruce, *Legends of People, Myths of State: violence, intolerance and political culture in Sri Lanka and Australia*, London, Berghahn, 2012.

Kearney, Robert N., *The Politics of Ceylon (Sri Lanka)*, London, Cornell University Press, 1973.

Kemper, Stephen, *The Presence of the Past: chronicles, politics and culture in Sinhala life*, Ithaca and London, Cornell University Pres, 1991.

Khan, M. S., *Tilak and Gokhale: a comparative study of their socio-political-economic programmes of reconstruction*, New Delhi, Ashish Publishing House, 1992.

King, Richard, *Orientalism and Religion: post-colonial theory, India and 'the mystic East'*, London, Routledge, 1999.

King, Richard D., *Nehru and the Language Politics of India*, Delhi, Oxford University Press, 1998

Kohn, Hans, *The Idea of Nationalism*, Macmillan, 1945.

Kopf, David, *British Orientalism and the Bengal Renaissance: the dynamics of Indian modernization 1773–1885*, Berkeley, University of California Press, 1969.

Kothari, Rajni, *Politics in India*, New Delhi, Little, Brown, 1970.

Krishna, Gopal, 'The Development of the Indian National Congress as a Mass Organisation, 1918–1923', *Journal of Asian Studies* 25.3 (1966), pp. 413–30.

Krishna, Sankaran, *Postcolonial Insecurities: India, Sri Lanka, and the question of nationhood*, Minneapolis, University of Minnesota Press, 1999.

Kumar, Dharma, *Land and Caste in South Asia: agricultural labour in the Madras*

Presidency during the nineteenth century, Cambridge, Cambridge University Press, 1965.

Kumar, Krishna, 'Hindu Revivalism and Education in North-Central India', *Social Scientist* 18.10 (1990), pp. 4–26.

Kumar, Sanjay, 'Bihar: interpreting the massive mandate', *The Hindu*, 23 May 2014, http://www.thehindu.com/opinion/op-ed/bihar-interpreting-the-massive-mandate/article6037680.ece?homepage=true, last accessed 30 May 2014.

Kumaradoss, Y. Vincent, 'Kamaraj Remembered', *Economic and Political Weekly* 39.17 (2004), pp. 1655–7.

Kumaratunga-Bandaranaike, Chandrika, *Profiles of Freedom, selected speeches by Chandrika Bandaranaike Kumaratunga*, Colombo, Government Information Department, 1996.

Laffey, Mark and Suthaharan Nadarajah, 'The hybridity of liberal peace: states, diasporas and insecurity', *Security Dialogue* 43.5 (2012), pp. 403–20.

Leary, Virginia A., *Ethnic Conflict and Violence in Sri Lanka: report of a mission to Sri Lanka in July–August 1981 on behalf of the International Commission of Jurists*, International Commission of Jurists, 1981.

LTTE, *Socialist Tamil Eelam: political programme of the LTTE*, Liberation Tigers of Tamil Eelam, undated.

Lunstead, Jeffrey, 'The United States' Role in Sri Lanka Peace Process 2002–2006', Asia Foundation, 2007, available at www.asiafoundation.org/resources/pdfs/SLSupplementarytoSCA.pdf, last accessed 12 June 2012.

Malathy, N., *A Fleeting Moment in my Country: the last years of the LTTE de facto state*, Atlanta, GA, Clearday Books, 2012.

Mandelbaum, Michael, *The Ideas that Conquered the World: peace, democracy, and free markets in the twenty-first century*, New York, Public Affairs, 2002.

Manogaran, Chelvaduri, *Ethnic Conflict and Reconciliation in Sri Lanka*, Honolulu, University of Hawaii Press, 1987.

——, 'Colonization as Politics: political use of space in Sri Lanka's ethnic conflict', in Manogaran, Chelvadurai and Bryan Pfaffenberger, eds, *The Sri Lankan Tamils: ethnicity and identity*, Boulder, CO, Westview Press, 1994, pp. 84–125.

Manogaran, Chelvadurai and Bryan Pfaffenberger, *The Sri Lankan Tamils: ethnicity and identity*, Boulder, CO, Westview Press, 1994.

Manor, James, 'The Failure of Political Integration in Sri Lanka (Ceylon)', *Commonwealth and Comparative Politics* 17.1 (1979), pp. 21–47.

——, *The Expedient Utopian: Bandaranaike and Ceylon*, Cambridge, Cambridge University Press, 1989.

Marks, Thomas A., 'Ideology of Insurgency: new ethnic focus or old Cold War distortions?' *Small Wars and Insurgencies* 15.1 (2004), pp. 107–28.

Marshall, P. J., *The Making and Unmaking of Empires: Britain, India, and America c.1750–1783*, Oxford, Oxford University Press, 2005.

McLane, John R., *Indian Nationalism and the Early Congress*, Princeton, NJ, Princeton University Press, 1977.

———, 'The early Congress, Hindu populism and the wider society', in Sisson, Rishard and Stanley Wolpert, eds, *Congress and Indian Nationalism: the pre-independence phase*, Berkeley, University of California Press, 1988.

Mehrotra, S. R., *Emergence of the Indian National Congress*, New Delhi, Vikas, 1971.

Mendelsohn, Oliver and Marika Vicziany, *The Untouchables: subordination, poverty and the state in modern India*, Cambridge, Cambridge University Press, 1988.

Mendis, G. C., *The Colebroke–Cameron papers: documents on British colonial policy in Ceylon, 1796–1833*, Oxford, University Press, 1956.

Metcalf, Thomas R., *The Aftermath of Revolt: India, 1857–1870*, London, Oxford University Press, 1965.

———, *Ideologies of the Raj*, Cambridge, Cambridge University Press, 1994.

Mill, John Stuart, *On Liberty and Other Essays*, Oxford, Oxford University Press, 1991.

Miller, Phil, *Britain's Dirty War against the Tamil People: 1970–2009*, Bremen, International Human Rights Association, 2014, http://www.ptsrilanka.org/images/documents/britains_dirty_war.pdf, last accessed April 2015.

Mills, Lennox A., *Ceylon under British rule, 1795–1932, with an account of the East India Company's embassies to Kandy, 1762–1795*, London, Frank Cass, 1964.

Mitchell, Lisa, *Language, Emotion, and Politics in South India: the making of a mother tongue*, Bloomington, Indiana University Press, 2009.

More, J. B. P., *The Political Evolution of Muslims in Tamilnadu and Madras, 1930–1947*, Hyderabad, Orient Longman, 1997.

———, *Muslim Identity, Print Culture and the Dravidian Factor in Tamil Nadu*, London, Orient Longman, 2004.

Moore, Mick, *The State and Peasant Politics in Sri Lanka*, Cambridge, Cambridge University Press, 1985.

———, 'Economic Liberalisation versus Political Pluralism in Sri Lanka?' *Modern Asian Studies* 24.2 (1990), pp. 341–83.

Muggah, R., *Relocation Failures in Sri Lanka: a short history of internal displacement and resettlement*, London and New York, Zed Books, 2008.

Mundy, Jacob, 'Deconstructing civil wars: beyond the new wars debate', *Security Dialogue* 42 (2011), pp. 279–95.

Murray, Nancy, 'The state against the Tamils', *Race and Class* 26.1 (1984), pp. 97–109.

Myilvaganam, M., 'The re-emergence of the Tamil Nadu factor in India's Sri Lanka policy', *Strategic Analysis* 31.6 (2007), pp. 943–64.

Nadarajah, Suthaharan and Dhananjayan Sriskandarajah, 'Liberation struggle or terrorism? The politics of naming the LTTE', *Third World Quarterly* 26.1 (2005), pp. 87–100.

Nadarajah, Suthaharan and Luxshi Vimalarajah, *The Politics of Transformation: the*

LTTE and the 2002–2006 peace process in Sri Lanka, Transitions No. 4, Berlin, Berghof Research Center for Constructive Conflict Management, 2008, available at www.berghofcenter.org/uploads/download/transitions_ltte.pdf, last accessed 12 June 2012.

Nadarajah, Suthaharan, '"Conflict sensitive" Aid and Making Liberal Peace', in Duffield, Mark and Vernon Hewitt, eds, *Empire, Development and Colonialism: the past in the present*, Martlesham, Suffolk, James Currey, 2009, pp. 109–29.

Nadarajah Suthaharan, 'Clash of Governmentalities: liberal peace, Tamil freedom and the 2001–2006 Peace Process in Sri Lanka', PhD Dissertation, University of London, 2010.

Nadarajah, Suthaharan and David Rampton, 'The limits of hybridity and the crisis of liberal peace', *Review of International Studies* 41.1 (2015), pp. 49–72.

Nadarajah, Suthaharan and Vicki Sentas, 'The Politics of State Crime and Resistance: Self determination in Sri Lanka', in Elizabeth Stanley and Jude McCulloch, eds, *State Crime* and Resistance, Abingdon, Oxon: Routledge, 2013.

Nambi Arooran, K, *Tamil Renaissance and Dravidian Nationalism 1905–1944*, Madurai, Koodal Publishers, 1980.

Natarajan, Srividya, 'Another stage in the life of the nation: Sadir, Bharathanatyam, Feminist theory', PhD Dissertation, School of Humanities, University of Hyderabad, 1997.

Navaratnam, Vaithianathan, *The Fall and Rise of the Tamil Nation: events leading to the Tamil war of independence and resumption of Eelam sovereignty*, Madras, Kaanthalakam, 1991.

Nehru, Jawaharlal, *The Discovery of India*, London, Meridian Books, 1947.

Neminathan, M., ed., *Tamil Eelam Literature*, Tamil Information Centre, 1996.

Neumann, Iver B. and Ole Jacob Sending, *Governing the Global Polity: practice, mentality, rationality*, Ann Arbor, University of Michigan Press, 2010.

New York Times, 'Sri Lanka's Tamil minority grows impatient with just promises', 15 March 2015.

Nithiyanandam, Vaithianathan, 'Ethnic politics and third world development: some lessons from Sri Lanka's experience', *Third World Quarterly* 21.2 (2000), pp. 283–311.

O'Duffy, Brendan, 'LTTE: Liberation Tigers of Tamil Eelam, majoritarianism, self-determination, and military-to-political transition in Sri Lanka', in Heiberg, Marianne, Brendan O'Leary and John J. Tirman, eds, *Terror, Insurgency and the State: ending protracted conflicts*, Philadelphia, University of Philadelphia Press, 2007, pp. 257–87.

O'Malley, L. S. S., *The Indian Civil Service, 1601–1930*, London, Frank Cass, 1965.

O'Sullivan, Meghan, 'Household entitlements during wartime: The experience of Sri Lanka', *Oxford Development Studies* 25.1 (1997), pp. 95–121.

Orjuela, Camilla, 'Building peace in Sri Lanka: A role for civil society?' *Journal of Peace Research* 40.2 (2003), pp. 195–212.

Orland, Brian, 'India's Sri Lanka Policy: Towards Economic Engagement', *Institute of Peace and Conflict Studies Research Papers* 16, New Delhi, Institute of Peace and Conflict Studies, 2008.

Owen, John M., *Liberal Peace, Liberal War: American politics and international security*, London, Cornell University Press, 1997.

Özkirimli, Umut, *Theories of Nationalism: a critical introduction*, New York, St Martin's Press, 2000.

Pandey, Gyanendra, *The Construction of Communalism in Colonial North India*, Delhi, Oxford University Press, 1990.

Pandian, M. S. S., '"Nation" from its margins: notes on E. V. Ramaswamy's "impossible" nation', in Bhargava, R., A. K. Bagchi and R. Sudarshan, eds, *Multiculturalism, Liberalism and Democracy*, Calcutta, Oxford University Press, 1999.

———, *Brahmin and non-Brahmin: genealogies of the Tamil political present*, Delhi, Permanent Black, 2007.

Paris, Roland, *At War's End: peace building after civil conflict*, Cambridge, Cambridge University Press, 1997.

———, 'Saving Liberal Peacebuilding', *Review of International Studies* 36.2 (2010), pp. 337–65.

Paust, Jordan J., 'The Human Rights to Food, Medicine and Medical Supplies, and Freedom from Arbitrary and Inhumane Detention and Controls in Sri Lanka', *Vanderbilt Journal of Transnational Law* 31 (1998), pp. 617–42.

Pearson, Michael N., *The Portuguese in India*, Cambridge, Cambridge University Press, 1987.

Peebles, Patrick, 'Colonization and Ethnic Conflict in the Dry Zone of Sri Lanka', *Journal of Asian Studies* 49.1 (1990), pp. 30–55.

Perinbanayagam, Handy, *Handy Perinbanayagam, a memorial volume: the Jaffna Youth Congress and selections from his writings and speeches*, Jaffna, Thirumakal Press, 1980.

Pfaffenberger, Bryan, 'The Political Construction of Defensive Nationalism: the 1968 temple-entry crisis in northern Sri Lanka', *Journal of Asian Studies* 49.1 (1990), pp. 78–96.

Phillips, Cyril Henry, *The Evolution of India and Pakistan, 1858–1947: select documents*, Oxford, Oxford University Press, 1962.

Piyadasa, L., *Sri Lanka: the holocaust and after*, London, Marram Books, 1984.

Ponnambalam, Ganapathipillai Gangaser, *The Marathon Crusade for 'fifty, fifty' in the State Council, 1939: a commemorative publication*, Chennai, Manimekalai Prasuram, 2001.

Ponnambalam, Satchi, *Sri Lanka: national conflict and the Tamil liberation struggle*, London, Zed Books, 1983.

Press conference on Tokyo donors conference, 21 November 2006, US Department of State Archive, http://2001-2009.state.gov/p/us/rm/2006/76483.htm, last accessed April 2014.

Purfield, Catriona, *Mind the Gap—is economic growth in India leaving some states behind?* IMF Working Paper, IMF, 2006.

Radhakrishnan, P., 'Backward Classes in Tamil Nadu: 1872–1988', *Economic and Political Weekly* 25.10 (1990), pp. 509–20.

Rajadurai, S. V. and V. Geetha, 'A Response to John Harriss', *Commonwealth and Comparative Politics* 40.3 (2002), pp. 118–24.

Rajapaksa, Mahinda, 'Address by his Excellency President Mahinda Rajapaksa at the ceremonial opening of Parliament', Sri Jayawardhanapura, Kotte, 19 May 2009, available at http://www.priu.gov.lk/news_update/Current_Affairs/ca200905/20090519terrorism_defeated.htm, last accessed 16 January 2015.

Ramaswamy, Sumathi, *Passions of the Tongue: language devotion in Tamil India, 1891–1970*, Berkeley, University of California Press, 1997.

Rampton, David, '"Deeper hegemony": the populist politics of Sinhala nationalist discontent and the JVP in Sri Lanka', doctoral dissertation, University of London, 2010.

———, '"Deeper hegemony": the politics of Sinhala nationalist authenticity and the failures of power-sharing in Sri Lanka', *Commonwealth and Comparative Politics* 49.2 (2011), pp. 256–8.

Rampton, David and Asanga Welikala, *The Politics of the South*, Asia Foundation, 2005, available at www.asiafoundation.org/resources/pdfs/SLPoliticsoftheSouth.pdf, last accessed 12 June 2012.

Rasaratnam, Madura and Mara Malagodi, 'Eyes Wide Shut: persistent conflict and liberal peace building in Nepal and Sri Lanka', *Conflict, Security and Development* 12.3 (2012), pp. 299–327.

Ravindran, V., 'Discourses of empowerment: missionary Orientalism in the development of Dravidian nationalism', in Brook, Timothy and André Schmid, eds, *Nation Work: Asian elites and national identities*, Ann Arbor, University of Michigan Press, 2000.

Rengaswamy, M., *Tamil Nationalism: political identity of the Tamil Arasu Kazhagam*, Chennai, Hema Publishers, 2006.

Reporters without Borders, 'Press Freedom Prize goes to Uzbek journalist and Sri Lankan daily', 27 November 2013, http://en.rsf.org/press-freedom-prize-goes-to-uzbek-27-11-2013,45522.html, last accessed April 2015.

Richmond, Oliver P., *The Transformation of Peace*, Basingstoke, Palgrave Macmillan, 2005.

Roberts, Michael, *Caste Conflict and Elite Formation: the rise of a Karava elite in Sri Lanka, 1500–1931*, Cambridge, Cambridge University Press, 1982.

———, 'Elite formation and elites: 1832–1921', in Roberts, Michael, ed., *Sri Lanka: collective identities revisited*, Colombo, Marga Institute, 1997.

———, 'Stimulants and ingredients in the awakening of latter day nationalism', in Roberts, Michael, ed., *Sri Lanka: collective identities revisited*, Colombo: Marga Institute, 1997.

Rogers, John D., 'Historical images in the British period', in Spencer, Jonathan, ed., *Sri Lanka: history and the roots of conflict*, London, Routledge, 1990.

———, 'Post Orientalism and the Interpretation of Pre-modern Political Identities: the case of Sri Lanka', *Journal of Asian Studies* 53.1 (1994), p13.

———, 'Caste as a social category and identity in colonial Lanka', *Indian Economic and Social History Review* 41.5 (2004), pp. 51–77.

———, 'Early British Rule and Social Classification in Lanka', *Modern Asian Studies* 38.4 (2004), pp. 625–47.

Ross Barnett, Marguerite, *The Politics of Cultural Nationalism in South India*, Princeton, NJ, Princeton University Press, 1976.

Rousseau, Jean-Jacques, *The Basic Political Writings*, translated by D. A. Cress, Indianapolis, Hackett Publishing Company, 1987.

Russell, Jane, *Communal Politics under the Donoughmore Constitution, 1931–1947*, Dehiwala, Sri Lanka, Tisara Prakasakayo, 1982.

Samaraweera, V., 'The Muslim revivalist movement 1880–1915', in Roberts, Michael, ed., *Sri Lanka: collective identities revisited*, Colombo, Marga Institute, 1997.

Sánchez-Cacicedo, Amaia, *Building States, Building Peace: global and regional involvement in Sri Lanka and Myanmar*, London, Palgrave Macmillan, 2014.

Sarkar, Sumit, *Modern India: 1885–1947*, Basingstoke, Macmillan, 1989.

———, 'Indian democracy: the historical inheritance', in Kohli, Atul, ed., *The Success of India's Democracy*, Cambridge, Cambridge University Press, 2001.

Saveri, Nicholapillai Maria, *A Catholic–Hindu Encounter: relations between Roman Catholics and Hindus in Jaffna, Sri Lanka, 1900–1926*, Jaffna, Sri Lanka, Centre for Performing Arts, 1993.

Schwarz, Walter and Murray Dickson, *The Tamils of Sri Lanka*, London, Minority Rights Group, 1975.

Schwarz, Walter, *The Tamils of Sri Lanka*, London, Minority Rights Group, 1983.

Scott, David, *Refashioning Futures: criticism after postcoloniality*, Princeton, NJ, Princeton University Press, 1999.

Seal, Anil, *The Emergence of Indian Nationalism: competition and collaboration in the later nineteenth century*, Cambridge, Cambridge University Press, 1968.

Seneviratne, H. L., *The Work of Kings: the new Buddhism in Sri Lanka*, Chicago, IL, University of Chicago Press, 1999.

Sentas, Vicki, 'One More Successful War? Tamil diaspora and counter-terrorism after the LTTE', in Poynting, S and D. Whyte, eds, *Counter-Terrorism and State Political Violence*, Abingdon, Oxon: Routledge, 2012.

Shashikumar, V. K., 'Winning wars: political will is the key—defense secretary', *Indian Defense Review* 24, July–Sept 2009, available at http://www.defence.lk/new.asp?fname=20100429_05, last accessed April 2015.

Shastri, Amita, 'The material basis for separatism: the Tamil Eelam movement in Sri Lanka', in Manogran C. and B. Pfaffenberger, eds, *The Sri Lankan Tamils: ethnicity and identity*, Boulder, CO, Westview Press, 1994.

————, 'An Open Economy in a Time of Intense Civil War: Sri Lanka, 1994–2000', in Winslow, Deborah W. and Michael D. Woost, eds, *Economy, Culture and Civil War in Sri Lanka*, Bloomington and Indianapolis, Indiana University Press, 2004, pp. 73–93.

Sieghart, Paul, *Sri Lanka: A mounting tragedy of errors*, International Commission of Jurists, 1984.

Singh, Pritam, 'Hindu bias in India's "secular" constitution: probing flaws in the instruments of governance', *Third World Quarterly* 26.6 (2005), pp. 909–26.

Sinha, Mrinalini, *Colonial Masculinity: the 'manly Englishman' and the 'effeminate Bengali' in the late nineteenth century*, Manchester, Manchester University Press, 1995.

Sivasundaram, Sujit, *Islanded: Britain, Sri Lanka, and the bounds of an Indian Ocean colony*, Chicago, IL, University of Chicago Press, 2013.

Smith, Anthony D., *The Ethnic Origins of Nations*, Oxford, Basil Blackwell, 1986.

Smith, Donald E., 'Religion, Politics and the Myth of Reconquest', in Fernando, Tissa, Robert N. Kearney and Nagalingam Balakrishnan, eds, *Modern Sri Lanka: a society in transition*, Syracuse, NY, Maxwell School of Citizenship and Public Affairs, 1979.

Snodgrass, Donald R., *Ceylon: an export economy in transition*, Homewood, ILL, Irwin, 1966.

Sooka, Yasmin, the Bar Human Rights Committee of England and Wales and the International Truth and Justice Project, Sri Lanka, 'An unfinished war: torture and sexual violence in Sri Lanka 2009–14', 2014, https://www.barhumanrights.org.uk/unfinished-war-torture-and-sexual-violence-sri-lanka-2009–2014, last accessed April 2015.

Spratt, Philip, *D.M.K. in Power*, Bombay, Nachiketa Publications, 1970.

Sri Lanka Campaign for Peace and Justice, 'The Sri Lankan army is seizing land that could be worth $2billion', 30 May 2013, available at http://www.srilankacampaign.org/the-sri-lankan-army-is-seizing-land-that-could-be-worth-2bn/, last accessed April 2015.

Sriskandarajah, Dhananjayan, 'The returns of peace in Sri Lanka: the development cart before the conflict resolution horse?' *Journal of Peacebuilding and Development* 1.2 (2003), pp. 21–35.

Staniland, Paul, *Networks of Rebellion: explaining insurgent cohesion and collapse*, Ithaca, NY, Cornell University Press, 2014.

Stepan, Alfred, Juan J. Linz and Yogendra Yadav, *Crafting State-Nations: India and other multinational democracies*, Baltimore, MD, Johns Hopkins University Press, 2011.

Stokes, Eric, *The English Utilitarians and India*, Oxford, Clarendon Press, 1959.

Stokke, Kristian, 'Sinhalese and Tamil nationalism as post-colonial political projects from "above", 1948–1983', *Political Geography* 17.1 (1998), pp. 83–113.

————, 'Building the Tamil Eelam state: emerging state institutions and forms of governance in LTTE-controlled areas in Sri Lanka', *Third World Quarterly* 27.6 (2006), pp. 1021–40.

Subramanian, Lakshmi, 'The reinvention of a tradition: nationalism, Carnatic music and the Madras Music Academy, 1900–1947', *Indian Economic and Social History Review* 36.2 (1999) pp. 131–63.

Subramanian, Narendra, *Ethnicity and Populist Mobilization: political parties, citizens, and democracy in South India*, Delhi and New York, Oxford University Press, 1999.

Subramanian, Nirupama, 'Back to the Freezer', *Frontline* 17 (19 Aug–1 Sept 2000), available at http://www.frontline.in/static/html/fl1717/17171100.htm, last accessed 16 January 2015.

Sunday Leader, 'President Kumaratunga promises Buddhist High Priests "political package will not be finalized until war is over"', 6 August 1995.

Sunday Times, 'Government to water down devolution', 20 August 1995.

———, 'HSZ Row, story behind the story', 29 December 2012.

———, 'When Reagan hosted JR to a White House dinner', 13 February 2011, http://www.sundaytimes.lk/110213/Timestwo/t2_14.html, last accessed April 2015.

Suntharalingam, R., *Politics and Nationalist Awakening in South India, 1852–1891*, Tucson, AZ, University of Arizona Press, 1974.

Swamy, Arun, 'Parties, Political Identities and the Absence of Mass Political Violence in South India', in Basu, Amitra and Atul Kohli, eds, *Community Conflicts and the State in India*, New Delhi, Oxford University Press, 1998.

Tambiah, Stanley J., *Sri Lanka: ethnic fratricide and the dismantling of democracy*, Chicago, IL, University of Chicago Press, 1986.

———, *Buddhism Betrayed? Religion, politics, and violence in Sri Lanka*, Chicago and London, University of Chicago Press, 1992.

———, *Leveling Crowds: ethno-nationalist conflicts and collective violence in South Asia*, Berkeley, CA, University of California Press, 1997.

Tamils Against Genocide, 'Intent to destroy, ongoing violence and violations against Tamil women', 2014, http://www.tamilsagainstgenocide.org/read.aspx?storyid=125, last accessed April 2015.

———, 'Silencing the press: an analysis of violence against the media in Sri Lanka', 2013, http://www.tamilsagainstgenocide.org/read.aspx?storyid=123, last accessed November 2013.

———, 'Grand jury indictment for genocide: proposed to the United States Department of Justice', 2009, Columbia, MD, http://www.tamilsagainstgenocide.org/Research.aspx, last accessed April 2015.

Tamil Guardian, 'International Mandate' Editorial, 13 December 2006, available at http://www.tamilguardian.com/article.asp?articleid=1027, last accessed April 2015.

———, 'TNA sets out to win support of the masses', 18 September 2013, available at http://www.tamilguardian.com/article.asp?articleid=8750, last accessed 15 January 2015.

———, 'Silences between the shouts', 13 May 2014, available at http://www.tamilguardian.com/article.asp?articleid=10894, last accessed May 2015.

Tamil Information Centre, 'Militarisation in Sri Lanka', London, 1986.

———, 'The Mossad connection and state terrorism in Sri Lanka', London, 1986.

———, 'The ethnic conflict in Sri Lanka: economic aspects', London, 1986.

———, 'Sri Lanka Devolution Proposals, August 1995–January 1996', London, 1996.

TamilNet, 'Pirapaharan's Heroes' day address', 27 November 2003, https://www.tamilnet.com/art.html?catid=13&artid=10554, last accessed April 2015.

———, 'Thousands attends Jaffna Pongu Thamil rally, seek Army withdrawal', 30 September 2005, https://www.tamilnet.com/art.html?catid=13&artid=15986, last accessed April 2015.

———, 'Grand finale for Pongku Thamizh in London', 13 July 2008, http://www.tamilnet.com/art.html?artid=26338&catid=79, last accessed April 2015.

Teenekoon, Serena N., 'Rituals of development: the accelerated Mahaveli development program of Sri Lanka', *American Ethnologist* 15.2 (1988).

Thornton, E. M. and R. Nithyananthan, *Sri Lanka, Island of Terror*, London, Eelam Research Organisation, 1984.

Tilly, Charles, 'War Making and State Making as Organized Crime' in Evans, Peter, Dietrich Rueschemeyer and Theda Skocpol, eds, *Bringing the State Back In*, Cambridge, Cambridge University Press, 1985.

Time Magazine, 'President Kumaratunga "conquers" Jaffna and holds a medieval victory ceremony', 18 December 1995.

TNA, 'Our Election Manifesto, Tamil National Alliance, 2001', available at https://www.tamilnet.com/img/publish/2010/03/TNA_Election_Manifesto_2001.pdf, last accessed May 2015.

———, 'Tamil National Alliance Election Manifesto, 2004', available at https://www.tamilnet.com/img/publish/2010/03/TNA_Election_Manifesto_2004pdf.pdf, last accessed May 2015.

Trautmann, Thomas R., *Aryans and British India*, Delhi, Yoda Press, 2004.

———, *Languages and Nations: the Dravidian proof in colonial Madras*, Berkeley and London, University of California Press, 2006.

Udalagama, Tharindi and Premakumara de Silva, 'Group Violence Against the State', in Hawden, John Ryan and Marc Lucht, eds, *The Causes and Consequences of Group Violence: from bullies to terrorists*, Lanham, MD, Lexington Books, 2014.

UK Government, 'UK Peace Building Strategy for Sri Lanka: A Joint DFID, FCO, MOD Strategy (2006–2009)', London, UK Government, 2007.

United Nations, 'Report of the Secretary General's Panel of Experts on Accountability in Sri Lanka', 31 March 2011, available at http://www.un.org/News/dh/infocus/Sri_Lanka/POE_Report_Full.pdf, last accessed 12 June 2012.

Uyangoda, Jayadeva, *Ethnic Conflict in Sri Lanka: changing dynamics*, Washington, DC, East–West Centre, 2007.

Van der Veer, Peter, *Imperial Encounters: religion and modernity in India and Britain*, Princeton, NJ, Princeton University Press, 2001.

———, 'Hindus: a superior race', *Nations and Nationalism* 5.3 (1999), pp. 419–30.

Varshney, Ashutosh, *Ethnic Conflict and Civic Life: Hindus and Muslims in India*, New Haven, CT, Yale University Press, 2003.

Verma, A. K., Beg Mizra Asmer and Kumar Sudhir, 'A saffron sweep in Uttar Pradesh', *The Hindu*, 23 May 2014, http://www.thehindu.com/opinion/op-ed/a-saffron-sweep-in-uttar-pradesh/article6037683.ece?homepage=true, last accessed 30 May 2014.

Vije, Mayan and Ratneswaren Suppiah, 'Enduring war and health inequality in Sri Lanka', Tamil Information Centre, 2009.

Vimalarajah, Luxshi and R. Cheran, *Empowering Diasporas: the politics of post-war transnational Tamil politics*, Berlin, Berghof Peace Support, Occasional Paper No. 31, 2010, available at http://www.berghof-peacesupport.org/publications/SL_Empowering_Diasporas.pdf, last accessed 12 June 2012.

Visswanathan, E. S., *The Political Career of Ramasami Naicker: a study in the politics of Tamil Nadu 1920–1949*, Madras, Ravi and Vasanth, 1983.

Vythilingam, M., *The Life of Sir Ponnambalam Ramanathan*, Jaffna, Thirumakal Press, 1971.

Washbrook, David A., *The Emergence of Provincial Politics: the Madras Presidency, 1870–1920*, University of Cambridge, Centre of South Asian Studies, 1976.

———, 'Law, State and Agrarian Society in Colonial India', *Modern Asian Studies* 15.3 (1981), p. 22.

———, 'Caste, Class and Dominance in Modern Tamil Nadu: Non Brahminism, Dravidianism and Tamil Nationalism', in Frankel, F. and M. Rao, eds, *Dominance and State Power in Modern India: decline of a social order*, Delhi, Oxford University Press, 1989.

———, 'India, 1818–1860: the two faces of colonialism', in Porter, A., ed., *The Oxford History of the British Empire: The Nineteenth Century (Volume III)*, Oxford, Oxford University Press, 1999.

———, 'South India 1770–1840: the colonial transition', *Modern Asian Studies* 38.3 (2004).

Wayland, Sarah, 'Ethno-nationalist Networks and Transnational Opportunities: The Sri Lankan Tamil Diaspora', *Review of International Studies* 30.3 (2004), pp. 405–26.

Webster, John C. B., 'Who is a Dalit?' in Michael, S. M., ed., *Untouchable: Dalits in modern India*, Boulder, CO, Lynne Rienner, 1999.

Westad, Odd Arne, *The Global Cold War: third world interventions and the making of our times*, Cambridge, Cambridge University Press, 2005.

Whitaker, Mark P., 'Tamilnet.com: some reflections on popular anthropology, nationalism, and the internet', *Anthropological Quarterly* 77.3 (2004) pp. 469–98.

Wickramasinghe, Nira, *Ethnic Politics in Colonial Sri Lanka, 1927–1947*, New Delhi, Vikas, 1995.

——, *Sri Lanka in the Modern Age: a history*, London, Hurst & Co., 2014.

Wilkinson, Steven, *Votes and Violence: electoral competition and ethnic violence in India*, Cambridge and New York, Cambridge University Press, 2004.

Wilson, A. Jeyaratnam, 'Politics and Political Development since 1948', in de Silva, K. M., ed., *Sri Lanka: a survey*, London, Hurst & Co., 1977.

——, *Politics in Sri Lanka 1947–1979*, London, Macmillan, 1979.

——, *The Break-up of Sri Lanka: the Sinhalese–Tamil conflict*, London, Hurst & Co., 1988.

——, *S. J. V. Chelvanayakam and the Crisis of Sri Lankan Tamil Nationalism, 1947–1977, a political biography*, London, Hurst & Co., 1994.

——, *Sri Lankan Tamil Nationalism: its origins and development in the nineteenth and twentieth centuries*, London, Hurst & Co., 2000.

Wills, Ashley, 'The US Stand on Sri Lanka's Conflict—Speech at Jaffna Public Library', 7 March 2001, http://www.tamilnation.co/intframe/us/01willis.htm, last accessed 30 May 2014.

Wimmer, Andreas, *Nationalist Exclusion and Ethnic Conflict: shadows of modernity*, Cambridge, Cambridge University Press, 2002.

Winslow, Deborah, 'Introduction to Part I', in Winslow, Deborah W. and Michael D. Woost, eds, *Economy, Culture and Civil War in Sri Lanka*, Bloomington and Indianapolis, Indiana University Press, 2004, pp. 31–40.

Winslow, Deborah and Michael Woost, 'Articulations of Economy and Ethnic Conflict in Sri Lanka', in Winslow, Deborah W. and Michael D. Woost, eds, *Economy, Culture and Civil War in Sri Lanka*, Bloomington and Indianapolis, Indiana University Press, 2004, pp. 1–27.

Winslow, Deborah W. and Michael D. Woost, eds, *Economy, Culture and Civil War in Sri Lanka*, Bloomington and Indianapolis, Indiana University Press, 2004.

Wolpert, Stanley A., *Tilak and Gokhale: revolution and reform in the making of modern India*, Berkeley, CA, University of California Press, 1962.

Wood, Elisabeth Jean, 'Armed Groups and Sexual Violence: when is wartime rape rare?' *Politics and Society* 37.1 (2009), pp. 131–61.

Yack, Bernard, 'The myth of the civic nation', *Critical Review* 10.2 (1996), pp. 193–211.

——, 'Popular Sovereignty and Nationalism', *Political Theory* 29.4 (2001), pp. 517–36.

Yadav, Yogendra, 'Reconfiguration in Indian politics: state assembly elections in 1993–1995', in Chatterjee, Partha, ed., *State and Politics in India*, Oxford, Oxford University Press, 1997.

Zachariah, Cherian Mampilly, *Rebel Rulers: insurgency, governance and civilian life during war*, Ithaca, NY, Cornell University Press, 2011.

Zelliot, Eleanor, 'Congress and the Untouchables, 1917–1950', in Sission, Richard and Stanley Wolpert, eds, *Congress and Indian Nationalism: the pre-independence phase*, Berkeley, CA, University of California Press, 1988.

INDEX

Adeney, Katharine: 20
Afghanistan: 52
African National Congress: 179
Ahmed, Sayid: 58; followers of, 57
Akali Dal: 119
Ali, Amir: founder of National
  Mohammedan Association, 59
Ali, Haider: territory ruled by, 31
All Ceylon Tamil Conference:
  members of, 97
All Ceylon Tamil Congress (ACTC):
  150–1, 159, 180, 208; electoral
  performance of (1947), 103;
  member of TNA, 195; members of,
  151, 156–7, 227; political strategies
  of, 151–2
All-India Congress: members of, 73
All-India Muslim League: 75
All India Students Federation:
  demonstration organised by (2008),
  232–3
All Party Representative Committee
  (ARPC): formation of, 198
Ananda Vikadan: 233
Andhras: 9
All India/Anna Dravida Munnetra
  Kazhagam (ADMK): 2, 118, 130,
  231, 234; development of, 128–9;
  electoral performance of, 119–20,

127–8; formation of (1972), 114,
  128; ideology of, 122, 130; state
  assembly electoral performance
  (2011), 233–4; World Tamil Studies
  Conference (1984), 122, 131
Annadurai, C.N.: 119, 126
anti-colonialism: 83, 105; mobilisation
  efforts, 20, 22, 66, 77
Arabic (language): 109
Arulampalam, C.: electoral perfor-
  mance of (1970), 156–7
Arunachalam, P.: 93, 95, 150; ideology
  of, 95–7; support for Sinhalese
  Buddhism, 95
Arya Samaj: 76; founding of (1875), 56
Aryan: 22, 40–1, 45, 47, 56–7, 59, 61,
  74, 84, 100, 238; concept of national
  identity, 56; culture associated with,
  42; role in Hindu nationalism, 55–6;
  Sinhalese, 84, 87, 95–6; theory of Sri
  Lankan history, 84–5
Asoka: 174
Australia: 219, 221; Tamil diaspora in,
  171

Babri Masjid: demolition of (1992), 20
Backward Classes/Castes (BCs): 117,
  123; mobilisation of, 117
Baker, Christopher: 16

socialism: 109, 116
Soulbury, Lord: 98
Soulbury Commission (1944–5):
recommendations of, 98, 104
South Africa: 171, 229
South Indian Political Association
(Justice Party/SIPA): 70; *Andhra
Prakasika*, 69; disintegration of, 73;
formation of, 68–9; *Justice*, 69;
merger with Self-Respect Movement
(1944), 74; Non-Brahmin
Manifesto, 69
sovereignty: popular, 14, 35
Soviet Union (USSR): collapse of
(1991), 167, 190
Sri Lanka: 1, 3–6, 10, 15–16, 19, 22,
24–5, 29–30, 32, 35–40, 43, 45, 62,
105, 135, 150, 171–3, 177–8,
189–90, 198–9, 206, 222, 225–6,
237–8, 242; Air Force, 233;
Anuradhapura, 84–5, 104;
attempted coup (1962), 143–4, 146;
Batticaloa, 153–4, 207; Black July
(1983), 2, 178–9, 230; British
Ceylon (1815–1948), 29–30, 33–5,
38–9, 79, 83–4, 89, 140, 150;
Catholic-Buddhist tensions
(1959–62), 143; Colombo, 1, 33,
89–92, 94, 147, 153, 194, 204, 229,
235; constitution of, 140; Dry Zone,
103, 138; Eastern Province, 89;
franchise rights in, 90; government
of, 1, 25, 92, 168–9, 229, 235;
Independence of (1972), 10, 13, 81,
140, 147, 229; Jaffna, 33, 89–90,
92–3, 102, 104, 139, 147, 149,
154–5, 157–8, 180, 185–6, 188,
194, 198, 201, 207, 211; Kandy, 33,
93–4, 96, 98–9, 137, 142, 153;
Kilinochchi, 188; Mannar, 188;
military of, 143–4, 172, 179, 197;

Mullaitivu, 188; Muslim population
of, 17, 34, 40, 138, 147, 149, 157,
188, 226; Muslim-Sinhalese violence
in, 94; Northern Province, 159, 188;
Polonnaruva, 84–5, 104; Sinhala-
Tamil violence in, 146, 149, 153,
159–60; Sinhalese population of, 18,
34, 37, 93–4, 99, 105, 134, 144–6,
160–1; State Council, 102, 104;
Supreme Council, 200; Tamil
population of, 7, 15, 17–18, 23–4,
34, 37, 42, 45, 79, 81, 89, 91, 93–4,
134, 141–2, 144, 166, 230;
Trincomalee, 154–5; Vanni, 89, 188,
194, 198, 210–11, 217, 220, 223;
Vavuniya, 154, 207; Western aid
provided to, 173–5; Western
Province, 93
Sri Lanka Freedom Party (SLFP): 152,
161, 170, 177, 203; electoral
performance of, 135, 155, 157;
formation of (1951), 136, 139;
ideology of, 138–9, 145, 189;
member of MEP, 139; members of,
145, 149, 160, 171, 187; supporters
of, 141
Sri Lankan Civil War (1983–2009): 6,
18, 24–5, 165–6, 175–6, 184–5,
187, 191–3, 213, 215, 228;
assassinations during, 193, 197, 207;
capture of Kilinochchi (2008),
216–17; Ceasefire Agreement
(CFA), 195–7, 199, 207; Colombo
Airport Attack (2001), 194;
destruction of Elephant Pass
complex (2000), 194; ethnic
cleansing during, 188; international
intervention during, 172–3, 181,
185, 188, 191, 193; LTTE capture of
Jaffna (1995), 198; media coverage
of, 204–5; Northern Offensive